Pro Design Patterns
in Swift

Adam Freeman

Apress®

Pro Design Patterns in Swift

ISBN-13 (pbk): 978-1-4842-0395-8

ISBN-13 (electronic): 978-1-4842-0394-1

Managing Director: Welmoed Spahr
Lead Editor: James DeWolf
Development Editor: Douglas Pundick
Technical Reviewer: Fabio Claudio Ferracchiati
Editorial Board: Steve Anglin, Mark Beckner, Gary Cornell, Louise Corrigan, James DeWolf, Jonathan Gennick, Jonathan Hassell, Robert Hutchinson, Michelle Lowman, James Markham, Matthew Moodie, Jeff Olson, Jeffrey Pepper, Douglas Pundick, Ben Renow-Clarke, Gwenan Spearing, Matt Wade, Steve Weiss
Coordinating Editor: Kevin Walter
Copy Editor: Kim Wimpsett
Compositor: SPi Global
Indexer: SPi Global
Artist: SPi Global
Cover Designer: Anna Ishchenko

Distributed to the book trade worldwide by Springer Science+Business Media New York, 233 Spring Street, 6th Floor, New York, NY 10013. Phone 1-800-SPRINGER, fax (201) 348-4505, e-mail orders-ny@springer-sbm.com, or visit www.springeronline.com. Apress Media, LLC is a California LLC and the sole member (owner) is Springer Science + Business Media Finance Inc (SSBM Finance Inc). SSBM Finance Inc is a Delaware corporation.

For information on translations, please e-mail rights@apress.com, or visit www.apress.com.

Apress and friends of ED books may be purchased in bulk for academic, corporate, or promotional use. eBook versions and licenses are also available for most titles. For more information, reference our Special Bulk Sales–eBook Licensing web page at www.apress.com/bulk-sales.

Any source code or other supplementary material referenced by the author in this text is available to readers at www.apress.com. For detailed information about how to locate your book's source code, go to www.apress.com/source-code/.

Dedicated to my lovely wife, Jacqui Griffyth.

Contents at a Glance

Contents

About the Author

Adam Freeman is an experienced IT professional who has held senior positions in a range of companies, most recently serving as chief technology officer and chief operating officer of a global bank. Now retired, he spends his time writing and running.

About the Technical Reviewer

Fabio Claudio Ferracchiati is a senior consultant and a senior analyst/developer using Microsoft technologies. He works at BluArancio SpA (www.bluarancio.com) as Senior Analyst/Developer and Microsoft Dynamics CRM Specialist. He is a Microsoft Certified Solution Developer for .NET, a Microsoft Certified Application Developer for .NET, a Microsoft Certified Professional, and a prolific author and technical reviewer. Over the past ten years, he's written articles for Italian and international magazines and coauthored more than ten books on a variety of computer topics.

Part I

Getting Ready

Understanding Design Patterns

Design patterns are insurance policies for software development. Insurance policies work by trading a little cost now to avoid the possibility of a lot of cost later. The premium you pay to insure a car against theft, for example, costs a few percent of the value of the car, but when the car is stolen, your overall costs are minimized. You still have to go through the inconvenience of having your car stolen, but at least you don't have to bear the financial loss as well.

In software development, design patterns are insurance against the time taken to solve problems. The premium is the time it takes to add extra flexibility to your code now, and the payout is avoiding a painful and protracted rewrite to change the way the application works later. Like real insurance policies, you may not benefit from paying the premium because the problem you anticipate might never happen, but software development rarely goes smoothly and problems often arise, so that additional flexibility is usually a good investment.

This is a book for hands-on professional programmers. I focus on the practical applications of design patterns and focus on code examples instead of abstract descriptions. I describe the most important design patterns and demonstrate how they can be applied to iOS using Swift. Some of the patterns I describe are already implemented in the Cocoa framework classes, and I show you how use them to create more robust and adaptable applications.

By the time you have finished reading this book, you will understand the most important design patterns in contemporary software development, the problems they are intended to solve, and how to apply them to your Swift projects.

Putting Design Patterns into Context

Every experienced programmer has a set of informal strategies that shape their coding style. These strategies are insurance policies against the recurrence of problems from earlier projects. If you have spent a week dealing with a last-minute database schema change, for example, then you will take a little extra time on future projects making sure that dependencies on the schema are not hard-coded throughout the application, even though you don't know for certain that the schema will change this time around. You pay a little premium now to avoid the potential for a bigger cost in the future.

You may still have to make changes, but the process will be more pleasant, just like the process of shopping for a replacement car is made more pleasant when the insurance company pays for the stolen one.

There are two problems with informal strategies. The first problem is *inconsistency*. Programmers with similar experiences *may* have different views about what the nature of a problem is and *will* disagree about the best solution.

The second problem is that informal strategies are driven by personal experiences, which can be associated with strong emotions. Describing the difficulty of fixing a problem rarely conveys the pain and misery you endured, and that makes it hard to convince others of the need to invest in preventative measures. It also makes it difficult to be objective about the importance of the problem. Bad experiences linger, and you may find it hard to accept that there is little support for making the changes that would avoid problems you have encountered on previous projects.

Introducing Design Patterns

A *design pattern* identifies a common software development problem and provides a strategy for dealing with it, rather like the informal approach that I described earlier but that is expressed objectively, consistently, and free from emotional baggage.

The strategies that design patterns describe are proven to work, which means you can compare your own approach to them. And, since they cover the most common problems, you will find that there are design patterns for problems that you have not had to personally endure.

Most of the other design patterns in this book originate from a classic book called *Design Patterns: Elements of Reusable Object-Oriented Software* by Erich Gamma, Richard Helm, Ralph Johnson, and John Vlissides (Addison-Wesley, 1995). The authors of this book are referred to as the *Gang of Four (GoF)* , and the patterns they describe are some of the most important and fundamental in modern software development.

The GoF book is worth reading but is somewhat academic in nature. Design patterns are expressed abstractly without reference to a particular programming language or platform. This abstraction makes them hard to use; it can be difficult to figure out whether a pattern describes a problem that you are concerned about and difficult to be sure that you have correctly implemented the solution.

My goal in this book is to put design patterns in context and give you all the information you need to easily identify and apply the patterns that you need, along with a Swift implementation that you can apply directly to your project.

Understanding the Structure of a Design Pattern

Most design patterns apply to small groups of objects in an application and solve a problem that arises when one object—known as the *calling component*—needs to perform an operation on one or more other objects in the application.

For each of the design patterns in this book, I describe the problem the pattern solves, explain how the pattern works, and show you how to implement the pattern using Swift. I also describe common variations on the pattern and describe the pitfalls most closely associated with the pattern.

> **WHERE IS THE UML?**
>
> The Unified Modeling Language (UML) is often used to describe patterns, but I don't use it in this book. I am not a fan of UML for several reasons. First, most developers don't completely understand UML and take in little information from a UML diagram. There are exceptions, of course, and these tend to be people who work in large corporations where there is a detailed analysis and design phase before development commences. For the rest of the world, UML is a poorly defined and misinterpreted mess of boxes and lines.
>
> I find that UML is good for expressing some kinds of relationship but fails dismally at representing others. To a great extent, understanding patterns means understanding where logic that represents knowledge of other components exists, which is hard to convey using UML.
>
> Finally, and rather less objectively, UML is symptomatic of many aspects of software development that I don't like. All too often, UML is used as a weapon to enforce static and inflexible designs and inhibits adapting a development process to meet evolving customer needs because the UML becomes an unchanging reference point.
>
> For these reasons, as subjective as they are, I don't use UML in this book. Instead, I'll use free-form diagrams to illustrate the points that I want to emphasize.

Quantifying the Value of Design Patterns

It is easy to accept that design patterns are a good thing. Everyone understands the appeal of proven solutions used on countless projects to solve difficult problems. It is much harder to convince other programmers on the team that a specific pattern should be adopted in a project.

You can assess whether an insurance policy represents value for money by asking yourself some questions:

- Does the policy address something bad that is likely to happen to me?
- How often does the bad thing occur?
- Is the cost of the policy a small fraction of the cost of dealing with the bad thing?

These simple questions make it easy to understand that there is no point in buying car insurance if you don't have a car or if there are no car thieves in your town. They also highlight the poor value in paying $10,000 per year to insure an $11,000 car unless you anticipate multiple thefts (in which case, you might also consider moving to a different area).

The point is clear even though this is a simplistic view of insurance: don't buy a policy unless it offers some benefit. The same is true for design patterns: don't adopt a pattern unless it offers value that you can quantify and articulate to others. The questions needed to assess the value for design patterns are similar:

- Does the pattern identify a problem that I am likely to encounter?
- How often does this problem occur?
- Do I care enough about avoiding the risk of having to fix the problem in the future to undertake the work of implementing the design pattern today?

It can be hard to answer these questions. There are no actuarial tables for software development, and it can be hard to estimate the amount of future effort that will be required to fix a problem (especially one that may not arise).

Instead, it can be easier to focus on the immediate benefits that a design pattern can offer. For example, those patterns that increase the modularity of an application generally do so to minimize the effect of a future change, but a modular application has fewer tightly coupled components, which means that it is easy to isolate units of code. Being able to isolate units of code is essential for effective unit testing, and so adopting a change-insurance pattern has an immediate benefit of improving the testability of code.

Equally, design patterns that increase the amount of abstraction in an application allow new features to be added with less effort and less code duplication. Almost everyone can agree that quicker and easier development is a good thing, even if they don't agree with the need to avoid the problem that a design pattern is intended to guard against.

There are no easy answers, however, and the final decision to adopt a design pattern will be driven by the combined experience of the development team, the confidence in the completeness of the specification, and the competence of individual developers.

Using a Design Pattern After the Problem Occurred

You will find it hard to drive the adoption of patterns if you are the sole voice promoting them in a team that has no experience of them and little time to consider them. The chances are that you will fail to convince others. Don't be frustrated.

My advice is not to push too hard. If you force the team into following new practices, you will be held accountable for every problem and delay they cause, which will be especially difficult if the problem you are trying to guard against never happens. Advocates for design patterns are, sadly, often seen predictors of unlikely doom.

Don't lose hope, but put this book away and wait. If the problem you are concerned about doesn't occur—if, for example, the database schema doesn't change—then take pleasure in that the project dodged a bullet and move on to the next assignment.

Don't worry if the problem does occur; you can still benefit from design patterns. Your project is now in a situation that you had hoped to avoid, but you can use the patterns as a framework for digging yourself out of the hole. Select the most appropriate design pattern and use it as a framework to structure the clean code around which you drive the resolution of the problem. In this way, you can leverage a bad situation to introduce the team to a proven solution to the problem. This isn't as good as avoiding the problem in first place, but at least you will be able to create a long-term solution and lend some credibility to your enthusiasm for design patterns.

Understanding the Limitations of Design Patterns

There is a lot to like about design patterns, but they have their limitations. By their nature, design patterns are solutions to problems that other people have encountered on other projects. Design patterns are a starting point for avoiding or solving a problem and not a precisely tailored solution. That doesn't mean they are not useful, but they do require some work in order to adapt them to fit into your project.

Treat design patterns as recipes. Tinker, adapt, and adjust a pattern, and you will end up with something that works for you. You might need to refine your implementation a few times, and your use of a pattern is likely to get better with insight gained from several projects, but you'll end up with something that improves on your starting position and that helps minimize the impact of a common problem.

Some programmers treat design patterns as immutable laws. They are *pattern zealots*, someone who promotes the use of patterns as an inflexible "best practice" that should always be followed and cannot be adapted. That's rubbish. Applying patterns that you don't need or resisting adapting a pattern to fit into a project misses the point entirely.

There is no point trying to argue with a pattern zealot. They get their pleasure from being able to reference ever more obscure sources, and there is no effective way to ground their views in reality. My advice is to ignore them and focus on building good software by making it robust, scalable, and flexible enough to cope with changes, all of which can be aided by the design patterns described in this book.

About This Book

In this book, I describe how to use the most important design patterns using Swift and the Cocoa frameworks. Swift has attracted many new developers to the Apple platform, so I have written this book to provide all of the information you will need about Swift and the Cocoa classes I use. I also show you how to create the example projects using Xcode, which can be a confusing tool if you are new to the world of Swift development. You can download all of the examples from `Apress.com` if you don't want to type in the code yourself.

What Do You Need to Know?

You need to be an experienced developer to follow the concepts in book. No prior experience of Swift is required, but you should understand the basic concepts of object-oriented programming and have used a modern language such as Objective-C, C#, Java, or JavaScript.

What Software Do You Need?

You need to have a Mac running OS X 10.10 (Yosemite) and have downloaded and installed Xcode 6.1. To get Xcode, you will need to sign up as an Apple Developer, which you can do at `https://developer.apple.com`. Don't worry if you are new to Xcode; I'll show you everything you need to know to follow the examples in Chapter 2.

What Is the Structure of This Book?

This book is split into five parts, each of which covers a set of related topics. Part 1 contains this chapter and an Xcode primer for the techniques you will need to follow for the example in this book. I also build an example application called SportsStore that I return to throughout this book to demonstrate how to apply design pattern in context.

Each of the other four parts of the book focuses on a specific type of pattern. Part 2 covers the creational design patterns, which are concerned with how objects are created in an application. Part 3 describes the structural design patterns, which define and manage the relationship between objects in an application. Part 4 of this book focuses on the patterns that describe how objects communicate with one another. In the final part of this book, I describe the Model/View/Controller (MVC) pattern, which applies to the structure of the entire application and is commonly used for Mac OS and iOS UI applications.

Where Can You Get the Example Code?

You can download all the examples for all the chapters in this book from www.apress.com. The download is available without charge and includes everything you need to re-create the examples without having to type them in. You don't have to download the code, but it is the easiest way of experimenting with the examples and cutting and pasting into your own projects.

If you do want to re-create the examples from scratch, then you will find that every chapter contains detailed listings of all the files that I create and modify. I never refer you to an external file or hand-wave about leaving the rest of the example as an exercise; every detail you need to re-create every example is contained within this book.

Summary

In this chapter, I outlined the content and structure of this book and set out the experience and software required. In the next chapter, I provide a brief primer to Xcode and describe the features I rely on in this book.

Chapter 2

Getting Used to Xcode

In this chapter, I use Xcode to demonstrate the ways in which I present examples throughout this book. *Playgrounds*, which are one of the most useful features of Xcode 6, allow for code experiments to be created and evaluated without needing to create an application project. I use playgrounds to help describe the problems that patterns are intended to solve and use them to demonstrate simple implementations.

Many of the design patterns I describe in this book rely on restricting access to classes, methods, and properties. Swift supports access protection keywords, but they operate on a per-file basis. This is a problem for playgrounds because all the code is in a single file, and so access protections are not enforced. Many of the design patterns I describe require support for concurrent access, which is something that playgrounds do not handle at all well.

For these reasons, I also use OS X Command Line Tool projects, which are the simplest Xcode projects that support multiple files. Command Line Tool projects do not present a windowed UI to the user and are limited to reading from and writing to the console. The benefit of using such a simple project type is that it allows me to focus on just the design pattern I am describing and the code required to implement it, without the complexity of dealing with a user interface.

Few real-world projects are so simple, of course, and in Chapter 3, I create an iOS app called SportsStore, which does present a graphical user interface and which I use in every chapter to provide additional context for applying the patterns I describe.

Working with Xcode Playgrounds

Xcode playgrounds are a good way to prototype code and test ideas without needing to create an iOS application project. Playgrounds are a new feature in Xcode 6, and many developers are unfamiliar with them, especially those who have been attracted to iOS and Mac OS development by Swift and have not used earlier Xcode releases to develop in Objective-C.

Creating a Playground

When you start Xcode, you will be presented with a splash screen that lets you select between creating a new playground, creating a new project, or checking out an existing project from a source code repository, as shown in Figure 2-1.

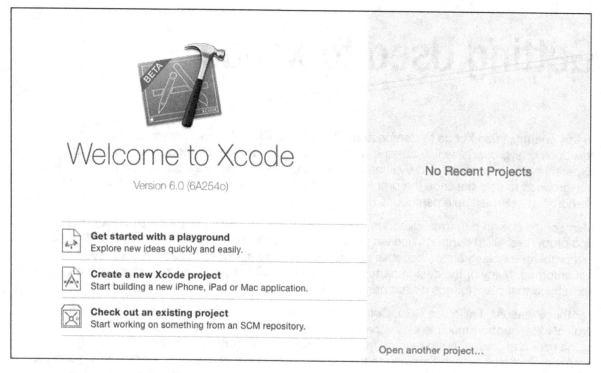

Figure 2-1. *The Xcode 6 splash screen*

Tip   Select New ➤ Playground from the File menu if the splash window is not shown.

Click "Get started with a playground." Xcode will prompt you for a location to name and save the playground file. Change the name to MyFirstPlayground and ensure that iOS is selected for Platform, as shown in Figure 2-2.

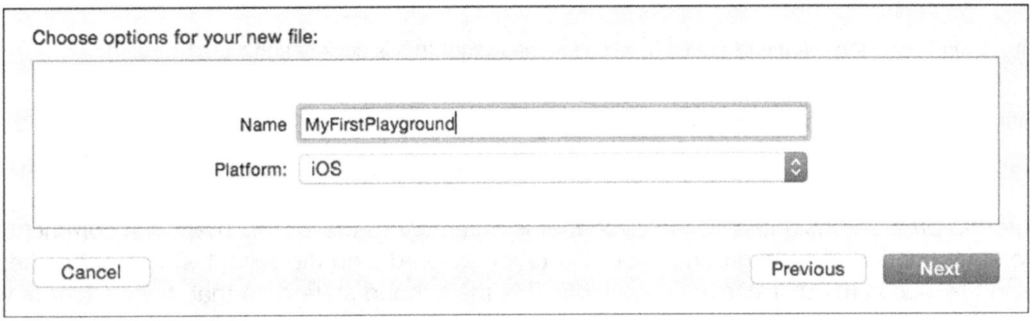

Choose options for your new file:

Name   MyFirstPlayground

Platform: iOS

Cancel   Previous   Next

Figure 2-2. Naming the playground and selecting the platform

Click the Next button and select a location where you will be easily able to find the playground in the future, as shown in Figure 2-3.

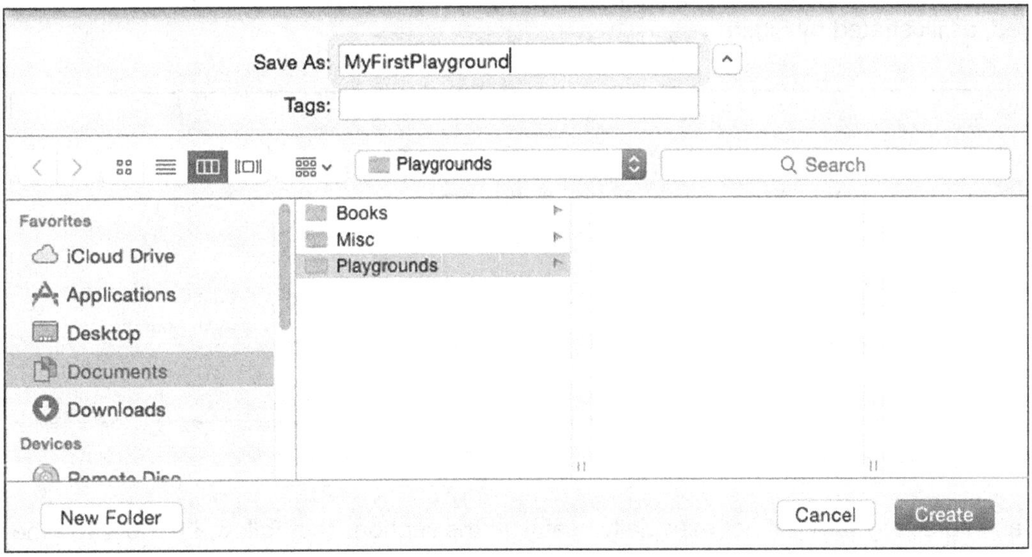

Save As: MyFirstPlayground

Tags:

Playgrounds   Q Search

Favorites
  iCloud Drive   Books
  Applications   Misc
  Desktop   Playgrounds
  Documents
  Downloads
Devices
  Remote Disc

New Folder   Cancel   Create

Figure 2-3. Changing the name of the playground file and selecting a save location

Xcode will create a file called MyFirstPlayground.playground in the location you selected, the contents of which are shown in Listing 2-1. If this is the first time you have used Xcode, you will be asked to enable developer mode.

Listing 2-1. The Contents of the MyFirstPlayground.playground File

```
import UIKit

var str = "Hello, playground"
```

> **Tip**   I don't show the comments added by Xcode in the listings in this book or add any of my own comments. In real projects I incessantly comment code, but in this book I'll be explaining the effect of the statements I write in the accompanying text.

A playground provides insights into the code that is entered into the editor. There is a comment and two statements in the playground. Comments are ignored, and the `import` statement makes classes in the Cocoa UIKit framework available. It is the second statement that gives a hint of what playgrounds can do.

```
...
var str = "Hello, playground"
...
```

This statement creates a variable called `str` and uses a literal string value to set its value. If you look to the right of this statement in the playground, you will see that the value of the variable is displayed, as illustrated by Figure 2-4.

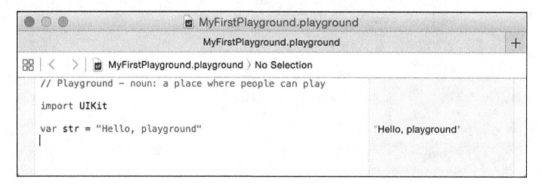

Figure 2-4. A simple playground

This is an interesting start but not especially useful. In the sections that follow, I'll show you the different playground features that I rely on in this book.

Displaying the Value History of a Variable

Modify the code in the playground to match Listing 2-2, and you will get a sense of the power of a playground.

Listing 2-2. Defining a Loop in the MyFirstPlayground.playground File

```
import UIKit

var str = "Hello, playground"

var counter = 0;
for (var i = 0; i < 10; i++) {
    counter += i;
    println("Counter: \(counter)");
}
```

Tip You don't have to compile—or even save—the playground file to see the effect of changes. The code statements are automatically evaluated after every edit.

I have defined a `counter` variable with an initial value of 0 and a `for` loop that increases the `counter` value with each iteration and writes the current value to the console using the `println` function. The right-hand panel updates, displaying (`10 times`) next to the statement that changes the `counter` value. To the right of the (`10 times`) message is a small circular plus button, as shown in Figure 2-5.

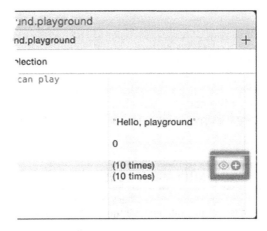

Figure 2-5. The button that shows value history

Tip Be sure to click the button next to the statement that changes the value of the `counter` variable and not the one that calls the `println` function.

This symbol is labeled *Value History*, and clicking it opens a panel that shows how the value of the `counter` variable changed as the code was executed and shows the console output generated through the `println` function. Figure 2-6 illustrates the view.

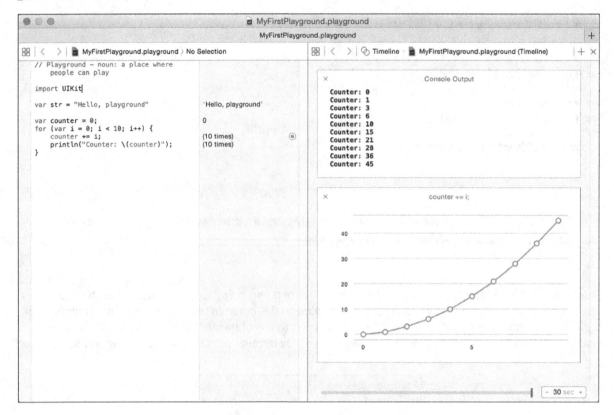

Figure 2-6. *Displaying the value history in a playground*

The chart shows how the value of the counter variable changes for each iteration of the for loop. You can display the value history for any variable defined in the playground, but numeric values are the most usefully presented.

A NOTE ABOUT CODING STYLE

You will notice that I use semicolons to terminate statements throughout this book, even though Swift doesn't require the use of semicolons after statements unless you need to separate multiple statements on the same line.

Although it's not a requirement of Swift, I have been writing code for decades with languages that do require semicolons, and—try as I might—I can't break the habit. There is something about an unterminated statement that just looks wrong to me, and I hit the semicolon key automatically. I considered going through each chapter and removing the semicolons, but that is a path that leads to broken examples, which I work hard to avoid in my books. And so, with a note of apology, I decided to let my preferences manifest themselves and use semicolons in the listings. You don't have to follow my style, however: one of the nice features of Swift is its relaxed approach to code style, and you are entirely free to express your own preferences and habits (including, if you want, the addition of unneeded semicolons).

Using the Value Timeline

At the bottom of the Value History panel is a slider that you can use to see how the value of variables changed during the execution of the code. The effect of this slider is easier to see when there are multiple variables to look at, and in Listing 2-3 I have updated the playground with some additional statements.

Listing 2-3. Adding Additional Statements to the MyFirstPlayground.playground File

```
import UIKit

var str = "Hello, playground"

var counter = 0;
var secondCounter = 0;

for (var i = 0; i < 10; i++) {
    counter += i;
    println("Counter: \(counter)");
    for j in 1...10 {
        secondCounter += j;
    }
}
```

Display the value histories for the counter and secondCounter variables by clicking the circular button to the right of the statements in the for loops. You will see two separate charts, and you can see the relationship between the values of the variables by dragging the playback head (the red vertical bar at the bottom of the panel) left and right to move to different points in the execution of the code, as shown in Figure 2-7.

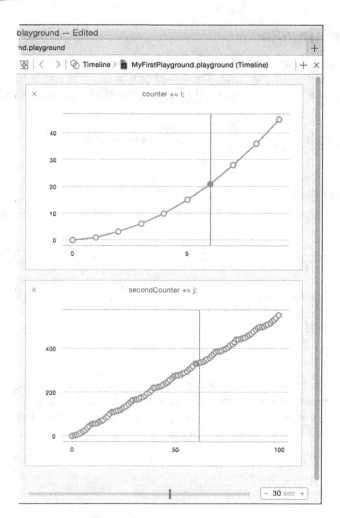

Figure 2-7. *Reviewing the variable value timelines in a playground*

Displaying UI Components in a Playground

Playgrounds can also be used to display UI components, which I rely on to demonstrate how Cocoa implements some patterns. Listing 2-4 shows how I modified the playground to show a text field.

Listing 2-4. Adding a UI Component to the MyFirstPlayground.playground File

```
import UIKit

var str = "Hello, playground"

var counter = 0;
var secondCounter = 0;

for (var i = 0; i < 10; i++) {
    counter += i;
    println("Counter: \(counter)");
    for j in 1...10 {
        secondCounter += j;
    }
}

let textField = UITextField(frame: CGRectMake(0, 0, 200, 50));
textField.text = "Hello";
textField.borderStyle = UITextBorderStyle.Bezel;

textField;
```

There are two important differences when using UI components in a playground from a regular Xcode project. The first is that you must use the initializer with the frame argument and generate a frame to contain the component using the CGRectMake function, like this:

```
...
let textField = UITextField(frame: CGRectMake(0, 0, 200, 50));
...
```

The arguments to the GCRectMake functions are the bounds of the frame that will contain the component, where the third and fourth values define the width and height. I have specified a frame that is 200 pixels wide and 50 high, which is sufficient for a text field.

The second difference is the last statement in the playground, which simply contains the name of the variable to which I have assigned the UI component.

```
...
textField;
...
```

This is required so that Xcode will provide the plus icon to the right of the statement; clicking the icon displays the component in the assistant editor, as shown in Figure 2-8. The assistant editor panels display the result of statements, so a statement that returns the configured UI component object is required.

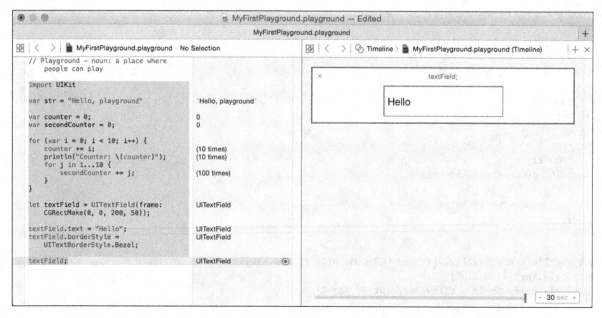

Figure 2-8. *Displaying a UI component in a playground*

Working with OS X Command Line Tool Projects

OS X Command Line Tool projects are ideally suited to demonstrating design patterns in Swift. This kind of project supports multiple files and concurrency, which makes it possible to demonstrate the effect of access protections and the effect of working with multiple threads.

Creating a Command-Line Project

Click "Create a new Xcode project" on the Xcode splash screen or select New ➤ Project from the Xcode File menu if the splash screen isn't visible. Select the Command Line Tool template, which is found in the OS X ➤ Application category, as shown in Figure 2-9.

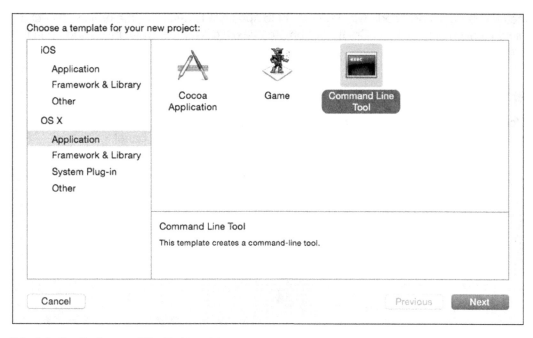

Figure 2-9. Selecting the Command Line Tool template

Click the Next button, and Xcode will prompt you for details of the project you want to create. Set the name to MyCommandLine and ensure that the Language option is set to Swift, as shown in Figure 2-10. I have specified Apress as the organization for the project, but I don't rely on these values in this book, and you can set them to your own organization.

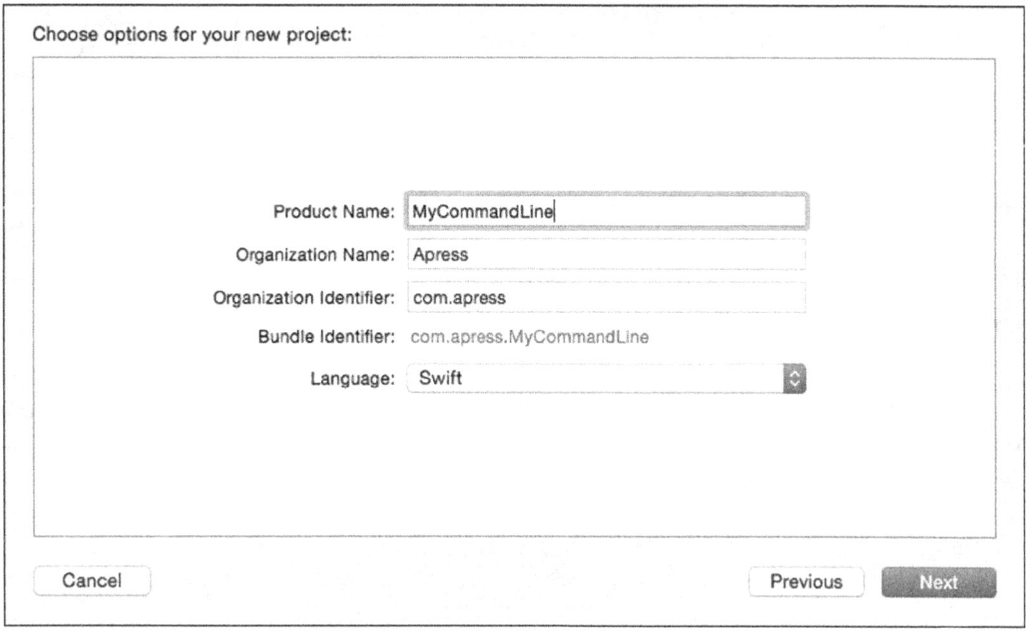

Figure 2-10. Specifying details for the project

Click the Next button, and Xcode will prompt you to specify a location for the project. Select a convenient location and click the Create button. Xcode will create the project files and open the main project window.

Understanding the Xcode Layout

When Xcode shows the project, you will see a layout that is similar to the one shown in Figure 2-11. You may see a slightly different layout, but I'll explain how to open each panel.

Figure 2-11. The Xcode layout for a Command Line Tool project

I have numbered the main panes that Xcode presents, and I describe them in Table 2-1 for readers who are new to Xcode. The content of some panes changes based on the task being performed by Xcode, so I have included details of how the content can be selected.

Table 2-1. The Default Xcode Panes

Number	Description
1	This is the navigator pane, which presents the contents of the project in different views that are selected using the row of buttons at the top edge. I use the Project Navigator view, which is displayed by clicking the first button in the row. The visibility of the navigator pane is controlled through the View ➤ Navigators menu.
2	This is the main editor window, which adapts to the file being edited. Different editors are available, includes one for project settings (which is what is shown when the project is first created), a code editor for .swift files, and a drag-and-drop editor called UI Builder that deals with .storyboard files. (I use .storyboard files in Chapter 3.) Select View ➤ Standard Editor ➤ Show Standard Editor to open the code editor.
3	This is the inspector pane, which reveals information about components in the application and is used when creating the application layout. I describe this pane further in Chapter 3.
4	This is the utility pane. The content of this pane is set using the four buttons at the top edge, and the view shown in the figure is the Object Library, which contains the UI controls used to create an application layout, which I use in Chapter 3. You can display the Object Library by selecting the View ➤ Utilities ➤ Show Object Library menu.
5	This is the Debug pane, which is used to interact with the debugger and to display console messages written using the Swift println function. This is where the output from Command Line Tool applications appears. This pane is controlled through the View ➤ Debug Area menu.

Adding a New Swift File

The reason that I use Command Line Tool projects is so I can create multiple code files and enforce access protection with keywords such as private. To add a new file to the project, select the Project Navigator view in the navigator pane and right-click the MyCommandLine folder item, which currently contains a file called main.swift, as shown in Figure 2-12.

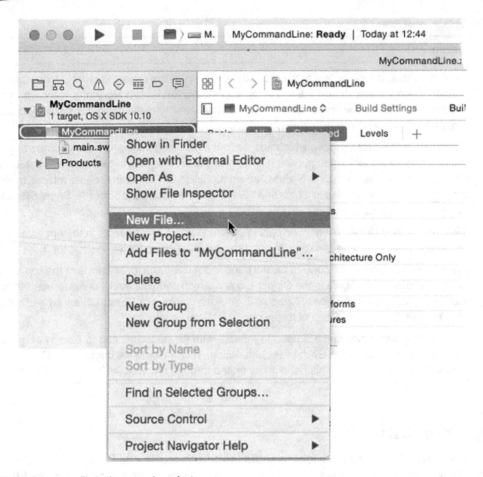

Figure 2-12. Adding a new file to the example project

Xcode will display the set of file templates available for new files. Select the Swift File template, as shown in Figure 2-13.

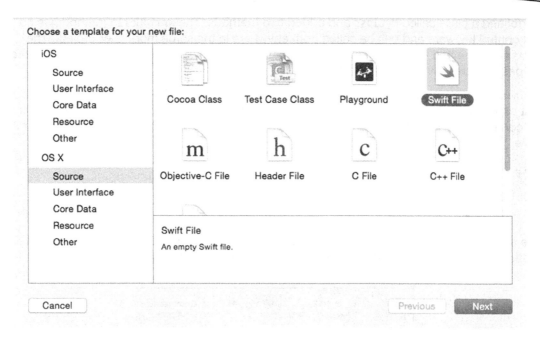

Figure 2-13. Selecting the Swift file template

Click the Next button and set the name of the new file to MyCode.swift, as shown in Figure 2-14.

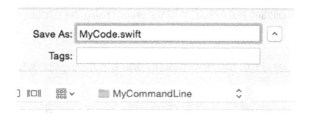

Figure 2-14. Setting the name of the code file

Click the Create button, and Xcode will create the file and open it for editing. Replace the default content with the statements shown in Listing 2-5.

Listing 2-5. The Contents of the MyCode.swift File

```swift
class MyClass {

    func writeHello() {
        println("Hello!");
    }

    private func writePassword() {
        println("secret");
    }
}
```

I have defined a class called MyClass and added two methods. The writeHello method has no access control keyword and can be called from anywhere in the same module or project. The writePassword method is decorated with the private keyword, which means it can be accessed only from types that are defined in the MyCode.swift file.

The main.swift file contains the statements that will be executed when the application is executed. In most of the examples in this book, I will add statements to the main.swift file to represent the calling component in a design pattern. Listing 2-6 shows the statements I added to the file for this example.

Listing 2-6. The Contents of the main.swift File

```
let myObject = MyClass();
myObject.writeHello();
```

I create an object from the MyClass class and call the writeHello method. To compile and run the application, click the play icon at the top of the Xcode window, as shown in Figure 2-15.

Figure 2-15. The Xcode button that compiles and runs the application

> **Tip**   If you don't see the button shown in the figure, then select Show Toolbar from the Xcode View menu. You can also control the compilation and execution of the project using the Product menu.

Xcode will compile the code and run the application, and the following output will appear in the debug console window:

```
Hello!
Program ended with exit code: 0
```

The first line of the output comes from the call to the println function. The second line indicates that the example program has terminated. I won't usually show the second line, and some of the example applications that I build won't terminate on their own.

Summary

In this chapter, I explained how Xcode can be used to create playgrounds and Command Line Tool projects, which are the main ways in which I introduce design patterns in this book. In the next chapter, I walk through the process of creating an iOS application called SportsStore, to which I apply every pattern in this book, in order to provide as many examples as possible and to put the patterns into a more realistic setting.

Chapter 3

Creating the SportsStore App

In the previous chapter, I showed you how Xcode can be used to create playgrounds and command-line tools, which are how I introduce each of the design patterns in the chapters that follow.

I like to provide as many code examples as I can in my books, so in this chapter I create an iOS app called SportsStore. The app I create is entirely unstructured, which means I simply bolt the code and the UI together as directly as possible without any thought to the long-term consequences. This is, of course, the antithesis to design patterns, but it is a surprisingly common development style. Throughout this book, I apply the design patterns to the unstructured application to provide additional context for their use.

Creating an Unstructured iOS App Project

In this section, I create a simple iOS app that allows a user to buy products from a retailer called SportsStore. I am going to implement only part of the shopping process in order to create an easy-to-understand example that doesn't require complex visual layouts and lets me focus on the structure of the code.

This is fortunate because I am one of the worst interface designers in the world. You will get a sense of my lack of aesthetic when you see the iOS layout I create—let's just call it minimalistic chic and move on. (In my own projects, I work with a professional designer, and I encourage you to do the same if you are similarly style-challenged).

The style of development I use in this section is known as a *single-class application*, which has no structure or design. This is a common development style, especially for programmers who have little experience of object-oriented languages.

This is the "before" in my proposition for the value of design patterns, and I introduce the "after" as I show you each pattern. I have, therefore, built this app so that I can emphasize the impact of the design patterns I describe, but this style of development is pretty common, and you can see code like this in just about any project, especially from developers who have recently made the transition to object-oriented languages. I am confident that if you think about the programmers you know, there will be at least person you can think of who writes similar code.

> **Tip**   I describe the process for creating the application step by step because many readers will be new to
> the world of Xcode and Swift. If you are an experienced Xcode user, then you can skip to Chapter 4 and just
> download the project from Apress.com.

The application that I am going to create is a simple stock management tool for an imaginary sports
equipment retailer called SportsStore. I use SportsStore in one form or another in most of my books,
and it lets me highlight the way that common problems can be addressed using different languages,
platforms, and patterns. Figure 3-1 shows a mock-up of the initial interface that I will create for the
SportsStore application.

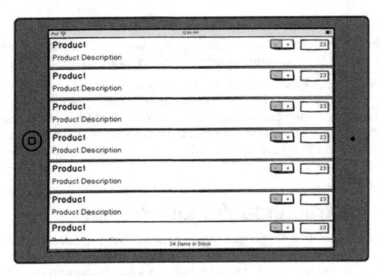

Figure 3-1. The mock-up for the SportsStore example application

The user will be presented with a list of products displayed in a table. For each product, the name and
a description will be displayed along with the current number of items in stock. The user will be able to
edit the stock level directly using a text field or increment and decrement the value with a stepper.

THE VALUE OF EXAMPLE APPLICATIONS

I am not for a second going to pretend that the SportsStore application is useful in its own right—but that is not the point
of an example. The goal is to give me a framework that I can use to demonstrate different patterns in a broader context
than just a fragment of code in a playground or command-line tool.

The SportsStore example is just complex enough to me to demonstrate how to apply patterns without causing me to deal
with difficult issues such as data persistence, security, data validation, and all of the other matters that have to be taken
into account in a real project.

The problem with creating a more realistic application is that too much of the book is then given over to writing code that isn't
directly related to the subject at hand. That is not the kind of book I want to write and, I hope, not the kind you want to read.

Creating the Project

To create a new project, select New ➤ Project from the Xcode File menu. You will be presented with the range of project types that Xcode supports. Select Single View Application from the iOS ➤ Application section, as shown in Figure 3-2.

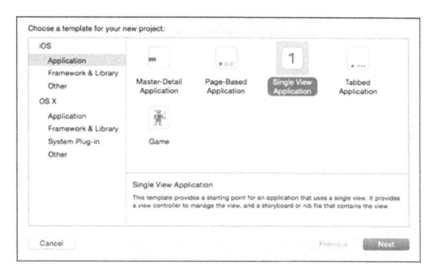

Figure 3-2. *Selecting the Xcode project type*

Click the Next button, and you will be asked to choose options for the new project. Set Product Name to SportsStore and enter **Apress** and **com.apress** for Organization Name and Identifier, respectively. Ensure that Swift is selected for Language, that iPad is selected for the Devices option, and that the Use Core Data option unchecked, as shown in Figure 3-3.

Figure 3-3. *Choosing options for the new Xcode project*

Click the Next button, and you will be prompted for a save location for the project files. Select a convenient location and click the Create button to generate the initial content for the project.

Understanding the Xcode Layout

Xcode will create the project, and you will be presented with the default view of the project, which I have shown in Figure 3-4. The layout and the panes it contains are the same ones I described in Chapter 2.

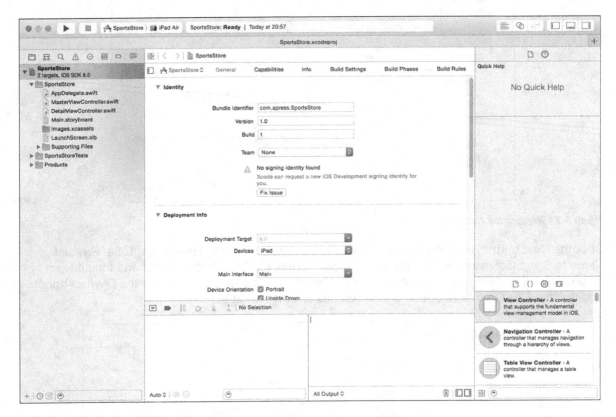

Figure 3-4. The Xcode project layout

Defining the Data

To keep the example application simple, I am going to define the product data statically. This wouldn't be useful in a real app because the changes the user makes are not persistent, but it is sufficient for this book, in which I want to focus on the design patterns rather than setting up data services.

I am going to define all of the code in the ViewController.swift file, which Xcode created when the project was set up. Locate the file in the navigation pane and click it. Xcode will switch to its code editor. Listing 3-1 shows the contents of the ViewController.swift file and the changes I made to define the data.

Listing 3-1. Adding Data to the ViewController.swift File

```swift
import UIKit

class ViewController: UIViewController {

    var products = [
        ("Kayak", "A boat for one person", "Watersports", 275.0, 10),
        ("Lifejacket", "Protective and fashionable", "Watersports", 48.95, 14),
        ("Soccer Ball", "FIFA-approved size and weight", "Soccer", 19.5, 32),
        ("Corner Flags", "Give your playing field a professional touch",
            "Soccer", 34.95, 1),
        ("Stadium", "Flat-packed 35,000-seat stadium", "Soccer", 79500.0, 4),
        ("Thinking Cap", "Improve your brain efficiency by 75%", "Chess", 16.0, 8),
        ("Unsteady Chair", "Secretly give your opponent a disadvantage",
            "Chess", 29.95, 3),
        ("Human Chess Board", "A fun game for the family", "Chess", 75.0, 2),
        ("Bling-Bling King", "Gold-plated, diamond-studded King",
            "Chess", 1200.0, 4)];

    override func viewDidLoad() {
        super.viewDidLoad()
    }

    override func didReceiveMemoryWarning() {
        super.didReceiveMemoryWarning()
    }
}
```

> **Tip** The term *view controller* refers to parts of one of the most important patterns for Swift/Cocoa development, called Model/View/Controller (MVC). This pattern is woven throughout iOS development, and I describe it in depth in Part 5. For this chapter, I am going to ignore the MVC pattern and consolidate as much of the code I require into a single class.

I have created a variable called `products` and assigned to it an array of tuples that represent products. A *tuple* allows several values to be easily grouped. See the "Working with Tuples" sidebar for a quick explanation of how tuples are defined and used.

> **Tip** Swift assigns literal floating-point values such as `19.5` using the `Double` type even when it could have used the smaller `Float` type. I could have enforced the use of `Float` values by specifying the type explicitly—in other words, `Float(19.5)`—but I am going to accept the use of `Double` values in order to keep the example simple.

WORKING WITH TUPLES

To demonstrate the use of tuples, I created a new playground called `Tuples.playground`. I have included the playground in the free source code download that accompanies this book. It contains the following code:

```
import Foundation;

var myProduct = ("Kayak", "A boat for one person", "Watersports", 275.0, 10);

func writeProductDetails(product: (String, String, String, Double, Int)) {
    println("Name: \(product.0)");
    println("Description: \(product.1)");
    println("Category: \(product.2)");
    let formattedPrice = NSString(format: "$%.2lf", product.3);
    println("Price: \(formattedPrice)");
}

writeProductDetails(myProduct);
```

The code in this playground defines a tuple and a function that prints details of its values to the console. Notice that to accept a tuple as a parameter in the function, I specify the types of the individual values as a comma-separated list, similar to the way that a tuple is created, as follows:

```
...
func writeProductDetails(product: (String, String, String, Double, Int)) {
...
```

You have to be careful when using literal numeric values in tuples because Swift will select the type for the value automatically. This is why I have specified the price of the product in the playground as `275.0`. If I had omitted the decimal fraction, then Swift would have created a `(String, String, String, Int, Int)` tuple, which would not have been accepted as an argument to the `writeProductDetails` function.

Within the function, I access the values within the tuple by referring to their index, like this:

```
...
println("Description: \(product.1)");
...
```

The expression `product.1` refers to the value at index 1 in the tuple passed as the argument to the `writeProductDetails` function. Tuple indexes are zero-based, which means that this expression evaluates to `A boat for one person`.

I used the `NSString` class to format the price of the product in the playground. Swift makes it easy to work with the different Cocoa frameworks, including the `Foundation` framework that provides core features such as string formatting.

To see the effect of the code in the playground, select Assistant Editor ➤ Show Assistant Editor from the View menu. The console output will be as follows:

```
Name: Kayak
Description: A boat for one person
Category: Watersports
Price: $275.00
```

Tuples are a convenient way of defining data types, but they have their limitations, as I explain in Chapter 4.

Creating the Basic Layout

The next change that I am going to make to the example project is to define a basic layout, consisting of a table that will display a row for each product and a label that will display the total number of products in stock.

In this section, I use the Xcode Interface Builder (IB), which is a drag-and-drop interface layout tool. It can take a while to get used to the way that IB works, so I will explain the process I followed step by step. If you an experienced Xcode developer, then you can skip ahead.

The first step is to open the Main.storyboard file for editing by clicking it in the navigation pane. This opens the IB window, which shows the views that the application will present to the user, as shown in Figure 3-5.

Figure 3-5. Using the Interface Builder to edit a storyboard

The main part of the display shows the view that the application will display to the user. There is only one view in this application because I selected the Single View Application template when I created the project. The view is shown as an empty box because there are no user interface components currently.

One the left is the hierarchy of controls, with View Controller Scene as the top-level item. There isn't much there at the moment, but it will be populated as I add the components I need for the SportsStore application. The control hierarchy is a useful part of the Interface Builder editor because it makes it easy to select components and create relationships between them, as you will see as I build out the view.

Adding the Basic Components

To add components to the view, you drag them from the Object Library, which is in the bottom-right corner of the Xcode window, onto the view and release them. You can then position the component on the layout.

The first component I require is a Label, which I will use to display the number of products in stock. You can locate the Label component in the Object Library by scrolling down the list or by entering the component name in the search box at the bottom of the pane. Drag the Label to the view. It doesn't matter where it is positioned at the moment.

Once you have added the Label, you can configure it using the inspectors pane, which is in the top-right corner of the Xcode window. At the top of the pane, there are buttons that allow different inspectors to be selected, as shown in Figure 3-6.

Figure 3-6. *The inspector pane selector buttons*

Select the Attributes Inspector using the buttons at the top of the pane and make the changes described in Table 3-1.

Table 3-1. *The Configuration Changes Required for the Label Control*

Attribute	Change
Color	This attribute controls the color of the label text. Select white for this property.
Alignment	This attribute controls the horizontal alignment of the text in the label. Click the button that centers the text.
Background	This attribute sets the background color for the label. Select black for this property.
Font	This attribute sets the font used for the text displayed by the label and should be set to System Bold 30.

When you have set the attributes, adjust the position of and size of the label so that it is aligned to the bottom edge of the view and touches the left and right edges, as shown in Figure 3-7. You can size and position the label by using the Size Inspector or by using the grab handles shown by the label in the view. I positioned my label at the (0, 550) coordinate and made the label 600 by 50 pixels.

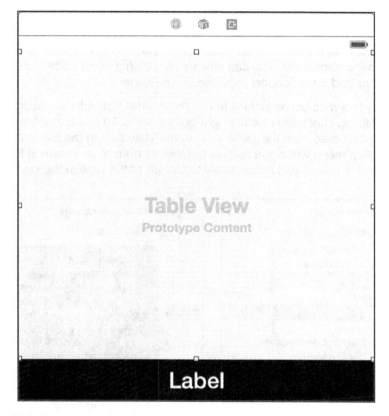

Figure 3-7. Adding the basic layout components

The next step is to add the table. Locate the Table View component in the Object Library, drag it to the view, and release. Resize the table so that it occupies all of the space in the view that is not occupied by the label. As you drag the top edge upward, you will see it snap to a guide that is just below the battery icon. This is the top layout guide, and it allows the application to fit into the device window without obscuring the status bar, as shown in Figure 3-7.

Caution   Use the Table View component and not the Table View Controller.

Configuring Auto Layout

The next step is to specify how the components will be positioned on the device screen. The layout looks fine in the storyboard editor, but iOS devices support a range of resolutions, and the application may be displayed in portrait and landscape modes. Auto layout is the feature that allows the size and position of a component to be specified relative to its container or other components, and in this section, I will define the layout for the table.

Auto layout works by specifying *constraints*, which fix the position and size of components relative to its container or other components. You can specify constraints using code statements, but it is simpler to use the drag-and-drop support provided by UI Builder.

The most reliable way to set up constraints is to use the control hierarchy because it makes it easy to be sure you are defining constraints for the right components. To create the first constraint, hold down the Control key and drag from the Table View to the View item in the hierarchy. You will be presented with a pop-up menu when you release the mouse button, as shown in Figure 3-8, which shows the object hierarchy displayed immediately to the left of the view in the storyboard.

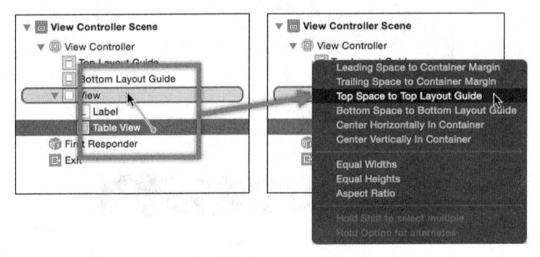

Figure 3-8. Applying a constraint using the component hierarchy

Hold the Shift key and select the following items:

- Leading Space to Container Margin
- Trailing Space to Container Margin
- Top Space to Top Layout Guide

Once you have selected all three menu items, click outside of the pop-up menu to dismiss it. A new `Constraints` item will appear in the component hierarchy to contain the constraints, which have the effect of ensuring that the top, left, and right edges of the table view are always in contact with the edges of the container, regardless of the size of the layout.

Table 3-2 shows the remaining constraints that are required, all of which are created using the same technique.

Table 3-2. *The Constraints Required for the Basic Layout*

Drag From	Drag To	Constraints
Label	View	Leading Space to Container Margin Trailing Space to Container Margin Bottom Space to Bottom Layout Guide
Table View	Label	Vertical Spacing
Label	Label	Height

Tip   For the last constraint in the table, Control-drag and release so that both ends of the line are within the boundaries of the Label item in the control hierarchy.

Testing the Basic Layout

Before going any further, I want to check that the layout and its constraints are set up correctly. To build and test the application, click the Play button in the Xcode toolbar, which runs across the top of the Xcode window, as shown in Figure 3-9. (The button is really labeled "Build and then run the current scheme," but that is an unwieldy name.)

Figure 3-9. *The Xcode button that builds and starts the application*

Tip   Select Show Toolbar from the Xcode View menu if you cannot see the button.

Xcode comes with an iOS simulator, and clicking the Play button will compile the code and send it to the simulator. You can change the device that is simulated using the selector next to the Play button, and as Figure 3-9 shows, I have selected the iPad 2. You can use any device, but the iPad 2 is convenient for generating compact screenshots, which is useful for page layouts.

Click the Play button, and Xcode will compile the project and start the simulator, as shown in Figure 3-10.

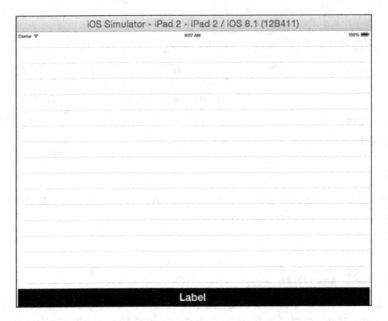

Figure 3-10. Running the example application in the iOS simulator

> **Note**   I have shown the simulator in its landscape mode, which is displayed using the Rotate Left and Rotate Right items on the simulator Hardware menu. I usually display landscape screenshots in books because they better suit the layout of a book and minimize the amount of empty space on the page.

Implementing the Total Label

It is time to start implementing the code that will drive the layout, and in this section I am going to wire up the label so that it displays the total number of products in stock. In the sections that follow, I will walk through the process of creating a relationship between the layout and the code.

Creating the Reference

The storyboard file that I edited with the Interface Builder in the previous section is an XML file. This file defines the layout and configuration of the user interface components, but an extra step is required to access the instances of the components—such as the label—that are created at runtime from the application code.

> **Tip**   You can see the XML content by right-clicking or Control-clicking the file in the navigator pane and selecting Open As ➤ Source Code from the pop-up menu.

Xcode has a feature called the *Assistant Editor*, which displays content that is logically related to the file displayed in the main editor area. Select Assistant Editor ➤ Show Assistant Editor from the View menu, and Xcode will add a new pane to its layout, which will display the contents of the ViewController.swift file.

> **Tip**   Xcode selects the file that the Assistant Editor displays automatically, but it won't always display the file you want. You can explicitly select a file to display in the Assistant Editor pane by Option-clicking a file in the navigator pane.

Control-click the Label in the View Controller Scene hierarchy of components and drag it to the Assistant Editor. Position the mouse pointer to be below the class definition and the product variable and let go. A pop-up will appear that lets you configure an *outlet*, which is the association between the instance of the label created for the app layout and the UIViewController class, as shown in Figure 3-11.

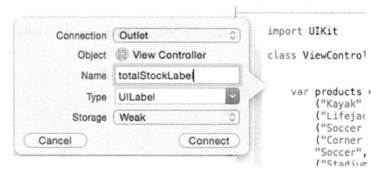

Figure 3-11. Creating an outlet for a label

Set the Name field to totalStockLabel and click the Connect button. Xcode will add a new variable to the ViewController class, as shown in Listing 3-2. (You can't add this code statement manually because Xcode makes other changes to the project behind the scenes).

Listing 3-2. Adding an Outlet in the ViewController.swift File

```
import UIKit

class ViewController: UIViewController {

    @IBOutlet weak var totalStockLabel: UILabel!

    var products = [
        ("Kayak", "A boat for one person", "Watersports", 275.0, 10),
        ("Lifejacket", "Protective and fashionable", "Watersports", 48.95, 14),
        ("Soccer Ball", "FIFA-approved size and weight", "Soccer", 19.5, 32),
```

```
        ("Corner Flags", "Give your playing field a professional touch", "Soccer", 34.95, 1),
        ("Stadium", "Flat-packed 35,000-seat stadium", "Soccer", 79500.0, 4),
        ("Thinking Cap", "Improve your brain efficiency by 75%", "Chess", 16.0, 8),
        ("Unsteady Chair", "Secretly give your opponent a disadvantage", "Chess", 29.95, 3),
        ("Human Chess Board", "A fun game for the family", "Chess", 75.0, 2),
        ("Bling-Bling King", "Gold-plated, diamond-studded King", "Chess", 1200.0, 4)];

    override func viewDidLoad() {
        super.viewDidLoad()
    }

    override func didReceiveMemoryWarning() {
        super.didReceiveMemoryWarning()
    }
}
```

The type of the variable is UILabel, which is the name of the class in the UIKit framework that implements the label functionality. The @IBOutlet attribute identifies the new variable as an outlet.

Updating the Display

Listing 3-3 shows how I used the outlet to update the text displayed by the label in order to display the number of items in stock.

Listing 3-3. Displaying the Total Stock in the ViewController.swift File

```
import UIKit

class ViewController: UIViewController {
    @IBOutlet weak var totalStockLabel: UILabel!
    var products = [
        ("Kayak", "A boat for one person", "Watersports", 275.0, 10),
        ("Lifejacket", "Protective and fashionable", "Watersports", 48.95, 14),
        ("Soccer Ball", "FIFA-approved size and weight", "Soccer", 19.5, 32),
        ("Corner Flags", "Give your playing field a professional touch", "Soccer", 34.95, 1),
        ("Stadium", "Flat-packed 35,000-seat stadium", "Soccer", 79500.0, 4),
        ("Thinking Cap", "Improve your brain efficiency by 75%", "Chess", 16.0, 8),
        ("Unsteady Chair", "Secretly give your opponent a disadvantage", "Chess", 29.95, 3),
        ("Human Chess Board", "A fun game for the family", "Chess", 75.0, 2),
        ("Bling-Bling King", "Gold-plated, diamond-studded King", "Chess", 1200.0, 4)];

    override func viewDidLoad() {
        super.viewDidLoad();
        displayStockTotal();
    }

    override func didReceiveMemoryWarning() {
        super.didReceiveMemoryWarning()
    }
```

```
func displayStockTotal() {
    let stockTotal = products.reduce(0,
        {(total, product) -> Int in return total + product.4});
    totalStockLabel.text = "\(stockTotal) Products in Stock";
}
}
```

I have defined a new method called displayStockTotal, which uses the reduce extension from the Swift standard library. The reduce method invokes a function for each item in the array. I expressed the function as a closure, which totals the value at index 4 for each data tuple.

Once I have generated the total, I set the text property of the label, which changes the string displayed by the UILabel component in the application layout.

I call the displayStockTotal method from viewDidLoad, which is invoked when the application is initialized and the view is loaded. To test the changes, click the Play button in the Xcode toolbar. The effect is shown in Figure 3-12.

Figure 3-12. Displaying the total number of products

Implementing the Table Cells

In this section, I am going to implement support for the table in order to provide the user with information about the stock level of each product and to change the stock level. I will create a custom table cell that contains other controls and wire everything up into the ViewController class, following the premise of creating a single-class application. (However, as you will see, I cannot get away with just one class, and I will end up with a simple second class that contains some IBOutlet properties).

Defining the Custom Table Cell and Layout

Click the `Main.storyboard` file in the navigator pane to open the Interface Builder editor. Ensure that the hierarchy is expanded so that you can see the components in the layout. Locate the `Table View Cell` component in the Object Library, drag it to the `Table View` component in the hierarchy, and release the mouse.

A new `Content View` item will appear in the hierarchy, which corresponds to a `Prototype Cells` object in the main IB view—this is the template that will be used to generate table cells.

Locate the `Text Field` item in the Object Library and drag it to the `Content View` item in the hierarchy. The `Text Field` component presents an editable text field. Position and resize the text field so that it occupies the right side of the table cell, as shown in Figure 3-13. The dotted blue lines in the figure are layout guides that Xcode provides to help position components.

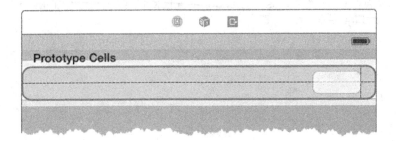

Figure 3-13. Positioning the first label in the custom table cell

---

Tip   You can drag the labels directly to the layout in the main part of the editor pane, but it is easy to add components to the wrong part of the layout. I find using the hierarchy to be more reliable, especially for complex layouts.

Ensure that the text field is selected, either in the main editor pane or in the component hierarchy, and use the Attributes Inspector to set the values shown in Table 3-3.

Table 3-3. The Configuration Changes Required for the Text Field

Attribute	Change
Font	Set this attribute to `System 20.0`.
Alignment	Set this attribute so that the text is aligned to the right edge of the component.

Now drag Label and Stepper items in the Object Library to create the layout shown in Figure 3-14, dragging the components to the Content View item in the hierarchy.

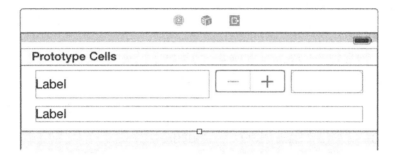

Figure 3-14. Adding the remaining components to the custom table cell layout

Tip   Don't worry about getting the layout pixel-perfect—a rough approximation will do. I enabled the blue lines in the figure to show the bounds of each component by selecting Canvas ➤ Show Bounds Rectangles from the Editor menu.

You will have to select the Table View Cell item in the hierarchy and use the grab bars to increase the height of the table cell to make everything fit.

To make it easier to differentiate between the two Label components, click the entry in the hierarchy for the topmost one and change its name to Name Label. Click the other Label and change its name to Description Label. Finally, click the entry for the Text Field and change its name to Text Field (the default name includes details of the style of the field).

The final step is to configure the components. Table 3-4 lists the new names for the components and the attributes that should be changed using the Attributes Inspector.

Table 3-4. The Attribute Changes Required for the Custom Table Cell Components

Component	Attribute	Value
Name Label	Font	System Bold 30
Description Label	Font	System 25
Text Field	Font	System 30

Setting the Table Cell Layout Constraints

Use the component hierarchy to set the layout constraints shown in Table 3-5. These ensure that the contents of the table cell will be visible regardless of the device and orientation used to display the app.

Table 3-5. *The Constraints Required for the Custom Table Cell Components*

Drag From	Drag To	Constraints
Text Field	Content View	Trailing Space to Container Margin Top Space to Container Margin
Text Field	Text Field	Width
Stepper	Content View	Top Space to Container Margin
Stepper	Text Field	Horizontal Spacing
Name Label	Content View	Leading Space to Container Margin Top Space to Container Margin
Name Label	Stepper	Horizontal Spacing
Name Label	Name Label	Height
Description Label	Content View	Leading Space to Container Margin Trailing Space to Container Margin Bottom Space to Container Margin

Creating the Table Cell Class and Outlets

To be able to display details of each product in a table cell, I need to be able to refer to the components added to the layout in the previous section. I do this by creating variables that are decorated with the IBOutlet attribute, just as I did for the UILabel component that displays the total number of items in stock. There is a wrinkle, however: I need to define a class that will be used to instantiate each cell in the table, which I can then use as a container for the outlets. I can't handle this in the ViewController class because custom data cell classes must be derived from UITableViewCell and Swift doesn't support multiple class inheritance. Listing 3-4 shows the addition of a new class to the ViewController.swift file.

Listing 3-4. *Adding a Table Cell Class to the ViewController.swift File*

```
import UIKit

class ProductTableCell : UITableViewCell {

}

class ViewController: UIViewController {

    //...statements omitted for brevity...
}
```

I have defined a new class called ProductTableCell, which will be instantiated for the cells in the table. To apply this class, select the Table View Cell item in the component hierarchy and use the Identity Inspector to change the value of the Class attribute to ProductTableCell and the value of the Module attribute to SportsStore.

Next, switch to the Attributes Inspector and set the Identifier attribute to ProductCell.

> **Tip**   Changing the Class attribute tells iOS to use the ProductTableCell class when it needs table cells. Setting the Identifier will allow me to request ProductTableCell objects to be created automatically, which I do in the next section.

Control-drag each of the four components added in the previous section—two labels, a text field, and a stepper—in turn to the new ProductTableCell class in the code editor to create new outlet properties; you can drag the items in the component hierarchy or the ones in the storyboard. Table 3-6 shows the mapping between the names of the components and the names I used for the outlets.

Table 3-6. The Mapping of Components Names to Outlet Property Names in the ProductTableCell Class

Name	Description
Name Label	nameLabel
Description Label	descriptionLabel
Stepper	stockStepper
Text Field	stockField

> **Tip**   Restart Xcode if you see an error telling you that there is no information available for the ProductTableCell class when you create an outlet.

When you have created all four outlets, the ProductTableCell class should match Listing 3-5.

Listing 3-5. Adding Outlet Properties to the ProductTableCell Class in the ViewController.swift File

```
...
class ProductTableCell : UITableViewCell {
    @IBOutlet weak var nameLabel: UILabel!
    @IBOutlet weak var descriptionLabel: UILabel!
    @IBOutlet weak var stockStepper: UIStepper!
    @IBOutlet weak var stockField: UITextField!
}
...
```

The order of the properties doesn't matter as long as you have defined all four and they correspond to the components shown in the table.

Implementing the Data Source Protocol

To provide a table with data, I must implement two methods from the UITableViewDataSource protocol that give me the opportunity to tell the table how many rows there are and to generate each cell. Before I do that, I need to create an outlet property so that I can refer to the table view from the ViewController class.

Control-drag the Table View item in the component hierarchy to the ViewController class and release the mouse so that Xcode creates the property under the totalStockOutlet property. Set the name of the property to tableView. The result should be the addition of the property shown in Listing 3-6.

Listing 3-6. Adding an Outlet Property for the Table View to the ViewController.swift File

```
import UIKit

class ProductTableCell : UITableViewCell {
    // ...statements omitted for brevity...
}

class ViewController: UIViewController {

    @IBOutlet weak var totalStockLabel: UILabel!
    @IBOutlet weak var tableView: UITableView!
    // ...statements omitted for brevity...
}
```

Now I can add the protocol to the UIViewController class and implement the two methods from the UITableViewDataSource protocol, which you can see in Listing 3-7.

Listing 3-7. Implementing the Data Source Protocol Methods in the ViewController.swift File

```
import UIKit

class ProductTableCell: UITableViewCell {
    @IBOutlet weak var nameLabel: UILabel!
    @IBOutlet weak var descriptionLabel: UILabel!
    @IBOutlet weak var stockStepper: UIStepper!
    @IBOutlet weak var stockField: UITextField!
}

class ViewController: UIViewController, UITableViewDataSource {

    @IBOutlet weak var totalStockLabel: UILabel!
    @IBOutlet weak var tableView: UITableView!

    var products = [
        ("Kayak", "A boat for one person", "Watersports", 275.0, 10),
        ("Lifejacket", "Protective and fashionable", "Watersports", 48.95, 14),
        ("Soccer Ball", "FIFA-approved size and weight", "Soccer", 19.5, 32),
        ("Corner Flags", "Give your playing field a professional touch", "Soccer", 34.95, 1),
        ("Stadium", "Flat-packed 35,000-seat stadium", "Soccer", 79500.0, 4),
```

```
                ("Thinking Cap", "Improve your brain efficiency by 75%", "Chess", 16.0, 8),
                ("Unsteady Chair", "Secretly give your opponent a disadvantage", "Chess", 29.95, 3),
                ("Human Chess Board", "A fun game for the family", "Chess", 75.0, 2),
                ("Bling-Bling King", "Gold-plated, diamond-studded King", "Chess", 1200.0, 4)];

    override func viewDidLoad() {
        super.viewDidLoad();
        displayStockTotal();
    }

    override func didReceiveMemoryWarning() {
        super.didReceiveMemoryWarning();
    }

    func tableView(tableView: UITableView,
        numberOfRowsInSection section: Int) -> Int {
        return products.count;
    }

    func tableView(tableView: UITableView,
        cellForRowAtIndexPath indexPath: NSIndexPath) -> UITableViewCell {
        let product = products[indexPath.row];
        let cell = tableView.dequeueReusableCellWithIdentifier("ProductCell")
        as ProductTableCell;
        cell.nameLabel.text = product.0;
        cell.descriptionLabel.text = product.1;
        cell.stockStepper.value = Double(product.4);
        cell.stockField.text = String(product.4);
        return cell;
    }

    func displayStockTotal() {
        let stockTotal = products.reduce(0,
        {(total, product) -> Int in return total + product.4});
        totalStockLabel.text = "\(stockTotal) Products in Stock";
    }
}
```

The methods from the UITableDataViewDataSource protocol are all called tableView and are differentiated by the parameters they define. The version of the tableView method that defines a numberOfRowsInSection parameter is called to find out how many rows there will be in the table, which I have implemented by returning the number of tuples in the product array.

The other version of the tableView method creates instances of the UITableViewCell class, which represents a row in the table. Information about the row is accessed through the row property of the indexPath parameter. The reason that I added an outlet property for the table view is so that I can call the dequeueReusableCellWithIdentifier method, which reuses cells that have been created to display content that is no longer visible. The argument to the dequeueReusableCellWithIdentifier method is the value I used to set the Identifier attribute for the custom table cell, which is how the table knows to create an instance of the ProductTableCell class.

Registering the Data Source

The final step toward displaying the data is to register the View Controller class as the data source for the table. Control-drag the Table View item to the View Controller item in the component hierarchy. When you release the mouse, a pop-up menu will appear—select the dataSource item to link the ViewController and the table, as shown in Figure 3-15.

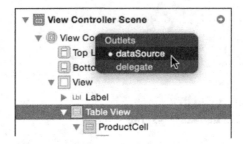

Figure 3-15. *Setting the data source for the table view*

Testing the Data Source

To test the data provided by the ViewController class, click the Play button on the Xcode toolbar, which will build the project and send the application to the iOS simulator, as shown in Figure 3-16.

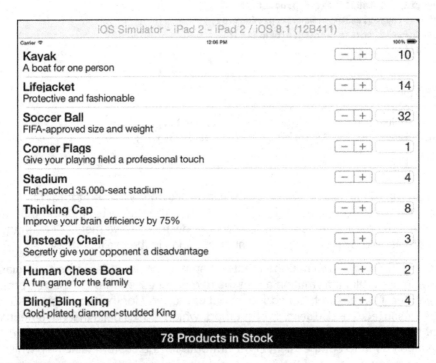

Figure 3-16. *Testing the SportsStore application*

Handling the Editing Actions

In this section, I am going to complete the SportsStore application by wiring up the Stepper and Text Field components so that the user can change the stock level for a product. To provide visual confirmation of changes, I will update the text displayed by the Label component at the bottom of the screen.

Switch to the Connections Inspector and then click the Text Field item in the component hierarchy. The Inspector will show a list of the events that are supported. Drag from the circle to the right of the Editing Changed event, known as the *connection well*, to the ViewController class in the Assistant Editor and position the line so that it terminates above the definition of the displayStockTotal method. Release the mouse and a pop-up menu will appear, as shown in Figure 3-17.

Figure 3-17.   Creating the Action method

Set Name to stockLevelDidChange and click the Connect button. Xcode will add the method shown in Listing 3-8 to the ViewController class.

Listing 3-8.   Adding an Action Method to the ViewController.swift File

```
...
@IBAction func stockLevelDidChange(sender: AnyObject) {
}
...
```

The IBAction attribute indicates that this is a method that will be invoked in response to a change in a layout component—in this case, whenever the text field is edited.

I want the same method to be invoked when the value of the stepper changes, so click the Stepper item in the component hierarchy, move to the Connections Inspector, and drag from the Value Changed connection well.

Position the pointer over the method stockLevelDidChange so that the method is highlighted and the text balloon changes from Insert Action to Connection Action and release the mouse button.

> **Tip**   Xcode can be unreliable when it comes to connecting to existing events. If you don't see the method highlighting, then simply create a new action and set the name to `stockLevelDidChange`, just like for the text field. This will create two methods with the same name in the code file. Delete one of the methods—it doesn't matter which one. The relationship between components and methods is handled through the method name, so this alternative technique can be used to work around one of Xcode's limitations.

Handling the Events

The `stockLevelDidChange` method will be invoked when the user interacts with the `Stepper` or `Text Field` components and that allows me to update the stock levels accordingly. Listing 3-9 shows the changes I made to the `ViewController` class to handle the events.

Listing 3-9. Handling Events in the ViewController.swift File

```swift
import UIKit

class ProductTableCell : UITableViewCell {

    @IBOutlet weak var nameLabel: UILabel!
    @IBOutlet weak var descriptionLabel: UILabel!
    @IBOutlet weak var stockStepper: UIStepper!
    @IBOutlet weak var stockField: UITextField!

    var productId:Int?;
}

class ViewController: UIViewController, UITableViewDataSource {

    @IBOutlet weak var totalStockLabel: UILabel!
    @IBOutlet weak var tableView: UITableView!

    var products = [
        ("Kayak", "A boat for one person", "Watersports", 275.0, 10),
        ("Lifejacket", "Protective and fashionable", "Watersports", 48.95, 14),
        ("Soccer Ball", "FIFA-approved size and weight", "Soccer", 19.5, 32),
        ("Corner Flags", "Give your playing field a professional touch", "Soccer", 34.95, 1),
        ("Stadium", "Flat-packed 35,000-seat stadium", "Soccer", 79500.0, 4),
        ("Thinking Cap", "Improve your brain efficiency by 75%", "Chess", 16.0, 8),
        ("Unsteady Chair", "Secretly give your opponent a disadvantage", "Chess", 29.95, 3),
        ("Human Chess Board", "A fun game for the family", "Chess", 75.0, 2),
        ("Bling-Bling King", "Gold-plated, diamond-studded King", "Chess", 1200.0, 4)];

    override func viewDidLoad() {
        super.viewDidLoad()
        displayStockTotal();
    }
```

```
override func didReceiveMemoryWarning() {
    super.didReceiveMemoryWarning()
}

func tableView(tableView: UITableView,
    numberOfRowsInSection section: Int) -> Int {
    return products.count;
}

func tableView(tableView: UITableView,
    cellForRowAtIndexPath indexPath: NSIndexPath) -> UITableViewCell {
    let product = products[indexPath.row];
    let cell = tableView.dequeueReusableCellWithIdentifier("ProductCell")
    as ProductTableCell;
    cell.productId = indexPath.row;
    cell.nameLabel.text = product.0;
    cell.descriptionLabel.text = product.1;
    cell.stockStepper.value = Double(product.4);
    cell.stockField.text = String(product.4);
    return cell;
}

@IBAction func stockLevelDidChange(sender: AnyObject) {
    if var currentCell = sender as? UIView {
        while (true) {
            currentCell = currentCell.superview!;
            if let cell = currentCell as? ProductTableCell {
                if let id = cell.productId? {

                    var newStockLevel:Int?;

                    if let stepper = sender as? UIStepper {
                        newStockLevel = Int(stepper.value);
                    } else if let textfield = sender as? UITextField {
                        if let newValue = textfield.text.toInt()? {
                            newStockLevel = newValue;
                        }
                    }

                    if let level = newStockLevel {
                        products[id].4 = level;
                        cell.stockStepper.value = Double(level);
                        cell.stockField.text = String(level);
                    }
                }
            }
            break;
        }
    }
    displayStockTotal();
    }
}
```

```
func displayStockTotal() {
    let stockTotal = products.reduce(0,
    {(total, product) -> Int in return total + product.4});
    totalStockLabel.text = "\(stockTotal) Products in Stock";
  }
}
```

The first change I made was to add a `productId` property to the `ProductTableCell` class, which I set in the `tableView` method that creates the table cells. I use this property in the `stockLevelDidChange` to map between the component that has invoked the method and the product whose stock level has to be changed. The argument to the `setLevelDidChange` method is the component that triggered the event, which I use to figure out how to get the new stock level and update the display to the user. At the end of the `stockLevelDidChange` method, I call `displayStockTotal` to provide visual reinforcement of the change to the user.

Testing the SportsStore App

The unstructured version of the SportsStore application is now complete. To see the finished result, click the Play button on the Xcode toolbar. Figure 3-18 shows the app in its landscape orientation.

Figure 3-18. The finished unstructured SportsStore application

The user is presented with a list of products and can use the Stepper and Text Field components to change the stock level for each of them. The total number of stock items is displayed at the bottom of the screen.

This application is undeniably basic, but it has allowed me to demonstrate the Xcode techniques required for this book and provides an example to which I can apply different patterns in addition to showing you fragments of code.

Summary

Xcode is an idiosyncratic development tool that can be confusing at first but that has some nice tools for creating apps. In this chapter, I created an iOS app with as little structure as possible. I rely on this app to demonstrate the design patterns in greater context in order to provide more realistic scenarios for their use.

Part II

The Creation Patterns

Chapter 4

The Object Template Pattern

In this chapter I describe a technique that is so fundamental to object-oriented programming that it isn't usually classified as a design pattern at all: creating new objects directly from classes or structs. In later chapters, I describe different techniques for managing the creation of objects, but I want to start by explaining the benefit of using classes and structs as templates from which objects are created. Not only is it an important topic in its own right, but it allows me to illustrate the problems that arise when templates are not used to create objects; it also sets the foundation for explaining the benefits of more advanced patterns later. Table 4-1 puts the object template pattern into context.

Table 4-1. *Putting the Object Template Pattern into Context*

Question	Answer
What is it?	The object template pattern uses a class or struct as the specification for the data types and logic for a given data type. Objects are created using the template, and values for the data are set during initialization, either through the use of default values in the template or using values provided by the component to the class or struct initializer, also known as the *constructor*.
What are the benefits?	The object template pattern provides the foundation for grouping data values and the logic that manipulates them together, known as *encapsulation*. Encapsulation allows an object to present an API to its consumers while hiding the private implementation of that API. This helps prevent the tight coupling of components.
When should you use this pattern?	You should use this pattern in all but the simplest of projects. Swift tuples are an interesting feature, but they can present a long-term maintenance problem, and only a little extra work is required to create a simple class or struct instead.
When should you avoid this pattern?	These are no drawbacks in using this pattern, but later patterns in this part of the book will show you more advanced techniques for its use.

(*continued*)

Table 4-1. (*continued*)

Question	Answer
How do you know when you have implemented the pattern correctly?	The pattern is implemented correctly when you can make changes to the private implementation of a class or struct without making corresponding changes to the components that use it.
Are there any common pitfalls?	The only pitfall with this pattern is using a struct as a template when you intended to use a class. Structs and classes have a lot in common, but they behave differently when objects created from them are assigned to new variables, as I explain in Chapter 5. (There are other differences, but they are not pertinent for this chapter.)
Are there any related patterns?	The prototype pattern, which I describe in Chapter 5, provides an alternative technique for creating objects.

Preparing the Example Project

For this chapter, I created an Xcode OS X Command Line Tool project called ObjectTemplate following the same process I described in Chapter 3. No other preparation is required at the moment.

Understanding the Problem Addressed by the Pattern

In Chapter 3, I used Swift tuples to define the data that the SportsStore application works with. Here is an example of a tuple from that code:

```
...
("Kayak", "A boat for one person", "Watersports", 275.0, 10)
...
```

Tuples are a set of values grouped together and are convenient and easy to use, but they present problems that mean their use should be limited. Listing 4-1 shows the statements I added to the main.swift file, which Xcode adds to Command Line Tool projects.

Listing 4-1. The Contents of the main.swift File

```
var products = [
    ("Kayak", "A boat for one person", 275.0, 10),
    ("Lifejacket", "Protective and fashionable", 48.95, 14),
    ("Soccer Ball", "FIFA-approved size and weight", 19.5, 32)];

func calculateTax(product:(String, String, Double, Int)) -> Double {
    return product.2 * 0.2;
}
```

```
func calculateStockValue(tuples:[(String, String, Double, Int)]) -> Double {
    return tuples.reduce(0, {
        (total, product) -> Double in
            return total + (product.2 * Double(product.3))
    });
}

println("Sales tax for Kayak: $\(calculateTax(products[0]))");
println("Total value of stock: $\(calculateStockValue(products))");
```

In this code, I defined an array of tuples representing products and two functions that operate on them. The calculateTax function defines a tuple parameter that it uses to calculate the sales tax on a price (I live in London and have set the rate to 20 percent, which is the sales tax for the United Kingdom). The calculateStockValue function operates on the array of tuples to calculate the total value of the products by multiplying the number of items in stock by the price of the product. I call both functions and write out the results using the println function. Running the project produces the following output in the Xcode debug console:

```
Sales tax for Kayak: $55.0
Total value of stock: $4059.3
```

One of the recurring themes in this book is that tightly coupled components are the antithesis of design patterns. Two components are tightly coupled when one depends on the inner workings of another, or, put another way, when you can make a change to one component without also updating the other.

The term *component* is loosely defined, and in this case I am using it to refer to the array of tuples and the functions that operate on it. Figure 4-1 shows the tight couplings from the playground that exist between two functions and the tuples.

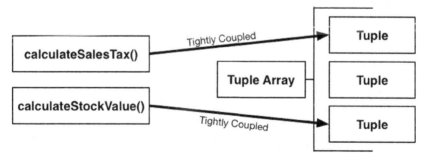

Figure 4-1. The tight couplings in the playground

Both functions are tightly coupled to the tuples, both in the way they define their parameters and in the function bodies. When defining parameters for functions that operate on tuples, the number, order, and types of the tuple values have to match exactly. When operating on tuples in a function body, the index values used to get or set values have to be defined explicitly. Here is the calculateSalesTax function, in which I have highlighted the dependencies on the tuples:

```
...
func calculateTax(product:(String, String, String, Double, Int)) -> Double {
    return product.3 * 0.2;
}
...
```

And here are the dependencies that the calculateStockValue function has:

```
...
func calculateStockValue(tuples:[(String, String, Double, Int)]) -> Double {
    return tuples.reduce(0, {(total, product) -> Double in
        return total + (product.2 * Double(product.3))
    });
}
...
```

The dependency on the structure of the tuples means that the functions and the tuples are tightly coupled. The most obvious impact of tight coupling is that a change to the tuples forces corresponding changes wherever there is a dependency. In Listing 4-2, you can see what happens when I remove a value from the tuples.

Listing 4-2. Removing a Value from the Tuples in the main.swift File

```
var products = [("Kayak", 275.0, 10),
    ("Lifejacket", 48.95, 14),
    ("Soccer Ball", 19.5, 32)];

func calculateTax(product:(String, Double, Int)) -> Double {
    return product.1 * 0.2;
}

func calculateStockValue(tuples:[(String, Double, Int)]) -> Double {
    return tuples.reduce(0, {(total, product) -> Double in
        return total + (product.1 * Double(product.2))
    });
}

println("Sales tax for Kayak: $\(calculateTax(products[0]))");
println("Total value of stock: $\(calculateStockValue(products))");
```

UNDERSTANDING WHY TIGHT COUPLINGS CAN BE A PROBLEM

Tightly coupled components make code harder to maintain, which means that it takes more effort to make changes and test their impact. As Listing 4-2 shows, a change in one component requires a change in those that depend on its implementation. In an application that contains lots of tight coupling, these changes can cascade through the code, and the act of making a simple fix or adding a new feature becomes a substantial rewrite.

Loosely coupled components are a key goal in design patterns, but, as I explained in Chapter 1, it doesn't always make sense to apply a pattern to an application. There are some kinds of development where tight couplings are perfectly reasonable, either because they offer performance gains (such as real-time software) or because the application is unlikely to require any maintenance (because it is extremely simple or has a short life). Be careful when deciding you don't expect to maintain the code; there are few applications where this turns out to be true, even if that was the original intent.

I removed the value that describes the product, and the highlighted statements show the corresponding changes required in the functions. In a real project, these changes can mount up, and if they affect other tight couplings, then number of changes can lead to a substantial portion of the code in the application being modified. This level of change is hard to manage and requires thorough testing to ensure that the changes have been applied consistently and that the changes have not introduced any new bugs.

Understanding the Object Template Pattern

The *object template pattern* uses a class or struct to define a template from which objects are created. When an application component requires an object, it calls on the Swift runtime to create it by specifying the name of the template and any runtime initialization data values that are required to configure the object. There are three operations that make up the object template pattern, as illustrated by Figure 4-2.

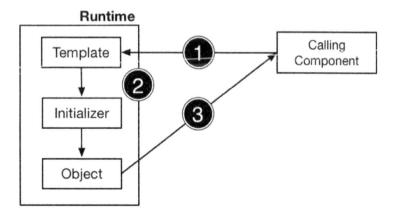

Figure 4-2. The object template pattern

The first operation is the calling component asking the Swift runtime to create an object, providing the name of the template to use and any runtime data values that are required to customize the object that will be created.

In the second operation, the Swift runtime allocates the memory required to store the object and uses the template to create it. Templates contain initializer methods that are used to prepare the object for use by settings its initial state, through either the runtime values supplied by the calling component or the values defined in the template (or both), and the Swift runtime calls the initializer to prepare the object for use. In the final operation, the Swift runtime gives the object it has created to the calling component. This three-step process can be repeated over and over again so that a single template can be used to create multiple objects.

UNDERSTANDING CLASSES STRUCTS, OBJECTS, AND INSTANCES

There are some object-oriented programing terms that are used loosely in day-to-day development but that can be confusing when it comes to understanding design patterns. The critical terms for this pattern are *class*, *struct*, *object*, and *instance*.

Classes and structs are both templates, which are the recipes that Swift follows for the object template pattern. Swift follows the instructions in the template to create new *objects*. The same template can be reused to create multiple objects. Each object is different, but it is created using the same instructions, just like a recipe can be used to create multiple cakes (add one Int, a method to change its value, and so on).

The word *instance* has the same meaning as object, but it is used to refer to the name of the pattern used to create that object so that a Product object can also be called an instance of the Product class.

The important point is that classes and structs are the instructions you write during development and objects are created when the application. When you change the value stored by an object, for example, it doesn't change the pattern used to create it.

Implementing the Object Template Pattern

Listing 4-3 shows the contents of a new file called Product.swift that I added to the example project and used to define a class called Product.

Listing 4-3. The Contents of the Product.swift File

```
class Product {
    var name:String;
    var description:String;
    var price:Double;
    var stock:Int;

    init(name:String, description:String, price:Double, stock:Int) {
        self.name = name;
        self.description = description;
        self.price = price;
        self.stock = stock;
    }
}
```

I have created a simple class in the listing to replicate the tuple-based approach as closely as possible, but I will add features to the class shortly. Listing 4-4 shows how I have updated the main.swift file to use the Product class.

Listing 4-4. Using the Product Class in the main.swift File

```
var products = [
    Product(name: "Kayak", description: "A boat for one person",
        price: 275, stock: 10),
    Product(name: "Lifejacket", description: "Protective and fashionable",
        price: 48.95, stock: 14),
    Product(name: "Soccer Ball", description: "FIFA-approved size and weight",
        price: 19.5, stock: 32)];

func calculateTax(product:Product) -> Double {
    return product.price * 0.2;
}

func calculateStockValue(productsArray:[Product]) -> Double {
    return productsArray.reduce(0, {(total, product) -> Double in
            return total + (product.price * Double(product.stock))
        });
}

println("Sales tax for Kayak: $\(calculateTax(products[0]))");
println("Total value of stock: $\(calculateStockValue(products))");
```

Like most patterns, using a class to define a template for objects requires some additional work, but it has substantial benefits; in fact, the benefits are so fundamental to effective OO programming that the uses of classes and structs are often taken as givens even when quicker and more direct approaches, such as tuples, are available.

When using a tuple, the definitions of the structure of the data and a set of values are performed in a simple step, but there are two steps when using a template: defining the template and creating objects using the template.

Understanding the Benefits of the Pattern

The benefits of using a template are significant and are generally worth the effort required to define the template, whether it is a class or a struct. Tuples are a nice feature, but for the serious software developer, classes and structs are usually preferable because they provide a level of control and loose coupling that tuples can't match, as I explain in the sections that follow.

The Benefit of Decoupling

I made the example in Listing 4-4 as simple as possible. It doesn't take advantage of the features that classes and structs provide, but it does allow me to demonstrate that even the simplest template reduces the impact of changes. Listing 4-5 shows how I removed the description property from the Product class.

Listing 4-5. Removing a Property from the Product Class

```
class Product {
    var name:String;
    var price:Double;
    var stock:Int;

    init(name:String, price:Double, stock:Int) {
        self.name = name;
        self.price = price;
        self.stock = stock;
    }
}
```

Listing 4-6 shows the corresponding changes I made to the main.swift file.

Listing 4-6. Updating the main.swift File to Reflect the Product Class Change

```
var products = [
    Product(name: "Kayak", price: 275, stock: 10),
    Product(name: "Lifejacket", price: 48.95, stock: 14),
    Product(name: "Soccer Ball", price: 19.5, stock: 32)];

func calculateTax(product:Product) -> Double {
    return product.price * 0.2;
}

func calculateStockValue(productsArray:[Product]) -> Double {
    return productsArray.reduce(0, {
        (total, product) -> Double in
            return total + (product.price * Double(product.stock))
    });
}

println("Sales tax for Kayak: $\(calculateTax(products[0]))");
println("Total value of stock: $\(calculateStockValue(products))");
```

I have updated the statements that create instances of the Product class so they no longer provide a value for the description property. The important point to note is that the change I made to the Product class has no impact on the calculateTax and calculateStockValue functions at all, and that's because each property in the class is defined and accessed independently of the other properties and because neither of the functions relies on the description property.

The use of classes and structs limits the scope of changes to just the code that is directly impacted by the change and prevents the widespread change cascades that can arise when using less structured data types, such as tuples.

The Benefit of Encapsulation

The most important benefit from using classes or structs as templates for data objects is the support for *encapsulation*. Encapsulation is one of the core ideas behind object-oriented programming, and there are two aspects of this idea that have a bearing on this chapter.

The first aspect is that encapsulation allows data values and the logic that operates on those values to be combined in a single component. Combining the data and logic makes it easier to read the code because everything related to the data type is defined in the same place. Listing 4-7 shows how I have updated the Product class so that it includes some logic.

Listing 4-7. Adding Logic in the Product.swift File

```swift
class Product {
    var name:String;
    var price:Double;
    var stock:Int;

    init(name:String, price:Double, stock:Int) {
        self.name = name;
        self.price = price;
        self.stock = stock;
    }

    func calculateTax(rate: Double) -> Double {
        return self.price * rate;
    }

    var stockValue: Double {
        get {
            return self.price * Double(self.stock);
        }
    }
}
```

I have added a calculateTax method, which accepts a tax rate as an argument and uses it to calculate the sales tax, and a stockValue computed property, which implements a getter clause that calculates the total value of the stock. To reflect these changes, I updated the code statements in the main.swift file that operate on Product objections to use the new method and property, as shown in Listing 4-8.

Listing 4-8. Updating the Code in the main.swift File

```swift
var products = [
    Product(name: "Kayak", price: 275, stock: 10),
    Product(name: "Lifejacket", price: 48.95, stock: 14),
    Product(name: "Soccer Ball", price: 19.5, stock: 32)];

func calculateStockValue(productsArray:[Product]) -> Double {
    return productsArray.reduce(0, {(total, product) -> Double in
            return total + product.stockValue;
        });
}

println("Sales tax for Kayak: $\(products[0].calculateTax(0.2))");
println("Total value of stock: $\(calculateStockValue(products))");
```

These may seem like simple changes, but something important has happened: the `Product` class now has a public presentation and a private implementation, as illustrated by Figure 4-3.

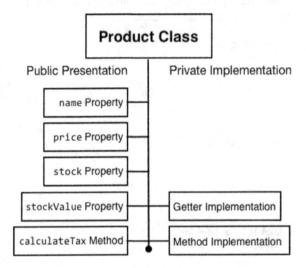

Figure 4-3. The public and private aspects of the Product class

The public presentation is the API that other components can use. Any component can get or set the values of the `name`, `price`, and `stock` properties and use them in any way they need. The public presentation also includes the `stockValue` property and the `calculateTax` method, but—and this is the important part—not their implementations.

> **Tip** Don't confuse the idea of a private implementation with the use of the `private` keyword. The `private` keyword limits who can use a class, method, or property, but even when the `private` keyword isn't used, the implementation of methods and computed properties isn't visible to calling components.

The ability to present a property or method without exposing its implementation makes it easy to break tight couplings because it is impossible for another component to depend on the implementation. As an example, Listing 4-9 shows how I have changed the implementation of the `calculateTax` method to define a maximum tax amount. Because the calculation is performed in the implementation of the `Product` object, the change is invisible to other components, which trust that the `Product` class knows how to perform its calculations.

Listing 4-9. Changing a Method Implementation in the Product.swift File

```
...
func calculateTax(rate: Double) -> Double {
    return min(10, self.price * rate);
}
...
```

I have used the min function from the Swift standard library to cap the amount of sales tax at $10. I have shown only the calculateTax method in Listing 4-9 because no other code statement in the playground has to change to accommodate the new tax calculation; the change is in the private implementation part of the Product class, with which other components are unable to create dependencies. Running the application produces the following results:

```
Sales tax for Kayak: $10.0
Total value of stock: $4059.3
```

The Benefit of an Evolving Public Presentation

A nice feature of Swift is the way that you can evolve the public presentation of a class over time as the application changes. As matters stand, the stock property is a standard stored property that can be set to any Int value, but it doesn't make sense to have a negative number of items in stock, and doing so will affect the result returned by the stockValue calculated property.

Swift allows me to seamlessly replace the stock-stored property with a calculated property whose implementation can enforce a validation policy to ensure that the stock level is never less than zero. Listing 4-10 shows the change that I made to alter the way the property is handled.

Listing 4-10. Adding a Calculated Property in the Product.swift File

```swift
class Product {

    var name:String;
    var price:Double;
    private var stockBackingValue:Int = 0;

    var stock:Int {
        get {
            return stockBackingValue;
        }
        set {
            stockBackingValue = max(0, newValue);
        }
    }

    init(name:String, price:Double, stock:Int) {
        self.name = name;
        self.price = price;
        self.stock = stock;
    }

    func calculateTax(rate: Double) -> Double {
        return min(10, self.price * rate);
    }
}
```

```
    var stockValue: Double {
        get {
            return self.price * Double(self.stock);
        }
    }
}
```

I have defined a backing variable that will hold the value of the stock property and have replaced the stored stock property with a calculated property that has a getter and setter. The getter simply returns the value of the backing property, which I have named stockBackingValue, but the setter uses the max function from the standard library to set the backing value to zero when a negative value is used to set the property. The effect of this change is that the public and private parts of the Product class have changed, but in a way that does not impact the code that uses the class, as shown in Figure 4-4.

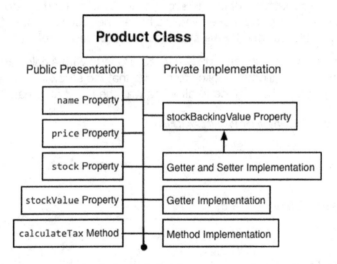

Figure 4-4. *The effect of changing a stored property to a calculated property*

Listing 4-11 shows the changes I made to the main.swift file to check the new validation property.

Listing 4-11. *Checking Validation in the main.swift File*

```
var products = [
    Product(name: "Kayak", price: 275, stock: 10),
    Product(name: "Lifejacket", price: 48.95, stock: 14),
    Product(name: "Soccer Ball", price: 19.5, stock: 32)];

func calculateStockValue(productsArray:[Product]) -> Double {
    return productsArray.reduce(0, {(total, product) -> Double in
            return total + product.stockValue;
        });
}
```

```
println("Sales tax for Kayak: $\(products[0].calculateTax(0.2))");
println("Total value of stock: $\(calculateStockValue(products))");
products[0].stock = -50;
println("Stock Level for Kayak: \(products[0].stock)");
```

I added two statements to the end of the playground to test the stock property's ability to deal with negative values, but no other changes are required. In particular, the code statements that rely on the stock property are unaware of the change from a stored property to a calculated one. Here is the console output that is produced when the example application is run:

```
Sales tax for Kayak: $10.0
Total value of stock: $4059.3
Stock Level for Kayak: 0
```

The last message shows the effect of the calculated property: I set the stock property to -50, but when I get the property value, I receive 0.

Understanding the Pitfalls of the Pattern

The pitfall to avoid with this pattern is choosing the wrong kind of template, and that usually means using a struct when a class would be more appropriate. Swift classes and structs have a lot in common, but there is one important difference in the context of this pattern: structs are value objects, and classes are reference objects. I explain this difference in more detail in Chapter 5, in which I describe the prototype pattern.

Examples of the Object Template Pattern in Cocoa

Because this is such a fundamental pattern, classes and structs can be found throughout the Cocoa frameworks and the built-in Swift types. Basic types such as strings, arrays, and dictionaries are implemented as structs, and classes are used to represent everything from network connections to user interface components. I am not going to list all of the classes and structs that are used in iOS and the Cocoa frameworks, but if you want to get a sense of how deeply rooted this pattern is in iOS development, take a look at the classes I used to create the SportsStore application. In addition to the Product class I created in this chapter, I have relied on NSNumberFormatter to format currency strings, UIViewController to manage the view presented by the app, and classes such as UILabel, UITextField, and UIStepper to preset layout components to the user.

Applying the Pattern to the SportsStore App

In this section, I will create and apply a Product class and use it to remove the tuples from the SportsStore app. Don't worry if you didn't follow the step-by-step instructions in Chapter 3; you can download the project from Apress.com along with all of the source code for this book.

Preparing the Example Application

The preparation for this chapter is to create a Swift file that I will use to define utility functions that are not directly related to design patterns. To add a new file to the project, Control-click the SportsStore folder in the project navigator and select New File from the menu. Xcode will present a choice of different files types, as illustrated in Figure 4-5.

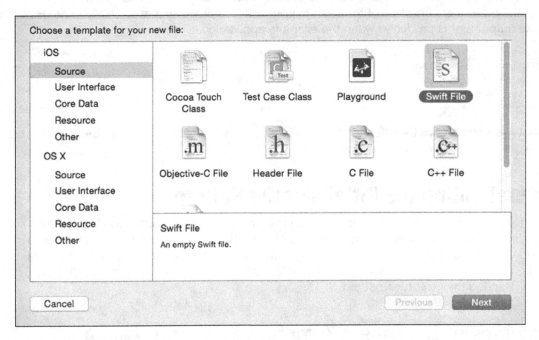

Figure 4-5. *Selecting the type of a new file*

Select Swift File from the iOS ➤ Source category and click the Next button. Set the file name to Utils.swift and ensure that SportsStore is checked in the Targets list, as shown in Figure 4-6.

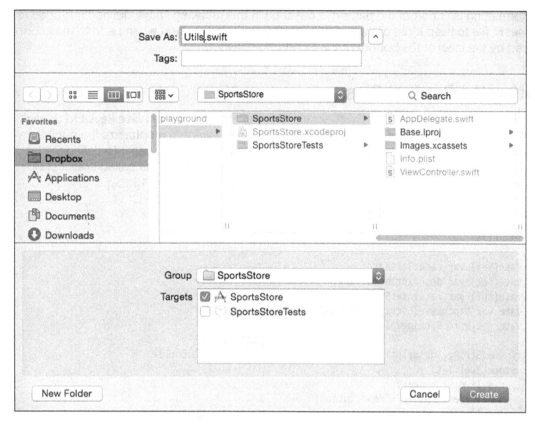

Figure 4-6. Creating the Product.swift file

Xcode will create the new file and open it for editing. Listing 4-12 shows how I used the file to define the Utils class.

Listing 4-12. The Contents of the Utils.swift File

```
import Foundation;

class Utils {

    class func currencyStringFromNumber(number:Double) -> String {
        let formatter = NSNumberFormatter();
        formatter.numberStyle = NSNumberFormatterStyle.CurrencyStyle;
        return formatter.stringFromNumber(number) ?? "";
    }
}
```

I have defined a type method (also known as a *static* method) called currencyStringFromNumber that accepts a Double value and returns a number formatted as a currency value. For example, the value 1000.1 would be formatted into the string $1,000.10. (The currency sign is applied based on the locale settings of the device. Outside of the United States, the dollar sign may be replaced with another symbol, such as those for the euro or the British pound.)

String formatting isn't part of the patterns I describe in this table, so I have defined this code in the Utils.swift file to keep it out of the way. I'll use the new type method when I add to the information displayed by the label at the bottom of the SportsStore layout.

Creating the Product Class

As I explain in the "Understanding Swift Access Control" sidebar, the private keyword doesn't restrict access to code defined in the same class file. Since I want to emphasize the public/private separation provided by this pattern, I am going to create a new file and use it to define the Product class. Following the process I described in the previous section, add a file called Product.swift to the SportsStore project and use it to define the class shown in Listing 4-13.

Listing 4-13. The Contents of the Product.swift File

```
class Product {

    private(set) var name:String;
    private(set) var description:String;
    private(set) var category:String;
    private var stockLevelBackingValue:Int = 0;
    private var priceBackingValue:Double = 0;

    init(name:String, description:String, category:String, price:Double,
        stockLevel:Int) {
            self.name = name;
            self.description = description;
            self.category = category;
            self.price = price;
            self.stockLevel = stockLevel;
    }

    var stockLevel:Int {
        get { return stockLevelBackingValue;}
        set { stockLevelBackingValue = max(0, newValue);}
    }

    private(set) var price:Double {
        get { return priceBackingValue;}
        set { priceBackingValue = max(1, newValue);}
    }

    var stockValue:Double {
        get {
            return price * Double(stockLevel);
        }
    }
}
```

The Product class shown in Listing 4-13 puts emphasis on the separation of the public presentation from the private implementation, which I have achieved in a couple of ways. The first way is by annotating the properties with private or private(set). The private keyword hides whatever it is applied to from code outside of the current file, and this has the effect of making the priceBackingValue and stockLevelBackingValue properties entirely invisible to the rest of the SportsStore application because the Product class is the only thing in the Product.swift file.

Annotating a property with private(set) means that a property can be read from code in other files in the same module but set by code only in the Product.swift file. I have used private(set) for most of the properties in Listing 4-13, which has the effect of allowing the values to be set using the arguments passed to the class initializer but not otherwise.

> **Tip**   I could have achieved a similar effect using constants, but I want to emphasize the object template pattern in this chapter, and private(set) is a more useful example.

The other technique I used is a calculated property that defines only a get clause. The implementation of the calculated property is private even though the property itself is available throughout the current module.

UNDERSTANDING SWIFT ACCESS CONTROL

Swift takes an unusual approach to access control, which can catch out the unwary. There are three levels of access control, which are applied using the public, private, and internal keywords. The private keyword is the most restrictive; it restricts access to the classes, structs methods, and properties to code defined in the same file. Restricting access on a per-file basis is a different approach from most languages and means that private has no effect in Xcode playgrounds.

The internal keyword denotes that access is allowed within the current module. This is the default level of access control that is used if no keyword is applied. For most iOS developers, internal protection will have the effect of allowing a class, struct, method, function, or property to be used throughout a project.

The public keyword applies the least restrictive level of control and allows access from anywhere, including outside the current module. This is of most use to developers who are creating frameworks and who will need to use the public keyword to define the API that the framework presents to other developers.

If you have moved to Swift from a language such as C# or Java, then you can most closely re-create the access controls you are used to by defining each class or struct in its own .swift file and using the private and internal access levels.

Applying the Product Class

Applying the `Product` class is a simple process. To use the `Product` class, I need to replace the tuples in the `ViewController.swift` file with `Product` instances and replace the references to individual tuple values with the corresponding `Product` properties. Listing 4-14 shows the changes I made.

Listing 4-14. Applying the Product Class in the ViewController.swift File

```swift
import UIKit

class ProductTableCell : UITableViewCell {

    @IBOutlet weak var nameLabel: UILabel!
    @IBOutlet weak var descriptionLabel: UILabel!
    @IBOutlet weak var stockStepper: UIStepper!
    @IBOutlet weak var stockField: UITextField!

    var product:Product?;
}

class ViewController: UIViewController, UITableViewDataSource {

    @IBOutlet weak var totalStockLabel: UILabel!
    @IBOutlet weak var tableView: UITableView!

    var products = [
        Product(name:"Kayak", description:"A boat for one person",
            category:"Watersports", price:275.0, stockLevel:10),
        Product(name:"Lifejacket", description:"Protective and fashionable",
            category:"Watersports", price:48.95, stockLevel:14),
        Product(name:"Soccer Ball", description:"FIFA-approved size and weight",
            category:"Soccer", price:19.5, stockLevel:32),
        Product(name:"Corner Flags",
            description:"Give your playing field a professional touch",
            category:"Soccer", price:34.95, stockLevel:1),
        Product(name:"Stadium", description:"Flat-packed 35,000-seat stadium",
            category:"Soccer", price:79500.0, stockLevel:4),
        Product(name:"Thinking Cap",
            description:"Improve your brain efficiency by 75%",
            category:"Chess", price:16.0, stockLevel:8),
        Product(name:"Unsteady Chair",
            description:"Secretly give your opponent a disadvantage",
            category: "Chess", price: 29.95, stockLevel:3),
        Product(name:"Human Chess Board",
            description:"A fun game for the family", category:"Chess",
            price:75.0, stockLevel:2),
        Product(name:"Bling-Bling King",
            description:"Gold-plated, diamond-studded King",
            category:"Chess", price:1200.0, stockLevel:4)];
```

```swift
override func viewDidLoad() {
    super.viewDidLoad()
    displayStockTotal();
}

override func didReceiveMemoryWarning() {
    super.didReceiveMemoryWarning()
}

func tableView(tableView: UITableView,
    numberOfRowsInSection section: Int) -> Int {
    return products.count;
}

func tableView(tableView: UITableView,
    cellForRowAtIndexPath indexPath: NSIndexPath) -> UITableViewCell {
    let product = products[indexPath.row];
    let cell = tableView.dequeueReusableCellWithIdentifier("ProductCell")
    as ProductTableCell;
    cell.product = products[indexPath.row];
    cell.nameLabel.text = product.name;
    cell.descriptionLabel.text = product.description;
    cell.stockStepper.value = Double(product.stockLevel);
    cell.stockField.text = String(product.stockLevel);
    return cell;
}

@IBAction func stockLevelDidChange(sender: AnyObject) {
    if var currentCell = sender as? UIView {
        while (true) {
            currentCell = currentCell.superview!;
            if let cell = currentCell as? ProductTableCell {
                if let product = cell.product? {
                    if let stepper = sender as? UIStepper {
                        product.stockLevel = Int(stepper.value);
                    } else if let textfield = sender as? UITextField {
                        if let newValue = textfield.text.toInt()? {
                            product.stockLevel = newValue;
                        }
                    }
                    cell.stockStepper.value = Double(product.stockLevel);
                    cell.stockField.text = String(product.stockLevel);
                }
                break;
            }
        }
        displayStockTotal();
    }
}
```

```
    func displayStockTotal() {
        let stockTotal = products.reduce(0,
        {(total, product) -> Int in return total + product.stockLevel});
        totalStockLabel.text = "\(stockTotal) Products in Stock";
    }
}
```

The transition to using the Product class is simple. In preparing the code for Listing 4-14, I started by using the class in the products data array and then fixed all of the compiler errors until all references to the tuples had been replaced. This is a dull and error-prone process, which is why it is a good idea to start a project with classes and structs if you can (something that, sadly, isn't always possible when taking over existing code).

Ensuring View and Model Separation

There are a couple of points to note about the code in Listing 4-14. The first is that the ViewController.swift file defines a class called ProductTableCell that I used to contain the references to the UI components that represent a product in the app layout and to locate a product when the user changes a stock level. In Listing 4-14, I replaced a variable that referred to the index position of a tuple in the products array with references to a Product object instead, like this:

```
...
class ProductTableCell : UITableViewCell {

    @IBOutlet weak var nameLabel: UILabel!
    @IBOutlet weak var descriptionLabel: UILabel!
    @IBOutlet weak var stockStepper: UIStepper!
    @IBOutlet weak var stockField: UITextField!

    var product:Product?;
}
...
```

You may be wondering why I didn't combine the ProductTableCell with the Product class and have a single entity that represents a product and the UI components that are used to display it. I explain the reasons in detail in Part 5 when I describe the Model/View/Controller (MVC) pattern, but the short answer is that it is good practice to separate the data in the application from the way it is presented to the user (in MVC parlance, separating the model from the view). Enforcing this separation allows the same data to be displayed in different ways more easily. I might need to add a second view to the app that presents the products in a grid, and without separation between the model and the view, the combined class would need to have references to every UI component that is involved in both views, which quickly becomes unwieldy and makes applying changes a tricky and error-prone process.

Expanding the Summary Display

I have been critical of tuples throughout this chapter, but they can be a useful language feature when they are used in a self-contained way, rather than to represent application-wide data.

In Listing 4-15, you can see an example of how I like to use tuples. I have changed the implementation of the `displayStockTotal` method of the `ViewController` class so that a single call to the global `reduce` function is used to calculate the number of items in stock and the total value of that stock (which I format using the `currencyStringFromNumber` method I defined in Listing 4-12).

Listing 4-15. Using Tuples in the ViewController.swift File

```
...
func displayStockTotal() {
    let finalTotals:(Int, Double) = products.reduce((0, 0.0),
        {(totals, product) -> (Int, Double) in
            return (
                totals.0 + product.stockLevel,
                totals.1 + product.stockValue
            );
        });

    totalStockLabel.text = "\(finalTotals.0) Products in Stock. "
        + "Total Value: \(Utils.currencyStringFromNumber(finalTotals.1))";
}
...
```

Tuples allow me to generate two total values (one for the number of items in stock and one for the value of that stock) for each iteration of the `reduce` function. I could have achieved this in different ways—such as by defining a struct that has two properties or by using a `for` loop to enumerate the array and update two local variables—but using tuples works nicely with Swift closures and produces code that is simple and easy to read. This kind of use, where creating a class or struct would be overkill since the data isn't exported outside the method, plays to the strengths of the tuples and doesn't cause the tight coupling and maintenance problems that arise when passing tuples more widely within the application.

You can see the effect of the additional total I calculate by starting the application. The label at the bottom of the layout will display the number and value of the items in stock, as illustrated by Figure 4-7.

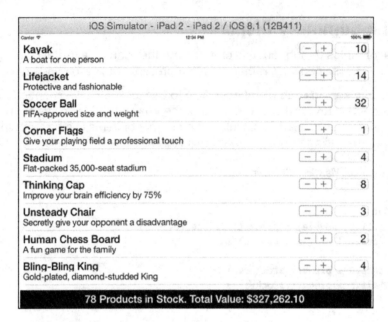

Figure 4-7. Adding to the information summary displayed by the SportsStore app

Summary

In this chapter, I described a pattern that is at the heart of Swift development: defining a template that is used to create objects. The benefit of this pattern is that it provides the basic tools that can be used to break tightly coupled components apart, allowing a public API to be presented to the consumers of an object and a hidden private implementation. In the next chapter, I turn to a different way of creating objects: using a *prototype*.

Chapter 5

The Prototype Pattern

In this chapter I describe the *prototype pattern*, in which you create new objects by copying an existing object, known as the *prototype*. The prototype itself is created using a template, as described in Chapter 4, but subsequent instances are *clones*. Table 5-1 puts the prototype pattern in context.

Table 5-1. *Putting the Prototype Pattern into Context*

Question	Answer
What is it?	The prototype pattern creates new objects by copying an existing object, known as the prototype.
What are the benefits?	The main benefit is to hide the code that creates objects from the components that use them; this means that components don't need to know which class or struct is required to create a new object, don't need to know the details of initializers, and don't need to change when subclasses are created and instantiated. This pattern can also be used to avoid repeating expensive initialization each time a new object of a specific type is created.
When should you use this pattern?	This pattern is useful when you are writing a component that needs to create new instances of objects without creating a dependency on the class initializer.
When should you avoid this pattern?	There are no drawbacks to using this pattern, but you should understand the other patterns in this part of the book to ensure that you pick the most suitable for your application.
How do you know when you have implemented the pattern correctly?	To test for an effective implementation of this pattern, change the initializer for the class or struct used for the prototype object and check to see whether a corresponding change is required in the component that creates clones. As a second test, create a subclass of the prototype's class and ensure that the component can clone it without requiring any changes. See the "Implementing the Prototype Pattern" section.

(continued)

Table 5-1. (*continued*)

Question	Answer
Are there any common pitfalls?	The main pitfall is selecting the wrong style of copying when cloning the prototype object. There are two kinds of copying available—shallow and deep—and it is important to select the correct kind for your application. See the "Understanding Shallow and Deep Copying" section for details.
Are there any related patterns?	The most closely related pattern is the object template pattern, which I describe in Chapter 4. Also see the singleton pattern, which provides a means by which a single object can be shared to avoid needing to create additional instances.

Understanding the Problem Addressed by the Pattern

In Chapter 4, I explained how to use templates to create objects, but this is an approach that has its own drawbacks, as I describe in the sections that follow.

Incurring Expensive Initializations

Some class or struct templates are expensive to use, meaning that initializing a new instance of an object can consume a substantial amount of memory or computation in order to prepare the object for use. To demonstrate this kind of problem, I created the `Initialization.playground` file, the contents of which are shown in Listing 5-1.

Listing 5-1. The Contents of the Initialization.playground File

```
class Sum {
    let resultsCache: [[Int]];
    var firstValue:Int;
    var secondValue:Int;

    init(first:Int, second:Int) {
        resultsCache = [[Int]](count: 10, repeatedValue:
            [Int](count:10, repeatedValue: 0));
        for i in 0..<10 {
            for j in 0..<10 {
                resultsCache[i][j] = i + j;
            }
        }
        self.firstValue = first;
        self.secondValue = second;
    }
```

```
    var Result:Int {
        get {
            return firstValue < resultsCache.count
                && secondValue < resultsCache[firstValue].count
            ? resultsCache[firstValue][secondValue]
            : firstValue + secondValue;
        }
    }
}

var calc1 = Sum(first:0, second: 9).Result;
var calc2 = Sum(first:3, second: 8).Result;

println("Calc1: \(calc1) Calc2: \(calc2)");
```

I have defined a class called Sum that produces the sum of two integer values passed to its initializer. As an optimization, the initializer for the Sum class creates a two-dimensional Int array and populates it with precalculated values with the intention of trading time spent during initialization against faster calculations later.

Having defined the Sum class, I then create two instances and use them to perform calculations. Each time that I create a new Sum object, I incur the cost of creating and populating the two-dimensional array—a cost that can be measured both in terms of memory required to store the calculated values and in computation. I finish by writing the results of the two calculations to the console, producing the following output:

```
Calc1: 9 Calc2: 11
```

This may seem like an unrealistic example, but this style of coding is surprisingly common and is usually a result of *premature optimization*, where a programmer tries to speculatively improve the performance of code as it is being written, rather than as a result of subsequent performance testing—something that usually results in worse performance and less readable code. There are, however, two aspects of this example that are unrealistic. The first is that the work performed by the Sum class is so simple that even the most enthusiastic optimizer is unlikely to see the cost of adding two integers as being worth caching. The second aspect is that the playground shows the Sum class and the two statements that create instances from it in the same file. In a real project, the initialization code is lost in a deep hierarchy of classes, and the statements that use the class will be in entirely different parts of the app.

Creating Template Dependencies

To create a new object from a template, a component must possess three pieces of information.

- The template that is associated with the object
- The initializer that must be called
- The names and types of the initializer arguments

This information becomes disseminated throughout an app wherever a new instance of an object is required. The problem this presents is that it creates a dependency on the template, such that when the template changes, all of the components that use the template to create new objects must be updated to reflect that change. You can see this in Listing 5-2, where I have reworked the Sum class so that it defines an additional initializer parameter.

Listing 5-2. Adding an Initializer in the Initialization.playground File

```
class Sum {
    let resultsCache: [[Int]];
    var firstValue:Int;
    var secondValue:Int;

    init(first:Int, second:Int, cacheSize:Int) {
        resultsCache = [[Int]](count: cacheSize, repeatedValue:
            [Int](count:cacheSize, repeatedValue: 0));
        for i in 0 ..< cacheSize {
            for j in 0 ..< cacheSize {
                resultsCache[i][j] = i + j;
            }
        }
        self.firstValue = first;
        self.secondValue = second;
    }

    var Result:Int {
        get {
            return firstValue < resultsCache.count
                && secondValue < resultsCache[firstValue].count
            ? resultsCache[firstValue][secondValue]
            : firstValue + secondValue;
        }
    }
}

var calc1 = Sum(first:0, second: 9, cacheSize:100).Result;
var calc2 = Sum(first:3, second: 8, cacheSize:20).Result;

println("Calc1: \(calc1) Calc2: \(calc2)");
```

The initializer parameter is used to control the number of cached results that are generated. As the listing demonstrates, I have had to update the statements that create Sum objects to use the revised initializer. The changes are trivial when the only two statements that create Sum objects are next to each other, but these construction statements can be distributed throughout a real project, and each one is required to have enough knowledge about the implementation of the Sum class to provide a sensible value for the cacheSize initializer parameter.

> **Tip**   My goal in this chapter is to showcase the prototype pattern, but there are other ways to solve this kind of problem. I could, for example, have defined a convenience initializer that calls the designated initializer and provided a default value for the cacheSize parameter. As I explained in Chapter 1, patterns are not always the only solution to a problem.

Understanding the Prototype Pattern

The *prototype pattern* uses an existing object—rather than a class or struct—to create new objects. This is often referred to as *cloning*, since the new object is an identical copy of the existing one, including any changes made to the object's stored properties that have been made since it was created. Figure 5-1 shows how the prototype pattern works.

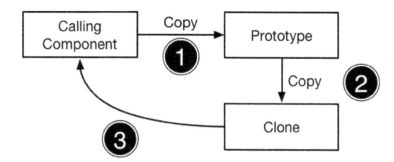

Figure 5-1. The prototype pattern

There are three operations in the prototype pattern. First, the component that needs an object calls on the original object (known as the *prototype*) to copy itself. The second operation is the copying process in which a new object (known as the *clone*) is created. In the final operation, the prototype gives the calling component the clone, completing the copying process.

Implementing the Prototype Pattern

Swift automatically applies the prototype pattern when you assign a value type to a new variable. Values types are defined using structs, and all of the built-in Swift types are implemented as structs behind the scenes, meaning that you can clone strings, Booleans, collections, enumerations, tuples, and numeric types just by assigning them to a new variable. Swift will copy the value of the prototype and use it to create a clone. Listing 5-3 shows the contents of the ValueTypes.playground file, which I created to demonstrate how value types are cloned.

Listing 5-3. The Contents of the ValueTypes.playground File

```
struct Appointment {
    var name:String;
    var day:String;
    var place:String;

    func printDetails(label:String) {
        println("\(label) with \(name) on \(day) at \(place)");
    }
}

var beerMeeting = Appointment(name: "Bob", day: "Mon", place: "Joe's Bar");

var workMeeting = beerMeeting;
workMeeting.name = "Alice";
workMeeting.day = "Fri";
workMeeting.place = "Conference Rm 2";

beerMeeting.printDetails("Social");
workMeeting.printDetails("Work");
```

I have defined a struct called `Appointment` that has stored `name`, `day`, and `place` properties and a `printDetails` method that writes these values to the console. I start by using the struct as a template for creating a new object like this:

```
...
var beerMeeting = Appointment(name: "Bob", day: "Mon", place: "Joe's Bar");
...
```

The prototype pattern relies on there being—obviously enough—a prototype object, which is commonly created from a template. This may seem counterintuitive, but you have to be able to get the prototype somehow. Once I have the prototype, I create a copy by assigning it to a new variable, like this:

```
...
var workMeeting = beerMeeting;
...
```

At this point, I have two separate `Appointment` objects that are assigned to the `beerMeeting` and `workMeeting` variables. The `name`, `day`, and `place` properties for both objects have the same values, as shown in Figure 5-2.

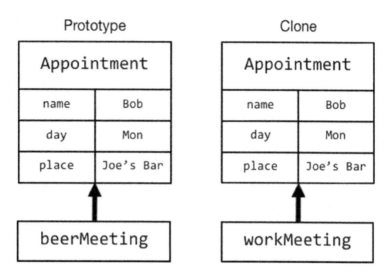

Figure 5-2. *The effect of cloning a struct prototype*

Once I have created the clone, I assign new values to the name, day, and place properties, configuring the clone to represent a different appointment from the one represented by the prototype, as shown in Figure 5-3.

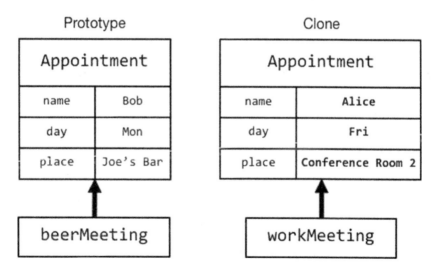

Figure 5-3. *Configuring the clone*

I finish by calling the printDetails method on both of the Appointment objects, which produces the following results:

```
Social with Bob on Mon at Joe's Bar
Work with Alice on Fri at Conference Rm 2
```

Once I have created the prototype, I can create and configure as many clones as I need without incurring the overhead associated with using the struct template.

Cloning Reference Types

Objects created using classes are reference types, and Swift doesn't copy these objects when you assign them to a new variable. Instead, a new reference to the object is created so that both variables refer to the same object. Listing 5-4 shows the content of the ReferenceTypes.playground file, in which I have reworked the Appointment example from the previous chapter to use a class as the template instead of a struct.

Listing 5-4. The Contents of the ReferenceTypes.playground File

```
class Appointment {
    var name:String;
    var day:String;
    var place:String;

    init(name:String, day:String, place:String) {
        self.name = name; self.day = day; self.place = place;
    }

    func printDetails(label:String) {
        println("\(label) with \(name) on \(day) at \(place)");
    }
}

var beerMeeting = Appointment(name: "Bob", day: "Mon", place: "Joe's Bar");

var workMeeting = beerMeeting;
workMeeting.name = "Alice";
workMeeting.day = "Fri";
workMeeting.place = "Conference Rm 2";

beerMeeting.printDetails("Social");
workMeeting.printDetails("Work");
```

In addition to using the class keyword, I have added an initializer to the Appointment class. Swift creates a default initializer for structs but not for classes. Aside from using a class to define the Appointment type, this example contains the same code as Listing 5-3. The results shown in the consoler, however, are different.

```
Social with Alice on Fri at Conference Rm 2
Work with Alice on Fri at Conference Rm 2
```

The problem here is that there is one Appointment object, and it is referred to by both the workMeeting and beerMeeting variables, as shown in Figure 5-4.

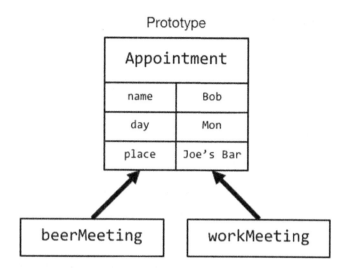

Prototype

Figure 5-4. *Assigning a reference object to a new variable*

Since there is only one Appointment object, the changes that I make to the stored properties via the workMeeting variable are read back when I access the properties via the beerMeeting variable, which is why I get the unexpected—and unhelpful—output in the console.

Implementing the NSCopying Protocol

Assigning new references to existing objects is an important part of object-oriented programming, but it doesn't help with the prototype pattern. To support cloning, the Foundation framework defines the NSCopying protocol, which lets you specify how an object should be cloned. Listing 5-5 shows how I updated the Appointment class to implement the NSCopying protocol.

Listing 5-5. Implementing the NSCopying Protocol in the ReferenceTypes.playground File

```
import Foundation

class Appointment : NSObject, NSCopying {
    var name:String;
    var day:String;
    var place:String;

    init(name:String, day:String, place:String) {
        self.name = name; self.day = day; self.place = place;
    }

    func printDetails(label:String) {
        println("\(label) with \(name) on \(day) at \(place)");
    }

    func copyWithZone(zone: NSZone) -> AnyObject {
        return Appointment(name:self.name, day:self.day, place:self.place);
    }
}
```

```
var beerMeeting = Appointment(name: "Bob", day: "Mon", place: "Joe's Bar");
var workMeeting = beerMeeting.copy() as Appointment;

workMeeting.name = "Alice";
workMeeting.day = "Fri";
workMeeting.place = "Conference Rm 2";

beerMeeting.printDetails("Social");
workMeeting.printDetails("Work");
```

> **Tip**   You can implement the NSCopying protocol only on classes and not structs. Structs are always subject to shallow copying.

The NSCopying protocol defines the copyWithZone method, which is called when the object is copied. The mechanism that is used to copy the object is left to the class to implement, and in this case, I create a new instance of the Appointment class using the stored property values from the current object.

> **Tip**   You can ignore the NSZone argument when implementing the copyWithZone method.

To take advantage of the NSCopying protocol, I have to change the Appointment class so that it is derived from NSObject, which defines the copy method. To copy an Appointment, I call the copy method—and not copyWithZone—on the prototype, like this:

```
...
var workMeeting = beerMeeting.copy() as Appointment;
...
```

The copyWithZone method returns AnyObject, which means that I have to downcast the object created by the copy method with the as keyword so that the workMeeting variable is correctly typed.

> **Caution**   Implementing the NSCopying protocol doesn't change a reference type into a value type. You must call the copy method to clone the prototype. If you simply assign the prototype to a new variable, you will end up with a new reference to the prototype and not a new object.

Understanding Shallow and Deep Copying

An important aspect of the prototype pattern is whether objects are cloned using *deep copying* or *shallow copying*, which relates to how stored properties that refer to other reference types are handled. In Listing 5-6, I have defined a new class in the ReferenceTypes playground and added a new property to the Appoinment class that refers to an instance of it.

Listing 5-6. Adding a Reference Type Property in the ReferenceTypes.playground File

```
import Foundation

class Location {
    var name:String;
    var address:String;

    init(name:String, address:String) {
        self.name = name; self.address = address;
    }
}

class Appointment : NSObject, NSCopying {
    var name:String;
    var day:String;
    var place:Location;

    init(name:String, day:String, place:Location) {
        self.name = name; self.day = day; self.place = place;
    }

    func printDetails(label:String) {
        println("\(label) with \(name) on \(day) at \(place.name), "
            + "\(place.address)");
    }

    func copyWithZone(zone: NSZone) -> AnyObject {
        return Appointment(name:self.name, day:self.day,
            place:self.place);
    }

}

var beerMeeting = Appointment(name: "Bob", day: "Mon",
    place: Location(name:"Joe's Bar", address: "123 Main St"));

var workMeeting = beerMeeting.copy() as Appointment;
workMeeting.name = "Alice";
workMeeting.day = "Fri";
workMeeting.place.name = "Conference Rm 2";
workMeeting.place.address = "Company HQ";

beerMeeting.printDetails("Social");
workMeeting.printDetails("Work");
```

I have created a simple Location class and used it for the place property of the Appointment object. Here is the output shown in the console:

```
Social with Bob on Mon at Conference Rm 2, Company HQ
Work with Alice on Fri at Conference Rm 2, Company HQ
```

Once again, the changes that I have applied through the workMeeting variable have affected the stored values available through the workMeeting variable. This is because I changed the type for the place property from a value type (String) to a reference type (Location) and my implementation of the NSCopying protocol creates a new reference to the prototype's Location object, as illustrated in Figure 5-5.

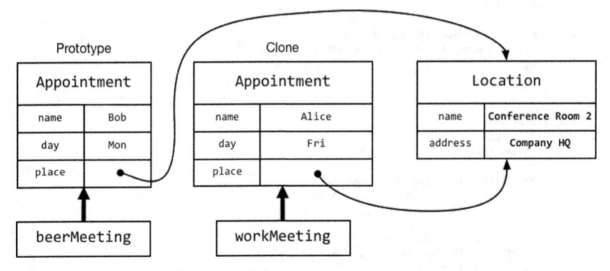

Figure 5-5. *The effect of copying references when cloning a prototype*

This is known as a *shallow copy*, in which references to objects are copied, not the objects themselves. As Figure 5-5 shows, there are two Appointment objects, but their place properties refer to the same Location object. This is why the changes that I applied via the workMeeting.place property affect the values I got through the beerMeeting.place property.

Tip   Related to the NSCopying protocol is the @NSCopying property attribute, which can be applied to stored properties. The @NSCopying attribute automatically invokes the copyWithZone method of objects that are assigned to the annotated property, and I demonstrate its use in the "Examples of the Prototype Pattern in Cocoa" section later in this chapter.

Implementing Deep Copying

Deep copying creates copies of all the objects referred to by the prototype, which in this case will ensure that each `Appointment` object refers to a different `Location` object via its `place` property. Listing 5-7 shows how I implemented deep copying in the `ReferenceTypes` playground.

Listing 5-7. Implementing Deep Copying in the ReferenceTypes.playground File

```
import Foundation

class Location : NSObject, NSCopying {
    var name:String;
    var address:String;

    init(name:String, address:String) {
        self.name = name; self.address = address;
    }

    func copyWithZone(zone: NSZone) -> AnyObject {
        return Location(name: self.name, address:self.address);
    }
}

class Appointment : NSObject, NSCopying {
    var name:String;
    var day:String;
    var place:Location;

    init(name:String, day:String, place:Location) {
        self.name = name; self.day = day; self.place = place;
    }

    func printDetails(label:String) {
        println("\(label) with \(name) on \(day) at \(place.name), "
            + "\(place.address)");
    }

    func copyWithZone(zone: NSZone) -> AnyObject {
        return Appointment(name:self.name, day:self.day,
            place:self.place.copy() as Location);
    }
}

var beerMeeting = Appointment(name: "Bob", day: "Mon",
    place: Location(name:"Joe's Bar", address: "123 Main St"));

var workMeeting = beerMeeting.copy() as Appointment;
```

```
workMeeting.name = "Alice";
workMeeting.day = "Fri";
workMeeting.place.name = "Conference Rm 2";
workMeeting.place.address = "Company HQ";

beerMeeting.printDetails("Social");
workMeeting.printDetails("Work");
```

To create a deep copy, I have to implement the NSCopying protocol on the Location class, change the base class to NSObject, and define the copyWithZone method. All the reference types that you want to deep-copy must implement the NSCopying protocol, so you must repeat this process throughout the classes referred to by your prototype, including those that are referred to via other references.

CHOOSING SHALLOW OR DEEP COPYING

There are no hard-and-fast rules for choosing between shallow and deep copying, and the decision has to be made on a class-by-class basis. You should consider three factors: the amount of work required to copy an object, the amount of memory required to store the copy, and the way that the copied object will be used.

It is the last factor—how the copied object will be used—that is the most important. In the case of the Location class in Listing 5-7, sharing objects between Appointment objects doesn't make any sense because a change made to the location of one appointment is unlikely to apply to the other appointments that refer to the same Location object, especially when social and work appointments are mixed together.

It is possible that there is a group of related appointments that would benefit from a shared location. Imagine, as an example, a daylong series of meetings that are all held in the same conference room—your application might benefit from optimizing the creation of Location objects for related meetings. In such cases, you should balance the amount of computation and memory required to create and store a new object against the complexity of managing references to a shared object. In the Appointment/Location example, the Location objects are so easily created and require such little storage (just two String values) that the overhead and complexity of having to work out when Location objects can be shared and when they can't just isn't justified.

The best advice I can give is to think through the purpose of objects and figure out which ones are intended to be common across all of the copies you create from the prototype. If you are unsure, then start with shallow copying because it is the simplest to perform—it won't always be the right technique, but it allows you to test the effect of changes without having to implement the NSCopying protocol throughout your application.

As I noted earlier, implementing the NSCopying protocol doesn't change a reference type into a value type, so I must call the copy method to create a clone of the Appointment prototype's Location object, which I do in the copyWithZone method defined by the Appointment class.

```
...
func copyWithZone(zone: NSZone) -> AnyObject {
    return Appointment(name:self.name, day:self.day,
        place:self.place.copy() as Location);
}
...
```

These changes mean that the Appointment prototype and its Location object are cloned, as illustrated by Figure 5-6.

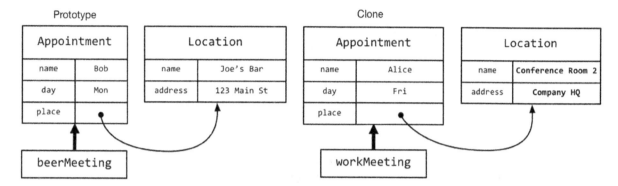

Figure 5-6. *The effect of deep copying*

You can see the effect of the deep copy by looking at the console output from the example code, shown here:

```
Social with Bob on Mon at Joe's Bar, 123 Main St
Work with Alice on Fri at Conference Rm 2, Company HQ
```

Since the Appointment objects have their own Location objects, the changes that I apply via the workMeeting variable have no effect on the object accessed via the beerMeeting variable.

Copying Arrays

Swift arrays are implemented as structs, which makes them value types. When you assign an array to a new variable, the array itself is copied along with any value types it contains. Reference types contained in the array are shallow copied, such that the prototype array and the clone array will both contain references to the same objects. Listing 5-8 shows the contents of the ArrayCopy.playground file, which I created to provide a demonstration.

Listing 5-8. The Contents of the ArrayCopy.playground File

```
import Foundation

class Person : NSObject, NSCopying {
    var name:String;
    var country:String;

    init(name:String, country:String) {
        self.name = name; self.country = country;
    }
```

```
    func copyWithZone(zone: NSZone) -> AnyObject {
        return Person(name: self.name, country: self.country);
    }
}

var people = [Person(name:"Joe", country:"France"),
              Person(name:"Bob", country:"USA")];
var otherpeople = people;

people[0].country = "UK";
println("Country: \(otherpeople[0].country)");
```

> **Tip**   As a performance optimization, Swift arrays are not copied until you modify them, known as
> *lazy copying*. This isn't something you need to worry about on a day-to-day basis because it happens
> seamlessly behind the scenes, but it means that cloned arrays behave like reference types if you are just
> reading the contents of the array and behave like value types once you make a modification.

I create an array called people containing two Person objects. I assign the array to a variable called
otherpeople and then modify the first object in the people array. Here is the console output, which
shows that the contents of the array are shallow copied, even though the array itself is a struct:

```
Country: UK
```

To deeply copy an array, you must inspect each item in the array and look for objects whose classes
are derived from NSObject and that implement the NSCopying protocol, as shown in Listing 5-9.

Listing 5-9. Deep Copying an Array in the ArrayCopy.playground File

```
import Foundation

class Person : NSObject, NSCopying {
    var name:String;
    var country:String;

    init(name:String, country:String) {
        self.name = name; self.country = country;
    }

    func copyWithZone(zone: NSZone) -> AnyObject {
        return Person(name: self.name, country: self.country);
    }
}
```

```
func deepCopy(data:[AnyObject]) -> [AnyObject] {
    return data.map({item -> AnyObject in
        if (item is NSCopying && item is NSObject) {
            return (item as NSObject).copy();
        } else {
            return item;
        }
    })
}

var people = [Person(name:"Joe", country:"France"),
                Person(name:"Bob", country:"USA")];
var otherpeople = deepCopy(people) as [Person];

people[0].country = "UK";
println("Country: \(otherpeople[0].country)");
```

> **Tip** In the "Examples of the Prototype Pattern in Cocoa" section, I explain how to copy Cocoa arrays, which are implemented by the NSArray and NSMutableArray classes. These classes behave differently to the built-in Swift arrays I describe in this section, and understanding how they work can be useful when working with Objective-C code.

I have defined a function called deepCopy that accepts an array and uses the map method to copy the array. The closure that I pass to the map method checks to see whether the object can be deep-copied and, if it can, calls the copy method. Other objects are added to the result array without modification. As this console output shows, the deeply copied arrays no longer contain references to the same objects:

```
Country: France
```

Understanding the Benefits of the Prototype Pattern

In the following sections, I describe the benefits that the prototype pattern provides. Some of them address the problems I identified at the start of the chapter, but there are additional benefits that arise from the way that objects are copied through the NSCopying protocol.

Avoiding Expensive Initializations

Using the NSCopying protocol allows objects to take responsibility for copying themselves, which means that cloning can avoid expensive initialization operations. At the start of the chapter, I used the Initialization.playground file to define a Sum class that generated an array of cached results in its initializer, which I have repeated in Listing 5-10.

Listing 5-10. The Contents of the Initialization.playground File

```
class Sum {
    let resultsCache: [[Int]];
    var firstValue:Int;
    var secondValue:Int;

    init(first:Int, second:Int) {
        resultsCache = [[Int]](count: 10, repeatedValue:
            [Int](count:10, repeatedValue: 0));
        for i in 0..<10 {
            for j in 0..<10 {
                resultsCache[i][j] = i + j;
            }
        }
        self.firstValue = first;
        self.secondValue = second;
    }

    var Result:Int {
        get {
            return firstValue < resultsCache.count
                && secondValue < resultsCache[firstValue].count
            ? resultsCache[firstValue][secondValue]
            : firstValue + secondValue;
        }
    }
}

var calc1 = Sum(first:0, second: 9).Result;
var calc2 = Sum(first:3, second: 8).Result;

println("Calc1: \(calc1) Calc2: \(calc2)");
```

Each time I create a Sum object, I incur the cost of allocating and populating the two-dimensional resultsCache array. By implementing the NSCopying protocol, I can apply the prototype pattern and selectively clone the object in the copyWithZone method, as shown in Listing 5-11.

Listing 5-11. Applying the Prototype Pattern in the Initialization.playground File

```
import Foundation

class Sum : NSObject, NSCopying {
    let resultsCache: [[Int]];
    var firstValue:Int;
    var secondValue:Int;

    init(first:Int, second:Int) {
        resultsCache = [[Int]](count: 10, repeatedValue:
            [Int](count:10, repeatedValue: 0));
```

```
        for i in 0..<10 {
            for j in 0..<10 {
                resultsCache[i][j] = i + j;
            }
        }
        self.firstValue = first;
        self.secondValue = second;
    }

    private init(first:Int, second:Int, cache:[[Int]]) {
        self.firstValue = first;
        self.secondValue = second;
        resultsCache = cache;
    }

    var Result:Int {
        get {
            return firstValue < resultsCache.count
                && secondValue < resultsCache[firstValue].count
            ? resultsCache[firstValue][secondValue]
            : firstValue + secondValue;
        }
    }

    func copyWithZone(zone: NSZone) -> AnyObject {
        return Sum(first:self.firstValue,
            second: self.secondValue,
            cache: self.resultsCache);
    }
}

var prototype = Sum(first:0, second:9);
var calc1 = prototype.Result;
var clone = prototype.copy() as Sum;
clone.firstValue = 3; clone.secondValue = 8;
var calc2 = clone.Result;

println("Calc1: \(calc1) Calc2: \(calc2)");
```

I changed the class declaration so that the base class is NSObject (which provides the copy method)
and implemented the NSCopying protocol. To support cloning, I have added a new initializer that
accepts cached data as an argument rather than generating the data itself. I have annotated the
initializer with the private keyword so that I can use it in the copyWithZone function to clone an
object using the cached data generated by the prototype but prevent other components from
providing their own results data.

Separating Object Creation from Object Use

As I explained earlier in the chapter, three pieces of knowledge are required to create an object from its template.

- The template that is associated with the object
- The initializer that must be called
- The names and types of the initializer arguments

The prototype pattern allows components to create new objects from the prototype without needing any information about its template, which means you can change the class or struct without having to change the components that need to create instances of it. Put another way, you can minimize the number of dependencies on the templates you define by separating the way that objects are created from the way objects are used. Components that follow the prototype pattern do not need to know the type of the prototype objects they clone, which makes it possible to limit the amount of knowledge about subclasses in components that need to create new objects. This is a benefit that causes some confusion, so I will build up the example in stages. Listing 5-12 shows the contents of the Hiding.playground file, which I created for this example.

Listing 5-12. The Contents of the Hiding.playground File

```
import Foundation

class Message {
    var to:String;
    var subject:String;

    init(to:String, subject:String) {
        self.to = to; self.subject = subject;
    }
}

class MessageLogger {
    var messages:[Message] = [];

    func logMessage(msg:Message) {
        messages.append(msg);
    }

    func processMessages(callback:Message -> Void) {
        for msg in messages {
            callback(msg);
        }
    }
}

var logger = MessageLogger();

var message = Message(to: "Joe", subject: "Hello");
logger.logMessage(message);
```

```
message.to = "Bob";
message.subject = "Free for dinner?";
logger.logMessage(message);

logger.processMessages({msg -> Void in
    println("Message - To: \(msg.to) Subject: \(msg.subject)");
});
```

I have defined a Message class that has to and subject stored properties and a MessageLogger class that stores Message objects passed to its logMessage method and processes the stored objects using a closure passed to its processMessages method.

The problems in this example start with the fact that I am reusing Message objects, which is a common optimization—albeit for more complex types. (Ignore, if you will, the benefit of reusing objects; it is an optimization that is often applied almost without thought, even when the cost of creating objects is trivial.)

```
...
message.to = "Bob";
message.subject = "Free for dinner?";
logger.logMessage(message);
...
```

The effect of reusing the Message objects is that the array defined by the MessageLogger class is filled with references to the same object. You can see the effect of this problem in the console output, which is generated by the closure I pass to the processMessages method.

```
Message - To: Bob Subject: Free for dinner?
Message - To: Bob Subject: Free for dinner?
```

(Not Really) Solving the Problem

If you were unfamiliar with the prototype pattern or if you don't like the way that the NSCopying protocol works, you might be tempted to modify the MessageLogger class so that it creates its own Message objects using the class initializer, as shown in Listing 5-13.

Listing 5-13. Modifying the MessageLogger Class in the Hiding.playground File

```
...
class MessageLogger {
    var messages:[Message] = [];

    func logMessage(msg:Message) {
        messages.append(Message(to: msg.to, subject: msg.subject));
    }
}
```

```
func processMessages(callback:Message -> Void) {
    for msg in messages {
        callback(msg);
    }
}
}
...
```

> **Tip**   I can't solve this problem by just storing the data values because the closure passed to the process
> expects to be dealing with `Message` objects. And, as you will learn shortly, there is a more serious underlying
> problem to be solved that extracting the data values would not solve.

This approach solves the problem, as the following console output shows:

```
Message - To: Joe Subject: Hello
Message - To: Bob Subject: Free for dinner?
```

Revealing the Underlying Problem

The immediate problem has been solved, but I have just stored up trouble for the future because
the `MessageLogger` class is now dependent on being able to create `Message` objects by invoking
the `Message` class initializer. My solution falls apart when I subclass `Message` to produce a more
specialized class, as shown in Listing 5-14.

Listing 5-14. Adding a Subclass in the Hiding.playground File

```
import Foundation

class Message {
    var to:String;
    var subject:String;

    init(to:String, subject:String) {
        self.to = to; self.subject = subject;
    }
}

class DetailedMessage : Message {
    var from:String;

    init(to: String, subject: String, from:String) {
        self.from = from;
        super.init(to: to, subject: subject);
    }
}
```

```
class MessageLogger {
    var messages:[Message] = [];

    func logMessage(msg:Message) {
        messages.append(Message(to: msg.to, subject: msg.subject));
    }

    func processMessages(callback:Message -> Void) {
        for msg in messages {
            callback(msg);
        }
    }
}

var logger = MessageLogger();

var message = Message(to: "Joe", subject: "Hello");
logger.logMessage(message);

message.to = "Bob";
message.subject = "Free for dinner?";
logger.logMessage(message);

logger.logMessage(DetailedMessage(to: "Alice", subject: "Hi!", from: "Joe"));

logger.processMessages({msg -> Void in
    if let detailed = msg as? DetailedMessage {
        println("Detailed Message - To: \(detailed.to) From: \(detailed.from)"
            + " Subject: \(detailed.subject)");
    } else {
        println("Message - To: \(msg.to) Subject: \(msg.subject)");
    }
});
```

I have subclassed Message to define the DetailedMessage class, and I created an instance of the subclass so that I can pass it to the logMessage method defined by MessageLogger. I have also revised the closure that I pass to the processMessages method so that it writes the additional property stored by DetailedMessage objects.

The problem is that the MessageLogger class receives Message and DetailedMessage objects, but it only adds Message objects to its storage array. When the processMessage method is called, only to and subject properties are displayed, and the additional detail contained in the from property is forever lost. Here is the console output from Listing 5-14:

```
Message - To: Joe Subject: Hello
Message - To: Bob Subject: Free for dinner?
Message - To: Alice Subject: Hi!
```

(Not Really) Solving the Underlying Problem

Without using the prototype pattern, the obvious way to solve the second problem is to make the MessageLogger class aware that there are Message and DetailedMessage classes and how to create each of them, as shown in Listing 5-15.

Listing 5-15. Modifying the MessageLogger Class in the Hiding.playground File

```
...
class MessageLogger {
    var messages:[Message] = [];

    func logMessage(msg:Message) {
        if let detailed = msg as? DetailedMessage {
            messages.append(DetailedMessage(to: detailed.to,
                subject: detailed.subject, from: detailed.from));
        } else {
            messages.append(Message(to: msg.to, subject: msg.subject));
        }
    }

    func processMessages(callback:Message -> Void) {
        for msg in messages {
            callback(msg);
        }
    }
}
...
```

This solves the immediate problem by increasing the amount of knowledge that the MessageLogger class has about the Message class and its subclasses. I will need to update the logMessage class every time that I create a new subclass or when I change any of the initializers, which is an unwelcome increase in the work required to maintain the code.

Applying the Prototype Pattern

I can create a better approach by implementing the NSCopying protocol and using the prototype pattern to clone the objects handled by the MessageLogger class, as shown in Listing 5-16.

Listing 5-16. Applying the Prototype Pattern in the Hiding.playground File

```
import Foundation

class Message : NSObject, NSCopying {
    var to:String;
    var subject:String;

    init(to:String, subject:String) {
        self.to = to; self.subject = subject;
    }
```

```swift
    func copyWithZone(zone: NSZone) -> AnyObject {
        return Message(to: self.to, subject: self.subject);
    }
}

class DetailedMessage : Message {
    var from:String;

    init(to: String, subject: String, from:String) {
        self.from = from;
        super.init(to: to, subject: subject);
    }

    override func copyWithZone(zone: NSZone) -> AnyObject {
        return DetailedMessage(to: self.to,
            subject: self.subject, from: self.from);
    }
}

class MessageLogger {
    var messages:[Message] = [];

    func logMessage(msg:Message) {
        messages.append(msg.copy() as Message);
    }

    func processMessages(callback:Message -> Void) {
        for msg in messages {
            callback(msg);
        }
    }
}

var logger = MessageLogger();

var message = Message(to: "Joe", subject: "Hello");
logger.logMessage(message);

message.to = "Bob";
message.subject = "Free for dinner?";
logger.logMessage(message);

logger.logMessage(DetailedMessage(to: "Alice", subject: "Hi!", from: "Joe"));

logger.processMessages({msg -> Void in
    if let detailed = msg as? DetailedMessage {
        println("Detailed Message - To: \(detailed.to) From: \(detailed.from)"
            + " Subject: \(detailed.subject)");
    } else {
        println("Message - To: \(msg.to) Subject: \(msg.subject)");
    }
});
```

I have changed the base type for the Message class to NSObject and implemented the copyWithZone method in the Message and DetailedMessage classes. This allows me to clone the objects passed to the logMessage method without needing to worry about subclasses or initializers.

> **Tip**   Notice that I don't have to implement the NSCopying protocol in the DetailedMessage class because it is inherited from the Message class. All I need to do is override the copyWithZone method.

The output shown in the console shows that applying the prototype pattern ensures that the additional property defined by the DetailedMessage class isn't lost.

```
Message - To: Joe Subject: Hello
Message - To: Bob Subject: Free for dinner?
Detailed Message - To: Alice From: Joe Subject: Hi!
```

The advantage of applying the prototype pattern is that objects can be cloned as long as they were originally created from the Message class or one of its subclasses; creating new subclasses or modifying the class initializers doesn't require any changes to the MessageLogger class, which makes the code more flexible and easier to maintain.

> **Tip**   With a little extra effort, I can break the dependency on the Message class entirely and create a generic class that can clone objects. See the "Applying the Pattern to the SportsStore Application" section for details.

Understanding the Pitfalls of the Prototype Pattern

There are a few pitfalls to avoid when using the prototype pattern, which I describe in the sections that follow.

Understanding the Deep vs. Shallow Pitfall

The first pitfall to avoid is performing a shallow copy when a deep copy is required. When cloning an object, think carefully about whether you need to create a completely separate copy or whether a simple reference is sufficient. Creating references is quicker and simpler than performing deep copies, but it does mean that two or more references will point to the same object.

Also, don't forget that you need to consider the entire hierarchy of objects that you are cloning and not just the one on which you call the copy method. For each variable that points to a reference type, you must make a shallow versus deep decision. See the "Implementing Deep Copying" section earlier in this chapter for details and examples.

Understanding the Exposure Distortion Pitfall

A common pitfall is to enforce the existence of a single prototype objects from which all clones are created. This can lead to a distorted code structure, where the prototype is exposed to every component in the app, just in case copies are required. Don't be afraid to have multiple prototypes in each logical section of your app, and don't forget that you can make copies from clones.

> **Tip** Some proponents of the prototype pattern believe that you shouldn't use the prototype object exception to create clones. I don't agree with this restriction and believe that there is no harm in cloning any object that supports the prototype pattern, including objects that are being used to perform work and objects that are clones.

Understanding the Nonstandard Protocol Pitfall

The standard iOS way to implement the prototype pattern is by implementing the NSCopying protocol and to ensure that the prototype's base class is NSObject. This NSCopying protocol isn't especially Swift-friendly, so you may be tempted to create a more elegant solution by defining your own protocol or by defining copy constructors (which are initializers that accept an instance of the class and clone it).

Either approach will work, but one of the benefits of NSCopying is that it is well understood and used in the iOS frameworks. Departing from the standard protocol will limit the scope of the prototype pattern to your custom classes and makes it difficult to work with third-party code that expects the NSCopying protocol to be adopted. My advice is to stick with NSObject and NSCopying. They may be slightly awkward, but they work, and they are widely used.

Examples of the Prototype Pattern in Cocoa

The prototype pattern is used throughout Cocoa, especially in the Foundation framework, where you will find many classes that implement NSCopying. I describe one useful instance in the next section and explain how you can make using the NSCopying protocol more Swift-like by using a property attribute.

Using Cocoa Arrays

Of particular interest are the NSArray class and its subclass NSMutableArray. You will often receive data from Objective-C modules using these classes, and they follow a different path than the built-in Swift arrays. Listing 5-17 shows the contents of the NSArray.playground file, which I created to provide a demonstration.

Listing 5-17. The Contents of the NSArray.playground File

```
import Foundation

class Person : NSObject, NSCopying {
    var name:String
    var country: String

    init(name:String, country:String) {
        self.name = name; self.country = country;
    }

    func copyWithZone(zone: NSZone) -> AnyObject {
        return Person(name: self.name, country: self.country);
    }
}

var data = NSMutableArray(objects: 10, "iOS", Person(name:"Joe", country:"USA"));
var copiedData = data;

data[0] = 20;
data[1] = "MacOS";
(data[2] as Person).name = "Alice"

println("Identity: \(data === copiedData)");
println("0: \(copiedData[0]) 1: \(copiedData[1]) 2: \(copiedData[2].name)");
```

> **Tip** The NSArray class creates an immutable array, which cannot be modified. The NSMutableArray, which is a subclass of NSArray, does allow modifications. I have used the NSMutableArray class because I want to demonstrate how arrays and their contents are copied.

I have created an NSMutableArray object that contains an Int, a String, and a Person object, which I create from the Person class I defined in the playground and which implements the NSCopying protocol. (NSArray and NSMutableArray are not strongly typed, unlike the Swift built-in arrays.)

I assign the array to a new variable called copiedData and then modify each of the data array values. To complete the example, I use the Swift identity operator to see whether the data and copiedData variables reference the same object and print out the items in the copiedData array. Here is the console output produced by the playground:

```
Identity: true
0: 20 1: MacOS 2: Alice
```

Swift arrays are implemented as structs, which means that assigning a Swift array to a new variable creates a new array and duplicates its value objects. But that is not what has happened here. Instead, both the data and copiedData variables reference the same NSMutableArray object, and changing values in one of the variables affects the data obtained through both of them. NSArray and NSMutableArray are both reference types, which produces a different behavior than when using the built-in Swift arrays.

Shallow Copying a Cocoa Array

I can apply the prototype pattern and duplicate the array, which performs a shallow copy. In addition to the copy method that I have been using throughout this chapter, there is another prototype-related method to consider when working with Foundation classes: mutableCopy. Table 5-2 describes these methods.

Table 5-2. The Prototype Methods Defined by the NSArray and NSMutableArray Classes

Name	Description
copy()	Returns an instance of NSArray, which cannot be modified
mutableCopy()	Returns an instance of NSMutableArray, which allows modifications

These methods represent a clash between the way that Swift handles mutable and immutable arrays—which is dealt with by using the let and var keywords—and the approach taken by Cocoa and Objective-C. Listing 5-18 shows how I create a clone of the NSMutableArray object by calling the mutableCopy method, producing another NSAMutableArray as the clone.

Listing 5-18. Cloning a Cocoa Array in the NSArray.playground File

```
...
var data = NSMutableArray(objects: 10, "iOS", Person(name:"Joe", country:"USA"));
var copiedData = data.mutableCopy() as NSArray;
...
```

The effect of the cloning operation is that I have two separate NSMutableArray objects. The contents of the array are shallow-copied, which means that the value types are duplicated but that both arrays reference the same Person object, which can be seen in the console output.

```
Identity: false
0: 10 1: iOS 2: Alice
```

Creating a Deep Copy of a Cocoa Array

The NSArray and NSMutable array classes define copy constructors that duplicate the array and, optionally, perform a deep copy on the contents of the prototype array. I advised against copy constructors when I described the potential pitfalls of the prototype pattern, but they are a common Objective-C technique, and you will find them in key Cocoa classes. Listing 5-19 shows how I performed a deep copy on the data array in the NSArray.playground file.

Listing 5-19. Performing a Deep Copy in the NSArray.playground File

```
...
var data = NSMutableArray(objects: 10, "iOS", Person(name:"Joe", country:"USA"));
var copiedData = NSMutableArray(array: data, copyItems: true);
...
```

The arguments to the copy constructor are the prototype array and a `Bool` value that specifies whether objects that implement the `NSCopyable` protocol are cloned. I have specified `true` for the `copyItems` argument, which ensures that I end up with a separate `Person` object in each array, as confirmed by the console output.

```
Identity: false
0: 10 1: iOS 2: Joe
```

ONE-LEVEL DEEP COPIES AND THE NSCODING PROTOCOL

The `copy` and `mutableCopy` methods that I described in Table 5-2 perform a top-level deep copy, which means that the array class takes responsibility for cloning only the objects that it contains and not the nested objects. Some programmers don't consider this to be a true deep copy because it doesn't create clones of any objects that the array may refer to. As an alternative, you will sometimes see the `NSCoding` protocol recommended, which does force a complete deep copy.

There are two pitfalls here. The first is that the `NSCoding` protocol is responsible for serializing and deserializing objects, and using it to apply the prototype pattern is an expensive operation—the prototype has to be rendered into a serialized form and then restored and assigned to a new variable. This is a big job for large, complex objects with lots of nested references.

The more serious problem is that using `NSCoding` assumes that the programmer performing the deep copy knows more about the structure, purpose, and implementation of the objects than the programmer who wrote the original classes. Forcing a deep copy is often a bad idea because the private implementations of the objects that are being serialized may make assumptions about references being shared, and that can cause odd and unexpected defects when separate instances are created.

My advice is to trust the implementation of the `copyWithZone` method of the objects you are cloning to be the authoritative source of knowledge about how an object should be cloned and avoid imposing your own views without a compelling reason and a substantial amount of testing.

Using the NSCopying Property Attribute

Swift supports changing the behavior of properties by decorating them with attributes. One such attribute is `@NSCopying`, which can be applied to any stored property in order to synthesize a setter that calls the `copy` method for objects derived from `NSObject` and that implement the `NSCopying` protocol. The value used to call the property setter is treated as the prototype and is cloned in order to obtain a value to be stored. Listing 5-20 shows the contents of the `NSCopyingAttribute.playground` file, which I created to provide a demonstration.

Listing 5-20. The Contents of the NSCopyingAttribute.playground File

```
import Foundation

class LogItem {
    var from:String?;
    @NSCopying var data:NSArray?
}

var dataArray = NSMutableArray(array: [1, 2, 3, 4]);

var logitem = LogItem()
logitem.from = "Alice";
logitem.data = dataArray;

dataArray[1] = 10;
println("Value: \(logitem.data![1])");
```

In this example, I have defined a class called `LogItem` that has optional `from` and `data` variables.
I have applied the `@NSCopying` attribute to the `data` variable so that the array value is shallow-copied
when the property is set.

To demonstrate that the array is copied when the property is set, I create an `NSMutableArray` object
that I use to set the `data` property of the `LogItem` object. I then modify one of the items in the array
and print out the corresponding value from the array assigned to the `data` property of the `LogItem`
object. The playground produces the following console output, confirming that the prototype pattern
has been applied and the array was copied:

```
Value: 2
```

There are some limitations to the `@NSCopying` attribute. The first is that values set during initialization
are not cloned, which is why I defined the `data` property of the `LogItem` class as optional so that I
don't have to set values for them in an initializer.

The other limitation is that the `@NSCopying` attribute will call the `copy` method, even when the object
supports the `mutableCopy` method. This means that my `NSMutableArray` object was converted into an
immutable `NSArray` object when I assigned it to the `data` property of the `LogItem` method, preventing
me from performing further modifications.

Applying the Pattern to the SportsStore App

In this section, I will apply the prototype pattern to the SportsStore application in order to put the
pattern into a broader context. I am going to create a variation of one of the classes I introduced
earlier to log changes to the `Product` objects, which I will do by writing a message to the debug
console.

Preparing the Example Application

No preparation is required for this chapter, and I will pick up the SportsStore application as I left it in Chapter 4.

> **Tip**   You can download the SportsStore project from `Apress.com`, along with all of the source code for this book.

Implementing NSCopying in the Product Class

The first step is to update the Product class that I created in Chapter 4 so that it can be cloned. To do this, I must set the base class to NSObject and implement the NSCopying protocol, but there are some wrinkles to be worked around, as Listing 5-21 illustrates.

Listing 5-21. Implementing the NSCopying Protocol in the Product.swift File

```
import Foundation

class Product : NSObject, NSCopying {

    private(set) var name:String;
    private(set) var productDescription:String;
    private(set) var category:String;
    private var stockLevelBackingValue:Int = 0;
    private var priceBackingValue:Double = 0;

    init(name:String, description:String, category:String, price:Double,
            stockLevel:Int) {
        self.name = name;
        self.productDescription = description;
        self.category = category;

        super.init();

        self.price = price;
        self.stockLevel = stockLevel;
    }

    var stockLevel:Int {
        get { return stockLevelBackingValue;}
        set { stockLevelBackingValue = max(0, newValue);}
    }

    private(set) var price:Double {
        get { return priceBackingValue;}
        set { priceBackingValue = max(1, newValue);}
    }
```

```
var stockValue:Double {
    get {
        return price * Double(stockLevel);
    }
}

func copyWithZone(zone: NSZone) -> AnyObject {
    return Product(name: self.name, description: self.description,
        category: self.category, price: self.price,
        stockLevel: self.stockLevel);
}
}
```

The changes in Listing 5-21 highlight two common issues that arise when support for cloning is applied retrospectively to an existing class. The first is that I have had to change the name of the stored property that describes the product because the NSObject class defines a method called description. I change the name of the property as follows:

```
...
private(set) var productDescription:String;
...
```

I have not used this property in the application yet, so no additional changes are required. In a real application, some judicious refactoring would be required. This isn't the end of the world, but it is preferable to apply the prototype pattern as early as possible in the development process to avoid this kind of issue.

The second issue is also caused by the change to the NSObject base class. Initializers of subclasses invoke the initializer of their superclass, but this must be done *after* the stored properties have been set and *before* the computed properties are used. It is for this reason that I have called super.init in the middle of the Product class initializer.

Creating the Logger Class

I need a way of tracking the changes that are made to the Product objects in the application. I added a file called Logger.swift to the project, the contents of which are shown in Listing 5-22.

Listing 5-22. The Contents of the Logger.swift File

```
import Foundation

class Logger<T where T:NSObject, T:NSCopying> {
    var dataItems:[T] = [];
    var callback:(T) -> Void;

    init(callback:T -> Void) {
        self.callback = callback;
    }
```

```
    func logItem(item:T) {
        dataItems.append(item.copy() as T);
        callback(item);
    }

    func processItems(callback:T -> Void) {
        for item in dataItems {
            callback(item);
        }
    }
}
```

This is a generic version of the class I used in the "Implementing the Prototype Pattern" section. I have applied a constraint to the generic type parameter that ensures that the Logger class can be used to store only objects that are derived from NSObject and implement the NSCopying protocol. The Logger class defines an initializer that takes a callback function that is passed new items as they are logged. This allows me to dispatch details of new items in a rough and ready way, but I'll demonstrate a better approach in Chapter 22, when I describe the observer pattern.

Logging Changes in the View Controller

I can now log changes by creating an instance of the Logger class and using it to store Product objects when the user specifies a different stock level. Since I am still working with an unstructured app, these changes go into the ViewController.swift file, as shown in Listing 5-23. (I have omitted a lot of the content of this file from the listing because the changes are small but spread throughout the file.) The callback function I have provided as the Logger initializer argument writes out the name and stock level of the changed product.

Listing 5-23. Logging Product Changes in the ViewController.swift File

```
import UIKit

// ...ProductTableCell class omitted for brevity...

var handler = { (p:Product) in
    println("Change: \(p.name) \(p.stockLevel) items in stock");
};

class ViewController: UIViewController, UITableViewDataSource {

    @IBOutlet weak var totalStockLabel: UILabel!
    @IBOutlet weak var tableView: UITableView!

    let logger = Logger<Product>(callback: handler);
    var products = [
        Product(name:"Kayak", description:"A boat for one person",
            category:"Watersports", price:275.0, stockLevel:10),

        // ...other products omitted for brevity...
```

```
        Product(name:"Bling-Bling King",
            description:"Gold-plated, diamond-studded King",
            category:"Chess", price:1200.0, stockLevel:4)];

    // ...methods omitted for brevity...

    func tableView(tableView: UITableView,
        cellForRowAtIndexPath indexPath: NSIndexPath) -> UITableViewCell {
        let product = products[indexPath.row];
        let cell = tableView.dequeueReusableCellWithIdentifier("ProductCell")
            as ProductTableCell;

        cell.product = products[indexPath.row];
        cell.nameLabel.text = product.name;
        cell.descriptionLabel.text = product.productDescription;
        cell.stockStepper.value = Double(product.stockLevel);
        cell.stockField.text = String(product.stockLevel);
        return cell;
    }

    @IBAction func stockLevelDidChange(sender: AnyObject) {
        if var currentCell = sender as? UIView {
            while (true) {
                currentCell = currentCell.superview!;
                if let cell = currentCell as? ProductTableCell {
                    if let product = cell.product? {
                        if let stepper = sender as? UIStepper {
                            product.stockLevel = Int(stepper.value);
                        } else if let textfield = sender as? UITextField {
                            if let newValue = textfield.text.toInt()? {
                                product.stockLevel = newValue;
                            }
                        }
                        cell.stockStepper.value = Double(product.stockLevel);
                        cell.stockField.text = String(product.stockLevel);
                        logger.logItem(product);
                    }
                    break;
                }
            }
            displayStockTotal();
        }

    }
    // ...methods omitted for brevity...
}
```

> **Note** In Listing 5-23, I have defined the callback closure outside the ViewController class. As I write this, there is a bug in the Swift compiler that will not allow this kind of closure to be defined inline.

Testing the Changes

All that remains is to test the changes. Start the application and make changes to the stock levels of the products displayed. For each change, you will see a message written to the Xcode debug console, similar to the following:

```
Change: Kayak 11 items in stock
Change: Lifejacket 15 items in stock
Change: Soccer Ball 31 items in stock
Change: Corner Flags 2 items in stock
```

It is worth taking a moment to consider the effect of the changes that I made. The challenge in creating a generic Logger class is that it is passed objects that may change in the future, but by implementing the prototype pattern, the Logger class is able to create clones without knowing anything about the nature of the objects other than their base class and—implicitly—their implementation of the NSCopying protocol.

Tip   Select the Debug Area ➤ Activate Console from the Xcode View menu if the console isn't visible.

Decoupling the copying of objects from the class that defines them means I can change the Product initializer or create and use subclasses without needing to make corresponding changes in the Logger class. The overall effect is to simplify the code in the app and make it easier to extend and maintain over time.

Summary

In this chapter, I described the prototype pattern and demonstrated how it can be used to create new objects without having knowledge of the class that is used to define them. I explained how objects can be subjected to deep and shallow copying, and I explained the most common pitfalls that are associated with that process. In the next chapter, I describe the singleton pattern, which ensures that only one object of a given type exists in the application.

Chapter 6

The Singleton Pattern

I describe the *singleton pattern* in this chapter, which ensures that only one object of a given type exists in the application. This is one of the most commonly used design patterns because it solves problems that arise often, either because you need an object to represent a real-world resource or because you want to ensure that all activity of a certain kind—such as logging—is handled in a consistent way. Table 6-1 puts the singleton pattern in context.

Table 6-1. Putting the Singleton Pattern into Context

Question	Answer
What is it?	The singleton pattern ensures that only one object of a given type exists in the application.
What are the benefits?	The singleton pattern can be used to manage objects that represent real-world resources or to encapsulate a shared resource.
When should you use this pattern?	The singleton pattern should be used when creating further objects doesn't increase the number of real-world resources available or when you want to consolidate an activity such as logging.
When should you avoid this pattern?	The singleton pattern isn't useful if there are not multiple components that require access to a shared resource or if there are no objects that represent real-world resources in the application.
How do you know when you have implemented the pattern correctly?	The pattern has been correctly implemented when there is only one instance of a given type *and* when that instance cannot be copied and cloned *and* when further instances cannot be created.
Are there any common pitfalls?	The main pitfalls are using reference types (which can be copied) or classes that implement the NSCopying protocol (which can be cloned). The singleton pattern usually requires some protections against concurrent use, which is a common source of problems.
Are there any related patterns?	The object pool pattern, which I describe in Chapter 7, manages a fixed number of objects rather than the single object handled by the singleton pattern.

Preparing the Example Project

I created an OS X Command Line Tool project called `Singleton` for this chapter, following the same process I described in Chapter 2. No further preparation is required.

Understanding the Problem That the Pattern Solves

The singleton pattern ensures that only one object of a given type exists and that all components that depend on that object use the same instance. This is different from the prototype pattern I described in Chapter 5, which makes it easy to make copies of objects. By contrast, the singleton pattern permits the existence of just one object and prevents it from being copied.

The problem addressed by the singleton pattern arises when you have an object that you don't want duplicated throughout an application, either because it represents a real-world resource (such as a printer or server) or because you want to consolidate a set of related activities in one place. When it comes to real-world resources, the ability to create new objects that represent printers or servers is nonsensical because creating an object doesn't magically put new hardware into place.

Even for more abstract representations, being able to create multiple objects can be a problem. Listing 6-1 shows the contents of the `BackupServer.swift` file, which I added to the `Singleton` project.

Listing 6-1. The Contents of the BackupServer.swift File

```
import Foundation

class DataItem {

    enum ItemType : String {
        case Email = "Email Address";
        case Phone = "Telephone Number";
        case Card = "Credit Card Number";
    }

    var type:ItemType;
    var data:String;

    init(type:ItemType, data:String) {
        self.type = type; self.data = data;
    }
}

class BackupServer {
    let name:String;
    private var data = [DataItem]();

    init(name:String) {
        self.name = name;
    }
```

```
    func backup(item:DataItem) {
        data.append(item);
    }

    func getData() -> [DataItem]{
        return data;
    }
}
```

I have defined a `BackupServer` class to represent a server that archives data items, which are represented by instances of the `DataItem` class. I don't need to get into the details of creating archives to demonstrate the singleton pattern, so the `backup` method defined by the `BackupServer` class just appends its `DataItem` object to a stored instance property called `data`, which can later be accessed through the `getData` method. In Listing 6-2, you can see how I modified the `main.swift` file to use the `BackupServer` class.

Listing 6-2. Using the BackupServer Class in the main.swift File

```
var server = BackupServer(name:"Server#1");
server.backup(DataItem(type: DataItem.ItemType.Email, data: "joe@example.com"));
server.backup(DataItem(type: DataItem.ItemType.Phone, data: "555-123-1133"));

var otherServer = BackupServer(name:"Server#2");
otherServer.backup(DataItem(type: DataItem.ItemType.Email, data: "bob@example.com"));
```

The code in the project compiles and can be executed, but it doesn't make any practical sense. If the purpose of a `BackupServer` object is to represent a real-world backup server, then what does it mean when anyone can create a new object and start calling the `backup` method? Real servers are not provisioned just because a programmer creates a new object (although I admit that I like the sound of that), so the outcome is that some of the data that was backed up in Listing 6-2 won't arrive at a real server and won't be backed up. Even in the world of cloud servers, creating a new server instance generally requires more than instantiating a new Swift object.

Put another way, the code in Listing 6-2 doesn't make sense because an object that represents a real-world server can work only when it is associated with a server that exists and has been configured beforehand—and that means carefully controlling the creation of the object that does correspond to the real-world servers and preventing any other instances from being created.

> **Tip**   There is no output produced from the example project at the moment.

Understanding the Shared Resource Encapsulation Problem

Not all of the objects that can benefit from the singleton pattern represent real-world objects. There will be occasions where you want to create an object that can be used by all of the components in an application in a simple and consistent way. To demonstrate, Listing 6-3 shows the contents of the `Logger.swift` file, which I added to the example project.

Listing 6-3. The Contents of the Logger.swift File

```
class Logger {
    private var data = [String]()

    func log(msg:String) {
        data.append(msg);
    }

    func printLog() {
        for msg in data {
            println("Log: \(msg)");
        }
    }
}
```

This is a simple logging class of the kind I use to debug problems in my own projects. I like the modern debuggers like the one that comes with Xcode, but I often fall back on old-school techniques like this because you can learn a lot just by looking at the order in which messages appear in the console.

The Logger class defines a log method that accepts String message arguments and appends them to an array. The printLog method is called to display the messages, which it does by calling the global println function. Listing 6-4 shows how I updated the main.swift file to log details about the data items I back up.

Listing 6-4. Using the Logger Class in the main.swift File

```
let logger  = Logger();

var server = BackupServer(name:"Server#1");
server.backup(DataItem(type: DataItem.ItemType.Email, data: "joe@example.com"));
server.backup(DataItem(type: DataItem.ItemType.Phone, data: "555-123-1133"));

logger.log("Backed up 2 items to \(server.name)");

var otherServer = BackupServer(name:"Server#2");
otherServer.backup(DataItem(type: DataItem.ItemType.Email, data: "bob@example.com"));
logger.log("Backed up 1 item to \(otherServer.name)");

logger.printLog();
```

If you run the application, you will see this output shown in the console:

```
Log: Backed up 2 items to Server#1
Log: Backed up 1 item to Server#2
```

That all works as expected: I log some debugging messages using a local instance of the Logger class and call the printLog method to write out the messages once I have backed up all my data.

The problem arises when I want to log some debug messages in the BackupServer class, as shown in Listing 6-5.

Listing 6-5. Adding Logging in the BackupServer.swift File

```
...
class BackupServer {
    let name:String;
    private var data = [DataItem]();
    let logger = Logger();

    init(name:String) {
        self.name = name;
        logger.log("Created new server \(name)");
    }

    func backup(item:DataItem) {
        data.append(item);
        logger.log("\(name) backed up item of type \(item.type.rawValue)");
    }

    func getData() -> [DataItem]{
        return data;
    }
}
...
```

There are now two Logger objects, each of which maintains a set of messages. My call to the printLog method on the Logger object in the main.swift file doesn't print out the messages logged to the BackupServer class. What I require is a single Logger object that I can use to capture all of the debug messages in the application and a means for application components to locate that Logger object without creating tight coupling—known as *encapsulating* a shared resource.

Understanding the Singleton Pattern

The singleton pattern solves both the real-world object and shared resource encapsulation problems by ensuring that there is only ever one instance of a class in an application. This object—known as the *singleton*—is shared between all of the components that require its functionality, as shown in Figure 6-1.

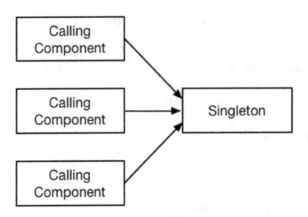

Figure 6-1. *The singleton pattern*

The figure looks simple, but the singleton pattern is unusual in that its implementation is closely tied to the language being used. Swift doesn't have some features that would be used to implement the pattern in languages such as C# and Java, and some ingenuity is required.

Implementing the Singleton Pattern

When implementing the singleton pattern, there are some important rules to follow:

- The singleton must be the only instance of its type that exists.
- The singleton cannot be replaced by another object, even of the same type.
- The singleton must be locatable by the components that need to use it.

There can never be more than one instance of the singleton, either because the object represents real-world resources or because you want to funnel all activity, such as logging, through the same object. In the sections that follow, I describe how to implement the singleton pattern in Swift.

> **Note**   The singleton pattern works only with reference types, which means that only classes are supported. Structs and other values types don't work because they are copied when they are assigned to a new variable. The only way to copy a reference type is to create a new instance via its initializer or to rely on it implementing the NSCopying protocol. See Chapter 5 for details.

The Quick Singleton Implementation

The quickest way to implement the singleton is to use a Swift global constant. Global constants have some useful behaviors that set the foundation for following the rules I listed in the previous section. Listing 6-6 shows how I have implemented the singleton pattern based on a global constant in the Logger.swift file.

Listing 6-6. Implementing the Singleton Pattern in the Logger.swift File

```swift
let globalLogger = Logger();

final class Logger {
    private var data = [String]()

    private init() {
        // do nothing - required to stop instances being
        // created by code in other files
    }

    func log(msg:String) {
        data.append(msg);
    }

    func printLog() {
        for msg in data {
            println("Log: \(msg)");
        }
    }
}
```

The first change I have made is to define the global constant, which I have called globalLogger. It may not look like much, but the Swift language makes two guarantees about global constants and variables. They will be initialized lazily, and that lazy initialization is thread-safe. These guarantees mean that the singleton object won't be created until the value of the globalLogger constant is read for the first time and that when it is read, only a single instance of the Logger class will be instantiated even if another thread tries to read the value while the singleton is being initialized.

The other changes I made in Listing 6-6 are to the Logger class. I marked the class as final to prevent subclasses from being defined and marked the initializer as private so that instances cannot be created from outside the Logger.swift file. Having defined the singleton and protected its class so that other instances cannot be created, I can update the BackupServer class, as shown in Listing 6-7.

Listing 6-7. Using the Singleton in the BackupServer.swift File

```swift
...
class BackupServer {
    let name:String;
    private var data = [DataItem]();

    init(name:String) {
        self.name = name;
        globalLogger.log("Created new server \(name)");
    }

    func backup(item:DataItem) {
        data.append(item);
        globalLogger.log("\(name) backed up item of type \(item.type.rawValue)");
    }
```

```
    func getData() -> [DataItem]{
        return data;
    }
}
...
```

I have removed the local Logger object and added calls to the log method of the singleton. The last rule I listed in the previous section was that components should be able to locate the singleton, and—as you can see—using a global constant makes that a simple process.

> **Tip**   This implementation also adheres to the other rules. The private initializer and the lazy initialization ensure that there is only one instance of the Logger class, and using the constant means that the object referred to by the globalLogger cannot be changed.

I also have to make changes to the main.swift file, as shown in Listing 6-8.

Listing 6-8. Using the Singleton in the main.swift File

```
var server = BackupServer(name:"Server#1");
server.backup(DataItem(type: DataItem.ItemType.Email, data: "joe@example.com"));
server.backup(DataItem(type: DataItem.ItemType.Phone, data: "555-123-1133"));

globalLogger.log("Backed up 2 items to \(server.name)");

var otherServer = BackupServer(name:"Server#2");
otherServer.backup(DataItem(type: DataItem.ItemType.Email, data: "bob@example.com"));
globalLogger.log("Backed up 1 item to \(otherServer.name)");

globalLogger.printLog();
```

If you run the application, you will see that the singleton pattern has allowed me to gather all of the logging messages and write them to the console.

```
Log: Created new server Server#1
Log: Server#1 backed up item of type Email Address
Log: Server#1 backed up item of type Telephone Number
Log: Backed up 2 items to Server#1
Log: Created new server Server#2
Log: Server#2 backed up item of type Email Address
Log: Backed up 1 item to Server#2
```

Creating a Conventional Singleton Implementation

Using a global variable works perfectly well, but you will be used to the convention of accessing a singleton via its class if you have come to Swift from C# or Java. The problem is that Swift doesn't support type stored properties, and some ingenuity is required to apply the singleton pattern in the conventional way. Listing 6-9 shows how I have used a struct with a static property to solve the problem.

Listing 6-9. Implementing the Singleton Pattern in the BackupServer.swift File

```
...
final class BackupServer {
    let name:String;
    private var data = [DataItem]();

    private init(name:String) {
        self.name = name;
        globalLogger.log("Created new server \(name)");
    }

    func backup(item:DataItem) {
        data.append(item);
        globalLogger.log("\(name) backed up item of type \(item.type.rawValue)");
    }

    func getData() -> [DataItem]{
        return data;
    }

    class var server:BackupServer {
        struct SingletonWrapper {
            static let singleton = BackupServer(name:"MainServer");
        }
        return SingletonWrapper.singleton;
    }
}
...
```

> **Note**   The choice between a global constant and a nested struct is a personal one. I like the simplicity of the global variable, but years of Java and C# development mean that I am more comfortable with the nested struct. If you do use global constants, then make sure you use a naming convention that is unambiguous and consistent throughout your application.

Within the computed type property server, I have defined a struct called SingletonWrapper that has a static stored property called singleton. I create the singleton BackupServer object and assign it to the singleton property. Finally, I return the value of the singleton property as the value of the server property.

Do not worry if the last sentence doesn't make immediate sense. This technique relies on the way that Swift processes `struct` definitions and static stored properties to ensure that only one instance of the `BackupServer` class is created, even though the code is a little mind-bending.

To access the singleton, I read the value of the `BackupServer.server` property, as shown in Listing 6-10.

Listing 6-10. Using the Singleton in the main.swift File

```
var server = BackupServer.server;

server.backup(DataItem(type: DataItem.ItemType.Email, data: "joe@example.com"));
server.backup(DataItem(type: DataItem.ItemType.Phone, data: "555-123-1133"));

globalLogger.log("Backed up 2 items to \(server.name)");

var otherServer = BackupServer.server;
otherServer.backup(DataItem(type: DataItem.ItemType.Email, data: "bob@example.com"));
globalLogger.log("Backed up 1 item to \(otherServer.name)");

globalLogger.printLog();
```

The `server` and `otherServer` variables in the listing refer to the singleton, which means that all the `DataItem` objects are sent to the same server.

Dealing with Concurrency

If you are using a singleton in a multithreaded application, then you need to think through the consequences of different components performing simultaneous operations on the singleton and make sure you guard against any potential problems.

> **Caution**   Effective concurrent programming requires careful thought and experience. It is easy to set out with the best of intentions but end up with an app that is substantially slower or freezes up. Take the time to learn the concepts that underpin concurrency before you embark on a multithreaded project, and give yourself enough development time to get the code right and to test thoroughly.

Potential concurrency problems are common, and even my simple `Logger` and `BackupServer` classes have them because Swift arrays are not thread-safe. This means two more threads can call the append method on an array at the same time and corrupt the data structure. To demonstrate the problem, I made some changes to the `main.swift` file, as shown in Listing 6-11.

Listing 6-11. Performing Concurrent Requests in the main.swift File

```swift
import Foundation

var server = BackupServer.server;

let queue = dispatch_queue_create("workQueue", DISPATCH_QUEUE_CONCURRENT);
let group = dispatch_group_create();

for count in 0 ..< 100 {
    dispatch_group_async(group, queue, {() in
        BackupServer.server.backup(DataItem(type: DataItem.ItemType.Email,
            data: "bob@example.com"))
    });
}

dispatch_group_wait(group, DISPATCH_TIME_FOREVER);

println("\(server.getData().count) items were backed up");
```

This listing uses Grand Central Dispatch (GCD) to asynchronously call the backup method on the BackupServer singleton 100 times. If you are not familiar with GCD, see the "Understanding Grand Central Dispatch" sidebars for a brief explanation of the code in this and subsequent listings. There are several GCD sidebars in this chapter, and I use GCD to implement many of the patterns in this book. I explain how each feature I use works, but I don't get into a great deal of detail because concurrent programming—and GCD—is a topic beyond the scope of this book. For full details of GCD, see https://developer.apple.com/library/ios/documentation/Performance/Reference/GCD_libdispatch_Ref/index.html.

UNDERSTANDING GRAND CENTRAL DISPATCH: PART 1

Several techniques are available for Cocoa concurrent programming, but the one that I have used in this book is Grand Central Dispatch, which I find the easiest to work with. Concurrent programming is an advanced topic, and I am not going to describe GCD in detail, but I will briefly explain how I use GCD in the examples in this chapter. For more information about GCD, see https://developer.apple.com/library/ios/documentation/Performance/Reference/GCD_libdispatch_Ref/index.html.

GCD is a standard part of the Foundation framework and is based around the idea of *queues* of *blocks*, where each block performs some item of work. You select or create a queue and use create the blocks—expressed as Swift closures—that represent the concurrent tasks that will be performed. GCD is a C API, and the syntax isn't especially Swift-like, but it is simple enough to use once you get the hang of it. In Listing 6-11, I created a new queue like this:

```swift
...
let queue = dispatch_queue_create("workQueue", DISPATCH_QUEUE_CONCURRENT);
...
```

The dispatch_queue_create function takes two arguments that set the name and type of the queue. I have called the queue workQueue and used the DISPATCH_QUEUE_CONCURRENT constant to specify that the blocks in the queue should be processed by concurrently by multiple threads. I assign the object that represents the queue to a constant called queue. (The queue type is dispatch_queue_t, which you will see me use in some of the later examples in this chapter and in Chapter 7.)

I can group blocks together in order to receive a notification when all of them have been executed. Groups are created using the dispatch_group_create function like this:

```
...
let group = dispatch_group_create();
...
```

To submit work to be performed asynchronously, I use the dispatch_group_async function to add the block to a queue, like this:

```
...
dispatch_group_async(group, queue, {() in
    BackupServer.server.backup(DataItem(type: DataItem.ItemType.Email,
        data: "bob@example.com"))
});
...
```

The first argument is the group that the block is associated with, the second argument is the queue to which the block will be added, and the final argument is the block itself, expressed as a closure. The closure takes no arguments and returns no results. GCD will take each block of work from the queue and execute it asynchronously—although, as you will learn, queues can also be used to serialize work.

The final step is to wait until all 100 blocks have been completed, which I do like this:

```
...
dispatch_group_wait(group, DISPATCH_TIME_FOREVER);
...
```

The dispatch_group_wait function blocks the current thread until all of the blocks in the specified group have been completed. The first argument is the group to monitor, and the second argument is the duration to wait. By using the DISPATCH_TIME_FOREVER value, I specify that I want to wait indefinitely for the blocks in the group to complete.

To see the problem, simply start the application. Concurrency problems are all about timing and require two or more threads to be performing conflicting operations simultaneously. You might be lucky when you run the application and no such conflict will occur—but the likelihood is that two calls overlapping calls to the backup method will result in two threads trying to add data to an array through the append method at the same time, causing an error. When this happens, the debugger will break on the backup method, as shown in Figure 6-2.

```
        func backup(item:DataItem) {
            data.append(item);                                    Thread 2: EXC_BAD_A
            globalLogger.log("\(name) backed up item of type \(item.type.toRaw())");
        }
```

Figure 6-2. A concurrency problem

> **Tip**   If you are fortunate enough not to encounter an error, then run the application again. Many factors
> affect concurrency problems, but the code in the example is likely to fail most of the time.

The exact error reported by the debugger will differ, but the problem remains the same: manipulating
the contents of a Swift array isn't a thread-safe operation, and singletons that use arrays need
concurrency protections.

Serializing Access

To solve this problem, I need to ensure that only one block at a time is allowed to call the append
method on the array. Listing 6-12 shows how I have used GCD to solve the problem. (I explain the
GCD features I have used in the second "Understanding Grand Central Dispatch: Part 2" sidebar.)

Listing 6-12. Serializing Access to the Array in the BackupServer.swift File

```swift
import Foundation

class DataItem {

    enum ItemType : String {
        case Email = "Email Address";
        case Phone = "Telephone Number";
        case Card  = "Credit Card Number";
    }

    var type:ItemType;
    var data:String;

    init(type:ItemType, data:String) {
        self.type = type; self.data = data;
    }
}

final class BackupServer {
    let name:String;
    private var data = [DataItem]();
    private let arrayQ = dispatch_queue_create("arrayQ", DISPATCH_QUEUE_SERIAL);
```

```
private init(name:String) {
    self.name = name;
    globalLogger.log("Created new server \(name)");
}

func backup(item:DataItem) {
    dispatch_sync(arrayQ, {() in
        self.data.append(item);
        globalLogger.log(
            "\(self.name) backed up item of type \(item.type.rawValue)");
    })
}

func getData() -> [DataItem]{
    return data;
}

class var server:BackupServer {
    struct SingletonWrapper {
        static let singleton = BackupServer(name:"MainServer");
    }
    return SingletonWrapper.singleton;
}
}
```

In this listing, I perform the opposite action of the one in Listing 6-11: I take a set of asynchronous blocks and force them to be performed serially in order to ensure that only one block calls the append method on the array at any one time.

This may appear self-defeating, but in a real application multiple components will create the blocks, rather than a single for loop. These components won't be able to coordinate their activities and usually won't know anything about each other, so it falls to the singleton to protect the resources it relies on.

UNDERSTANDING GRAND CENTRAL DISPATCH—PART 2

In Listing 6-12, I create a queue using the dispatch_queue_create function, like this:

```
...
private let arrayQ = dispatch_queue_create("arrayQ", DISPATCH_QUEUE_SERIAL);
...
```

The first argument is the name of the queue, and the second argument—the DISPATCH_QUEUE_SERIAL value—specifies that the blocks will be taken from the queue and executed one after the other, such that a block won't be started until the previous one has been completed.

Within the backup method I use the `dispatch_sync` function to add blocks to the queue.

```
...
dispatch_sync(arrayQ, {() in
    self.data.append(item);
    globalLogger.log(
            "\(self.name) backed up item of type \(item.type.toRaw())");
})
...
```

The `dispatch_sync` function adds work to the queue just like the `dispatch_group_async` function I used in Listing 6-11, but it waits until the block has been completed before it returns, whereas the `dispatch_group_async` function returns immediately, leaving the block to be executed at some future point when it reached the front of the queue. (It also doesn't specify a group. The asynchronous equivalent of `dispatch_sync` is `dispatch_async`.)

The function used to add a block to the method doesn't affect the way that the block is processed—just whether the function returns immediately after adding the block to the queue or blocks until it has been processed.

The effect I have created is that calling the `backup` method is a synchronous operation that will not return until the data has been added to the array, and since I have specified a serial queue, this means that the method won't return until all of the other backups ahead in the queue are processed too.

The changes I made in Listing 6-12 ensure that the array used in the BackupServer singleton is protected, but the backup method uses the Logger class, and that presents a similar problem. Although calls to the log method are serialized within the BackupServer class, another component could use the singleton and call the log method at the same time, which would lead to the same kind of data corruption I described earlier. For completeness, I have used GCD to protect the data array in the Logger class, as shown in Listing 6-13.

Listing 6-13. Adding Concurrency Protection in the Logger.swift File

```
import Foundation;

let globalLogger = Logger();

final class Logger {
    private var data = [String]()
    private let arrayQ = dispatch_queue_create("arrayQ", DISPATCH_QUEUE_SERIAL);

    private init() {
        // do nothing - required to stop instances being
        // created by code in other files
    }

    func log(msg:String) {
        dispatch_sync(arrayQ, {() in
            self.data.append(msg);
        });
    }
}
```

```
func printLog() {
    for msg in data {
        println("Log: \(msg)");
    }
}
}
```

The Logger class exposes its singleton using the global constant technique, but the technique for protecting the data array from corruption is just the same—I create a serial GCD queue and use the dispatch_sync method to ensure that array modifications are performed only once at a time. If you run the application, there will be no data corruption, and the following output will be shown in the console window:

```
100 items were backed up
```

Understanding the Pitfalls of the Singleton Pattern

There are several pitfalls to avoid when implementing the singleton pattern, and it is important to think through your implementation carefully in order to ensure you adhere to the rules I described earlier in the chapter. In the sections that follow, I highlight the most common problems.

Understanding the Leakage Pitfall

The most common problem when implementing a singleton is producing an object that can be copied, either because it was created from a struct (or one of the built-in reference types) or because it was created from a class that implements the NSCopying protocol (which I described in Chapter 5).

Structs do not work as singletons because they are copied whenever they are assigned to a new variable or constant or passed as an argument, but you may be tempted to use a class that implements the NSCopying protocol because you trust that the components that will consume the singleton will not make copies. I advise caution: other developers may not realize the importance of not copying the singleton, and you should take steps to create a strict implementation of the pattern. Allowing other components to copy or clone the prototype breaks the first of the three singleton rules.

> **Tip**   You can apply the decorator pattern if you don't have control over the class definition of the object that you need as a singleton in order to prevent an object from being treated like a prototype. See Chapter 14 for details.

Understanding the Shared Code File Pitfall

The Swift access protection keywords operate at the file level, which means that applying the `private` keyword to an initializer affects only code outside of the file that contains the singleton. You should always define the singleton and the global constant—if you are using one—in their own file so that no other component is able to create its own instances of the singleton class, which breaks the first singleton rule.

Understanding the Concurrency Pitfalls

The most intractable problems with the singleton pattern are related to concurrency, which can be a difficult topic even for experience programmers. In the sections that follow, I describe the most common problems.

Not Applying Concurrency Protections

The first problem is not applying concurrency protections when they are needed. Not every singleton faces concurrency problems, but it is something that you should give serious consideration to. If you are relying on shared data structures, such as arrays, or on global functions, such as `println`, then you need to ensure that your singleton's code cannot be accessed by multiple threads concurrently. If in doubt, assume that there will be a problem because the overhead of serializing access to shared resources is less of an issue than an app that crashed once it has been deployed to customers.

Applying Concurrency Protections Consistently

Concurrency protections must be applied throughout a singleton so that all of the code that operates on a common resource, such as an array, is serialized in the same way. If you leave just one method or block of code that accesses the array without serialization, then you run the risk of two threads conflicting and corrupting the data. If you are finding it hard to track down all of the code that modifies a shared resource, then you should reconsider the design of your code and extract the resource—and the code that manipulates it—into its own class so that you can apply concurrency protections in a more focused way.

Bad Optimization

There is a common belief that concurrency mechanisms like GCD offer poor performance and that concurrent protections should be low-level and applied minimally. I think this is nonsense. There are some applications where every CPU cycle counts, but these are few and far between, and the actual overhead of applying any concurrency—even higher-level abstractions like GCD—is minimal on modern operating systems.

The perception of performance problems usually arises because concurrency protections expose poor code design. If you have 200 threads queuing up to access the same array, then you should consider whether the number of threads and the ratio of threads to arrays makes sense, rather than decide to start messing around with low-level operating system locks. (One pattern that can help redress this kind of ratio is the object pool pattern, which I describe in Chapters 7 and 8.)

My advice is to use GCD because it is relatively simple to understand and easy to work with and makes good use of Swift closures. If you do have performance problems, then you should consider why this is the case and whether applying the patterns described in this book would allow you to minimize the points of contention in the application.

Examples of the Singleton Pattern in Cocoa

There are several singletons used in the Cocoa frameworks, and they are usually used to represent the top-level component in an application. The most commonly encountered example is the UIApplication class, which provides features that control the overall behavior of an app and provide integration into iOS features. The UIApplication singleton is accessed through the type method sharedApplication.

Applying the Pattern to the SportsStore Application

In this section, I will apply the singleton pattern to the SportsStore application in order to put the pattern into a broader context. There is only one area of the application that would benefit from the singleton pattern, and that is the Logger class that I created in Chapter 5 to demonstrate the prototype pattern and which is similar to the class of the same name that I used in this chapter to demonstrate using the singleton pattern to solve the shared resource encapsulation problem. Listing 6-14 shows the existing definition of the Logger class in the SportsStore project.

Listing 6-14. The Contents of the Logger.swift File in the SportsStore Project

```
import Foundation

class Logger<T where T:NSObject, T:NSCopying> {
    var dataItems:[T] = [];
    var callback:(T) -> Void;

    init(callback:T -> Void) {
        self.callback = callback;
    }

    func logItem(item:T) {
        dataItems.append(item.copy() as T);
        callback(item);
    }

    func processItems(callback:T -> Void) {
        for item in dataItems {
            callback(item);
        }
    }
}
```

> **Tip**   You can download the SportsStore project and the source for all the listings in this chapter
> from Apress.com.

I am going apply the singleton pattern by starting with the concurrency issues and then creating the
singleton. There are two potential concurrency issues presented by the SportsStore Logger class.
The first issue is that the dataItems array is used in the logItem and processItems methods, and it is
possible that multiple threads may try to add new items to the array in the logItem method, maybe
even while other threads try to read the contents of the array in the processItems method.

Protecting the Data Array

I am going to use GCD to protect the array, but I am going to vary the technique that I used in earlier
examples in order to differentiate between threads that are reading the contents of the array and
those that are writing them. Allowing multiple threads to simultaneously read the contents of the
array doesn't present any concurrency hazards, as long as no threads are modifying the array at the
same time. You can see how I have solved this problem in Listing 6-15.

Listing 6-15. Applying Concurrency Protections in the Logger.swift File

```
import Foundation

class Logger<T where T:NSObject, T:NSCopying> {
    var dataItems:[T] = [];
    var callback:(T) -> Void;
    var arrayQ = dispatch_queue_create("arrayQ", DISPATCH_QUEUE_CONCURRENT);

    init(callback:T -> Void) {
        self.callback = callback;
    }

    func logItem(item:T) {
        dispatch_barrier_async(arrayQ, {() in
            self.dataItems.append(item.copy() as T);
            self.callback(item);
        });
    }

    func processItems(callback:T -> Void) {
        dispatch_sync(arrayQ, {() in
            for item in self.dataItems {
                callback(item);
            }
        });
    }
}
```

I use the dispatch_sync function in the processItems method to add a block of work that enumerates the array, waiting until the block has completed before allowing the method to return. The difference is that I have used the dispatch_barrier_async function in the logItem method to create a block of work that adds an item to the array. The dispatch_barrier_async function adds a special block to the queue that changes its behavior. The queue will not start executing the barrier block until all of the blocks ahead of it have completed and will not process any subsequent blocks until the barrier itself has completed.

UNDERSTANDING GRAND CENTRAL DISPATCH: PART 3

In the context of the Logger class, read operations are contained in ordinary blocks, and write operations are in barrier blocks. When a barrier block reaches the head of the queue, GCD waits until all of the read operations that are still in process have completed. Once they are all done, GCD executes the barrier block—which modifies the array—and does not process any subsequent blocks until the barrier block has completed. Once the barrier block is complete, the following items in the queue are processed as normal and in parallel until the next barrier block comes along.

Put another way, using a barrier changes a concurrent queue into a serial queue for as long as it takes to process the barrier block, after which it returns to being a concurrent queue again. Whichever way you prefer to think of it, using a GCD barrier makes it easy to create a reader/writer lock.

Protecting the Callback

The second problem requires more thought. My use of a barrier to allow multiple readers means that the callback function that is set through the initializer may be called concurrently. This presents a common concurrency dilemma.

I have several choices. The first choice is to do nothing—which is the current state of the code—and assume that the code that has provided the callback is aware of the concurrency risk and has taken the required precautions. From the perspective of the Logger class, this is the simplest option because it shifts the burden elsewhere. This isn't an entirely bad idea because the Logger class has no insights into how the callback is implemented, and I may end up with concurrency protections in the Logger class and in the component that defines the callback. The risk with redundant concurrency protection is that the application can deadlock if written inexpertly. The other problem is that I may end up with no protection at all and risk data corruption. This is the simplest choice but is also the most uncertain.

The second choice is to assume responsibility in the Logger class. This is the safe option, but once again I may end up with redundant protections; however, it does mean that data corruption is avoided.

The third choice—and the one that I am going to follow in this example—is to allow the component to chose when it provides the callback. You can see how I have modified the Logger class to support this feature in Listing 6-16.

Listing 6-16. Adding Optional Concurrency Protection in the Logger.swift File

```swift
import Foundation

class Logger<T where T:NSObject, T:NSCopying> {
    var dataItems:[T] = [];
    var callback:(T) -> Void;
    var arrayQ = dispatch_queue_create("arrayQ", DISPATCH_QUEUE_CONCURRENT);
    var callbackQ = dispatch_queue_create("callbackQ", DISPATCH_QUEUE_SERIAL);

    init(callback:T -> Void, protect:Bool = true) {
        self.callback = callback;
        if (protect) {
            self.callback = {(item:T) in
                dispatch_sync(self.callbackQ, {() in
                    callback(item);
                });
            };
        }
    }

    func logItem(item:T) {
        dispatch_barrier_async(arrayQ, {() in
            self.dataItems.append(item.copy() as T);
            self.callback(item);
        });
    }

    func processItems(callback:T -> Void) {
        dispatch_sync(arrayQ, {() in
            for item in self.dataItems {
                callback(item);
            }
        });
    }
}
```

I have defined a separate queue and added an initializer parameter that has a default value, allowing me to apply the protections without changing code elsewhere in the application. If protection is required—or the caller omits the new argument—then I wrap the callback in the closure that adds a block to the new queue.

Defining the Singleton

Now that I have addressed the concurrency issues, I am going to define the singleton object and protect the Logger class so that it can't be instantiated elsewhere in the application. Listing 6-17 shows the changes that I made.

Listing 6-17. Creating the Singleton in the Logger.swift File

```
import Foundation

let productLogger = Logger<Product>(callback: {p in
    println("Change: \(p.name) \(p.stockLevel) items in stock");
});

final class Logger<T where T:NSObject, T:NSCopying> {
    var dataItems:[T] = [];
    var callback:(T) -> Void;
    var arrayQ = dispatch_queue_create("arrayQ", DISPATCH_QUEUE_CONCURRENT);
    var callbackQ = dispatch_queue_create("callbackQ", DISPATCH_QUEUE_SERIAL);

    private init(callback:T -> Void, protect:Bool = true) {
        self.callback = callback;
        if (protect) {
            self.callback = {(item:T) in
                dispatch_sync(self.callbackQ, {() in
                    callback(item);
                });
            };
        }
    }

    func logItem(item:T) {
        dispatch_barrier_async(arrayQ, {() in
            self.dataItems.append(item.copy() as T);
            self.callback(item);
        });
    }

    func processItems(callback:T -> Void) {
        dispatch_sync(arrayQ, {() in
            for item in self.dataItems {
                callback(item);
            }
        });
    }
}
```

It isn't possible to create the singleton using the struct for generic types, so I have had to define a global constant that instantiates the Logger class with the Product type. I prefer the struct approach, but I like being able to use generic classes with a range of types and will happily use the global constant approach in this situation. The remaining change is to update the only component that uses the Logger class in the application, as shown in Listing 6-18.

Listing 6-18. Using the Singleton in the ViewController.swift File

```swift
import UIKit

class ProductTableCell: UITableViewCell {
    @IBOutlet weak var nameLabel: UILabel!
    @IBOutlet weak var descriptionLabel: UILabel!
    @IBOutlet weak var stockStepper: UIStepper!
    @IBOutlet weak var stockField: UITextField!

    var product: Product?;
}

class ViewController: UIViewController, UITableViewDataSource {

    @IBOutlet weak var totalStockLabel: UILabel!
    @IBOutlet weak var tableView: UITableView!

    //let logger = Logger<Product>(callback: handler);

    var products = [
        Product(name:"Kayak", description:"A boat for one person",
            category:"Watersports", price:275.0, stockLevel:10),

    // ...code omitted for brevity...

    @IBAction func stockLevelDidChange(sender: AnyObject) {
        if var currentCell = sender as? UIView {
            while (true) {
                currentCell = currentCell.superview!;
                if let cell = currentCell as? ProductTableCell {
                    if let product = cell.product? {
                        if let stepper = sender as? UIStepper {
                            product.stockLevel = Int(stepper.value);
                        } else if let textfield = sender as? UITextField {
                            if let newValue = textfield.text.toInt()? {
                                product.stockLevel = newValue;
                            }
                        }
                        cell.stockStepper.value = Double(product.stockLevel);
                        cell.stockField.text = String(product.stockLevel);
                        productLogger.logItem(product);
                    }
                    break;
                }
            }
            displayStockTotal();
        }
    }
    // ...code omitted for brevity...
}
```

Summary

In this chapter, I described the singleton pattern and explained how it can be used to ensure that there is only one object of a specific type in the application. The singleton pattern is easy to understand but requires careful attention to implement correctly, especially when it comes to ensuring that the code is safe for concurrent use. In the next chapter, I describe the object pool pattern, which shares some common ideas with the singleton pattern but operates on several objects of the same type.

The Object Pool Pattern

The *object pool pattern* is a variation on the singleton pattern that provides access to multiple identical objects rather than a single instance. This is useful when you have objects that represent a set of fungible resources, each of which can be used by only one component at a time. In this chapter, I describe the basic object pool pattern, and in Chapter 8 I show you some useful variations that allow object pools to adapt to different situations. Table 7-1 puts the object pool pattern in context.

Table 7-1. *Putting the Object Pool Pattern into Context*

Question	Answer
What is it?	The object pool pattern manages a collection of reusable objects that are provided to calling components. A component obtains an object from the pool, uses it to perform work, and returns it to the pool so that it can be allocated to satisfy future requests. An object that has been allocated to a caller is not available for use by other components until it has been returned to the pool.
What are the benefits?	The object pool pattern hides the construction of objects from the components that use them and allows expensive initializations to be amortized through reusing objects repeatedly.
When should you use this pattern?	Use the object pool pattern when you have a number of identical objects whose creation you need to manage, either because the objects represent real-world resources or because creating new instances is expensive.
When should you avoid this pattern?	Do not use this pattern if there can be only one object in existence at any moment (use the singleton pattern instead) or if there are no limits on the number of objects that can exist (allow calling components to create their own instances or use one of the other patterns described in this book, such as the factory method pattern).

(continued)

Table 7-1. (Continued)

Question	Answer
How do you know when you have implemented the pattern correctly?	The pattern is implemented correctly when objects are allocated to calling components without the need to create new instances and when an object returned to the pool is used to satisfy a subsequent request.
Are there any common pitfalls?	The main pitfall is the implementation of concurrency protections that ensure that objects are allocated correctly and without corrupting the data structures used to implement the pattern.
Are there any related patterns?	The singleton pattern shares some common ideas with the object pool pattern but manages a single object.

Preparing the Example Project

For this chapter, I created an OS X Command Line Tool project called ObjectPool. No further preparation is required.

Understanding the Problem That the Pattern Solves

In many projects, there will be objects for which the number of instances must be restricted but not to the extent where there is just one. To help put this problem into a real-world context, I am going to create an example that represents the system used by a library to track books. Listing 7-1 shows the contents of a file called Book.swift that I added to the example project.

Listing 7-1. The Contents of the Book.swift File

```
class Book {
    let author:String;
    let title:String;
    let stockNumber:Int;
    var reader:String?
    var checkoutCount = 0;

    init(author:String, title:String, stock:Int) {
        self.author = author;
        self.title = title;
        self.stockNumber = stock;
    }
}
```

In a system that tracks library books, the creation or cloning of Book objects won't magically create real-world books in the library, but equally, it doesn't make sense to manage a Book using the singleton pattern because a library will have more than one copy of most books, any of which can be used to satisfy someone's desire to read it.

Each book in a library can be checked out by only one reader at a time and is not available for further use until it is returned. Readers can check books out immediately when they are in stock, but once the stock is exhausted, anyone who wants a copy will have to wait until one is returned or the library adds more books to its collection.

The problem I face is I need a pattern that manages a number of identical, interchangeable objects and provides the model by which they can be fairly and equitably used.

> **Tip**   Library books are a real-world example of groups of objects that are reusable and interchangeable, but there are also abstract examples that you will encounter in software development. The most common examples include threads and network connections, but this is a problem that manifests itself with some frequency and in a variety of ways.

Understanding the Object Pool Pattern

The *object pool pattern* manages a collection of fungible objects, known as the *object pool*—or just the *pool*. Components that need an object borrow one from the pool, use it to perform some work, and then return it to the pool when the work has been completed. Returned objects are then used to satisfy subsequent requests, either from the same component or from another component.

The object pool pattern can be used to manage objects that represent real-world resources and also to amortize expensive initialization procedures by reusing objects to satisfy requests from multiple components.

An object pool has four important operations, as illustrated by Figure 7-1. The first operation is *initialization*, in which the collection of objects to be managed is prepared.

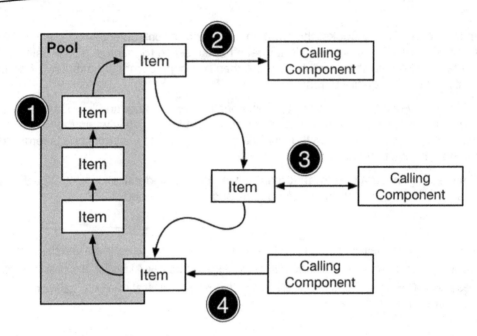

Figure 7-1. The basic operation of an object pool

The second operation is *checkout*, in which a component that requires an object borrows one from the pool.

The third operation is the component using the object to perform work of some sort. This doesn't require any activity from the pool, but it does mean that there is a period where an object managed by the pool is in use and cannot be loaned to other components.

The fourth and final operation is *check-in*, where the component returns the object to the pool so that it can be used to satisfy future loan requests.

In a multithreaded application, the second, third, and fourth operations may happen concurrently. Sharing objects between multiple components presents potential concurrency problems. Two or more components may ask to borrow or return objects simultaneously, and object pools must ensure that each request for a loan is satisfied with a different object when checked out and that objects are not lost when they are checked in again.

There will also be times when a request cannot be immediately satisfied because all of the objects in the pool have been checked out and are being used. A pool must be able to cope with these requests, either by indicating to the component that no object is available or by allowing the component to wait until an object is returned.

Implementing the Object Pool Pattern

In this chapter, I create a basic implementation of the pattern to demonstrate how the different operations are implemented. A basic object pool manages a fixed collection of objects and relies on the components that check objects out of the pool to return them when they are done. It is a good place to start because it allows me to address the basic concurrency techniques that are at the heart of a robust implementation of the pattern. In Chapter 8, I show you variations on the pattern that you can use to adapt the basic pool to your own projects.

Defining the Pool Class

The first step is to create a generic Pool class that will manage a collection of objects of a given type. This need not be a generic class, but the need to manage a pool is a common one, and a generic class makes it easy to reuse the code in different projects. I added a file called Pool.swift to the example project, the contents of which are shown in Listing 7-2.

Listing 7-2. The Contents of the Pool.swift File

```
import Foundation

class Pool<T> {
    private var data = [T]();

    init(items:[T]) {
        data.reserveCapacity(data.count);
        for item in items {
            data.append(item);
        }
    }

    func getFromPool() -> T? {
        var result:T?;
        if (data.count > 0) {
            result = self.data.removeAtIndex(0);
        }
        return result;
    }

    func returnToPool(item:T) {
        self.data.append(item);
    }
}
```

The Pool class—more correctly referred to as Pool<T>—is initialized with the collection of objects that it is to manage. The initializer copies the items into a local data array, which I use like a simple queue collection containing the objects that are available for use. When the getFromPool method is called, I return the object at the head of the array by calling the removeAtIndex method. The returnToPool method is called when a previously obtained object is finished, and I add it to the data array using the append method so that it is available for use for subsequent calls to the getFromPool method.

Protecting the Data Array

Handling concurrent requests is important in the object pool pattern, and there are two problems that I need to solve. The first problem is the same one I encountered when dealing with singleton pattern: the getFromPool and returnToPool methods contain statements that modify the data array, and I need to ensure that no two threads use these methods simultaneously. Listing 7-3 shows how I have added a Grand Central Dispatch (GCD) queue and applied the dispatch_sync function to protect the array from concurrent modifications.

Listing 7-3. Protecting the Array from Concurrent Modifications in the Pool.swift File

```swift
import Foundation

class Pool<T> {
    private var data = [T]();
    private let arrayQ = dispatch_queue_create("arrayQ", DISPATCH_QUEUE_SERIAL);

    init(items:[T]) {
        data.reserveCapacity(data.count);
        for item in items {
            data.append(item);
        }
    }

    func getFromPool() -> T? {
        var result:T?;
        if (data.count > 0) {
            dispatch_sync(arrayQ, {() in
                result = self.data.removeAtIndex(0);
            })
        }
        return result;
    }

    func returnToPool(item:T) {
        dispatch_async(arrayQ, {() in
            self.data.append(item);
        });
    }
}
```

> **Tip** You can implement the object pool pattern without adding concurrency protections, but only if you are sure that your application will only ever use one thread to access the objects in the pool. Be careful, though: applications have a habit of needing concurrency as they get more complicated, and an unprotected object pool will cause problems when that happens. My advice is to always add concurrency protections even if you don't expect to need them.

I have used the dispatch_sync and dispatch_async functions to create blocks using closures that contain the operations that manipulate the array. I add them to a queue I created with the dispatch_queue_create function, which I configured with the DISPATCH_QUEUE_SERIAL value so that only one block is executed at a time. This protects the array from corruption by ensuring that only one thread at a time can modify the array.

Ensuring Objects Are Available to Be Checked Out

There is a second concurrency problem in the Pool class, which means that the code may still encounter problems. In the getFromPool method, I check to see whether there are any free objects in the data array before adding a block to the queue to obtain an object, like this:

```
...
func getFromPool() -> T? {
    var result:T?;
    if (data.count > 0) {
        dispatch_sync(arrayQ, {() in
            result = self.data.removeAtIndex(0);
        })
    }
    return result;
}
...
```

This is a classic concurrency problem. Imagine that there is one free object in the data array and that two threads call the getFromPool method a few milliseconds apart. The first thread checks the data.count value, finds that there is a free object, and uses the dispatch_sync method to queue up a block that will remove it from the array so it can be used.

Shortly afterward, the second thread does the same thing. It, too, believes that there is a free object in the array because the block that the first thread created has yet to be executed. The second thread queues its own block in the expectation that it too will be able to obtain the object. The first thread's block executes and successfully removes the free object. The second thread's block is then executed and gets an error because the array is now empty.

To solve this problem, I need to ensure that a thread that calls the getFromPool method doesn't schedule a block to get a free object unless it is guaranteed to get one. Listing 7-4 shows how I solved this problem using the GCD *semaphore* feature.

Listing 7-4. Applying a Semaphore in the Pool.swift File

```
import Foundation

class Pool<T> {
    private var data = [T]();
    private let arrayQ = dispatch_queue_create("arrayQ", DISPATCH_QUEUE_SERIAL);
    private let semaphore:dispatch_semaphore_t;

    init(items:[T]) {
        data.reserveCapacity(data.count);
```

```
        for item in items {
            data.append(item);
        }
        semaphore = dispatch_semaphore_create(items.count);
    }

    func getFromPool() -> T? {
        var result:T?;
        if (dispatch_semaphore_wait(semaphore, DISPATCH_TIME_FOREVER) == 0) {
            dispatch_sync(arrayQ, {() in
                result = self.data.removeAtIndex(0);
            })
        }
        return result;
    }

    func returnToPool(item:T) {
        dispatch_async(arrayQ, {() in
            self.data.append(item);
            dispatch_semaphore_signal(self.semaphore);
        });
    }
}
```

At the heart of a semaphore is a counter, as you can see in the following statement that I used to create one:

```
...
semaphore = dispatch_semaphore_create(items.count);
...
```

The dispatch_semaphore_create function accepts an Int value that sets the initial value of the counter. The counter is decremented each time the dispatch_semaphore_wait function is called, like this:

```
...
if (dispatch_semaphore_wait(semaphore, DISPATCH_TIME_FOREVER) == 0) {
    dispatch_sync(arrayQ, {() in
        result = self.data.removeAtIndex(0);
    });
}
...
```

When the counter reaches zero, calls to the dispatch_semaphore_wait function will block. By calling the dispatch_semaphore_wait function in the getFromPool method, I decrement the counter each time an object is removed from the data array and cause calls to the method to block when there are no more items in the array to give out.

The counter is incremented by calling the dispatch_semaphore_signal function, which I do in the returnToPool method, after I have added the object to the data array.

```
...
dispatch_async(arrayQ, {() in
    self.data.append(item);
    dispatch_semaphore_signal(self.semaphore);
});
...
```

This increases the counter, allowing one of the threads blocking on the dispatch_semaphore_wait function to continue execution. The calls to the semaphore functions balance the number of requests to get and return pool objects and prevent calls to the getFromPool method from adding a block to the queue unless there is definitely an object waiting for it when it is executed.

Consuming the Pool Class

Now that I have created a generic pool class, I can complete my application of the object pool pattern by applying it to manage a collection of Book objects. Listing 7-5 shows the definition of a class called Library that I defined in a new file called Library.swift.

Listing 7-5. Consuming the Pool Class in the Library.swift File

```
import Foundation

final class Library {
    private let books:[Book];
    private let pool:Pool<Book>;

    private init(stockLevel:Int) {
        books = [Book]();
        for count in 1 ... stockLevel {
            books.append(Book(author: "Dickens, Charles", title: "Hard Times",
                stock: count))
        }
        pool = Pool<Book>(items:books);
    }

    private class var singleton:Library {
        struct SingletonWrapper {
            static let singleton = Library(stockLevel:2);
        }
        return SingletonWrapper.singleton;
    }

    class func checkoutBook(reader:String) -> Book? {
        var book = singleton.pool.getFromPool();
        book?.reader = reader;
        book?.checkoutCount++;
        return book;
    }
```

```
class func returnBook(book:Book) {
    book.reader = nil;
    singleton.pool.returnToPool(book);
}

class func printReport() {
    for book in singleton.books {
        println("...Book#\(book.stockNumber)...");
        println("Checked out \(book.checkoutCount) times");
        if (book.reader != nil) {
            println("Checked out to \(book.reader!)");
        } else {
            println("In stock");
        }
    }
}
}
```

The Library class implements the object pool pattern by combining the Pool class I defined in Listing 7-4 with the singleton pattern I described in Chapter 6. I need to use the singleton because there should be only one Library in this example, although the Library itself could have multiple pools, each of which manages copies of a single title. The code in Listing 7-5 represents a rather depressing library whose entire stock consists of two copies of a Charles Dickens novel.

When you visit a real library, you can borrow a copy of the book you want if one is available, and if it is not, you can join the queue and wait for one to be returned by another reader. The library provides these services but does so without making you understand how the process works behind the scenes. You are not, for example, required to find the other people waiting for a copy of the book and figure out the order in which returned copies should be distributed.

A RELAXED OBJECT CREATION POLICY

Notice that I have defined the Library and Book classes in different files and that I have not protected the Book class from being instantiated outside of the Library. When implementing the singleton pattern, I used a private constructor and defined the access class because I wanted to demonstrate how to control the creation of the singleton completely. In this chapter, I am taking a more relaxed approach because I am modeling an environment where there could be many sources of Book objects, representing the many real-world sources of books (publishers, book wholesalers, and online stores could all supply a library with books, for example). I am not going to build all of the possible sources into the example, but I wanted to demonstrate that you can use this pattern to manage objects without having to restrict the supply of them. My model remains true to the real world as long as the Books objects associated with the Library object cannot be altered without its consent.

The details of how a real-world library manages its books are hidden, and this is the approach that I have taken when implementing the Library class, too. Rather than expose the Pool<Book> object via the singleton, I have defined type methods called checkoutBook and returnBook that interact with the pool on behalf of callers. These methods also allow me to prepare a Book when it is checked out: I set the value of the reader property and increment the checkoutCount property. When a Book is returned, I clear the reader property.

The checkoutCount and reader properties are both used by the printReport method, which details each of the Book objects that the Library created, noting how many times the book has been checked out and whether it is currently in the pool. This is a diagnostic method that will allow me to see the state of the books being managed by the pool during testing. Listing 7-6 shows the code I used to test the Library class and its use of the Pool class in the main.swift file.

Listing 7-6. Testing the Library and Pool in the main.swift File

```
import Foundation

var queue = dispatch_queue_create("workQ", DISPATCH_QUEUE_CONCURRENT);
var group = dispatch_group_create();

println("Starting...");

for i in 1 ... 20 {
    dispatch_group_async(group, queue, {() in
        var book = Library.checkoutBook("reader#\(i)");
        if (book != nil) {
            NSThread.sleepForTimeInterval(Double(rand() % 2));
            Library.returnBook(book!);
        }
    });
}

dispatch_group_wait(group, DISPATCH_TIME_FOREVER);

println("All blocks complete");

Library.printReport();
```

This code uses a for loop to create asynchronous GCD blocks that check out and return Book objects from the Library. To make the example a little more realistic, I have added a delay after the Book is obtained from the Library and before it is returned again, like this:

```
...
NSThread.sleepForTimeInterval(Double(rand() % 2));
...
```

The NSThread.sleepForTimeInterval puts the thread executing the statement to sleep. I control the duration of the sleep so that it is randomly generated and forced to be either zero or one second, meaning that some blocks will return a book immediately and others will wait for a second before returning a book. I have done this because I want the use of the objects in the pool to overlap. Without this, the objects would be checked out and returned in strict rotation, which isn't how pool objects are used in real projects (or, of course, in the real world).

Start the application to see the results. It will take a few seconds to run, so be patient. When all of the blocks generated in the main.swift file have executed, you will see output similar to the following:

```
Starting...
All blocks complete
...Book#1...
Checked out 13 times
In stock
...Book#2...
Checked out 7 times
In stock
```

Your results may be different because the random nature of the delay I added will vary the sequence in which objects are taken from and returned to the pool.

Although your results may differ, the total number of times that the books were checked out should be 20, which is the same number of GCD blocks created in the main.swift file. In my case, one Book object was checked out 13 times and the other was checked out 7 times. The difference is caused by the delay I added, which has led to the first Book object cycling through the pool several times while slower readers were holding onto the other object.

Understanding the Pitfalls of the Object Pool Pattern

Care is required when implementing the object pool pattern because it is easy to create a pool that doesn't work or doesn't suit the application to which it has been applied. It is easy to get carried away trying to create the perfect pool, especially when considering the variations that I describe in Chapter 8. The result can be code that is difficult to maintain and an unstable object pool that behaves unpredictably once it has been deployed.

Care is also required when protecting an object pool against concurrent access in order to avoid creating a pool that locks up unexpectedly, even if it works during your development tests. Be conservative and give preference to safety over performance—and, most importantly, test your code with as many different usage scenarios as you can. I recommend keeping object pools as simple as you can and focus on producing something that works and can be easily tested.

Examples of the Object Pool Pattern in Cocoa

The Cocoa frameworks do not expose objects pools in their public APIs, with one commonly encountered exception: table cell objects. You can see an example in the SportsStore application, where UITableViewCell objects are used to display rows in the table view. Listing 7-7 shows the implementation of the tableView method in the ViewController.swift file from the SportsStore project.

Listing 7-7. Getting a (Potentially) Pooled UITableViewCell in the ViewController.swift File

```
...
func tableView(tableView: UITableView,
    cellForRowAtIndexPath indexPath: NSIndexPath) -> UITableViewCell {
    let product = products[indexPath.row];
    let cell = tableView.dequeueReusableCellWithIdentifier("ProductCell")
        as ProductTableCell;

    cell.product = products[indexPath.row];
    cell.nameLabel.text = product.name;
    cell.descriptionLabel.text = product.productDescription;
    cell.stockStepper.value = Double(product.stockLevel);
    cell.stockField.text = String(product.stockLevel);

    return cell;
}
...
```

This is the method that is called to obtain a UITableViewCell object for display, and the highlighted statement shows that I obtain the UITableView object by making a call to the dequeueReusableCellWithIdentifier method defined by the UITableView class. The UIKit framework manages the creation and allocation of UITableViewCell objects so they can be reused. Apple doesn't publish the source code to the UIKit framework, so it is not possible to see how the pool is implemented, but this is an example of a pool being used to offset an expensive initialization by reusing the object.

> **Tip**   The dequeueReusableCellWithIdentifier method combines the object pool and factory method patterns. I describe the factory method pattern in Chapter 9, but the short description is that tables can be populated with different types of table cells, and the method argument—ProductCell in this case—is used to differentiate between them.

Applying the Pattern to the SportsStore Application

I am going to apply the object pool pattern to the SportsStore application in order to manage a pool of network request objects. Currently, the SportsStore application has a static array of Product objects that are displayed to the user, and I am going to replace this with a series of network calls that get details of the products and update the server when the stock level changes.

Preparing the Example Application

I am going to pick up the SportsStore project as I left it as the end of Chapter 6, and no preparation is required for this chapter.

Tip   Remember that you can download the source code for every stage of the SportsStore project—along with every other example in this book—from Apress.com.

Creating the (Fake) Server

I don't want to get into the details of creating and setting up a server, so I am going to simulate the request and responses, but the demonstration of creating and applying the pool will be unaffected. I added a file called NetworkConnection.swift to the SportsStore project and used it to define the class shown in Listing 7-8.

Listing 7-8. The Contents of the NetworkConnection.swift File

```
import Foundation

class NetworkConnection {

    private let stockData: [String: Int] = [
        "Kayak" : 10, "Lifejacket": 14, "Soccer Ball": 32,"Corner Flags": 1,
        "Stadium": 4, "Thinking Cap": 8, "Unsteady Chair": 3,
        "Human Chess Board": 2, "Bling-Bling King":4
    ];

    func getStockLevel(name:String) -> Int? {
        NSThread.sleepForTimeInterval(Double(rand() % 2));
        return stockData[name];
    }
}
```

The NetworkConnection class is the template for the objects that I manage in the object pool. There is a private stockData property that is set to the dictionary containing the initial stock levels for the SportsStore products, indexed by name. The getStockLevel method looks up a product in the dictionary and returns the stock level value. I have used the NSThread.sleepForTimeInterval method to add a random delay of one second to some requests.

Creating the Object Pool

The pools I demonstrated in earlier examples were all generic classes, which make it easy to reuse classes in different projects. For variety I have implemented the object pool for the SportsStore to operate on a specific type: the NetworkConnection class. Listing 7-9 shows the contents of the NetworkPool.swift file, which I added to the SportsStore project.

Listing 7-9. The Contents of the NetworkPool.swift File

```swift
import Foundation

final class NetworkPool {
    private let connectionCount = 3;
    private var connections = [NetworkConnection]();
    private var semaphore:dispatch_semaphore_t;
    private var queue:dispatch_queue_t;

    private init() {
        for _ in 0 ..< connectionCount {
            connections.append(NetworkConnection());
        }
        semaphore = dispatch_semaphore_create(connectionCount);
        queue = dispatch_queue_create("networkpoolQ", DISPATCH_QUEUE_SERIAL);
    }

    private func doGetConnection() -> NetworkConnection {
        dispatch_semaphore_wait(semaphore, DISPATCH_TIME_FOREVER);
        var result:NetworkConnection? = nil;
        dispatch_sync(queue, {() in
            result = self.connections.removeAtIndex(0);
        });
        return result!;
    }

    private func doReturnConnection(conn:NetworkConnection) {
        dispatch_async(queue, {() in
            self.connections.append(conn);
            dispatch_semaphore_signal(self.semaphore);
        });
    }

    class func getConnection() -> NetworkConnection {
        return sharedInstance.doGetConnection();
    }

    class func returnConnecton(conn:NetworkConnection) {
        sharedInstance.doReturnConnection(conn);
    }

    private class var sharedInstance:NetworkPool {
        get {
            struct SingletonWrapper {
                static let singleton = NetworkPool();
            }
            return SingletonWrapper.singleton;
        }
    }
}
```

This is a pool that manages a collection of NetworkConnection objects, following the basic pattern I created earlier in the chapter. The NetworkPool class implements the object pool pattern, but it also uses the singleton pattern from Chapter 6 so that other components in the application can locate the pool easily.

Applying the Object Pool

To apply the pool, I have created a class called ProductDataStore, into which I have moved the statically defined product data—albeit without stock level information. Listing 7-10 shows the contents of the ProductDataStore.swift file, which I added to the SportsStore project.

Listing 7-10. The Contents of the ProductDataStore.swift File

```swift
import Foundation

final class ProductDataStore {
    var callback:((Product) -> Void)?;
    private var networkQ:dispatch_queue_t
    private var uiQ:dispatch_queue_t;
    lazy var products:[Product] = self.loadData();

    init() {
        networkQ = dispatch_get_global_queue(DISPATCH_QUEUE_PRIORITY_BACKGROUND, 0);
        uiQ = dispatch_get_main_queue();
    }

    private func loadData() -> [Product] {
        for p in productData {
            dispatch_async(self.networkQ, {() in
                let stockConn = NetworkPool.getConnection();
                let level = stockConn.getStockLevel(p.name);
                if (level != nil) {
                    p.stockLevel = level!;
                    dispatch_async(self.uiQ, {() in
                        if (self.callback != nil) {
                            self.callback!(p);
                        }
                    })
                }
                NetworkPool.returnConnecton(stockConn);
            });
        }
        return productData;
    }
}
```

```
    private var productData:[Product] = [
        Product(name:"Kayak", description:"A boat for one person",
            category:"Watersports", price:275.0, stockLevel:0),
        Product(name:"Lifejacket", description:"Protective and fashionable",
            category:"Watersports", price:48.95, stockLevel:0),
        Product(name:"Soccer Ball", description:"FIFA-approved size and weight",
            category:"Soccer", price:19.5, stockLevel:0),
        Product(name:"Corner Flags",
            description:"Give your playing field a professional touch",
            category:"Soccer", price:34.95, stockLevel:0),
        Product(name:"Stadium", description:"Flat-packed 35,000-seat stadium",
            category:"Soccer", price:79500.0, stockLevel:0),
        Product(name:"Thinking Cap", description:"Improve your brain efficiency",
            category:"Chess", price:16.0, stockLevel:0),
        Product(name:"Unsteady Chair",
            description:"Secretly give your opponent a disadvantage",
            category: "Chess", price: 29.95, stockLevel:0),
        Product(name:"Human Chess Board", description:"A fun game for the family",
            category:"Chess", price:75.0, stockLevel:0),
        Product(name:"Bling-Bling King",
            description:"Gold-plated, diamond-studded King",
            category:"Chess", price:1200.0, stockLevel:0)];
}
```

The ProductDataStore has become the authoritative source for Product objects in the SportsStore app. Product objects are obtained through the products property, which returns the contents of a private array. The Product objects are defined with zero stockLevel values, but the products property is lazily computed and uses the NetworkPool class to request the current stock levels for each product. When the request completes, the Product object is updated, and an optional callback is invoked to provide notification of the new information.

> **Tip**   In a real project, it would make sense to get all of the stock levels in a single request, but for the purposes of this chapter I want to exercise the pool with more requests than there are pooled objects.

Notice that I have used two GCD queues in this class. I obtain a global queue—one that is created automatically by GCD—with background priority in order to execute the simulated network requests. Using background priority means that delays in getting the stock information don't prevent more important tasks from being performed, such as responding to user interaction. When I handle the callback, I use the main application queue to ensure that updates are performed immediately and not deferred until the background tasks are complete.

Listing 7-11 shows the changes I have made to the ViewController.swift file to use the ProductDataStore class, rather than define the data locally.

Listing 7-11. Using the ProductDataSource Class in the ViewController.swift File

```swift
import UIKit

class ProductTableCell: UITableViewCell {
    // ...statements omitted for brevity...
}

class ViewController: UIViewController, UITableViewDataSource {

    @IBOutlet weak var totalStockLabel: UILabel!
    @IBOutlet weak var tableView: UITableView!
    var productStore = ProductDataStore();

    override func viewDidLoad() {
        super.viewDidLoad();
        displayStockTotal();

        productStore.callback = {(p:Product) in
            for cell in self.tableView.visibleCells() {
                if let pcell = cell as? ProductTableCell {
                    if pcell.product?.name == p.name {
                        pcell.stockStepper.value = Double(p.stockLevel);
                        pcell.stockField.text = String(p.stockLevel);
                    }
                }
            }
            self.displayStockTotal();
        }
    }

    override func didReceiveMemoryWarning() {
        super.didReceiveMemoryWarning();
    }

    func tableView(tableView: UITableView,
        numberOfRowsInSection section: Int) -> Int {
            return productStore.products.count;
    }

    func tableView(tableView: UITableView,
        cellForRowAtIndexPath indexPath: NSIndexPath) -> UITableViewCell {
        let product = productStore.products[indexPath.row];
        let cell = tableView.dequeueReusableCellWithIdentifier("ProductCell")
            as ProductTableCell;
        cell.product = product;
        cell.nameLabel.text = product.name;
        cell.descriptionLabel.text = product.productDescription;
        cell.stockStepper.value = Double(product.stockLevel);
        cell.stockField.text = String(product.stockLevel);
        return cell;
    }
```

```
@IBAction func stockLevelDidChange(sender: AnyObject) {
    // ...statements omitted for brevity...
}

func displayStockTotal() {
    let finalTotals:(Int, Double) = productStore.products.reduce((0, 0.0),
        {(totals, product) -> (Int, Double) in
            return (
                totals.0 + product.stockLevel,
                totals.1 + product.stockValue
            );
        });

    totalStockLabel.text = "\(finalTotals.0) Products in Stock. "
        + "Total Value: \(Utils.currencyStringFromNumber(finalTotals.1))";
    }
}
```

I have defined a productStore property that is assigned a ProductDataStore object and from which the Product objects are obtained for display. I have also defined the callback closure that locates the table cell being used to display the Product—if it is visible—and updates the stock level it displays.

The effect you will see when running the app is that the stock values will be initially displayed as zero and then updated as objects are checked out from the pool and used to make (simulated) network requests. The random delay that I added in the NetworkConnection class means that the updates will arrive gradually as the pool limits the number of concurrent requests.

Summary

In this chapter I explained how to apply the basic object pool pattern to manage a collection of objects. In the next chapter, I show you how to vary the way that the object pool works to manage objects with different usage patterns.

Chapter 8

Object Pool Variations

In this chapter, I explain how you can vary the basic implementation of the object pool pattern I described in Chapter 7 to manage objects with different characteristics. Each technique applies a strategy to handling an aspect of the pool's implementation to deal with calling components that require pool objects. Table 8-1 puts the variations into context.

Table 8-1. Putting the Object Pool Pattern Variations into Context

Question	Answer
What are they?	The variations on the object pool pattern allow you to change the way that the object pool works to operate in different situations.
What are the benefits?	These variations change the behavior of the pool so that it can service calling components with different expectations and needs and manage objects with a range of characteristics and life cycles.
When should you use these variations?	You should use these variations when the basic implementation of the pattern I described in Chapter 7 does not meet your needs.
When should you avoid these variations?	These variations require advanced concurrency techniques and should be avoided unless you can test them thoroughly and have a solid understanding of Cocoa concurrency.
How do you know when you have implemented the variations correctly?	The only way to be sure you have implemented these variations correctly is through thorough testing.
Are there any common pitfalls?	These are advanced techniques, and it is easy to misuse concurrency protections to create a pool that doesn't work or that performs poorly.
Are there any related patterns?	Not applicable.

Preparing the Example Project

I continue using the ObjectPool project I created in Chapter 7. No changes are required to prepare for this chapter.

Understanding the Object Pool Pattern Variations

The implementation of an object pool consists of four strategies that collectively form the behavior for allocating objects:

- The object creation strategy

- The object reuse strategy

- The empty pool strategy

- The allocation strategy

By changing these strategies, you can tailor the implementation of the object pool pattern to suit the kind of objects you need to manage. I explain each of the strategies in the sections that follow and demonstrate how to implement them.

Understanding the Object Creation Strategy

The object creation strategy governs how the objects that the pool manages are created. In the previous chapter, I implemented an *eager* strategy, which means that the objects are created before they are used. In fact, I create the Book objects in the Library class and pass them as an array to the Pool initializer, like this:

```
...
private init(stockLevel:Int) {
    books = [Book]();
    for count in 1 ... stockLevel {
        books.append(Book(author: "Dickens, Charles", title: "Hard Times",
            stock: count))
    }
    pool = Pool<Book>(items:books);
}
...
```

This is the strategy I adopt when I am working with objects that represent real-world resources because the number of objects that will be managed is typically known in advance (my library purchased two copies of *Hard Times*) and requires some level of configuration (allocating a unique stock reference).

The drawback of this approach is that all of the cost involved in creating and configuring the objects is incurred before there is any demand for them. I have created two Book objects to represent my Charles Dickens collection, but there may be little or no reader demand, and the overhead of creating and preparing the Book objects will never be justified by requests.

That is usually acceptable for objects that represent real-world objects because the state of the pool reflects a real-world situation: the library has purchased two copies of *Hard Times* in anticipation of reader demands. However, it isn't helpful if you are using an object pool to avoid incurring expensive initializations of objects that are not tied to the real-world, such as the Sum objects that I used to demonstrate the prototype pattern in Chapter 5.

The alternative is to use a *lazy creation* strategy, which means that objects are not created until they are required. For the purposes of my Library example, I am going to create a BookSeller class from which Book objects can be obtained. The library in my example will be able to obtain the books it needs from the seller the first time it is required. Listing 8-1 shows the contents of the BookSources. swift file, which I added to the project.

Listing 8-1. The Contents of the BookSources.swift File

```
import Foundation

class BookSeller {
    class func buyBook(author:String, title:String, stockNumber:Int) -> Book {
        return Book(author: author, title: title, stock: stockNumber);
    }
}
```

The BookSeller class defines a type method that creates a Book object. The implementation of the BookSeller class isn't important for the example—it's only important that there is a source of Book objects that will be called upon to supply the items in the pool. Listing 8-2 shows the changes that I made to the Pool class to support delaying the creation of items until they are required.

Listing 8-2. Implementing Lazy Object Creation in the Pool.swift File

```
import Foundation

class Pool<T> {
    private var data = [T]();
    private let arrayQ = dispatch_queue_create("arrayQ", DISPATCH_QUEUE_SERIAL);
    private let semaphore:dispatch_semaphore_t;
    private var itemCount = 0;
    private let maxItemCount:Int;
    private let itemFactory: () -> T;

    init(maxItemCount:Int, factory:() -> T) {
        self.itemFactory = factory;
        self.maxItemCount = maxItemCount;
        semaphore = dispatch_semaphore_create(maxItemCount);
    }

    func getFromPool() -> T? {
        var result:T?;
        if (dispatch_semaphore_wait(semaphore, DISPATCH_TIME_FOREVER) == 0) {
            dispatch_sync(arrayQ, {() in
                if (self.data.count == 0 && self.itemCount < self.maxItemCount) {
                    result = self.itemFactory();
                    self.itemCount++;
```

```
            } else {
                result = self.data.removeAtIndex(0);
            }
        })
    }
    return result;
}

func returnToPool(item:T) {
    dispatch_async(arrayQ, {() in
        self.data.append(item);
        dispatch_semaphore_signal(self.semaphore);
    });
}

func processPoolItems(callback:[T] -> Void) {
    dispatch_barrier_sync(arrayQ, {() in
        callback(self.data);
    });
}
}
```

I have changed the Pool initializer so that it receives a closure that can be used to create new items for the pool and an Int parameter that specifies the maximum number of times that the closure may be used. I set the initial counter value for the Grand Central Dispatch semaphore to the maximum number of items and perform a more complex check for the state of the pool in the getFromPool method, like this:

```
...
if (self.data.count == 0 && self.itemCount < self.maxItemCount) {
    result = self.itemFactory();
    self.itemCount++;
} else {
    result = self.data.removeAtIndex(0);
}
...
```

To reach this point in the method, a thread has passed through the semaphore, and that means either there is an object waiting for use in the data array or that I need to call the factory closure to create one. This allows me to defer the creation of the items in the pool until there is a demand for them.

The other change to the Pool class was to implement a type method called processPoolItems. In the original implementation of the pool, responsibility for creating the objects in the pool fell to the Library class, which kept references to all the Book objects it was responsible for and was able to generate a report about them using those local references. In this implementation, it is the Pool class that creates the objects, and the Library class has no reference to them at all— so I have added the processPoolItems method that accepts a callback closure that is passed the data array within a synchronous GCD barrier block.

> **Tip**   You can see how I have implemented the Book factory closure in Listing 8-3. I could have retained
> a reference to the Book objects as they are created, but the way that Swift deals with closures defined in
> initializers makes it a difficult process. Instead, I have made the Pool class the authoritative source for
> details of the Book objects in the example application.

Listing 8-3 shows the corresponding changes to the Library class to complete the implementation
of the lazy creation strategy.

Listing 8-3. Implementing Lazy Object Creation in the Library.swift File

```swift
import Foundation

final class Library {
    private let pool:Pool<Book>;

    private init(stockLevel:Int) {

        var stockId = 1;

        pool = Pool<Book>(maxItemCount: stockLevel, factory: {() in
            return BookSeller.buyBook("Dickens, Charles",
                title: "Hard Times", stockNumber: stockId++)
        });
    }

    private class var singleton:Library {
        struct SingletonWrapper {
            static let singleton = Library(stockLevel:200);
        }
        return SingletonWrapper.singleton;
    }

    class func checkoutBook(reader:String) -> Book? {
        var book = singleton.pool.getFromPool();
        book?.reader = reader;
        book?.checkoutCount++;
        return book;
    }

    class func returnBook(book:Book) {
        book.reader = nil;
        singleton.pool.returnToPool(book);
    }
}
```

```
class func printReport() {
    singleton.pool.processPoolItems({(books) in
        for book in books {
            println("...Book#\(book.stockNumber)...");
            println("Checked out \(book.checkoutCount) times");
            if (book.reader != nil) {
                println("Checked out to \(book.reader!)");
            } else {
                println("In stock");
            }
        }
        println("There are \(books.count) books in the pool");
    });
}
}
```

The changes are minor. I have defined the closure that will be used to create the Book objects through the BookSeller class, and I have updated the printReport method to get its data items from the pool. I have also increased the maximum number of books in the pool to 200, which is far more than is needed to satisfy the demand generated by the code in the main.swift file.

> **Note**   This simulates a situation where a real-world library has agreed to a line of credit with a bookseller that can be called upon as needed. The library holds no stock initially, but every time that there is a request for a book and there are no books in stock, the bookseller is asked to send a copy up until a predetermined limit—200 copies in this case. New copies are asked for only if there are none in stock, however—the library will reissue one of its existing copies if available.

You can see the effect of the lazy strategy by running the application. The report generated after all of the requests have been processed, which can take 15 to 20 seconds, finished with a statement that notes how many Book objects are in the pool.

```
...
There are 14 books in the pool
```

The exact number of books will differ each time you run the application because I add a delay to some of the request randomly, and this will affect how many often Book objects are reused by the pool.

The worst case is that 20 books will be created, which means that the 200 books that the library was willing to buy was a gross overestimate. If I had used an eager strategy, all 200 copies would have been purchased; with the lazy strategy, I am able to more closely match the actual demand.

Understanding the Object Reuse Strategy

The nature of the object pool pattern means that the objects managed by a pool will be allocated to consumers repeatedly, and this presents the risk that an object is returned in a poor state. In terms of a real-world library, this could mean torn or missing book pages. In software, it means an object that has inconsistent state or that has encountered an unrecoverable error.

The simplest approach is the *trusting strategy*, which is where you trust that objects will be returned to the pool in a reusable state. This isn't always a bad idea because not all objects have to deal with this kind of problem. The Book objects that the pool has managed so far are good examples because they present little mutable public state.

The alternative is an *untrusting strategy*, in which objects are inspected before they are returned to the pool to make sure they can be used again. Objects that cannot be reused are ejected from the pool.

Caution   An untrusting strategy should be used only on pools that have the ability to replace ejected objects. Without the ability to replace the objects, the pool may run out of items, and the application can grind to a halt. See the "Understanding the Empty Pool Strategy" section for details.

I am going to change the way that my Book objects are used so that they can be checked out of the pool only a certain number of times, reflecting that fact that books sustain wear and tear and eventually reach the point of being unreadable. I don't want to build any knowledge of the Book class into my generic Pool class, so I have defined a protocol called PoolItem in a new file called PoolItem.swift, the contents of which are shown in Listing 8-4.

Listing 8-4. The Contents of the PoolItem.swift File

```
@objc protocol PoolItem {

    var canReuse:Bool {get}
}
```

This PoolItem protocol defines a get-only property called canReuse. I will read this property when items are returned to the pool and discard any objects that return false. Listing 8-5 shows the corresponding changes in the Pool class.

Tip   Notice that I have applied the @objc attribute to the protocol. This will allow me to downcast objects to the protocol so I can read the canReuse property in the pool class.

Listing 8-5. Adding Support for the PoolItem Protocol in the Pool.swift File

```swift
import Foundation

class Pool<T:AnyObject> {
    private var data = [T]();
    private let arrayQ = dispatch_queue_create("arrayQ", DISPATCH_QUEUE_SERIAL);
    private let semaphore:dispatch_semaphore_t;

    private var itemCount = 0;
    private let maxItemCount:Int;
    private let itemFactory: () -> T;

    init(maxItemCount:Int, factory:() -> T) {
        self.itemFactory = factory;
        self.maxItemCount = maxItemCount;
        semaphore = dispatch_semaphore_create(maxItemCount);
    }

    func getFromPool() -> T? {
        var result:T?;
        if (dispatch_semaphore_wait(semaphore, DISPATCH_TIME_FOREVER) == 0) {
            dispatch_sync(arrayQ, {() in
                if (self.data.count == 0 && self.itemCount < self.maxItemCount) {
                    result = self.itemFactory();
                    self.itemCount++;
                } else {
                    result = self.data.removeAtIndex(0);
                }
            })
        }
        return result;
    }

    func returnToPool(item:T) {
        dispatch_async(arrayQ, {() in
            let pitem = item as AnyObject as? PoolItem;
            if (pitem == nil || pitem!.canReuse) {
                self.data.append(item);
                dispatch_semaphore_signal(self.semaphore);
            }
        });
    }

    func processPoolItems(callback:[T] -> Void) {
        dispatch_barrier_sync(arrayQ, {() in
            callback(self.data);
        });
    }
}
```

I don't want to limit the range of objects that the pool can work with, so I check for reusability only if the PoolItem protocol is implemented. Checking protocol conformance can be done only when the protocol is decorated with the @objc attribute, and applying the attribute means that it can be implemented only by classes and not structs. To give Swift the type information it needs to check conformance, I have restricted the Pool generic type parameter.

```
...
class Pool<T:AnyObject> {
...
```

The AnyObject protocol means that the Pool can work only with class-based objects, which is not a significant limitation because pooling value types doesn't make any sense given that they are copied when assigned to a variable. To check for conformance to the PoolItem protocol, I have to give Swift a helping hand.

```
...
let pitem = item as AnyObject as? PoolItem;
if (pitem == nil || pitem!.canReuse) {
    self.data.append(item);
    dispatch_semaphore_signal(self.semaphore);
}
...
```

If I used the as? operator directly on the item object (which is of type T—the generic type in the Pool class), then the compiler generates an error. I need to first cast to AnyObject (which is guaranteed to work because the type T is restricted to classes that implement the AnyObject protocol) and then use the as? operator to see whether the PoolItem protocol has been implemented.

The effect is that an item is returned to the pool if the PoolItem protocol isn't implemented or—if it is—the value of the canReuse property is true.

Applying the Protocol

The next step is to apply the PoolItem protocol so that Book objects can be loaned out a fixed number of times before they are ejected from the pool. Listing 8-6 shows how I have modified the Book class to implement the protocol.

> **Tip** Notice that I have added the @objc attribute to the Book class. This is required to support conformance to the PoolItem protocol in the Pool class.

Listing 8-6. Implementing the Protocol in the Book.swift File

```
import Foundation;

@objc class Book : PoolItem {
    let author:String;
    let title:String;
    let stockNumber:Int;
    var reader:String?
    var checkoutCount = 0;

    init(author:String, title:String, stock:Int) {
        self.author = author;
        self.title = title;
        self.stockNumber = stock;
    }

    var canReuse:Bool {
        get {
            let reusable = checkoutCount < 5
            if (!reusable) {
                println("Eject: Book#\(self.stockNumber)");
            }
            return reusable;
        }
    }
}
```

I return `false` from the `canReuse` property if a Book object has been checked out of the pool more than five times, and, so that I can see when items are being ejected, I write a message to the console.

Testing the Strategy

To test the strategy of ejecting items from the pool, I need to balance the maximum number of items that the pool will contain against the number of requests that will be made by the code in the `main.swift` file. I need to have enough books to allow some of them to be ejected while leaving enough slack in the system to service all of the requests. In the "Understanding the Empty Pool Strategy" section, I'll show you how to approach this properly by formalizing a strategy, but for the moment I will set the maximum number of items in the pool to 5 (which I settled on through trial and error). Listing 8-7 shows how I changed the limit in the `Library` class.

Listing 8-7. Changing the Maximum Number of Items in the Pool in the Library.swift File

```
...
private class var singleton:Library {
    struct SingletonWrapper {
        static let singleton = Library(stockLevel:5);
    }
    return SingletonWrapper.singleton;
}
...
```

Running the application will produce output similar to the following:

```
Starting...
Eject: Book#1
Eject: Book#2
All blocks complete

...Book#3...
Checked out 3 times
In stock

...Book#4...
Checked out 4 times
In stock

...Book#5...
Checked out 3 times
In stock
There are 3 books in the pool
Program ended with exit code: 0
```

You may get different results because of the random delays before items are returned to the pool, but the basic outcome should be the same: some of the Book objects are checked out more than others, and they are ejected from the pool when they have been checked out five times and replaced with new objects created by the pool.

Understanding the Empty Pool Strategy

As its name suggests, the *empty pool strategy* specifies how a pool responds when there are no items in the pool available to service new requests for objects. The simplest strategy is the one used by my example pool, which is the *blocking strategy* that forces the calling thread to wait until an object is returned to the pool.

A blocking strategy is simple, but it can cause an application to slow down if there is a mismatch between the number of objects in the pool and the level of demand for those objects. The application can also lock up if a blocking strategy is combined with the untrusting statement management strategy I described in the previous section.

In the previous example, I settled on the maximum number of Books objects that the pool could create by trial and error. It took only a moment because I was able to run the application several times to get a sense for how the requests for objects from the main.swift file affected the rate at which objects were ejected from the pool. In real applications, you can only guess at the demand, and some allowances have to be made for unusual periods of high demand, which puts additional pressure on the pool objects. To see the kind of problem that arises, I have increased the number of times that objects are requested from the pool, as shown in Listing 8-8.

Listing 8-8. Increasing the Number of Requests in the main.swift File

```
...
for i in 1 ... 35 {
    dispatch_group_async(group, queue, {() in
        var book = Library.checkoutBook("reader#\(i)");
        if (book != nil) {
            NSThread.sleepForTimeInterval(Double(rand() % 2));
            Library.returnBook(book!);
        }
    });
}
...
```

I have increased the number of requests to 35 because it is exceeds the number of times that the objects in the pool can be used. The pool is allowed to create a maximum of five items, and each can be used a maximum of five times. That means the pool won't have any objects to use for the 26th and all subsequent requests. You can see the effect by running the application, which will produce output like this:

```
Starting...
Eject: Book#4
Eject: Book#5
Eject: Book#1
Eject: Book#3
Eject: Book#2
```

Notice that there is no summary of the state of each book. That is because all five books have been ejected from the pool and the GCD blocks trying to get objects cannot get past the semaphore in the getFromPool method. The application is deadlocked: the GCD blocks won't be executed until the pool signals the semaphore to indicate that there are free objects, but the pool has reached the limit of the number of objects it can create.

Implementing the Failing Request Strategy

The failing request strategy deals with an empty pool by shifting responsibility to the components that request objects. The component has to specify how long it is willing to wait for an object to become available before its request should fail. A failed request means that the component has to be prepared for situations in which it will not receive the object it wanted and have some plan for continuing its operation or reporting an error. Listing 8-9 shows how I revised the implementation of the getFromPool method in the Pool class to implement this strategy.

Listing 8-9. Implementing the Strategy in the Pool.swift File

```
...
func getFromPool(maxWaitSeconds:Int = 5) -> T? {
    var result:T?;

    let waitTime = (maxWaitSeconds == -1)
        ? DISPATCH_TIME_FOREVER
```

```
        : dispatch_time(DISPATCH_TIME_NOW,
            (Int64(maxWaitSeconds) * Int64(NSEC_PER_SEC)));

    if (dispatch_semaphore_wait(semaphore, waitTime) == 0) {
        dispatch_sync(arrayQ, {() in
            if (self.data.count == 0 && self.itemCount < self.maxItemCount) {
                result = self.itemFactory();
                self.itemCount++;
            } else {
                result = self.data.removeAtIndex(0);
            }
        })
    }
    return result;
}
...
```

> **Caution**   This strategy should be used with caution because the components that consume objects from the pool have to be written to deal with requests that fail. I sometimes see components that wrap their requests for objects in a loop so they keep requesting objects until they get one. This is equivalent to making a request that waits forever, and the application still locks up—just in a different and more CPU-intensive way.

I have added a parameter called maxWaitSeconds with a default value to the getFromPool method that allows the caller to specify how many seconds they are prepared to wait for an object to become available. I interpret a value of -1 to mean wait forever and interpret any other value to be the number of seconds from the current time.

GCD defines the DISPATCH_TIME_FOREVER constant to represent an indefinite wait, and I create the value for any other duration using the dispatch_time function, whose arguments are an initial time and an additional number of nanoseconds that should be added to it:

```
...
let waitTime = (maxWaitSeconds == -1)
    ? DISPATCH_TIME_FOREVER
    : dispatch_time(DISPATCH_TIME_NOW,
        (Int64(maxWaitSeconds) * Int64(NSEC_PER_SEC)));
...
```

I use the DISPATCH_TIME_NOW constant for the first argument to specify that I want the time to be relative to the present moment, and I multiply the number of seconds specified by the caller by the NSEC_PER_SEC constant (which defines how many nanoseconds there are in a second) to get the number of nanoseconds.

> **Caution**   You can use the DISPATCH_TIME_NOW constant only as an argument to the dispatch_time function. If you use it outside of the function, it returns a value of zero.

I pass the waitTime value as the second argument to the dispatch_semaphore_wait function.

```
...
if (dispatch_semaphore_wait(semaphore, waitTime) == 0) {
...
```

The dispatch_semaphore_wait function will block until the semaphore is signaled in the returnToPool method or until the specified time is reached. If the DISPATCH_TIME_FOREVER value is used, then the semaphore will block forever, which is the behavior I relied on in previous sections. For other waitTime values, the dispatch_semaphore_wait function will let the thread continue after the time period has elapsed.

I need to know why the semaphore has allowed the thread to continue. If it is because there is an object available in the pool, then I want to get the object and return it to the caller If it is because the time period has elapsed, then I want to allow the method to return without assigning a value to the optional result variable. I can figure out what has happened by looking at the result returned by the dispatch_semaphore_wait function. A value of 0 means that the semaphore has been signaled, and a nonzero value means that the time has expired.

The signature of the getFromPool method already returns an optional Book object, which means that the Library class is already set up to deal with a call to the checkoutBook method that doesn't yield a Book object from the pool.

```
...
class func checkoutBook(reader:String) -> Book? {
    var book = singleton.pool.getFromPool();
    book?.reader = reader;
    book?.checkoutCount++;
    return book;
}
...
```

The result from the checkoutBook method is also an optional Book object, which makes it easy for me to detect timed-out requests in the main.swift file, as shown in Listing 8-10.

Listing 8-10. Dealing with Expired Requests in the main.swift File

```
import Foundation

var queue = dispatch_queue_create("workQ", DISPATCH_QUEUE_CONCURRENT);
var group = dispatch_group_create();

println("Starting...");

for i in 1 ... 35 {
    dispatch_group_async(group, queue, {() in
        var book = Library.checkoutBook("reader#\(i)");
        if (book != nil) {
            NSThread.sleepForTimeInterval(Double(rand() % 2));
            Library.returnBook(book!);
```

```
        } else {
            dispatch_barrier_async(queue, {() in
                println("Request \(i) failed");
            });
        }
    });
}

dispatch_group_wait(group, DISPATCH_TIME_FOREVER);

dispatch_barrier_sync(queue, {() in
    println("All blocks complete");
    Library.printReport();
});
```

If I do not receive a Book object from the Library class, then I write a message to the console indicating that the request has failed. The println function, which writes the message to the console, is not safe for concurrent use, so I have enclosed the function call in a GCD block. I have used a barrier because the queue is concurrent, and I don't want two failed requests to result in simultaneous calls to the println function, which would produce garbled output.

> **Tip**   Notice that I have enclosed the call to the Library.printReport method in a GCD block as well. This method uses the println function to write a report to the debug console, so I have used the same GCD queue to ensure that producing the report doesn't call the println function at the same time as a failed request message is being written.

If you run the application, you will see output like this:

```
Starting...
Eject: Book#4
Eject: Book#1
Eject: Book#5
Eject: Book#2
Eject: Book#3
All blocks complete
Request 26 failed
Request 30 failed
Request 28 failed
Request 31 failed
Request 29 failed
Request 27 failed
Request 32 failed
Request 33 failed
Request 34 failed
Request 35 failed
There are 0 books in the pool
```

The application runs to completion this time, and requests that are unable to obtain an object fail. The application no longer locks up, but it does mean that the consumers of the Library class have to be written to deal with the possibility that a Book object may not be available and know how to cope when this happens.

Dealing with Exhausted Pools

The problem with the strategy I implemented in the previous section is that it requires callers to wait even when the pool is exhausted, by which I mean that all of the objects have been ejected and the pool cannot create more because it has reached the limit set during initialization. This is far from ideal because calls that want to wait until an object is available will be allowed to do so, even though the pool is permanently exhausted. Listing 8-11 shows how I have enhanced the Pool class to fail requests when the pool is exhausted.

Listing 8-11. Handling Pool Expiry in the Pool.swift File

```swift
import Foundation

class Pool<T:AnyObject> {
    private var data = [T]();
    private let arrayQ = dispatch_queue_create("arrayQ", DISPATCH_QUEUE_SERIAL);
    private let semaphore:dispatch_semaphore_t;
    private var itemCount = 0;
    private let maxItemCount:Int;
    private let itemFactory: () -> T;
    private var ejectedItems = 0;
    private var poolExhausted = false;

    init(maxItemCount:Int, factory:() -> T) {
        self.itemFactory = factory;
        self.maxItemCount = maxItemCount;
        semaphore = dispatch_semaphore_create(maxItemCount);
    }

    func getFromPool(maxWaitSeconds:Int = -1) -> T? {
        var result:T?;

        let waitTime = (maxWaitSeconds == -1)
            ? DISPATCH_TIME_FOREVER
            : dispatch_time(DISPATCH_TIME_NOW,
                (Int64(maxWaitSeconds) * Int64(NSEC_PER_SEC)));

        if (!poolExhausted) {
            if (dispatch_semaphore_wait(semaphore, waitTime) == 0) {
                if (!poolExhausted) {
                    dispatch_sync(arrayQ, {() in
                        if (self.data.count == 0
                                && self.itemCount < self.maxItemCount) {
                            result = self.itemFactory();
                            self.itemCount++;
```

```
                        } else {
                            result = self.data.removeAtIndex(0);
                        }
                })
            }
        }
    }
    return result;
}

func returnToPool(item:T) {
    dispatch_async(arrayQ, {() in
        if let pitem = item as AnyObject as? PoolItem {
            if (pitem.canReuse) {
                self.data.append(item);
                dispatch_semaphore_signal(self.semaphore);
            } else {
                self.ejectedItems++;
                if (self.ejectedItems == self.maxItemCount) {
                    self.poolExhausted = true;
                    self.flushQueue();
                }
            }
        } else {
            self.data.append(item);
        }
    });
}

private func flushQueue() {
    var dQueue = dispatch_queue_create("drainer", DISPATCH_QUEUE_CONCURRENT);
    var backlogCleared = false;

    dispatch_async(dQueue, {() in
        dispatch_semaphore_wait(self.semaphore, DISPATCH_TIME_FOREVER);
        backlogCleared = true;
    });

    dispatch_async(dQueue, {() in
        while (!backlogCleared) {
            dispatch_semaphore_signal(self.semaphore);
        }
    });
}

func processPoolItems(callback:[T] -> Void) {
    dispatch_barrier_sync(arrayQ, {() in
        callback(self.data);
    });
}
}
```

The changes in the listing address two problems: recognizing when the pool is exhausted and rejecting any pending requests. To recognize when the pool is exhausted, I keep track of the number of objects that are rejected from the pool in the returnToPool method, and when all of the objects that the pool is able to create have been ejected, I set an instance variable called poolExhausted to true and invoke a new method called flushQueue.

> **Tip**   I have had to rewrite the returnToPool method to deal with three possible conditions. The first is that the object implements the PoolItem protocol and can be reused. The second is that the object implements the PoolItem protocol and cannot be reused—and may be the last object to be ejected. The final condition is that the item doesn't implement the PoolItem protocol, in which case ejection and exhaustion are not of concern and the item can be added back into the pool.

I have modified the getFromPool method so that requests check the value of the poolExhausted property before waiting for the semaphore, which means that any new requests that arrive after the pool has been exhausted return immediately.

The second problem is dealing with the outstanding requests for objects that arrived before the pool became exhausted. The threads making the requests will be waiting for the GCD semaphore and will continue to do so until they are signaled. Unfortunately, the GCD semaphore doesn't provide a means for me to wake up all of the waiting threads, so I have had to take an indirect route when implementing the flushQueue method.

I create a separate GCD queue and add two blocks to it. The first block waits for the semaphore and sets the value of a local variable called backLogCleared to true when the semaphore lets it pass.

```
...
dispatch_async(dQueue, {() in
    dispatch_semaphore_wait(self.semaphore, DISPATCH_TIME_FOREVER);
    backlogCleared = true;
});
...
```

GCD semaphores allow threads to pass in first-in first-out (FIFO) order, which means that this block won't be allowed to pass the semaphore until all of the waiting requests that arrived before the queue was exhausted have also been allowed to pass.

The second block repeatedly signals the semaphore until the value of the backLogCleared property changes.

```
...
dispatch_async(dQueue, {() in
    while (!backlogCleared) {
        dispatch_semaphore_signal(self.semaphore);
    }
});
...
```

The queue to which I add these blocks is concurrent, and the semaphore will be signaled until the backlog is cleared. I want to prevent calls that were waiting for the semaphore from adding blocks to the array modification queue, which is why I check the value of the poolExhausted property before and after waiting for the semaphore in the getFromPool method.

```
...
if (!poolExhausted) {
    if (dispatch_semaphore_wait(semaphore, waitTime) == 0) {
        if (!poolExhausted) {
...
```

I changed the default value of the maxWaitSeconds parameter in the getFromPool method to -1 to test the new functionality easier; a request for an object will be rejected only when the pool is exhausted. Run the application, and you will see output similar to the previous example—but this implementation of the code prevents callers who are willing to wait for an object being locked up when the pool is exhausted.

Creating an Elastic Pool

You don't have to reject requests for objects if the pool is able to create the number it needs to meet demand. This is known as an *elastic pool*, and it can be used where there is a preferred number of objects and a separate maximum number.

In terms of software development, elastic pools can be used in any situation where it is feasible to create additional objects to cope with increased demand. A common example is network connections, where there is a preferred number of connections for normal operation and some headroom for peak periods.

In terms of a real-world library, peak demand for a popular title may be satisfied by borrowing books from nearby branches. This isn't ideal because it reduces availability elsewhere in the library network, but it means that requests for books can be satisfied without long waits under exceptional circumstances. To map this into my example, I have added a class called LibraryNetwork to the BookSources.swift file, as shown in Listing 8-12.

Listing 8-12. The Contents of the BookSources.swift File

```
import Foundation

class BookSeller {
    class func buyBook(author:String, title:String, stockNumber:Int) -> Book {
        return Book(author: author, title: title, stock: stockNumber);
    }
}

class LibraryNetwork {

    class func borrowBook(author:String, title:String, stockNumber:Int) -> Book {
        return Book(author: author, title: title, stock: stockNumber);
    }

    class func returnBook(book:Book) {
        // do nothing
    }
}
```

The LibraryNetwork class is a placeholder that allows me to demonstrate temporarily obtaining additional books. I am not going to implement any logic in this class because my focus is on the pool. Listing 8-13 shows how I have implemented elasticity in the Pool class.

Listing 8-13. Adding Item Elasticity in the Pool.swift File

```swift
import Foundation

class Pool<T:AnyObject> {
    private var data = [T]();
    private let arrayQ = dispatch_queue_create("arrayQ", DISPATCH_QUEUE_SERIAL);
    private let semaphore:dispatch_semaphore_t;

    private let itemFactory: () -> T;
    private let peakFactory: () -> T;
    private let peakReaper:(T) -> Void;

    private var createdCount:Int = 0;
    private let normalCount:Int;
    private let peakCount:Int;
    private let returnCount:Int;
    private let waitTime:Int;

    init(itemCount:Int, peakCount:Int, returnCount: Int, waitTime:Int = 2,
            itemFactory:() -> T, peakFactory:() -> T, reaper:(T) -> Void) {

        self.normalCount = itemCount; self.peakCount = peakCount;
        self.waitTime    = waitTime; self.returnCount = returnCount;
        self.itemFactory = itemFactory; self.peakFactory = peakFactory;
        self.peakReaper  = reaper;
        self.semaphore   = dispatch_semaphore_create(itemCount);
    }

    func getFromPool() -> T? {
        var result:T?;

        let expiryTime = dispatch_time(DISPATCH_TIME_NOW,
            (Int64(waitTime) * Int64(NSEC_PER_SEC)));

        if (dispatch_semaphore_wait(semaphore, expiryTime) == 0) {
            dispatch_sync(arrayQ, {() in
                if (self.data.count == 0) {
                    result = self.itemFactory();
                    self.createdCount++;
                } else {
                    result = self.data.removeAtIndex(0);
                }
            })
        } else {
            dispatch_sync(arrayQ, {() in
```

```
            result = self.peakFactory();
            self.createdCount++;
        });
    }
    return result;
}

func returnToPool(item:T) {
    dispatch_async(arrayQ, {() in
        if (self.data.count > self.returnCount
                && self.createdCount > self.normalCount) {
            self.peakReaper(item);
            self.createdCount--;
        } else {
            self.data.append(item);
            dispatch_semaphore_signal(self.semaphore);
        }
    });
}

func processPoolItems(callback:[T] -> Void) {
    dispatch_barrier_sync(arrayQ, {() in
        callback(self.data);
    });
}
}
```

> **Note**   I have removed the code that deals with exhausted pools and ejecting items to make the example simpler and because they are not usually used with elasticity (because the code gets complicated and hard to maintain).

This pool uses a GCD semaphore to wait for an object to become available for a specified period, which defaults to three seconds. If the `semaphore wait` operation expires before an item becomes available, then a factory closure is used to create a temporary item to cope with demand. (There are two factory closures—one for normal lazy object creation and one for creating temporary peak items).

The defining characteristic of an elastic pool is what you do with the temporary objects. You can keep them in the pool forever, you can let the reference go so that the object will be deleted, or—as I have done here—you can define a *reaper*, which is used to dispose of items when they are longer required. In this case, I accept the reaper as an initializer argument and invoke it when the demand for objects falls.

> **Tip**   You can create sophisticated policies for deciding when temporary objects are no longer required, but I recommend keeping it as simple as possible. Complex schemes work well during development but tend to fall apart in the face of real usage patterns, which are hard to predict in advance.

To use the elastic pool, I need to change the initializer in the `Library` class to provide the additional closures and item counts, as shown in Listing 8-14.

Listing 8-14. Updating the Library Initializer in the Library.swift File

```
...
private init(stockLevel:Int) {

    var stockId = 1;

    pool = Pool<Book>(
        itemCount:stockLevel,
        peakCount: stockLevel * 2,
        returnCount: stockLevel / 2,
        itemFactory: {() in
            return BookSeller.buyBook("Dickens, Charles",
            title: "Hard Times", stockNumber: stockId++)},
        peakFactory: {() in
            return LibraryNetwork.borrowBook("Dickens, Charles",
                title: "Hard Times", stockNumber: stockId++)},
        reaper: LibraryNetwork.returnBook
    );
}
...
```

The normal pool items will be `Book` objects obtained from the `BookSeller` class. When demand is twice the normal level, additional `Book` objects will be obtained from the `LibraryNetwork.borrowBook` method, and when the number of objects falls to 50 percent of the normal level, the additional objects are reaped by the `LibraryNetwork.return` book method.

You can see the effect of item elasticity by running the application, which will produce output like this:

```
...Starting...
All blocks complete
...Book#2...
Checked out 4 times
In stock
...Book#15...
Checked out 1 times
In stock
...Book#19...
Checked out 1 times
In stock
...Book#17...
Checked out 1 times
In stock
...Book#18...
Checked out 1 times
In stock
There are 5 books in the pool
...
```

This example borrows Book objects to satisfy demand, which is reflected in the number of times that the books shown in the output have been checked out of the pool. The code in the main.swift file requests 35 Book objects, but the report shows only 8 checkouts. The remaining requests have been satisfied using objects obtained from—and subsequently returned to—the LibraryNetwork class.

Understanding the Allocation Strategy

The allocation strategy determines how an available object is selected to service a request. The strategy I have been using so far in this chapter is first-in first-out, based on treating an array like a queue. The advantage of this approach is that it is simple to implement, but it does mean that objects can be allocated unevenly so that some are checked out of the pool many more times than others.

For most applications, the FIFO allocation strategy will be appropriate, but some applications will require a different approach to allocating objects. For my example application, I am going to allocate the least-used available book, but—as you will see—the impact of such a strategy is limited when demand for objects is high. Listing 8-15 shows how I have added support for a custom allocation strategy in the Pool class.

Listing 8-15. Adding Support for an Allocation Strategy in the Pool.swift File

```
import Foundation

class Pool<T:AnyObject> {
    private var data = [T]();
    private let arrayQ = dispatch_queue_create("arrayQ", DISPATCH_QUEUE_SERIAL);
    private let semaphore:dispatch_semaphore_t;

    private let itemFactory: () -> T;
    private let itemAllocator:[T] -> Int;
    private let maxItemCount:Int;
    private var createdCount:Int = 0;

    init(itemCount:Int, itemFactory:() -> T, itemAllocator:([T] -> Int)) {
        self.maxItemCount = itemCount;
        self.itemFactory = itemFactory;
        self.itemAllocator = itemAllocator;
        self.semaphore = dispatch_semaphore_create(itemCount);
    }

    func getFromPool() -> T? {
        var result:T?;

        if (dispatch_semaphore_wait(semaphore, DISPATCH_TIME_FOREVER) == 0) {
            dispatch_sync(arrayQ, {() in
                if (self.data.count == 0) {
                    result = self.itemFactory();
                    self.createdCount++;
```

```
            } else {
                result = self.data.removeAtIndex(self.itemAllocator(self.data));
            }
        })
    }
    return result;
}

func returnToPool(item:T) {
    dispatch_async(arrayQ, {() in
        self.data.append(item);
        dispatch_semaphore_signal(self.semaphore);
    });
}

func processPoolItems(callback:[T] -> Void) {
    dispatch_barrier_sync(arrayQ, {() in
        callback(self.data);
    });
}
}
```

This is a fixed-size pool that creates its objects lazily. I have defined an initializer parameter called `itemAllocator` that is a closure to which the array of available items is passed. The closure returns the position in the array of the item that should be allocated to service the request. Listing 8-16 shows how I have updated the initializer of the `Library` class to implement an allocation strategy.

Listing 8-16. Adding an Allocation Strategy in the Library.swift File

```
...
private init(stockLevel:Int) {

    var stockId = 1;

    pool = Pool<Book>(
        itemCount:stockLevel,
        itemFactory: {() in
            return BookSeller.buyBook("Dickens, Charles",
            title: "Hard Times", stockNumber: stockId++)},
        itemAllocator: {(var books) in return 0; }
    );
}
...
```

I have started with the FIFO strategy, and the closure selects the first item in the array. I recommend that you start with this strategy in order to measure the impact of any alternatives. Depending on the pattern of requests that are made to the pool, you may well find that the FIFO allocation strategy gives you something close to your goal. Here is a formatted version of the output from running the application using FIFO:

```
...
...Book#4...Checked out 10 times
...Book#3...Checked out 6 times
...Book#2...Checked out 5 times
...Book#1...Checked out 5 times
...Book#5...Checked out 9 times
...
```

There is some variation between how often the objects have been used but not an enormous amount. In a real project, I would consider sticking with the FIFO strategy with these results (although I would also look at the variation in production to ensure that my tests are realistic).

Listing 8-17 shows a least-used strategy. This strategy selects the least-used *available* object. There could be objects that are checked out that have been used less. Taking into account all of the objects is called a *perfect allocation strategy*, but it is rarely useful because it means you block a request until the absolute least-used object becomes available, which may not happen for some time.

Listing 8-17. Implementing a Different Allocation Strategy in the Library.swift File

```
...
private init(stockLevel:Int) {

    var stockId = 1;

    pool = Pool<Book>(
        itemCount:stockLevel,
        itemFactory: {() in
            return BookSeller.buyBook("Dickens, Charles",
            title: "Hard Times", stockNumber: stockId++)},
        itemAllocator: {(var books) in
            var selected = 0;
            for index in 1 ..< books.count {
                if (books[index].checkoutCount < books[selected].checkoutCount) {
                    selected = index;
                }
            }
            return selected;
        }
    );
}
...
```

In the new closure, I check each of the available objects and select the one with the lowest checkoutCount property value. Here is the edited output from using this strategy:

```
...
...Book#2...Checked out 8 times
...Book#3...Checked out 5 times
...Book#5...Checked out 8 times
...Book#4...Checked out 8 times
...Book#1...Checked out 6 times
...
```

The exact results will vary because of the randomness in the main.swift code, but the overall effect is to allocate the objects more evenly. This is a more balanced allocation strategy, but it requires more work each time an object is allocated, and (at least for my test code) the impact is relatively small. That doesn't mean you should always use the FIFO allocation strategy, but you should make sure that the additional work is justified by the results.

Understanding the Pitfalls of the Pattern Variations

The main danger presented by these variations is complexity, which can manifest itself in concurrency problems and in code that is harder to read and harder to maintain. Beyond these problems, there are specific pitfalls that these strategies can lead to, as described in the following sections.

Understanding the Expectation Gap Pitfall

As this chapter has demonstrated, it is possible to create object pools that look superficially similar but that implement different strategies behind the scenes. You must ensure that the external impact of these strategies is obvious to calling components because otherwise you will find that the efficacy of the object pool is undermined.

For example, you may choose to deal with an empty pool by rejecting requests for objects. If you do this, ensure that the return type of the pool object checkout method is an optional type, such as Book? and not simply Book. Using optional results makes it clear that it is possible that a call to the method will not yield an object.

Not every behavior can be expressed using language features, and I recommend you provide API documentation that describes how the pool operates in some detail. For example, you will need to document the fact that you deal with an exhausted pool by rejecting requests in order to avoid calling components using a for loop until they receive an object—a behavior that can lead to the application locking up.

Understanding the Over- and Under-utilization Pitfalls

Once you start implementing the object pool pattern, it is easy to become emotionally invested in selecting and creating the strategies you need and making them fit together. A well-written implementation of the object pool pattern is a thing of beauty, but you must keep one eye on how the pool performs during testing and deployment because it is easy to create a pool that is perfect in implementation but that impairs the performance of the application or consumes too many resources.

An over-utilized pool is a performance hazard because it spends most of its time empty and has a long queue of calling components waiting for objects. An under-utilized pool is a resource hazard because it manages a collection of objects that are rarely used. Balancing the size and behavior of an object pool against its workload requires some trial and error—and realistic usage data for testing. Also, you must be prepared to change the size and behavior of your pool to match the application needs, even if that means discarding a strategy of which you are particularly proud.

Examples of the Pattern Variations in Cocoa

There are no obvious uses of these pattern variations in the Cocoa frameworks, although it is hard to be sure because Apple does not publish the source code.

Applying a Pattern Variation to SportsStore

To finish this chapter, I am going to change the object creation strategy to the pool that I added to the SportsStore application in Chapter 7. Currently, the NetworkPool class eagerly creates its objects.

```
...
private init() {
    for _ in 0 ..< connectionCount {
        connections.append(NetworkConnection());
    }
    semaphore = dispatch_semaphore_create(connectionCount);
    queue = dispatch_queue_create("networkpoolQ", DISPATCH_QUEUE_SERIAL);
}
...
```

I am going to switch to a lazy strategy. I used a closure to do this for the generic pool class earlier in the chapter because I didn't want the pool to have directly knowledge of how the objects it manages are created. By contrast, the SportsStore NetworkPool class is already aware of the NetworkConnection class and how it is created, which simplifies the implementation of the strategy. Listing 8-18 shows the changes I made to implement the new strategy.

Listing 8-18. Changing the Object Creation Strategy in the NetworkPool.swift File

```swift
import Foundation

final class NetworkPool {
    private let connectionCount = 3;
    private var connections = [NetworkConnection]();
    private var semaphore:dispatch_semaphore_t;
    private var queue:dispatch_queue_t;
    private var itemsCreated = 0;

    private init() {
        semaphore = dispatch_semaphore_create(connectionCount);
        queue = dispatch_queue_create("networkpoolQ", DISPATCH_QUEUE_SERIAL);
    }

    private func doGetConnection() -> NetworkConnection {
        dispatch_semaphore_wait(semaphore, DISPATCH_TIME_FOREVER);
        var result:NetworkConnection? = nil;
        dispatch_sync(queue, {() in
            if (self.connections.count > 0) {
                result = self.connections.removeAtIndex(0);
            } else if (self.itemsCreated < self.connectionCount) {
                result = NetworkConnection();
                self.itemsCreated++;
            }
        });
        return result!;
    }

    private func doReturnConnection(conn:NetworkConnection) {
        dispatch_async(queue, {() in
            self.connections.append(conn);
            dispatch_semaphore_signal(self.semaphore);
        });
    }

    class func getConnection() -> NetworkConnection {
        return sharedInstance.doGetConnection();
    }

    class func returnConnecton(conn:NetworkConnection) {
        sharedInstance.doReturnConnection(conn);
    }
```

```
private class var sharedInstance:NetworkPool {
    get {
        struct SingletonWrapper {
            static let singleton = NetworkPool();
        }
        return SingletonWrapper.singleton;
    }
}
}
```

The changes are simple. I have removed the code that eagerly creates the NetworkConnection objects from the initializer and added code that lazily creates them in the doGetConnection method. It is always easier to work on a pool class that manages a specific type, but I still prefer to use generic pool classes because it means I always get a consistent pool implementation because I copy the code from one project to another, and to me, that is worth the additional complexity.

Summary

In this chapter, I showed you how you can change the four strategies that define the way an object pool works so that you can use different implementations of the pattern to handle a variety of objects. Few patterns require as much detail as the object pool pattern, and I return to simpler territory in the next chapter, in which I describe the factory method pattern.

Chapter 9

The Factory Method Pattern

The factory method pattern is used when there is a choice to be made between classes that implement a common protocol or share a common base class. This pattern allows implementation subclasses to provide specializations without requiring the components that rely on them to know any details of those classes and how they relate to each other. Table 9-1 puts the factory method into context.

Table 9-1. *Putting the Factory Method Pattern into Context*

Question	Answer
What is it?	The factory method pattern selects an implementation class to satisfy a calling component's request without requiring the component to know anything about the implementation classes or the way they relate to one another.
What are the benefits?	This pattern consolidates the logic that decides which implementation class is selected and prevents it from being diffused throughout the application. This also means that calling components rely only on the top-level protocol or base class and do not need any knowledge about the implementation classes or the process by which they are selected.
When should you use this pattern?	Use this pattern when you have several classes that implement a common protocol or that are derived from the same base class.
When should you avoid this pattern?	Do not use this pattern when there is no common protocol or shared base class because this pattern works by having the calling component rely on only a single type.
How do you know when you have implemented the pattern correctly?	This pattern is implemented correctly when the appropriate class is instantiated without the calling component knowing which class was used or how it was selected.
Are there any common pitfalls?	No. The factory method pattern is simple to implement.
Are there any related patterns?	The factory method pattern is often combined with the singleton and object pool patterns.

> **Note**   The factory method pattern is closely related to the abstract factory pattern. See Chapter 10 for details of the abstract factory pattern and guidance for choosing between them.

Preparing the Example Project

For this chapter, I created an OS X Command Line Tool project called FactoryMethod. I added a file called RentalCar.swift to the project, the contents of which are shown in Listing 9-1.

Listing 9-1. The Contents of the RentalCar.swift File

```
protocol RentalCar {
    var name:String { get };
    var passengers:Int { get };
    var pricePerDay:Float { get };
}

class Compact : RentalCar {
    var name = "VW Golf";
    var passengers = 3;
    var pricePerDay:Float = 20;
}

class Sports : RentalCar {
    var name = "Porsche Boxter";
    var passengers = 1;
    var pricePerDay:Float = 100;
}

class SUV : RentalCar {
    var name = "Cadillac Escalade";
    var passengers = 8;
    var pricePerDay:Float = 75;
}
```

This file contains a protocol called RentalCar and three conforming classes: Compact, Sports, and SUV. Listing 9-2 shows the contents of the CarSelector.swift file, which I added to the project and which defines a class that relies on the RentalCar protocol and its implementations.

Listing 9-2. The Contents of the CarSelector.swift File

```
class CarSelector {
    class func selectCar(passengers:Int) -> String? {
        var car:RentalCar?;
        switch (passengers) {
            case 0...1:
                car = Sports();
            case 2...3:
                car = Compact();
```

```
        case 4...8:
            car = SUV();
        default:
            car = nil;
    }
        return car?.name;
    }
}
```

The CarSelector class defines a type method called selectCar that instantiates an implementation of the RentalCar protocol that can accommodate the number of passengers (excluding the driver) specified by the passengers parameter. The result of the selectCar method is the value of the name property of the RentalCar implementation class that is selected and instantiated. I also added the statements shown in Listing 9-3 to the main.swift file.

Listing 9-3. The Contents of the main.swift File

```
import Foundation

let passengers = [1, 3, 5];

for p in passengers {
    println("\(p) passengers: \(CarSelector.selectCar(p)!)");
}
```

The code in the main.swift file calls the CarSelector.selectCar method for different numbers of passengers and writes the results to the debug console. You will see the following output when you run the application:

```
1 passengers: Porsche Boxter
3 passengers: VW Golf
5 passengers: Cadillac Escalade
```

Understanding the Problem That the Pattern Solves

The factory method pattern solves a problem that arises when there are multiple classes that conform to a protocol and you need to select the one that should be instantiated. You can see this at work in Listing 9-2, in which the CarSelector.selectCar method selects and instantiates one of the classes that conforms to the RentalCar protocol based on the value of the passengers parameter.

This approach has two related issues. The first issue is that by needing to instantiate the implementation classes, the CarSelector class doesn't benefit from the abstraction offered by the RentalCar protocol. In fact, the RentalCar protocol doesn't deliver any real benefit at all, which you can see when I add a new implementation class, as shown in Listing 9-4.

Listing 9-4. Adding a New Implementation Class in the RentalCar.swift File

```
protocol RentalCar {
    var name:String { get };
    var passengers:Int { get };
    var pricePerDay:Float { get };
}

// ...other implementation classes omitted for brevity...

class Minivan : RentalCar {
    var name = "Chevrolet Express";
    var passengers = 14;
    var pricePerDay:Float = 40;
}
```

The listing shows the addition of the Minivan class, and you can see the impact it has on the CarSelector class in Listing 9-5.

Listing 9-5. Adding Support for a New Implementation Class in the CarSelector.swift File

```
class CarSelector {
    class func selectCar(passengers:Int) -> String? {
        var car:RentalCar?;
        switch (passengers) {
            case 0...1:
                car = Sports();
            case 2...3:
                car = Compact();
            case 4...8:
                car = SUV();
            case 9...14:
                car = Minivan();
            default:
                car = nil;
        }
        return car?.name;
    }
}
```

The CarSelector class has to know about every implementation of the RentalCar protocol that it wants to use, and it has to know when each should be created. This is different from tight coupling because the CarSelector class doesn't depend on the implementation of the classes it uses, but it is still a problem because it depends on knowledge about the classes that implement the protocol. New implementation classes require updates to the CarSelector class, as do changes in the circumstances for which a specific implementation class is appropriate. For example, if I change the car model used for the Sports class so that it has four seats, then I must update the CarSelector class so that it knows it can be used for one to three passengers.

The second issue is that the knowledge about how to select an implementation class will become diffused throughout the application as I add components that need to select implementations of the RentalCar protocol. In Listing 9-6, you can see the contents of the PriceCalculator.swift file that I added to the project.

Listing 9-6. The Contents of the PriceCalculator.swift File

```swift
class PriceCalculator {
    class func calculatePrice(passengers:Int, days:Int) -> Float? {
        var car:RentalCar?;
        switch (passengers) {
        case 0...1:
            car = Sports();
        case 2...3:
            car = Compact();
        case 4...8:
            car = SUV();
        case 9...14:
            car = Minivan();
        default:
            car = nil;
        }
        return car == nil ? nil : car!.pricePerDay * Float(days);
    }
}
```

The PriceCalculator class defines a type method called calculatePrice that works out what it costs to rent a car for a given number of passengers and days. The code for selecting the RentalCar implementation class is just the same as in the CarSelector class and suffers from the same dependency on understanding the relationship between those classes.

> **Note** Duplicating the code like this seems obviously wrong in such a simple example, but in a complex project with multiple developers it is easy to end up with this situation because there is no other way of getting an instance of an implementation class.

Both of these problems are barriers to creating robust and easily maintained software. A diffused dependency on the relationship between classes causes cascades of changes throughout an application whenever you need to alter the relationships, and it is all too easy to omit a required change and create a bug that is hard to test for.

Understanding the Factory Method Pattern

The factory method pattern encapsulates the logic required to select an implementation class within a single method that is accessible to calling components. The factory method exposes only the protocol or base class to its callers and does not reveal the details of the implementation classes or the relationship between them. There are three operations in the factory method pattern, as illustrated by Figure 9-1.

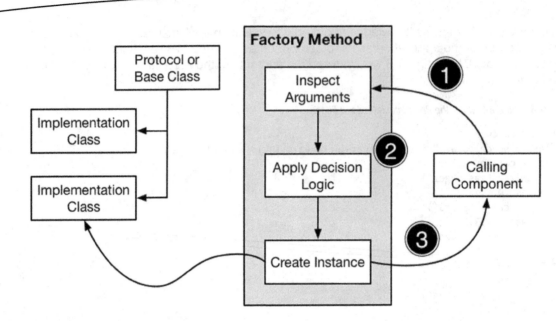

Figure 9-1. The factory pattern method

The first operation occurs when the calling component invokes the factory method, supplying it with the arguments needed to decide which implement class should be instantiated.

For the second operation, the factory method applies its decision logic to the arguments supplied by the calling component to decide which of the implementation classes will be instantiated. The final operation creates an instance of the implementation class and returns it to the calling component, completing the process and providing the caller with the object it needs to do its work.

The calling component does not need to understand the relationship between the implementation classes. In fact, it doesn't even need to know that they exist because the return type from the factory method is the protocol or base type and not the implementation that has been created (you will see how this works in the following section).

Implementing the Factory Method Pattern

The heart of the factory method pattern is—as the name suggests—a method. The method encapsulates the decision logic that selects the implementation class, it defines the parameters needed to execute the logic, and it returns an implementation of the protocol it operates on.

The standard mechanism used to implement the factory method in languages such as Java and C# is the *abstract class*, which is a type that defines some concrete functionality but which must be subclassed in order to be instantiated. There are two basic approaches to implementing the factory method in Swift, although they are somewhat less elegant, as I demonstrate in the sections that follow.

Defining a Global Factory Method

The simplest way to implement the pattern is to define a global function. Global functions are available throughout an application, which makes it easy for calling components to find and call them, as shown in Listing 9-7.

Listing 9-7. Implementing the Factory Method Pattern in the RentalCar.swift File

```swift
func createRentalCar(passengers:Int) -> RentalCar? {
    var car:RentalCar?;
    switch (passengers) {
        case 0...1:
            car = Sports();
        case 2...3:
            car = Compact();
        case 4...8:
            car = SUV();
        case 9...14:
            car = Minivan();
        default:
            car = nil;
    }
    return car;
}

protocol RentalCar {
    var name:String { get };
    var passengers:Int { get };
    var pricePerDay:Float { get };
}

class Compact : RentalCar {
    var name = "VW Golf";
    var passengers = 3;
    var pricePerDay:Float = 20;
}

// ...implementation classes omitted for brevity...
```

This may seem like a small change because the global function—called `createRentalCar`—contains the same decision logic that the `CarSelector` and `PriceCalculator` classes use. Even so, the effect it has on the calling components is profound. Listing 9-8 shows the changes to the `CarSelector` class to use the global function.

Listing 9-8. Calling the Global Function in the CarSelector.swift File

```swift
class CarSelector {
    class func selectCar(passengers:Int) -> String? {
        return createRentalCar(passengers)?.name;
    }
}
```

Not only is there a lot less code, but the CarSelector class has dependencies only on the global factory function and the RentalCar protocol. It no longer knows anything about the implementation classes and the relationship between them—it just knows that calling the createRentalCar global function will produce an object that conforms to the protocol. Listing 9-9 shows the corresponding changes to the PriceCalculator class.

Listing 9-9. Calling the Global Function in the PriceCalculator.swift File

```
class PriceCalculator {
    class func calculatePrice(passengers:Int, days:Int) -> Float? {
        var car = createRentalCar(passengers);
        return car == nil ? nil : car!.pricePerDay * Float(days);
    }
}
```

The added value that each class provides is intact, but exists without diffusing the decision logic and implementation classes throughout the application.

Using a Base Class

The global function approach works, but it can feel a little disconnected from the protocol and classes it operates on. An alternative approach is to replace the protocol with a base class that defines the factory function. Listing 9-10 shows the changes required to implement this approach. (I have also reduced the number of implementation classes to simplify the example and to prepare for future changes.)

Listing 9-10. Implementing the Pattern Using a Base Class in the RentalCar.swift File

```
class RentalCar {
    private var nameBV:String;
    private var passengersBV:Int;
    private var priceBV:Float;

    private init(name:String, passengers:Int, price:Float) {
        self.nameBV = name;
        self.passengersBV = passengers;
        self.priceBV = price;
    }

    final var name:String {
        get { return nameBV; }
    }

    final var passengers:Int {
        get { return passengersBV; }
    };

    final var pricePerDay:Float {
        get { return priceBV; }
    };
```

```
    class func createRentalCar(passengers:Int) -> RentalCar? {
        var car:RentalCar?;
        switch (passengers) {
            case 0...3:
                car = Compact();
            case 4...8:
                car = SUV();
            default:
                car = nil;
        }
        return car;
    }
}

class Compact : RentalCar {
    private init() {
        super.init(name: "VW Golf", passengers: 3, price: 20);
    }
    // functionality specific to compact cars goes here
}

class SUV : RentalCar {
    private init() {
        super.init(name: "Cadillac Escalade", passengers: 8, price: 75);
    }
    // functionality specific to SUVs cars goes here
}
```

> **Tip** This is just a difference in implementation style. I prefer it because I am used to relying on abstract classes in other languages, and this is as close to that approach as I can get with Swift. You should pick the approach that best suits your coding style.

I have replaced the RentalCar protocol with a RentalCar class. I want to use the class to capture the implementation contract that the protocol imposed on its implementations, so I have defined final computed properties that expose the name, the number of passengers, and the price, and I have defined backing properties that are set by a private constructor. Subclasses have to invoke the RentalCar initializer, which requires values for backing values that are used by the computed properties, creating an effect that is similar to using a protocol.

The RentalCar class defines a type method called createRentalCar that contains the decision logic and is responsible for creating the objects that are returned to calling components. Listing 9-11 shows how I have updated the CarSelector class to use the new implementation.

Listing 9-11. Consuming a Base Class in the CarSelector.swift File

```
class CarSelector {
    class func selectCar(passengers:Int) -> String? {
        return RentalCar.createRentalCar(passengers)?.name;
    }
}
```

Listing 9-12 shows the corresponding change to the PriceCalculator class.

Listing 9-12. Consuming a Base Class in the PriceCalculator.swift File

```
class PriceCalculator {
    class func calculatePrice(passengers:Int, days:Int) -> Float? {
        var car = RentalCar.createRentalCar(passengers);
        return car == nil ? nil : car!.pricePerDay * Float(days);
    }
}
```

Delegating Decisions for Deeper Class Hierarchies

If you are dealing with a deep hierarchy of implementation classes, then it can be useful to delegate some of the decision logic into the classes themselves, as shown in Listing 9-13.

Listing 9-13. Delegating Decision Logic in the RentalCar.swift File

```
class RentalCar {
    private var nameBV:String;
    private var passengersBV:Int;
    private var priceBV:Float;

    private init(name:String, passengers:Int, price:Float) {
        self.nameBV = name;
        self.passengersBV = passengers;
        self.priceBV = price;
    }

    final var name:String { get { return nameBV; }}
    final var passengers:Int { get { return passengersBV; }};
    final var pricePerDay:Float { get { return priceBV; }};

    class func createRentalCar(passengers:Int) -> RentalCar? {
        var carImpl:RentalCar.Type?;
        switch (passengers) {
            case 0...3:
                carImpl = Compact.self;
            case 4...8:
                carImpl = SUV.self
            default:
                carImpl = nil;
        }
```

```
        return carImpl?.createRentalCar(passengers);
    }
}

class Compact : RentalCar {
    private convenience init() {
        self.init(name: "VW Golf", passengers: 3, price: 20);
    }

    private override init(name: String, passengers: Int, price: Float) {
        super.init(name: name, passengers: passengers, price: price);
    }

    override class func createRentalCar(passengers:Int) -> RentalCar? {
        if (passengers < 2) {
            return Compact();
        } else {
            return SmallCompact();
        }
    }
}

class SmallCompact : Compact {

    private init() {
        super.init(name: "Ford Fiesta", passengers: 3, price: 15);
    }
}

class SUV : RentalCar {

    private init() {
        super.init(name: "Cadillac Escalade", passengers: 8, price: 75);
    }

    override class func createRentalCar(passengers:Int) -> RentalCar? {
        return SUV();
    }
}
```

> **Note**   There are some who believe that delegating object creation to the implementation classes is an essential part of the factory method pattern. I take a more relaxed view and generally use delegation only when dealing with complex hierarchies of classes. For simpler situations, I prefer to consolidate the decision logic in one place, as I did in the previous section, because I find it easier to test and maintain.

I have expanded the range of rental cars available by subclassing Compact to create the SmallCompact class. I could have included the decision logic for choosing between Compact or SmallCompact in the RentalCar class, but this can become awkward to maintain for deep hierarchies of classes (much deeper than the two classes I have used here).

The alternative approach is to push the decision into the implementation classes, on the basis that the Compact class, for example, is best placed to understand when it should be used and when the SmallCompact class is more appropriate, as illustrated by Figure 9-2.

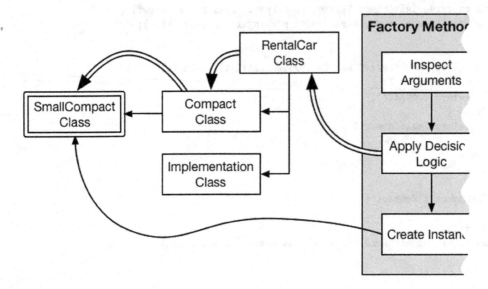

Figure 9-2. Delegating the decision into subclasses

When delegating the decision, the factory method has to break its work into two separate operations that were previously conflated. The first operation is to identify the type that will be instantiated to satisfy the request, like this:

```
...
var carImpl:RentalCar.Type?;
switch (passengers) {
    case 0...3:
        carImpl = Compact.self;
    case 4...8:
        carImpl = SUV.self
    default:
        carImpl = nil;
}
...
```

The `carImpl` variable is defined as an optional `RentalCar.Type`. The `Type` suffix specifies that this variable will be a metatype and not an object (meaning the implementation class and not an instance of it). The logic in the `RentalCar` factory method selects one of the top-level implementation classes and then invokes its `createRentalCar` method to create the result that will be returned to the caller.

```
...
return carImpl?.createRentalCar(passengers);
...
```

In part, the choice of where to place the decision logic is a matter of personal preference. I generally start by consolidating the decision logic in the factory method and start to delegate only once the conditional statements are hard to manage or when my unit tests for validating the decisions become unwieldy—at which point I start pushing the decisions down into the classes themselves. Bear in mind, however, that putting all of the logic in the factory method creates dependencies on all of the implementation classes and their subclasses, which can undermine the benefit of applying the pattern when there is a complex class hierarchy to deal with.

Variations on the Factory Method Pattern

The factory method pattern can be combined with other patterns to add structure to more complex applications by consolidating the decision logic. The most common combination is to use the factory method pattern to select different singleton objects that all implement a common protocol or that are all derived from a common base class. In Listing 9-14, you can see how I have modified the implementation classes in the example project to be singletons.

Listing 9-14. Combining the Singleton and Factory Method Patterns in the RentalCar.swift File

```
class RentalCar {
    private var nameBV:String;
    private var passengersBV:Int;
    private var priceBV:Float;

    private init(name:String, passengers:Int, price:Float) {
        self.nameBV = name;
        self.passengersBV = passengers;
        self.priceBV = price;
    }

    final var name:String { get { return nameBV; }}
    final var passengers:Int { get { return passengersBV; }};
    final var pricePerDay:Float { get { return priceBV; }};

    class func createRentalCar(passengers:Int) -> RentalCar? {
        var carImpl:RentalCar.Type?;
        switch (passengers) {
            case 0...3:
                carImpl = Compact.self;
            case 4...8:
                carImpl = SUV.self
```

```
                    default:
                        carImpl = nil;
                }
                return carImpl?.createRentalCar(passengers);
        }
}

class Compact : RentalCar {

    private convenience init() {
        self.init(name: "VW Golf", passengers: 3, price: 20);
    }

    private override init(name: String, passengers: Int, price: Float) {
        super.init(name: name, passengers: passengers, price: price);
    }

    override class func createRentalCar(passengers:Int) -> RentalCar? {
        if (passengers < 2) {
            return sharedInstance;
        } else {
            return SmallCompact.sharedInstance;
        }
    }

    class var sharedInstance:RentalCar {
        get {
            struct SingletonWrapper {
                static let singleton = Compact();
            }
            return SingletonWrapper.singleton;
        }
    }
}

class SmallCompact : Compact {

    private init() {
        super.init(name: "Ford Fiesta", passengers: 3, price: 15);
    }

    override class var sharedInstance:RentalCar {
        get {
            struct SingletonWrapper {
                static let singleton = SmallCompact();
            }
            return SingletonWrapper.singleton;
        }
    }
}
```

```
class SUV : RentalCar {

    private init() {
        super.init(name: "Cadillac Escalade", passengers: 8, price: 75);
    }

    override class func createRentalCar(passengers:Int) -> RentalCar? {
        return SUV();
    }
}
```

I have modified the Compact and Subcompact classes so that they define singletons using the struct technique I described in Chapter 6. These singletons are used by the modifications I applied to the implementation of the Compact.createRentalCar method, which returns the shared instances rather than creating new ones.

The outcome of combining the singleton and factory methods patterns is that knowledge about the singleton is tightly contained to the implementation classes. The calling component of the factory method doesn't know—or care—if it receives a new instance or a singleton and nor does the factory method itself. You can also mix singletons with new instances. This is illustrated by the SUV class, which does not employ a singleton and whose implementation of the createRentalCar method creates a new instance every time it is called.

> **Tip**   You can also use the factory method to manage access to a group of related object pools. If you do so, remember to create a pool for each class of implementation object. If you use a single pool for all objects, callers will receive the wrong kind of implementation.

Understanding the Pitfalls of the Pattern

There are no serious pitfalls with this pattern, other than to ensure that the factory method doesn't reveal any details of which implementation class has been selected to satisfy a request.

Examples of the Factory Method Pattern in Cocoa

The Objective-C Cocoa classes make extensive use of the factory method pattern, referring to classes that implement the pattern as *class clusters*. Class clusters are managed through factory methods, but these methods are mapped to convenience initializers for use in Swift, which hides the details away.

For example, the NSNumber class in the Foundation framework defines an Objective-C factory method called numberWithBool that accepts a BOOL value and returns an NSNumber object that represents it (with the numeric value 0 or 1).

This `numberWithBool` method is presented as a Swift convenience initializer that accepts a `Bool` value, like this:

```
...
var number = NSNumber(bool: true);
...
```

The result of calling this initializer is that an `NSBoolNumber` object is created, but this is hidden from the caller and presented as an `NSNumber` object.

> **Note** It isn't possible to use Swift initializers to implement the factory method pattern for your own classes. Only Objective-C factory methods are handled this way.

Applying the Pattern to the SportsStore Application

To complete this chapter, I am going to apply the factory method pattern to the SportsStore application in order to create variations on the `Product` class.

> **Tip** Remember that you can download the source code for all the projects in this book—including the SportsStore application in its different stages—from `Apress.com`.

Preparing the Example Application

To prepare for the pattern, I need to create implementation classes that will represent different kinds of product. Listing 9-15 shows the additional classes I created.

Listing 9-15. Defining Subclasses in the Product.swift File

```
import Foundation

class Product : NSObject, NSCopying {

    private(set) var name:String;
    private(set) var productDescription:String;
    private(set) var category:String;
    private var stockLevelBackingValue:Int = 0;
    private var priceBackingValue:Double = 0;
    private var salesTaxRate:Double = 0.2;

    required init(name:String, description:String, category:String, price:Double,
        stockLevel:Int) {
            self.name = name;
            self.productDescription = description;
            self.category = category;
```

```
            super.init();
            self.price = price;
            self.stockLevel = stockLevel;
    }

    var stockLevel:Int {
        get { return stockLevelBackingValue;}
        set { stockLevelBackingValue = max(0, newValue);}
    }

    private(set) var price:Double {
        get { return priceBackingValue;}
        set { priceBackingValue = max(1, newValue);}
    }

    var stockValue:Double {
        get {
            return (price * (1 + salesTaxRate)) * Double(stockLevel);
        }
    }

    func copyWithZone(zone: NSZone) -> AnyObject {
        return Product(name: self.name, description: self.description,
            category: self.category, price: self.price,
            stockLevel: self.stockLevel);
    }

    var upsells:[UpsellOpportunities] {
        get {
            return Array();
        }
    }
}

enum UpsellOpportunities {
    case SwimmingLessons;
    case MapOfLakes;
    case SoccerVideos;
}

class WatersportsProduct : Product {

    required init(name: String, description: String, category: String,
        price: Double, stockLevel: Int) {

        super.init(name: name, description: description, category: category,
            price: price, stockLevel: stockLevel);
        salesTaxRate = 0.10;
    }
```

```
        override var upsells:[UpsellOpportunities] {
            return [UpsellOpportunities.SwimmingLessons, UpsellOpportunities.MapOfLakes];
        }
    }

    class SoccerProduct: Product {

        required init(name: String, description: String, category: String,
            price: Double, stockLevel: Int) {

            super.init(name: name, description: description, category: category,
                price: price, stockLevel: stockLevel);
            salesTaxRate = 0.25;
        }

        override var upsells:[UpsellOpportunities] {
            return [UpsellOpportunities.SoccerVideos];
        }
    }
```

I have enhanced the Product class by adding a tax rate that is used to calculate the stock value.
I also defined an enumeration called UpsellOpportunities that lists additional products that may
interest customers.

I have created two subclasses derived from Product: WatersportsProduct and SoccerProduct. The
decision logic I define when I implement the factory method pattern will select a subclass based
on the product category. Vanilla Product objects will represent products that have no specialized
subclass.

Implementing the Factory Method Pattern

To implement the pattern, I defined a type method on the Pattern class that contains all of
the decision logic. The object hierarchy for the SportsStore application is too simple to require
delegating the decisions. Listing 9-16 shows the factory method.

Listing 9-16. Implementing the Factory Method Pattern in the Product.swift File

```
...
class Product : NSObject, NSCopying {

    private(set) var name:String;
    private(set) var productDescription:String;
    private(set) var category:String;
    private var stockLevelBackingValue:Int = 0;
    private var priceBackingValue:Double = 0;
    private var salesTaxRate:Double = 0.2;

    required init(name:String, description:String, category:String, price:Double,
        stockLevel:Int) {
            self.name = name;
            self.productDescription = description;
```

```
        self.category = category;

        super.init();

        self.price = price;
        self.stockLevel = stockLevel;
    }

    // ...properties and method omitted for brevity...

    class func createProduct(name:String, description:String, category:String,
        price:Double, stockLevel:Int) -> Product {

        var productType:Product.Type;

        switch (category) {
            case "Watersports":
                productType = WatersportsProduct.self;
            case "Soccer":
                productType = SoccerProduct.self;
            default:
                productType = Product.self;
        }

        return productType(name:name, description: description, category: category,
            price: price, stockLevel: stockLevel);
    }
}
...
```

The factory method is called createProduct, and it selects a class using a switch statement on the category parameter. The class is instantiated to produce the object that is returned to the caller. The createProduct method returns an instance of the Product class and hides the details of which subclass has been selected and the process that led to the selection.

Consuming the Factory Method Pattern

To consume the factory method pattern, I have replaced the direct instantiation of the Product class with calls to the factory method, as shown in Listing 9-17.

Listing 9-17. Consuming the Factory Method in the ProductDataStore.swift File

```
import Foundation

final class ProductDataStore {
    var callback:((Product) -> Void)?;
    private var networkQ:dispatch_queue_t
    private var uiQ:dispatch_queue_t;
    lazy var products:[Product] = self.loadData();
```

```
// ...initializer and method omitted for brevity...

private var productData:[Product] = [
    Product.createProduct("Kayak", description:"A boat for one person",
        category:"Watersports", price:275.0, stockLevel:0),
    Product.createProduct("Lifejacket",
        description:"Protective and fashionable",
        category:"Watersports", price:48.95, stockLevel:0),
    Product.createProduct("Soccer Ball",
        description:"FIFA-approved size and weight",
        category:"Soccer", price:19.5, stockLevel:0),
    Product.createProduct("Corner Flags",
        description:"Give your playing field a professional touch",
        category:"Soccer", price:34.95, stockLevel:0),
    Product.createProduct("Stadium",
        description:"Flat-packed 35,000-seat stadium",
        category:"Soccer", price:79500.0, stockLevel:0),
    Product.createProduct("Thinking Cap",
        description:"Improve your brain efficiency",
        category:"Chess", price:16.0, stockLevel:0),
    Product.createProduct("Unsteady Chair",
        description:"Secretly give your opponent a disadvantage",
        category: "Chess", price: 29.95, stockLevel:0),
    Product.createProduct("Human Chess Board",
        description:"A fun game for the family",
        category:"Chess", price:75.0, stockLevel:0),
    Product.createProduct("Bling-Bling King",
        description:"Gold-plated, diamond-studded King",
        category:"Chess", price:1200.0, stockLevel:0)];
}
```

When you run the application, the appropriate class will be selected to represent each product, and you will see that the total value of the stock changes to reflect the different sales tax for each product category.

Summary

In this chapter, I showed you how to apply the factory method pattern to consolidate the logic that selects which subclasses are instantiated to satisfy a calling component's need. In the next chapter, I show you how to use the abstract factory pattern to create families of related objects.

10

Abstract Factory Pattern

In this chapter, I describe the abstract factory pattern. This pattern is similar to the factory method pattern that I described in Chapter 9 but allows a calling component to obtain a family or group of related objects without needing to know which classes were used to create them. Table 10-1 puts the abstract factory pattern in context.

Table 10-1. *Putting the Abstract Factory Pattern into Context*

Question	Answer
What is it?	The abstract factory pattern allows a calling component to create a group of related objects. The pattern hides the details of which classes are used to create the objects and the reason why they were selected from the calling component. This pattern is similar to the factory method pattern I described in Chapter 9 but presents the calling component with a set of objects.
What are the benefits?	The calling component doesn't know which classes are used to create the objects or why they were selected, which makes it possible to change the classes that are used without needing to change the components that consume them.
When should you use this pattern?	Use this pattern when you need to ensure that multiple compatible objects are used by a calling component without the component needing to know which objects are able to work together.
When should you avoid this pattern?	Do not use this pattern to create a single object; the factory method pattern is a simpler alternative that should be used instead.

(continued)

Table 10-1. (continued)

Question	Answer
How do you know when you have implemented the pattern correctly?	This pattern is implemented correctly when a calling component receives a set of objects without knowing which classes were used to instantiate them. The calling component should be able to access the object's functionality only through the protocols they implement or the base classes from which they are derived.
Are there any common pitfalls?	The main pitfall is to leak details of the classes that are used to the calling component, either creating a dependency on the decision-making process that selects classes or creating a dependency on specific classes.
Are there any related patterns?	The factory method pattern (Chapter 9) is a simpler pattern when only a single object is required. The abstract factory method is often combined with the singleton and prototype patterns (see the "Variations on the Abstract Factory Pattern" section).

Preparing the Example Project

For this chapter, I created a new OS X Command Line Tool project called AbstractFactory. The example in this chapter is based on creating the parts required for different models of car. To get started, I added a file called Floorplans.swift, the contents of which are shown in Listing 10-1.

Listing 10-1. The Contents of the Floorplans.swift File

```
protocol Floorplan {
    var seats:Int { get }
    var enginePosition:EngineOption { get };
}

enum EngineOption : String {
    case FRONT = "Front"; case MID = "Mid";
}

class ShortFloorplan: Floorplan {
    var seats = 2;
    var enginePosition = EngineOption.MID
}

class StandardFloorplan: Floorplan {
    var seats = 4;
    var enginePosition = EngineOption.FRONT;
}

class LongFloorplan: Floorplan {
    var seats = 8;
    var enginePosition = EngineOption.FRONT;
}
```

I have defined a protocol called `Floorplan` that represents the foundation for a car. It has a number of seats, expressed by the `Int` property `seats` and an engine mounted in a position expressed by the `enginePosition` property, which is a value from the `EngineOption` enumeration. I have defined three classes that conform to the protocol, each of which represents a different floor plan configuration: `ShortFloorplan`, `StandardFloorplan`, and `LongFloorplan`.

I repeated this process with another file called `Suspension.swift`, the contents of which are shown in Listing 10-2.

Listing 10-2. The Contents of the Suspension.swift File

```
protocol Suspension {
    var suspensionType:SuspensionOption { get };
}

enum SuspensionOption : String {
    case STANDARD = "Standard"; case SPORTS = "Firm"; case SOFT = "Soft";
}

class RoadSuspension : Suspension {
    var suspensionType = SuspensionOption.STANDARD;
}

class OffRoadSuspension : Suspension {
    var suspensionType = SuspensionOption.SOFT;
}

class RaceSuspension : Suspension {
    var suspensionType = SuspensionOption.SPORTS;
}
```

The protocol in this case is called `Suspension`, and it defines a property called `suspensionType`, which is set to a value from `SuspensionOption`. Like before, I have created three classes that conform to the protocol to represent three different suspension products.

i created a file called `Drivetrains.swift` for the last set of products, as shown in Listing 10-3.

Listing 10-3. The Contents of the Drivetrains.swift File

```
protocol Drivetrain {
    var driveType:DriveOption { get };
}

enum DriveOption : String {
    case FRONT = "Front"; case REAR = "Rear"; case ALL = "4WD";
}

class FrontWheelDrive : Drivetrain {
    var driveType = DriveOption.FRONT;
}
```

```
class RearWheelDrive : Drivetrain {
    var driveType = DriveOption.REAR;
}

class AllWheelDrive : Drivetrain {
    var driveType = DriveOption.ALL;
}
```

The protocol represents a drive train and defines a property that takes a value from the DriveOption
enumeration. The implementation classes represent three different types of drive train that can be
used in the production of cars.

To finish the preparation, I added a file called CarsParts.swift, the contents of which are shown in
Listing 10-4.

Listing 10-4. The Contents of the CarsParts.swift File

```
enum Cars: String {
    case COMPACT = "VW Golf";
    case SPORTS = "Porsche Boxter";
    case SUV = "Cadillac Escalade";
}

struct Car {
    var carType:Cars;
    var floor:Floorplan;
    var suspension:Suspension;
    var drive:Drivetrain;

    func printDetails() {
        println("Car type: \(carType.rawValue)");
        println("Seats: \(floor.seats)");
        println("Engine: \(floor.enginePosition.rawValue)");
        println("Suspension: \(suspension.suspensionType.rawValue)");
        println("Drive: \(drive.driveType.rawValue)");
    }
}
```

I have defined an enumeration called Cars that has values for each model of car that I am going
to create and a struct called Car that represents a completed car with properties for each type of
product in the example. The printDetails function writes out details of the car settings to the debug
console.

Tip   Notice that I have used String as the base type for all of the enumerations in this project. This isn't
something you would do in a real project, but it is helpful in an example because it allows me to easily
indicate which values have been selected by writing the raw values to the debug console.

Understanding the Problem That the Pattern Solves

In Chapter 9, I showed you how the factory method pattern can be used to allow calling components to obtain an instance of an implementation class without needing to know which class was selected or why it was selected.

The problem for this chapter is similar but applies to groups of related objects that do not share a common protocol or base class. In the previous section, I defined protocols for three car parts and created three implementation classes from them. For each of the values in the Cars enumeration, I want to select the appropriate product from each category, as shown in Table 10-2.

Table 10-2. The Car to Product Mappings

Car	Floorplan	Suspension	Drivetrain
COMPACT	StandardFloorplan	RoadSuspension	FrontWheelDrive
SPORTS	ShortFloorplan	RaceSuspension	RearWheelDrive
SUV	LongFloorplan	OffRoadSuspension	AllWheelDrive

Currently, the only way for a component to create a car is to have knowledge of at least part of the table in order to instantiate the classes it requires. Listing 10-5 shows how I create the implementation objects and use them to set the properties of a Car struct in the main.swift file.

Listing 10-5. The Contents of the main.swift File

```
var car = Car(carType: Cars.SPORTS,
    floor: ShortFloorplan(),
    suspension: RaceSuspension(),
    drive: RearWheelDrive());

car.printDetails();
```

You will see the following output in the debug console when you run the application:

```
Car type: Porsche Boxter
Seats: 2
Engine: Mid
Suspension: Firm
Drive: Rear
```

The problem presented by this approach is just the same as the one I faced in Chapter 9: the decision logic for selecting which implementation classes will be diffused and duplicated throughout the application, and dependencies are created on the existence of individual implementation classes. If there is a change in the product mappings in Table 10-2, then corresponding changes will be required in all of the components that need to work with those products. These types of changes are tedious, error-prone, and hard to test.

Understanding the Abstract Factory Pattern

The abstract factory pattern shares a common purpose with the factory method pattern, but it is used to create groups of objects whose relationship is not expressed through a common protocol or base class. In the case of the example application, three objects are required to populate a Car struct, and each of those objects will implement a different protocol: the Floorplan, Suspension, and Drivetrain protocols.

THE FACTORY METHOD VS. THE ABSTRACT FACTORY PATTERNS

There is endless debate about the differences between the factory method and abstract factory patterns and when each should be used. This debate is made more complicated by the way that features of different languages change the implementation and emphasize or hide subtle differences.

My advice is to focus on the intent and not the implementation. If you have a product matrix like the one in Table 10-2 and you need to make sure you don't end up with, for example, the suspension of a sports car being used with the floor plan of an SUV, then use the abstract factory pattern. The abstract factory pattern hides the details of which objects are in a group inside of concrete factory classes, which are in turn hidden from the calling component. This extra complexity makes it easy to add new rows to the product matrix (by creating a new concrete factory) or change the products in an existing row (by modifying a concrete factory).

The factory method pattern is much simpler because it deals with a single object and only has to hide which implementation class is selected. As you will see, I implement the abstract factory pattern by combining multiple factory methods into a single class.

So, in short, ignore the semantic debate and focus on the goal. Use the factory method pattern to create a single object and use the abstract factory pattern if you are trying to manage a set of objects.

The abstract factory pattern addresses the diffusion of the decision logic by consolidating it in one place. The pattern addresses the dependency on specific implementation classes by providing the calling component with access only to the protocols and not the classes that conform to them. There are four operations in the abstract factory pattern, as illustrated by Figure 10-1.

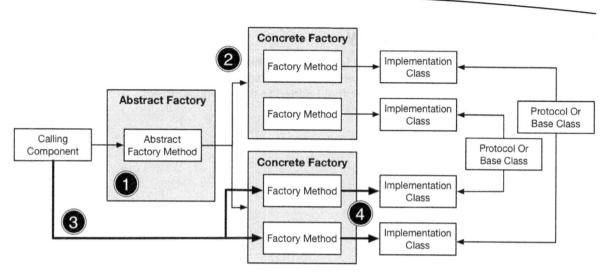

Figure 10-1. *The abstract factory pattern*

The pattern requires the use of an *abstract factory class*, which defines a method that will return an implementation of a protocol or base class. The first operation in the pattern occurs when the calling component invokes the abstract factory method to obtain an object.

For the second operation, the abstract factory method examines the request from the calling component and selects a *concrete factory class*, which is a class that implements the factory method pattern (as described in Chapter 9). An instance of the concrete factory class is created and returned to the caller.

In the third operation, the calling component invokes the factory methods defined by the concrete factory class. This leads to the fourth and final operation, in which the implementation classes are instantiated to provide the calling component with the objects it requires.

When trying to understand this pattern, it helps to focus on how knowledge of other classes is distributed throughout the pattern. The concrete factory knows which implementation classes belong together, and its methods create objects within the same group, even though the classes implement different protocols or are derived from different base classes.

The abstract factory doesn't know about which implementation classes will be used, but it does have knowledge of how to select the appropriate concrete factory for any given request.

The calling component knows only about the factories and the protocols or base classes used by the implementation classes but not directly about the implementation classes. It relies on the abstract factory to provide it with an appropriate concrete factory and relies on the concrete factory to select appropriate implementation classes.

Implementing the Abstract Factory Pattern

In the sections that follow, I show you how to implement the abstract factory pattern in order to create objects to represent the car products that I defined at the start of the chapter.

Creating the Abstract Factory

I am going to start by creating the abstract factory class. This class is at the heart of the pattern because it is used as the base class from which concrete factories are derived. Listing 10-6 shows the contents of a file called `Abstract.swift` that I added to the example project.

Listing 10-6. The Contents of the Abstract.swift File

```swift
class CarFactory {

    func createFloorplan() -> Floorplan {
        fatalError("Not implemented");
    }

    func createSuspension() -> Suspension {
        fatalError("Not implemented");
    }

    func createDrivetrain() -> Drivetrain {
        fatalError("Not implemented");
    }
}
```

The abstract factory is called `CarFactory`, and it defines `createFloorplan`, `createSuspension`, and `createDrivetrain` methods that return objects that implement the three product protocols: `Floorplan`, `Suspension`, and `Drivetrain`. There is just enough functionality in this class for it to be used as a base for the concrete factory classes, which I define in the next section. Once the concrete factory classes are defined, I will return to this class and complete it so that it is capable of selecting and using a concrete factory.

Creating the Concrete Factories

The next step is to create the concrete factory classes, which are responsible for creating a group of product objects that can be used together. I added a file called `Concrete.swift` to the project and used it to define the classes shown in Listing 10-7.

Listing 10-7. The Contents of the Concrete.swift File

```swift
class CompactCarFactory : CarFactory {
    override func createFloorplan() -> Floorplan {
        return StandardFloorplan();
    }
    override func createSuspension() -> Suspension {
        return RoadSuspension();
    }
    override func createDrivetrain() -> Drivetrain {
        return FrontWheelDrive();
    }
}
```

```
class SportsCarFactory : CarFactory {
    override func createFloorplan() -> Floorplan {
        return ShortFloorplan();
    }
    override func createSuspension() -> Suspension {
        return RaceSuspension();
    }
    override func createDrivetrain() -> Drivetrain {
        return RearWheelDrive();
    }
}

class SUVCarFactory : CarFactory {
    override func createFloorplan() -> Floorplan {
        return LongFloorplan();
    }
    override func createSuspension() -> Suspension {
        return OffRoadSuspension();
    }
    override func createDrivetrain() -> Drivetrain {
        return AllWheelDrive();
    }
}
```

Each concrete factory class is derived from the CarFactory class and overrides its methods to create one of the groups of products shown in Table 10-2.

Completing the Abstract Factory

I can now return to the abstract factory class and complete the implementation of the pattern. Listing 10-8 shows the changes that select concrete factories in order to provide calling components with the means to obtain a concrete factory.

Listing 10-8. Completing the Pattern Implementation in the Abstract.swift File

```
class CarFactory {

    func createFloorplan() -> Floorplan {
        fatalError("Not implemented");
    }

    func createSuspension() -> Suspension {
        fatalError("Not implemented");
    }

    func createDrivetrain() -> Drivetrain {
        fatalError("Not implemented");
    }
```

```
    final class func getFactory(car:Cars) -> CarFactory? {
        var factory:CarFactory?
        switch (car) {
            case .COMPACT:
                factory = CompactCarFactory();
            case .SPORTS:
                factory = SportsCarFactory();
            case .SUV:
                factory = SUVCarFactory();
        }
        return factory;
    }
}
```

I have added a type method called getFactory that accepts a value from the Cars enumeration and that selects a concrete factory and returns an instance of it to the calling component. The selected factory is presented to the calling component as a CarFactory object, and details of which concrete factory has been selected—and why—remain private.

Consuming the Abstract Factory Pattern

The last step is to update the code that creates the Car object so that it obtains its products through the abstract factory. Listing 10-9 shows the changes I made to the main.swift file.

Listing 10-9. Consuming the Abstract Factory Pattern in the main.swift File

```
let factory = CarFactory.getFactory(Cars.SPORTS);

if (factory != nil) {
    let car = Car(carType: Cars.SPORTS,
        floor: factory!.createFloorplan(),
        suspension: factory!.createSuspension(),
        drive: factory!.createDrivetrain());

    car.printDetails();
}
```

Rather than instantiate the implementation objects directly, I use the abstract factory class to obtain a concrete factory for the type of car I require and then call the create methods to obtain the implementation objects. If you run the application, you will see the following output:

```
Car type: Porsche Boxter
Seats: 2
Engine: Mid
Suspension: Firm
Drive: Rear
```

As the Listing 10-9 shows, there are no dependencies between the code in the `main.swift` file and the individual product classes. This means that if the matrix shown in Table 10-2 changes, I can update the corresponding concrete factory classes without having to make corresponding changes in the components that consume them. In Listing 10-10, you can see how I changed the drive train option for the sports car.

Listing 10-10. Changing an Implementation Class in the Concrete.swift File

```
...
class SportsCarFactory : CarFactory {
    override func createFloorplan() -> Floorplan {
        return ShortFloorplan();
    }
    override func createSuspension() -> Suspension {
        return RaceSuspension();
    }
    override func createDrivetrain() -> Drivetrain {
        return AllWheelDrive();
    }
}
...
```

The output produced by running the application shows the effect of the change.

```
Car type: Porsche Boxter
Seats: 2
Engine: Mid
Suspension: Firm
Drive: 4WD
```

By consolidating the decisions about which group of products belong together, the concrete factories reduce the impact of change in the application, which makes the decision logic easier to test and maintain. The abstract factory consolidates the decision logic for selecting the concrete factory, further isolating calling components from the details of how groups of implementation classes are associated with one another.

Variations on the Abstract Factory Pattern

There are common variations that you can use to adapt the way that the abstract factory is implemented. As I explain in the following sections, the basic mechanism remains the same, but the implementation is altered to control how objects are created.

Hiding the Abstract Factory Class

The first variation, and the most common, is to hide the implementation of the abstract factory pattern inside the class or struct that calling components use to store the implementation objects. In the case of the example application, this means the Car struct, and Listing 10-11 shows how I have modified it to deal directly with the abstract and concrete factory classes.

Listing 10-11. Hiding the Pattern in the CarParts.swift File

```
enum Cars: String {
    case COMPACT = "VW Golf";
    case SPORTS = "Porsche Boxter";
    case SUV = "Cadillac Escalade";
}

struct Car {
    var carType:Cars;
    var floor:Floorplan;
    var suspension:Suspension;
    var drive:Drivetrain;

    init(carType:Cars) {
        let concreteFactory = CarFactory.getFactory(carType);
        self.floor = concreteFactory!.createFloorplan();
        self.suspension = concreteFactory!.createSuspension();
        self.drive = concreteFactory!.createDrivetrain();
        self.carType = carType;
    }

    func printDetails() {
        println("Car type: \(carType.rawValue)");
        println("Seats: \(floor.seats)");
        println("Engine: \(floor.enginePosition.rawValue)");
        println("Suspension: \(suspension.suspensionType.rawValue)");
        println("Drive: \(drive.driveType.rawValue)");
    }
}
```

I have added an initializer that accepts the type of car that is required as a Cars value, which is used to ask the abstract factory for a concrete factory. The concrete factory is then used to obtain the Floorplan, Suspension, and Drivetrain objects that are required to initialize the object. The effect of this change is to drastically simplify the code in the main.swift file, as shown in Listing 10-12.

Listing 10-12. The Effect of Hiding the Factories in the main.swift File

```
let car = Car(carType: Cars.SPORTS);
car.printDetails();
```

> **Caution**   This approach makes two assumptions about what the calling component is trying to achieve.
> It assumes that it wants to create a Car object and that it requires all three objects. If you do adopt this
> variation, then ensure that the calling component can still access the abstract factory so that it can create the
> objects it needs for whatever purpose it requires them.

Applying the Singleton Pattern to the Concrete Factories

Another common variation is to apply the singleton pattern to the concrete factories. The concrete factories make good singletons because they contain only the logic that is required to create objects from the implementation classes. The first step in applying the singleton pattern is to update the abstract factory class, which is the base class for the concrete factories. Listing 10-13 shows the changes that I made.

Listing 10-13. Preparing for the Singleton Pattern in the Abstract.swift File

```swift
class CarFactory {

    required init() {
        // do nothing
    }

    func createFloorplan() -> Floorplan {
        fatalError("Not implemented");
    }

    func createSuspension() -> Suspension {
        fatalError("Not implemented");
    }

    func createDrivetrain() -> Drivetrain {
        fatalError("Not implemented");
    }

    final class func getFactory(car:Cars) -> CarFactory? {
        var factoryType:CarFactory.Type;
        switch (car) {
            case .COMPACT:
                factoryType = CompactCarFactory.self;
            case .SPORTS:
                factoryType = SportsCarFactory.self;
            case .SUV:
                factoryType = SUVCarFactory.self;
        }
        var factory = factoryType.sharedInstance;
        if (factory == nil) {
            factory = factoryType();
        }
        return factory;
    }

    class var sharedInstance:CarFactory? {
        get {
            return nil;
        }
    }
}
```

I have added a sharedInstance computed type property that the concrete factories can override if they want to be dealt with as singletons. I have changed the implementation of the getfactory method so that it reads the value of the sharedInstance property and returns the result, if there is one, to the caller. Concrete classes that don't override the sharedInstance property will inherit the default implementation, which I deal with by creating a new factory instance to deal with requests. Listing 10-14 shows how I have updated one of the concrete factories so that it will be treated as a singleton.

Listing 10-14. Applying the Singleton Pattern in the Concrete.swift File

```
...
class SportsCarFactory : CarFactory {
    override func createFloorplan() -> Floorplan {
        return ShortFloorplan();
    }
    override func createSuspension() -> Suspension {
        return RaceSuspension();
    }
    override func createDrivetrain() -> Drivetrain {
        return AllWheelDrive();
    }

    override class var sharedInstance:CarFactory? {
        get {
            struct SingletonWrapper {
                static let singleton = SportsCarFactory();
            }
            return SingletonWrapper.singleton;
        }
    }
}
...
```

I have overridden the sharedInstance property of the SportsCarFactory class to implement the singleton pattern, as described in Chapter 6. I have left the other two concrete factory classes unchanged, which means that new instances of those classes will be created each time they are selected to deal with a request from a calling component. By contrast, there will be only one instance of the SportsCarFactory class, which will be used to deal with all requests for which the abstract factory selects it.

Applying the Prototype Pattern to the Implementation Classes

You could also apply the singleton pattern to the implementation classes, but that means all components will operate on the same set of objects, which is suitable only when there is little or no mutable state or when concurrency protections are in place.

A more common variation is to use the prototype pattern to create implementation objects by cloning. In the sections that follow, I prepare the application for use with the prototype pattern and then show you how to implement it.

Preparing the Example Application

The first step is to update the implementation classes so that they can be cloned. This requires more work than you might expect because the NSCopying protocol that is used to implement the prototype pattern won't operate on Swift enumerations. This means I have to create an Objective-C enumeration and import it into Swift to get the behavior I require.

Start by right-clicking the AbstractFactory item in the Project Navigator and select New File from the pop-up menu. Select the Objective-C File template from the list, as shown in Figure 10-2.

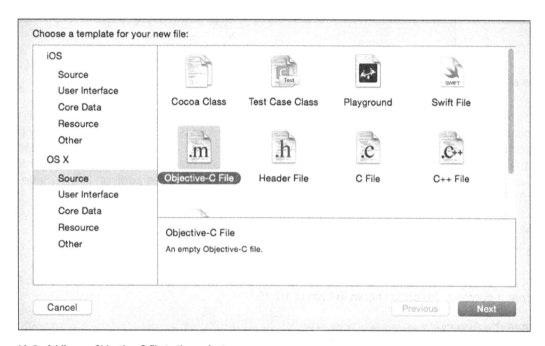

Figure 10-2. Adding an Objective-C file to the project

Click the Next button and set the name of the file to SuspensionOption, as shown in Figure 10-3.

Figure 10-3. Setting the name for the Objective-C file

Click the Next button and save the file alongside the Swift files that are already in the project. When you save the file, Xcode will prompt you to create a bridging header file, as shown in Figure 10-4.

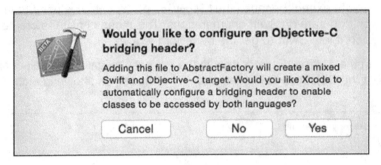

Figure 10-4. The Xcode prompt to create the bridging header file

Click the Yes button to create the file, which is required to import the Objective-C enumeration that I am going to write into Swift. Xcode will create two files. The first is SuspensionOption.m, which is the Objective-C file. I don't need to make any changes to this file; I just created it to get Xcode to set up the bridging header file, which is the other file that Xcode created. The bridging header file is called AbstractFactory-Bridging-Header.h, and Listing 10-15 shows the addition I have made in preparation for the enumeration I am going to define.

Listing 10-15. The Contents of the AbstractFactory-Bridging-Header.h File

```
#import "SuspensionOption.h"
```

Add another file to the project, but this time, add a header file called SuspensionOption.h. Edit the file so that it contains the code shown in Listing 10-16.

Listing 10-16. The Contents of the SuspensionOption.h File

```
#import <Foundation/Foundation.h>

typedef NS_ENUM(NSInteger, SuspensionOption) {
    SuspensionOptionSTANDARD,
    SuspensionOptionSPORTS,
    SuspensionOptionSOFT
};
```

This enumeration will be imported into Swift so that it is a compatible replacement for the one that I defined in the Suspension.swift file. Listing 10-17 shows how I removed the Swift enumeration and prepared for the prototype pattern.

Listing 10-17. Preparing for the Prototype Pattern in the Suspension.swift File

```
import Foundation

@objc protocol Suspension {
    var suspensionType:SuspensionOption { get };
}

//enum SuspensionOption : String {
//    case STANDARD = "Standard"; case SPORTS = "Firm"; case SOFT = "Soft";
//}

class RoadSuspension : Suspension {
    var suspensionType = SuspensionOption.STANDARD;
}

class OffRoadSuspension : Suspension {
    var suspensionType = SuspensionOption.SOFT;
}

class RaceSuspension : NSObject, NSCopying, Suspension {
    var suspensionType = SuspensionOption.SPORTS;

    func copyWithZone(zone: NSZone) -> AnyObject {
        return RaceSuspension();
    }
}
```

I have added the @objc attribute to the Suspension enumeration so that I can perform type casting when I implement the prototype pattern in the concrete factory class shortly. I have commented out the Swift SuspensionOption enumeration so that it doesn't conflict with its Objective-C counterpart. Finally, I modified the RaceSuspension class so that it implements the NSCopying protocol, which allows it to be treated as a prototype.

> **Tip**   The effect of applying the prototype pattern to the implementation classes is minimal because they are so simple. See Chapter 5 for details of when this pattern has more impact.

If you run the application, you will see the following output:

```
Car type: Porsche Boxter
Seats: 2
Engine: Mid
Suspension: 1
Drive: 4WD
```

Notice that the Suspension value is a number. Objective-C doesn't allow strings to be used as the underlying type for enumerations, so I used an integer when I defined the SuspensionOption enumeration in Listing 10-16. As a consequence, the output no longer shows a descriptive string for the suspension.

Applying the Prototype Pattern

It is important to apply the prototype pattern to the implementation classes and not the concrete factories. There are two reasons for this: the first is that you can end up with multiple prototypes unless all of the concrete factories are singletons, which undermines the effect of applying the pattern. The second reason is that knowledge about which implementation classes are treated as prototypes and which should be instantiated will be duplicated throughout the factories, which means that changing the behavior of one implementation class will require a corresponding change in all of the concrete factory classes that use it. Forgetting to make all of these changes will result in an implementation class that is treated inconsistently.

Listing 10-18 shows how I sidestep these problems by defining a method in Suspension protocol that factories will use to obtain a conforming object and allow each implementation class to decide how that object is created.

Listing 10-18. Applying the Prototype Pattern in the Suspension.swift File

```
import Foundation

@objc protocol Suspension {
    var suspensionType:SuspensionOption { get };

    class func getInstance() -> Suspension;
}

class RoadSuspension : Suspension {
    var suspensionType = SuspensionOption.STANDARD;

    private init() {};

    class func getInstance() -> Suspension {
        return RoadSuspension();
    }
}

class OffRoadSuspension : Suspension {
    var suspensionType = SuspensionOption.SOFT;

    private init() {};

    class func getInstance() -> Suspension {
        return OffRoadSuspension();
    }
}
```

```
class RaceSuspension : NSObject, NSCopying, Suspension {
    var suspensionType = SuspensionOption.SPORTS;

    private override init() {};

    func copyWithZone(zone: NSZone) -> AnyObject {
        return RaceSuspension();
    }

    private class var prototype:RaceSuspension {
        get {
            struct SingletonWrapper {
                static let singleton = RaceSuspension();
            }
            return SingletonWrapper.singleton;
        }
    }

    class func getInstance() -> Suspension {
        return prototype.copy() as Suspension;
    }
}
```

> **Tip**   You would apply the pattern to all of the implementation classes in a real project, but I am changing the suspension classes only to avoid repeating similar changes.

I have added a method called getInstance to the Suspension protocol. Each of the implementation classes is required to define this method, and the RoadSuspension and OffRoadSuspension simply create new objects. The RaceSuspension class defines a prototype as a singleton and copies it each time the getInstance method is called.

> **Tip**   I have defined empty private initializers on the implementation classes so they cannot be instantiated directly. Notice that I used the override keyword for the RaceSuspension class because it inherits an empty initializer from the NSObject class, which is the required base class for the NSCopying protocol. See Chapter 5 for details.

In Listing 10-19, you can see how I have updated the concrete factory classes to reflect the changes in the suspension classes.

Listing 10-19. Revising the Consumption of Suspension Classes in the Concrete.swift File

```swift
class CompactCarFactory : CarFactory {
    override func createFloorplan() -> Floorplan {
        return StandardFloorplan();
    }
    override func createSuspension() -> Suspension {
        return RoadSuspension.getInstance();
    }
    override func createDrivetrain() -> Drivetrain {
        return FrontWheelDrive();
    }
}

class SportsCarFactory : CarFactory {

    override func createFloorplan() -> Floorplan {
        return ShortFloorplan();
    }
    override func createSuspension() -> Suspension {
        return RaceSuspension.getInstance();
    }
    override func createDrivetrain() -> Drivetrain {
        return AllWheelDrive();
    }

    override class var sharedInstance:CarFactory? {
        get {
            struct SingletonWrapper {
                static let singleton = SportsCarFactory();
            }
            return SingletonWrapper.singleton;
        }
    }
}

class SUVCarFactory : CarFactory {
    override func createFloorplan() -> Floorplan {
        return LongFloorplan();
    }
    override func createSuspension() -> Suspension {
        return OffRoadSuspension.getInstance();
    }
    override func createDrivetrain() -> Drivetrain {
        return AllWheelDrive();
    }
}
```

With these changes in place, instances of the RaceSuspension class are created through the prototype pattern. This fact is hidden from the concrete factory classes, which makes it easy to change the behavior of individual implementation classes without further changes to the concrete factories.

Understanding the Pitfalls of the Pattern

The main pitfall for this pattern is blurring the lines between the different components. Specifically, the abstract factory class should contain the decision logic only for selecting a concrete factory and not for implementation classes. Equally, the concrete factories should contain the logic for selecting implementation classes and not provide any of the functionality defined by the product protocols.

The only other pitfall to avoid arises when combining this pattern with the object pool pattern that I described in Chapter 7. This is a disastrous combination if you try to manage separate pools for each implementation class and make calling components wait for a combination of objects to become available. Object pooling works best when all of the components require the same type of object, and trying to queue access to overlapping sets of objects will often lead to deadlocks when two components have acquired a free object required by the other. If you do try to combine these patterns, ensure that your calling components always acquire objects from the pools in the same order and that you pay particular attention to avoiding deadlocks.

Examples of the Pattern in Cocoa

It is not possible to tell whether the factory method or abstract factory pattern has been used when you create a Cocoa object. As the recipient of the object, you simply don't know whether you have received a concrete factory or just a regular object whose class was selected based on your request. It doesn't help that Apple conflates the factory method and abstract factory patterns in its documentation, which is why you will often hear class clusters described as an implementation of both patterns.

This is exactly how it should be because both patterns are all about hiding decisions and implementations from the calling components, and the only way you can tell which pattern has been used is to look at the source code. The implementation of either pattern would be flawed if you could tell by any other means.

Applying the Pattern to the SportsStore Application

To demonstrate how to apply the abstract factory pattern, I am going to change the way that the total value of the SportsStore stock is produced so that different currencies and currency rates can be selected. In the sections that follow, I'll walk through the process of defining the protocols and implementation classes that will convert the stock value and prepare it for display and of delivering those classes via abstract and concrete factories.

Preparing the Example Application

No preparation is required for this chapter; I am going to pick up the project just as I left it in Chapter 9.

> **Tip**   Do not forget that you can download the source code for every chapter from Apress.com in case you don't want to re-create the SportsStore project manually.

Defining the Implementation Protocols and Classes

The first step is to create a file that will contain the definitions for the implementation classes and the protocols through which their functionality will be expressed. Listing 10-20 shows the contents of the StockValueImplementations.swift file, which I added to the SportsStore project.

Listing 10-20. The Contents of the StockValueImplementations.swift File

```
import Foundation

protocol StockValueFormatter {
    func formatTotal(total:Double) -> String;
}

class DollarStockValueFormatter : StockValueFormatter {
    func formatTotal(total:Double) -> String {
        let formatted = Utils.currencyStringFromNumber(total);
        return "\(formatted)";
    }
}

class PoundStockValueFormatter : StockValueFormatter {
    func formatTotal(total:Double) -> String {
        let formatted = Utils.currencyStringFromNumber(total);
        return "£\(dropFirst(formatted))";
    }
}

protocol StockValueConverter {
    func convertTotal(total:Double) -> Double;
}

class DollarStockValueConverter : StockValueConverter {
    func convertTotal(total:Double) -> Double {
        return total;
    }
}

class PoundStockValueConverter : StockValueConverter {
    func convertTotal(total:Double) -> Double {
        return 0.60338 * total;
    }
}
```

I have defined two protocols and two families of implementation classes. The protocols are called StockValueFormatter and StockValueConverter. The StockValueConverter protocol is responsible for converting the currency amount from dollars, and the StockValueFormatter protocol is responsible for preparing the currency amount. I have created two families of implementation classes, one of which simply passes the dollar amount on without any modification and the other converts the amount to British pounds.

Defining the Abstract and Concrete Factory Classes

I defined the abstract factory and concrete factory classes in a new file called StockValueFactories. swift, the contents of which are shown in Listing 10-21.

Listing 10-21. The Contents of the StockValueFactories.swift File

```
import Foundation

class StockTotalFactory {

    enum Currency {
        case USD
        case GBP
    }

    private(set) var formatter:StockValueFormatter?;
    private(set) var converter:StockValueConverter?;

    class func getFactory(curr:Currency) -> StockTotalFactory {
        if (curr == Currency.USD) {
            return DollarStockTotalFactory.sharedInstance;
        } else {
            return PoundStockTotalFactory.sharedInstance;
        }
    }
}

private class DollarStockTotalFactory : StockTotalFactory {

    private override init() {
        super.init();
        formatter = DollarStockValueFormatter();
        converter = DollarStockValueConverter();
    }

    class var sharedInstance:StockTotalFactory {
        get {
            struct SingletonWrapper {
                static let singleton = DollarStockTotalFactory();
            }
            return SingletonWrapper.singleton;
        }
    }
}

private class PoundStockTotalFactory : StockTotalFactory {

    private override init() {
        super.init();
        formatter = PoundStockValueFormatter();
        converter = PoundStockValueConverter();
    }
```

```
class var sharedInstance:StockTotalFactory {
    get {
        struct SingletonWrapper {
            static let singleton = PoundStockTotalFactory();
        }
        return SingletonWrapper.singleton;
    }
}
}
```

The `StockTotalFactory` class is the abstract factory, and it selects between the concrete classes, `DollarStockTotalFactory` and `PoundStockTotalFactory`, based on a value from the `Currency` enumeration passed to the `getFactory` method. The effect is the matrix shown in Table 10-3.

Table 10-3. The Currency to Formatter/Converter Mappings

Currency	StockValueFormatter	StockValueConverter
USD	DollarStockValueFormatter	DollarStockValueConverter
GBP	PoundStockValueFormatter	PoundStockValueConverter

Consuming the Factories and Implementation Classes

The last step is to use the abstract factory to convert and format the value of the stock. Listing 10-22 shows the changes I made to the `ViewController.swift` file.

Listing 10-22. Consuming the Abstract Factory Pattern in the ViewController.swift File

```
...
func displayStockTotal() {
    let finalTotals:(Int, Double) = productStore.products.reduce((0, 0.0),
        {(totals, product) -> (Int, Double) in
            return (
                totals.0 + product.stockLevel,
                totals.1 + product.stockValue
            );
        });

    var factory = StockTotalFactory.getFactory(StockTotalFactory.Currency.GBP);
    var totalAmount = factory.converter?.convertTotal(finalTotals.1);
    var formatted = factory.formatter?.formatTotal(totalAmount!);

    totalStockLabel.text = "\(finalTotals.0) Products in Stock. "
        + "Total Value: \(formatted!)";
}
...
```

I have specified the GBP currency, which selects the implementation class family responsible for handling British pounds. When you run the application, the total value of the stock will be converted from dollars to pounds and displayed in the application, as shown in Figure 10-5.

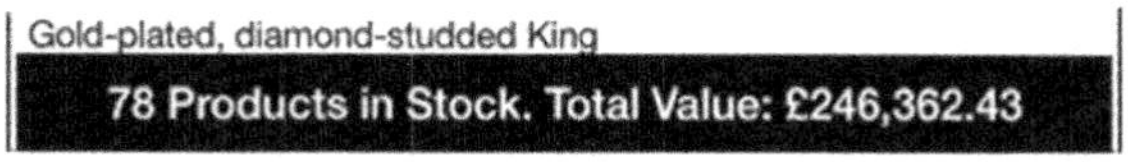

Figure 10-5. *Converting and formatting the value of the stock*

The ViewController class is able to format the stock value without needing any details about the concrete class that has been selected and the implementation classes that it provides.

Summary

In this chapter, I explained how the abstract factory pattern can be used to create objects that are part of a group or family but that do not conform to a common protocol or share a common base class. In the next chapter, I describe the builder pattern.

The Builder Pattern

The builder pattern is used to separate the configuration of an object from its creation. The calling component has the configuration data and passes it to an intermediary—the builder—that is responsible for creating an object on behalf of the component. This separation can reduce the amount of knowledge that the calling component has about the objects it uses and concentrates default configuration values in the builder class, rather than being required in every component that creates objects. Table 11-1 puts the builder pattern in context.

Table 11-1. *Putting the Builder Pattern into Context*

Question	Answer
What is it?	The builder pattern puts the logic and default configuration values required to create an object into a builder class. This allows calling components to create objects with minimal configuration data and without needing to know the default values that will be used to create the object.
What are the benefits?	This pattern makes it easier to change the default configuration values used to create an object and to change the class from which instances are created.
When should you use this pattern?	Use this pattern when a complex configuration process is required to create an object and you don't want the default configuration values to be disseminated throughout the application.
When should you avoid this pattern?	Don't use this pattern when every data value required to create an object will be different for each instance.
How do you know when you have implemented the pattern correctly?	The calling component can create objects by providing just the data values for which there are no default values (although values may also be provided to override some or all of the defaults).
Are there any common pitfalls?	No.
Are there any related patterns?	This pattern can be combined with the factory method or abstract factory patterns to change the implementation class used to create the object based on the configuration data provided by the calling component.

Preparing the Example Project

For this chapter, I created a new OS X Command Line Tool project called Builder. I added a file called **Food.swift** to the project and used it to define the class shown in Listing 11-1.

Listing 11-1. The Contents of the Food.swift File

```
class Burger {
    let customerName:String;
    let veggieProduct:Bool;
    let patties:Int;
    let pickles:Bool;
    let mayo:Bool;
    let ketchup:Bool;
    let lettuce:Bool;
    let cook:Cooked;

    enum Cooked : String {
        case RARE = "Rare";
        case NORMAL = "Normal";
        case WELLDONE = "Well Done";
    }

    init(name:String, veggie:Bool, patties:Int, pickles:Bool, mayo:Bool,
            ketchup:Bool, lettuce:Bool, cook:Cooked) {

        self.customerName = name;
        self.veggieProduct = veggie;
        self.patties = patties;
        self.pickles = pickles;
        self.mayo = mayo;
        self.ketchup = ketchup;
        self.lettuce = lettuce;
        self.cook = cook;
    }

    func printDescription() {
        println("Name \(self.customerName)");
        println("Veggie: \(self.veggieProduct)");
        println("Patties: \(self.patties)");
        println("Pickles: \(self.pickles)");
        println("Mayo: \(self.mayo)");
        println("Ketchup: \(self.ketchup)");
        println("Lettuce: \(self.lettuce)");
        println("Cook: \(self.cook.rawValue)");
    }
}
```

The **Burger** class represents an order in a restaurant and defines constant values for the different aspects of the order that are set through the constructor. The **printDescription** method writes out the values of the constants to the debug console. Listing 11-2 shows how I edited the **main.swift** file to create a **Burger** object and call the **printDescription** method.

Listing 11-2. The Contents of the main.swift File

```
let order = Burger(name: "Joe", veggie: false, patties: 2, pickles: true,
    mayo: true, ketchup: true, lettuce: true, cook: Burger.Cooked.NORMAL);

order.printDescription();
```

Running the application produces the following output:

```
Name Joe
Veggie: false
Patties: 2
Pickles: true
Mayo: true
Ketchup: true
Lettuce: true
Cook: Normal
```

Understanding the Problems That the Pattern Solves

The problem addressed by the builder pattern arises when an object requires a large number of configuration data values, not all of which the calling component has values for. In the case of the **Burger** class, the initializer requires values for every aspect of the burger it represents. Here is the ordering process that is followed in my imaginary restaurant:

1. The server asks the customer for their name.

2. The server asks the customer whether they require a vegetarian meal.

3. The server asks whether the customer wants to customize their burger.

4. The server asks whether the customer wants to upgrade and buy an additional patty.

There are only four steps in this process, but it throws up some issues. Listing 11-3 shows how I can model the process in the **main.swift** file to change the way I create **Burger** objects.

Listing 11-3. Implementing the Order Process in the main.swift File

```
// Step 1 - Ask for name
let name = "Joe";

// Step 2 - Is veggie meal required?
let veggie = false;

// Step 3 - Customize burger?
let pickles = true;
let mayo = false;
let ketchup = true;
let lettuce = true;
let cooked = Burger.Cooked.NORMAL;
```

```
// Step 4 - Buy additional patty?
let patties = 2;

let order = Burger(name: name, veggie: veggie, patties: patties, pickles: pickles,
    mayo: mayo, ketchup: ketchup, lettuce: lettuce, cook: cooked);

order.printDescription();
```

The **Burger** initializer requires calling components to understand the default configuration values when the customer doesn't want to change them—for example, knowing that a standard burger comes with two patties and has ketchup. Each component that requires a **Burger** object has to have this knowledge, and the effect is that a change in the default values must be implemented in every calling component.

UNDERSTANDING THE TELESCOPING INITIALIZER ANTI-PATTERN

In other languages, the builder pattern is used as an alternative to the *telescoping initializer* or *telescoping constructor* anti-pattern. Anti-patterns are commonly used techniques that don't solve the problem they are intended to address or solve a problem in a difficult or dangerous way. In some languages, the telescoping constructor pattern is a commonly used technique intended to simplify working with classes that define a lot of initializer parameters. Consider this class:

```
...
class Milkshake {

    enum Size { case SMALL; case MEDIUM; case LARGE };
    enum Flavor { case CHOCOLATE; case STRAWBERRY; case VANILLA };

    let count:Int;
    let size:Size;
    let flavor:Flavor;

    init(flavor:Flavor, size:Size, count:Int) {
        self.count = count;
        self.size = size;
        self.flavor = flavor;
    }
}
...
```

The **Milkshake** class defines an initializer with three parameters. This requires calling components to know what the default values are for the parameters and to provide values even when the defaults are required, like this:

```
...
var shake = Milkshake(
    flavor: Milkshake.Flavor.CHOCOLATE,
    size: Milkshake.Size.MEDIUM,
    count: 1
);
...
```

Most customers will want a single medium shake and specify only a flavor. The telescoping initializer anti-pattern tries to improve the situation by defining convenience initializers that provide default values, like this:

```
...
class Milkshake {

    enum Size { case SMALL; case MEDIUM; case LARGE };
    enum Flavor { case CHOCOLATE; case STRAWBERRY; case VANILLA };

    let count:Int;
    let size:Size;
    let flavor:Flavor;

    init(flavor:Flavor, size:Size, count:Int) {
        self.count = count;
        self.size = size;
        self.flavor = flavor;
    }

    convenience init(flavor:Flavor, size:Size) {
        self.init(flavor:flavor, size:size, count:1);
    }

    convenience init(flavor:Flavor) {
        self.init(flavor:flavor, size:Size.MEDIUM);
    }
}
...
```

Each convenience initializer omits an additional parameter and calls the preceding initializer with a default value. It allows objects to be created without the calling component knowing the default values for the parameters that it doesn't provide, like this:

```
...
var shake = Milkshake(flavor: Milkshake.Flavor.CHOCOLATE);
...
```

Telescoping initializers are considered to be an anti-pattern because they result in a large number of initializers that are hard to read and maintain. You can avoid telescoping initializers in Swift by using default parameter values, like this:

```
...
class Milkshake {

    enum Size { case SMALL; case MEDIUM; case LARGE };
    enum Flavor { case CHOCOLATE; case STRAWBERRY; case VANILLA };

    let count:Int;
    let size:Size;
    let flavor:Flavor;
```

```
init(flavor:Flavor, size:Size = Size.MEDIUM, count:Int = 1) {
    self.count = count;
    self.size = size;
    self.flavor = flavor;
}
}
...
```

The default values for the **size** and **count** parameters are used whenever the component that wants to create a **Milkshake** object omits them. This has the benefit of defining the default values within the **Milkshake** class without needing to define permutations of initializers.

Understanding the Builder Pattern

The builder pattern solves the problem by introducing an intermediary—called the *builder*—between a component and the object it needs to work with. As Figure 11-1 shows, there are three operations in the builder pattern.

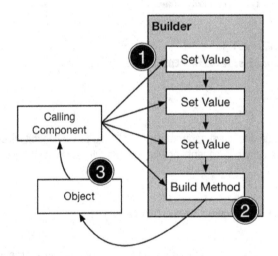

Figure 11-1. The builder pattern

In the first operation, the calling component provides the builder with an item of data that replaces one of the default values used to create an object. The operation is repeated each time the calling component obtains a new value from the process it is following. In the case of my burger-ordering process, the calling component is able to provide the builder with new data after each stage in the sequence.

In the second operation, the calling component asks the builder to create an object. This signals to the builder that there will be no new data and that an object should be created using the data values it has received so far, along with default values for the data items that were not specified by the calling component.

In the third operation, the builder creates an object and returns it to the calling component with an object.

The calling component knows *what* is required—a burger with no ketchup, for example—but it doesn't know *how* to create it. The builder class knows *how* to create a burger and knows the default configuration, but it doesn't know *what* the customer wants for any specific order. The builder pattern brings the "what" and the "how" together without letting the calling component become tightly coupled to the objects it requires.

Implementing the Builder Pattern

In the sections that follow, I demonstrate how to apply the builder pattern to the example project in order to decouple the creation process for the **Burger** class from the components that use **Burger** objects.

Defining the Builder Class

The first step is to define the builder class, which contains the default values for the **Burger** initializer parameters and contains the means to allow calling components to change those values. Listing 11-4 shows the contents of the **Builder.swift** file, which I added to the example project.

Listing 11-4. The Contents of the Builder.swift File

```
class BurgerBuilder {
    private var veggie  = false;
    private var pickles = true;
    private var mayo    = true;
    private var ketchup = true;
    private var lettuce = true;
    private var cooked  = Burger.Cooked.NORMAL;
    private var patties = 2;

    func setVeggie(choice: Bool)  { self.veggie  = choice; }
    func setPickles(choice: Bool) { self.pickles = choice; }
    func setMayo(choice: Bool)    { self.mayo    = choice; }
    func setKetchup(choice: Bool) { self.ketchup = choice; }
    func setLettuce(choice: Bool) { self.lettuce = choice; }
    func setCooked(choice: Burger.Cooked) { self.cooked = choice; }
    func addPatty(choice: Bool)   { self.patties = choice ? 3 : 2; }

    func buildObject(name: String) -> Burger {
        return Burger(name: name, veggie: veggie, patties: patties,
            pickles: pickles, mayo: mayo, ketchup: ketchup,
            lettuce: lettuce, cook: cooked);
    }
}
```

The **BurgerBuilder** class defines methods that will change the data values used to create a **Burger** object. Only the **name** parameter on the **Burger** initializer doesn't have a default value, so the **buildObject** method accepts a **name** argument. The class responds to the **buildObject** method being called by creating a **Burger** object using the **name** value, the values provided via the other methods, and the default values.

> **Tip**   I could have used properties in the class, but I prefer to use methods because I can clearly indicate the values for which there are no defaults by defining parameters on the **buildObject** method. I demonstrate how to use properties to create a builder when I apply the pattern to the SportsStore application later in this chapter.

There is a direct mapping to the underlying properties for almost all of the methods defined by the class. The exception is the **addPatty** method, which allows the calling component to specify a number of patties—just by specifying whether an extra one should be added. This approach allows me to handle extra patties without making the calling component aware of what the default number is.

Consuming the Builder

The next step is to use the builder to create an object. Listing 11-5 shows the changes I made to the **main.swift** file.

Listing 11-5. Consuming the Builder Pattern in the main.swift File

```
var builder = BurgerBuilder();

// Step 1 - Ask for name
let name = "Joe";

// Step 2 - Is veggie meal required?
builder.setVeggie(false);

// Step 3 - Customize burger?
builder.setMayo(false);
builder.setCooked(Burger.Cooked.WELLDONE);

// Step 4 - Buy additional patty?
builder.addPatty(false);

let order = builder.buildObject(name);

order.printDescription();
```

This may appear similar to the way I created **Burger** objects without the builder pattern, but using the builder as an intermediary leads to improvements in flexibility by isolating the impact of change.

Understanding the Impact of the Pattern

The first improvement is that it is possible to change a default value in the builder without having to make changes to the calling component or to the **Burger** class. If most customers choose not to have pickles—presumably because they are weird and horrible and ruin a good burger—then the restaurant can update its menu to make burgers without them. Listing 11-6 shows the change to the builder class.

Listing 11-6. Disabling Pickles in the Builder.swift File

```
class BurgerBuilder {
    private var veggie  = false;
    private var pickles = false;
    private var mayo    = true;
    private var ketchup = true;
    private var lettuce = true;
    private var cooked  = Burger.Cooked.NORMAL;
    private var patties = 2;

    func setVeggie(choice: Bool)  { self.veggie  = choice; }
    func setPickles(choice: Bool) { self.pickles = choice; }
    func setMayo(choice: Bool)    { self.mayo    = choice; }
    func setKetchup(choice: Bool) { self.ketchup = choice; }
    func setLettuce(choice: Bool) { self.lettuce = choice; }
    func setCooked(choice: Burger.Cooked) { self.cooked = choice; }
    func addPatty(choice: Bool)   { self.patties = choice ? 3 : 2; }

    func buildObject(name: String) -> Burger {
        return Burger(name: name, veggie: veggie, patties: patties,
            pickles: pickles, mayo: mayo, ketchup: ketchup,
            lettuce: lettuce, cook: cooked);
    }
}
```

The calling component isn't aware that the default has changed, and neither is the **Burger** class, but **Burger** objects will now be created without pickles unless the customer specifically asks for them. You can see the effect in the output produced by running the application.

```
Name Joe
Veggie: false
Patties: 2
Pickles: false
Mayo: false
Ketchup: true
Lettuce: true
Cook: Well Done
```

Changing the Process

The second improvement is that I can change or streamline the ordering process without needing to make changes in the builder or the **Burger** class. The upgrade of an additional patty may have been a limited-time offer, and the restaurant may have been asking all customers if they want a vegetarian burger in order to draw attention to a new product. I can still use the builder to create **Burger** objects, even if I omit these steps from the process, as shown in Listing 11-7.

Listing 11-7. Revising the Process in the main.swift File

```swift
var builder = BurgerBuilder();

// Step 1 - Ask for name
let name = "Joe";

// Step 2 - Customize burger?
builder.setMayo(false);
builder.setCooked(Burger.Cooked.WELLDONE);

let order = builder.buildObject(name);

order.printDescription();
```

The customer still gets the same order even though the process has changed. This isn't a universal benefit, however; adding new steps to the process can require other changes.

Changing the Object

The third improvement is that I can change the **Burger** class and absorb the impact of the change in the builder class so that it doesn't propagate to the calling components. Listing 11-8 shows what happens to the **Burger** class when the restaurant adds bacon to the menu.

Listing 11-8. Adding Bacon to the Food.swift File

```swift
class Burger {
    let customerName:String;
    let veggieProduct:Bool;
    let patties:Int;
    let pickles:Bool;
    let mayo:Bool;
    let ketchup:Bool;
    let lettuce:Bool;
    let cook:Cooked;
    let bacon:Bool;

    enum Cooked : String {
        case RARE = "Rare";
        case NORMAL = "Normal";
        case WELLDONE = "Well Done";
    }
```

```
init(name:String, veggie:Bool, patties:Int, pickles:Bool, mayo:Bool,
        ketchup:Bool, lettuce:Bool, cook:Cooked, bacon:Bool) {

    self.customerName  = name;
    self.veggieProduct = veggie;
    self.patties       = patties;
    self.pickles       = pickles;
    self.mayo          = mayo;
    self.ketchup       = ketchup;
    self.lettuce       = lettuce;
    self.cook          = cook;
    self.bacon         = bacon;
}

func printDescription() {
    println("Name     \(self.customerName)");
    println("Veggie:  \(self.veggieProduct)");
    println("Patties: \(self.patties)");
    println("Pickles: \(self.pickles)");
    println("Mayo:    \(self.mayo)");
    println("Ketchup: \(self.ketchup)");
    println("Lettuce: \(self.lettuce)");
    println("Cook:    \(self.cook.rawValue)");
    println("Bacon:   \(self.bacon)");
}
}
```

Adding bacon to the menu has changed the **Burger** initializer, which requires a corresponding change in the builder protocol and class, as shown in Listing 11-9.

Listing 11-9. Updating the Builder Protocol and Class in the Builder.swift File

```
class BurgerBuilder {
    private var veggie  = false;
    private var pickles = false;
    private var mayo    = true;
    private var ketchup = true;
    private var lettuce = true;
    private var cooked  = Burger.Cooked.NORMAL;
    private var patties = 2;
    private var bacon   = true;

    func setVeggie(choice: Bool)  { self.veggie  = choice; }
    func setPickles(choice: Bool) { self.pickles = choice; }
    func setMayo(choice: Bool)    { self.mayo    = choice; }
    func setKetchup(choice: Bool) { self.ketchup = choice; }
    func setLettuce(choice: Bool) { self.lettuce = choice; }
    func setCooked(choice: Burger.Cooked) { self.cooked = choice; }
    func addPatty(choice: Bool)   { self.patties = choice ? 3 : 2; }
    func setBacon(choice: Bool)   { self.bacon = choice; }
```

```
func buildObject(name: String) -> Burger {
    return Burger(name: name, veggie: veggie, patties: patties,
        pickles: pickles, mayo: mayo, ketchup: ketchup,
        lettuce: lettuce, cook: cooked, bacon: bacon);
  }
}
```

> **Tip** Notice that the default setting for bacon is contained in the builder and not the **Burger** class.

The components that require **Burger** objects can use the builder without modification, as long as they are happy to receive burgers that have bacon by default.

```
Name Joe
Veggie: false
Patties: 2
Pickles: false
Mayo: false
Ketchup: true
Lettuce: true
Cook: Well Done
Bacon: true
```

Avoiding Inconsistent Configurations

The final improvement is that the builder class can be used to avoid inconsistent configurations that prevent an object from being created. As an example, adding bacon by default to all burgers is unlikely to be popular with customers who order vegetarian burgers. Listing 11-10 shows how I can handle this situation in the builder class.

Listing 11-10. Dealing with Inconsistent Configurations in the Builder.swift File

```
...
func setVeggie(choice: Bool) {
    self.veggie = choice;
    if (choice) {
        self.bacon = false;
    }
}
...
```

I have updated the **setVeggie** method to remove bacon if a vegetarian burger is requested. This doesn't preclude customers from requesting bacon as a customization, however, and still leaves the calling component in charge of the ordering process.

Variations on the Builder Pattern

You can create variations on the builder pattern by combining it with other patterns, usually the factory method or abstract factory patterns (which I described in Chapter 9 and Chapter 10).

The combination that I use most often is to define multiple builder classes that define different sets of default values and apply them through the factory method pattern. Listing 11-11 shows how I have added a new builder for a different type of burger and added a factory method that allows a builder to be selected.

Listing 11-11. Combining the Builder and Factory Method Patterns in the Builder.swift File

```
enum Burgers {
    case STANDARD; case BIGBURGER; case SUPERVEGGIE;
}

class BurgerBuilder {
    private var veggie  = false;
    private var pickles = false;
    private var mayo    = true;
    private var ketchup = true;
    private var lettuce = true;
    private var cooked  = Burger.Cooked.NORMAL;
    private var patties = 2;
    private var bacon   = true;

    private init() {
        // do nothing
    }

    func setVeggie(choice: Bool) {
        self.veggie = choice;
        if (choice) {
            self.bacon = false;
        }
    }

    func setPickles(choice: Bool) { self.pickles = choice; }
    func setMayo(choice: Bool)    { self.mayo    = choice; }
    func setKetchup(choice: Bool) { self.ketchup = choice; }
    func setLettuce(choice: Bool) { self.lettuce = choice; }
    func setCooked(choice: Burger.Cooked) { self.cooked = choice; }
    func addPatty(choice: Bool)   { self.patties = choice ? 3 : 2; }
    func setBacon(choice: Bool)   { self.bacon   = choice; }

    func buildObject(name: String) -> Burger {
        return Burger(name: name, veggie: veggie, patties: patties,
            pickles: pickles, mayo: mayo, ketchup: ketchup,
            lettuce: lettuce, cook: cooked, bacon: bacon);
    }
```

```
    class func getBuilder(burgerType:Burgers) -> BurgerBuilder {
        var builder:BurgerBuilder;
        switch (burgerType) {
            case .BIGBURGER: builder    = BigBurgerBuilder();
            case .SUPERVEGGIE: builder = SuperVeggieBurgerBuilder();
            case .STANDARD: builder     = BurgerBuilder();
        }
        return builder;
    }
}

class BigBurgerBuilder : BurgerBuilder {

    private override init() {
        super.init();
        self.patties = 4;
        self.bacon = false;
    }

    override func addPatty(choice: Bool) {
        fatalError("Cannot add patty to Big Burger");
    }
}

class SuperVeggieBurgerBuilder : BurgerBuilder {

    private override init() {
        super.init();
        self.veggie = true;
        self.bacon = false;
    }

    override func setVeggie(choice: Bool) {
        // do nothing - always veggie
    }

    override func setBacon(choice: Bool) {
        fatalError("Cannot add bacon to this burger");
    }
}
```

I have created an enumeration called **Burgers** that details the range of burgers that are on offer, and I have defined a factory method in the **BurgerBuilder** class that accepts a **Burgers** value and selects a builder that will be returned to the caller. The **BurgerBuilder** class will continue to be used for the **STANDARD** burger, but I have created subclasses that will handle the new **BigBurger** and **SuperVeggieBurger** products.

The new builders revise the default values for the different burger components to create different starting points for the ordering process and to restrict the set of possible changes, such as preventing an extra patty from being added to the **BigBurger** or adding bacon to a **SuperVeggieBurger**.

To take advantage of these changes, I have to revise my ordering process so that the server asks what kind of burger the customer requires, as shown in Listing 11-12.

Listing 11-12. Revising the Ordering Process in the main.swift File

```
// Step 1 - Ask for name
let name = "Joe";

// Step 2 - Select a Product
let builder = BurgerBuilder.getBuilder(Burgers.BIGBURGER);

// Step 3 - Customize burger?
builder.setMayo(false);
builder.setCooked(Burger.Cooked.WELLDONE);

let order = builder.buildObject(name);

order.printDescription();
```

Understanding the Pitfalls of the Builder Pattern

There are no pitfalls to this pattern as long as you remember that the default values used to create the object should be defined in the builder class and not the calling component.

Examples of the Builder Pattern in Cocoa

The most commonly used example of the builder pattern can be found in the **NSDateComponents** class in the **Foundation** framework. The **NSDateComponents** class is a builder that allows a calling component to specify settings that can be used to produce an **NSDate** object that represents a calendar date. Listing 11-13 shows the contents of an Xcode playground I created called **DateBuilder.playground**.

Listing 11-13. The Contents of the DateBuilder.playground File

```
import Foundation;

var builder = NSDateComponents();

builder.hour     = 10;
builder.day      = 6;
builder.month    = 9;
builder.year     = 1940;
builder.calendar = NSCalendar(calendarIdentifier: NSGregorianCalendar);

var date         = builder.date;

println(date!);
```

I create the builder by instantiating the **NSDateComponents** class, and I configure the object that will be produced by setting the properties it defines. I have set values for the **hour**, **day**, **month**, **year**, and **calendar** properties to replace the default values defined by the builder.

To create the object, I read the value of the **date** property and receive an **NSDate** object that has been configured with the values I provided. I write the value to the console, which displays the following output in the playground console:

```
1940-09-06 09:00:00 +0000
```

I did not provide the builder with values for all the components that make up a date, so the builder has used its defaults for the minutes, seconds, and time zone components, which is why those parts of the date are set to zero.

By implementing the builder pattern, the **NSDateComponents** class allows me to configure a date by specifying a limited number of values in the order that suits me. The builder doesn't create the **NSDate** object until the **date** property is read, which allows me to provide data as it becomes available.

Applying the Pattern to the SportsStore Application

In this section, I will demonstrate a common use of the builder pattern and produce a serialized representation of an object. I'll also show you how to use properties rather than methods to create the builder.

Preparing the Example Application

I pick up the SportsStore application as I left it in Chapter 10. I am going to implement the builder pattern to create a serialized representation of a change to the product data. I added a new file called **ChangeRecord.swift** to the SportsStore project and used it to define the class shown in Listing 11-14.

Listing 11-14. The Contents of the ChangeRecord.swift File

```swift
class ChangeRecord : Printable {
    private let outerTag:String;
    private let productName:String;
    private let catName:String;
    private let innerTag:String;
    private let value:String;

    private init(outer:String, name:String, category:String,
            inner:String, value:String) {

        self.outerTag    = outer;
        self.productName = name;
        self.catName     = category;
        self.innerTag    = inner;
        self.value       = value;
    }

    var description : String {
        return "<\(outerTag)><\(innerTag) name=\"\(productName)\"" +
            " category=\"\(catName)\">\(value)</\(innerTag)></\(outerTag)>"
    }
}
```

The **ChangeRecord** class is used to create an XML-style string that represents change. The class defines a set of properties that are used to configure the string. The **ChangeRecord** class implements the **Printable** protocol, which means that its **description** property will be used when an instance of the class is passed to the **println** function.

Defining the Builder Class

To implement the builder pattern, I created a new class called **ChangeRecordBuilder**, as shown in Listing 11-15.

Listing 11-15. Defining a Builder Class in the ChangeRecord.swift File

```swift
class ChangeRecord : Printable {
    // ...statements omitted for brevity...
}

class ChangeRecordBuilder {
    var outerTag:String;
    var innerTag:String;
    var productName:String?;
    var category:String?;
    var value:String?;

    init() {
        outerTag = "change";
        innerTag = "product";
    }

    var changeRecord:ChangeRecord? {
        get {
            if (productName != nil && category != nil && value != nil) {
                return ChangeRecord(outer: outerTag, name: productName!,
                    category: category!, inner: innerTag, value: value!);
            } else {
                return nil;
            }
        }
    }
}
```

I have used properties to implement the pattern in the **ChangeRecordBuilder** class, which requires a different approach than when using methods. The **ChangeRecordBuilder** provides default values for the **outerTag** and **innerTag** properties but requires the calling component to provide values for the **productName**, **category**, and **value** properties.

The **changeRecord** property has to check to see that the required values are provided before it creates a **ChangeRecord** object, but there is no way for the **ChangeRecordBuilder** class to indicate when a required value is missing. The best I can do is to return an optional type from the **changeRecord** property when a value is missing. (It is for this reason that I prefer to use methods to implement the builder pattern.)

Using the Builder Class

To use the builder, I have updated the **Logger** class so that the default callback uses **ChangeRecord** objects to write messages to the console, as shown in Listing 11-16.

Listing 11-16. Using the Builder Class in the Logger.swift File

```
import Foundation;

let productLogger = Logger<Product>(callback: {p in

    var builder          = ChangeRecordBuilder();
    builder.productName = p.name;
    builder.category    = p.category;
    builder.value       = String(p.stockLevel);
    builder.outerTag    = "stockChange";

    var changeRecord = builder.changeRecord;
    if (changeRecord != nil) {
        println(builder.changeRecord!);
    }
});

final class Logger<T where T:NSObject, T:NSCopying> {
    // ...statements omitted for brevity...
}
```

You can see the effect of the changes by starting the application and changing the stock level for one of the products. The debug console will show a message like this one (I formatted it to make it easier to read):

```
<stockChange>
    <product name="Lifejacket" category="Watersports">15</product>
</stockChange>
```

Summary

I described the builder pattern in this chapter and showed you how it can be used to control the creation of objects when direct instantiation would cause calling components to know the default configuration values for an object and when configuration data is obtained gradually.

The builder pattern is the last of the construction patterns, and in Part 3 I describe a different type of pattern: the structural patterns.

Part III

The Structural Patterns

Chapter **12**

The Adapter Pattern

In this chapter, I describe the first of the structural patterns: the adapter pattern. This pattern allows two objects that provide related functionality to work together even when they have incompatible APIs. Table 12-1 puts the adapter pattern in context.

Table 12-1. Putting the Adapter Pattern into Context

Question	Answer
What is it?	The adapter pattern allows two components with incompatible APIs to work together by introducing an adapter that maps from one component to the other.
What are the benefits?	This pattern allows you to integrate components for which you cannot modify the source code into your application. This is a common problem when you use a third-party framework or when you are consuming the output from another project.
When should you use this pattern?	Use this pattern when you need to integrate a component that provides similar functionality to other components in the application but that uses an incompatible API to do so.
When should you avoid this pattern?	Do not use this pattern when you are able to modify the source code of the component that you want to integrate or when it is possible to migrate the data provided by the component directly into your application.
How do you know when you have implemented the pattern correctly?	The pattern is implemented correctly when the adapter allows the component to be integrated into the application without requiring modification of the application or the component.
Are there any common pitfalls?	The only pitfall is trying to extend the pattern to force integration of a component that does not provide the functionality intended by the API for which it is being adapted.
Are there any related patterns?	Many of the structural patterns have similar implementations but different intents. Ensure that you select the correct pattern from the ones I describe in this part of the book.

Preparing the Example Project

For this chapter, I created a new OS X Command Line Tool project called Adapter. I added a new file called Employees.swift to the project and used it to define the types shown in Listing 12-1.

Listing 12-1. The Contents of the Employees.swift File

```
struct Employee {
    var name:String;
    var title:String;
}

protocol EmployeeDataSource {
    var employees:[Employee] { get };
    func searchByName(name:String) -> [Employee];
    func searchByTitle(title:String) -> [Employee];
}
```

The example for this chapter will be a simple employee directory, and the Employee struct will be used to represent individual members of staff. Classes that provide employee data implement the EmployeeDataSource protocol.

Creating the Data Sources

I added a file called DataSources.swift to the project and used them to define the classes shown in Listing 12-2.

Listing 12-2. The Contents of the DataSources.swift File

```
import Foundation

class DataSourceBase : EmployeeDataSource {
    var employees = [Employee]();

    func searchByName(name: String) -> [Employee] {
        return search({e -> Bool in
            return e.name.rangeOfString(name) != nil;
        });
    }

    func searchByTitle(title: String) -> [Employee] {
        return search({e -> Bool in
            return e.title.rangeOfString(title) != nil;
        })
    }
```

```
        private func search(selector:(Employee -> Bool)) -> [Employee] {
            var results = [Employee]();
            for e in employees {
                if (selector(e)) {
                    results.append(e);
                }
            }
            return results;
        }
}

class SalesDataSource : DataSourceBase {

    override init() {
        super.init();
        employees.append(Employee(name: "Alice", title: "VP of Sales"));
        employees.append(Employee(name: "Bob", title: "Account Exec"));
    }
}

class DevelopmentDataSource : DataSourceBase {

    override init() {
        super.init();
        employees.append(Employee(name: "Joe", title: "VP of Development"));
        employees.append(Employee(name: "Pepe", title: "Developer"));
    }
}
```

The DataSourceBase class conforms to the EmployeeDataSource protocol and provides an implementation of the data source functionality that I can easily derive in order to add new data to the application. I have created two data source classes—SalesDataSource and DevelopmentDataSource—that provide employee information for two departments.

Defining the Application

To consume the data sources, I added a file to the project called EmployeeSearch.swift and used it to define the class shown in Listing 12-3.

Listing 12-3. The Contents of the EmployeeSearch.swift File

```
class SearchTool {

    enum SearchType {
        case NAME; case TITLE;
    }

    private let sources:[EmployeeDataSource];

    init(dataSources: EmployeeDataSource...) {
        self.sources = dataSources;
    }
```

```
    var employees:[Employee] {
        var results = [Employee]();
        for source in sources {
            results += source.employees;
        }
        return results;
    }

    func search(text:String, type:SearchType) -> [Employee] {
        var results = [Employee]();

        for source in sources {
            results += type == SearchType.NAME ? source.searchByName(text)
                : source.searchByTitle(text);
        }
        return results;
    }
}
```

The SearchTool class operates on a collection of data sources and consolidates their contents and search capabilities to provide uniform access to the employee data. Listing 12-4 shows the code I added to the main.swift file to test the functionality.

Listing 12-4. Testing the Example App in the main.swift File

```
let search = SearchTool(dataSources: SalesDataSource(), DevelopmentDataSource());

println("--List--");
for e in search.employees {
    println("Name: \(e.name)");
}

println("--Search--");
for e in search.search("VP", type: SearchTool.SearchType.TITLE) {
    println("Name: \(e.name), Title: \(e.title)");
}
```

Running the application produces the following output in the debug console:

```
--List--
Name: Alice
Name: Bob
Name: Joe
Name: Pepe
--Search--
Name: Alice, Title: VP of Sales
Name: Joe, Title: VP of Development
```

Understanding the Problem That the Pattern Solves

The problem that the adapter pattern solves arises when an existing system needs to integrate a new component that has a similar function but that doesn't present a common interface and that cannot be modified.

The example application represents the existing system—an employee directory that relies on classes that conform to the EmployeeDataSource protocol to provide it with search functionality. The problems start when a new source of data needs to be integrated into the directory that doesn't conform to the protocol.

There are lots of reasons why incompatible code will be introduced into an application. In the case of an employee directory, an acquisition or merger may require integration of another company's systems. On a smaller scale, incompatible code can be introduced into a project when a third-party component is used or when you depend on the code produced by another development team working on a related project.

To illustrate the problem, imagine that my example company acquires a rival and wants to extend the directory to include the staff of the new company. The good news is that the new company already has a solid employee directory, but the bad news is that it doesn't use the types needed by the parent company. To represent this problem, I added a file to the project called NewCo.swift and used it to define the simple directory types shown in Listing 12-5.

Listing 12-5. The Contents of the NewCo.swift File

```swift
class NewCoStaffMember {
    private var name:String;
    private var role:String;

    init(name:String, role:String) {
        self.name = name; self.role = role;
    }

    func getName() -> String {
        return name;
    }

    func getJob() -> String {
        return role;
    }
}

class NewCoDirectory {
    private var staff:[String: NewCoStaffMember];

    init() {
        staff = ["Hans": NewCoStaffMember(name: "Hans", role: "Corp Counsel"),
            "Greta": NewCoStaffMember(name: "Greta", role: "VP, Legal")];
    }
```

```
    func getStaff() -> [String: NewCoStaffMember] {
        return staff;
    }
}
```

The NewCoDirectory class provides a dictionary of NewCoStaffMember objects that are keyed on the employee's name. There is no search capability and no common types with the directory I created at the start of the chapter. The problem I face is integrating the NewCoDirectory class into the existing staff directory.

WHY NOT JUST CHANGE THE CODE?

I could solve this problem just by revising the NewCoDirectory class, but that isn't always possible in the real world, which is why the adapter pattern is so useful. The main reason that code cannot be modified is when a component is purchased from a third party, in which case you won't even see the source code, just the API it produces. The component developers are unlikely to adopt your private API when you are one customer out of the thousands they sell to.

You will also encounter code that cannot be changed when working in a large company. Common causes include dealing with legacy products ("We don't know how it works, and we are afraid to touch it"), dealing with projects that are under-resourced ("We'll have time to implement your API in about 2 years"), and dealing with politics ("You should implement *my* API instead").

Whatever the reason, the result is the same: an API that provides the functionality you require but not in a way you want. For the purposes of this chapter, imagine that I don't have the source code to the NewCoDirectory class—perhaps because it is an off-the-shelf product—and that I need to find a way to integrate the employee data it provides without being able to make any changes.

I could solve this problem by modifying the SearchTool application so that it knows how to query the new data source. This means I have to repeat that modification process for each component that I integrate and perform the modification for every part of the application that needs to query the data sources. The result is a complex set of changes required each time a new data source is added or an existing one is changed—and this, of course, is what design patterns are intended to avoid.

Understanding the Adapter Pattern

The adapter pattern allows two incompatible classes to work together by adapting the API that one of them presents via mapping the API expected by the application to the API provided by the component, as shown in Figure 12-1. In the case of the example application, I need to adapt the API defined by the NewCoDirectory class so that the SearchTool class can use it.

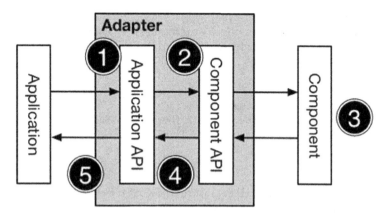

Figure 12-1. The adapter pattern

There are five operations in the adapter pattern. The first operation is a request from the application to the adapter using the API it expects to work with. In the second operation, the adapter uses its knowledge of both APIs to select a component method or property that can be used to handle the request.

In the third operation, the component receives the request from the adapter, does its work, and returns its result to the adapter.

For the fourth operation, the adapter uses its knowledge of both APIs to translate the result provided by the client into a result that the application is expecting and, in the final operation, returns the result.

The application and the component are unaware of each other. The adapter presents the application with an API it knows about and hides the details of how that API is mapped to the one provided by the component.

Implementing the Adapter Pattern

The most elegant way to implement the adapter pattern is with a Swift extension. Extensions allow you to add functionality to classes that you are unable to modify. This functionality includes adding conformance to a protocol, which is perfectly suited to implementing the adapter pattern. Listing 12-6 shows the contents of the Adapter.swift file that I added to the example file and that I used to implement the pattern with an extension.

Listing 12-6. The Contents of the Adapter.swift File

```
import Foundation

extension NewCoDirectory : EmployeeDataSource {

    var employees:[Employee] {
        return map(getStaff().values, { sv -> Employee in
            return Employee(name: sv.getName(), title: sv.getJob());
        });
    }
```

```
func searchByName(name:String) -> [Employee] {
    return createEmployees(filter: {(sv:NewCoStaffMember) -> Bool in
        return sv.getName().rangeOfString(name) != nil;
    });
}

func searchByTitle(title:String) -> [Employee] {
    return createEmployees(filter: {(sv:NewCoStaffMember) -> Bool in
        return sv.getJob().rangeOfString(title) != nil;
    });
}

private func createEmployees(filter filterClosure:(NewCoStaffMember -> Bool))
        -> [Employee] {
    return map(filter(getStaff().values, filterClosure), {entry -> Employee in
        return Employee(name: entry.getName(), title: entry.getJob());
    });
}
}
```

I have defined an extension that makes the NewCoDirectory class conform to the EmployeeDataSource protocol. The process of adapting an API is often more complex than just mapping between methods and properties and usually requires some logic in the adapter to handle type conversion and to plug small gaps in functionality. In Listing 12-6, you can see that I have to add the ability to search for names and titles as well as convert the NewCoStaffMember objects produced by the NewCoDirectory class into the Employee objects that the EmployeeDataSource protocol expects.

> **Tip**   Extensions can operate only on the accessible properties and methods defined by the class being extended. This is why I get details of the staff members through the getStaff method defined by the NewCoDirectory class and not the private property called staff.

Using an extension means that an instance of the NewCoDirectory class can be passed to the SearchTool initializer and be treated like any other data source, as shown in Listing 12-7. The methods and properties defined by the extension—as well as any protocols it conforms to—are applied to the class automatically, even though the class itself has not been modified.

Listing 12-7. Using the Adapter in the main.swift File

```
let search = SearchTool(dataSources: SalesDataSource(),
    DevelopmentDataSource(), NewCoDirectory());

println("--List--");
for e in search.employees {
    println("Name: \(e.name)");
}
```

```
println("--Search--");
for e in search.search("VP", type: SearchTool.SearchType.TITLE) {
    println("Name: \(e.name), Title: \(e.title)");
}
```

No changes to the SearchTool class are required, and you can see how the directory includes the NewCo employees by running the application.

```
--List--
Name: Alice
Name: Bob
Name: Joe
Name: Pepe
Name: Greta
Name: Hans
--Search--
Name: Alice, Title: VP of Sales
Name: Joe, Title: VP of Development
Name: Greta, Title: VP, Legal
```

WHY NOT JUST MIGRATE THE DATA?

In my example, an alternative approach would be to migrate the data from the acquired company's systems to those of the parent company. This isn't always a solution, of course, and it won't help when you are trying to integrate third-party code into your application.

Data migration has a lot of attractions over the long term, but it is hard to achieve quickly, especially for applications such as employee directories that are deeply tied into complex business processes and legacy applications. Migrating all the data to a single platform will eventually drive out cost by eliminating one of the systems—something that is important in mergers and acquisitions—but it requires a lot of effort and puts demands on key staff who are likely to be focused on other issues. Patterns such as adapter can help reduce the number of complex projects that get kicked off in the days following the deal and buy some time to see how other business processes are going to be changed.

Implementing a long-term strategic solution is always desirable, but getting some short-term benefit by using an adapter is often more pragmatic and more likely to succeed.

Variations on the Adapter Pattern

There are two useful variations in how the adapter pattern is implemented, which I describe in the sections that follow.

Defining an Adapter as a Wrapper Class

If you don't like using extensions, then you can implement an adapter as a class that wraps around the component. Listing 12-8 shows how I replaced the extension adapter with a class.

Listing 12-8. Implementing the Adapter as a Wrapper Class in the Adapter.swift File

```swift
class NewCoDirectoryAdapter : EmployeeDataSource {
    private let directory:NewCoDirectory;

    init() {
        directory = NewCoDirectory();
    }

    var employees:[Employee] {
        return map(directory.getStaff().values, { sv -> Employee in
            return Employee(name: sv.getName(), title: sv.getJob());
        });
    }

    func searchByName(name:String) -> [Employee] {
        return createEmployees(filter: {(sv:NewCoStaffMember) -> Bool in
            return sv.getName().rangeOfString(name) != nil;
        });
    }

    func searchByTitle(title:String) -> [Employee] {
        return createEmployees(filter: {(sv:NewCoStaffMember) -> Bool in
            return sv.getJob().rangeOfString(title) != nil;
        });
    }

    private func createEmployees(filter filterClosure:(NewCoStaffMember -> Bool))
            -> [Employee] {
        return map(filter(directory.getStaff().values, filterClosure),
            {entry -> Employee in
                return Employee(name: entry.getName(), title: entry.getJob());
        });
    }
}
```

> **Tip**   There is no advantage in using a wrapper class, but there are some advanced adaptions that can't be implemented using extensions, as I describe in the next section.

The logic contained in the adapter is the same as for an extension-based implementation, and only the way that the adapter is written is changed. I still have to implement support for performing searches, and I still have to map between the result types.

This approach requires that the adapter class be instantiated and used, rather than the (extended) component, as shown in Listing 12-9.

Listing 12-9. Using the Adapter Wrapper Class in the main.swift File

```
let search = SearchTool(dataSources: SalesDataSource(),
    DevelopmentDataSource(), NewCoDirectoryAdapter());

println("--List--");
for e in search.employees {
    println("Name: \(e.name)");
}

println("--Search--");
for e in search.search("VP", type: SearchTool.SearchType.TITLE) {
    println("Name: \(e.name), Title: \(e.title)");
}
```

Creating a Two-Way Adapter

The standard implementation of the adapter pattern assumes that the flow of method and property calls will flow in one direction: from the application to the component. This is usually the case, especially when dealing with third-party components like UI widgets, but there are occasions when the component expects to initiate its own actions, typically to query the application or to notify it about a change in its state or the services it provides. To demonstrate this problem, I created a playground called TwoWayAdapter.playground and used it to define the classes and protocols shown in Listing 12-10. (I have used a playground because demonstrating this problem in the example application would require me to list a lot of code for some minor changes).

Listing 12-10. The Contents of the TwoWayAdapter.playground File

```
// application

protocol ShapeDrawer {
    func drawShape();
}

class DrawingApp {
    let drawer:ShapeDrawer;
    var cornerRadius:Int = 0;

    init(drawer:ShapeDrawer) {
        self.drawer = drawer;
    }

    func makePicture() {
        drawer.drawShape();
    }
}
```

```
// component library

protocol AppSettings {
    var sketchRoundedShapes:Bool { get };
}

class SketchComponent {
    private let settings:AppSettings;

    init(settings:AppSettings) {
        self.settings = settings;
    }

    func sketchShape() {
        if (settings.sketchRoundedShapes) {
            println("Sketch Circle");
        } else {
            println("Sketch Square");
        }
    }
}
```

I have broken the code into two sections—one for the application and one for the component that needs to be integrated. On the application side, the DrawingApp class relies on the ShapeDrawer protocol to perform its work in the makePicture method. On the component side, the SketchComponent class relies on the AppSettings protocol to work out what type of shape it should draw.

The goal is to create an adapter that will let a DrawingApp object use a SketchComponent object to create a shape and, in return, let the SketchComponent query the application through the AppSettings protocol.

Using an adapter in a single direction is easy, but it is harder to adapt objects that communicate in both directions—not least because I have created the classes to have *dueling initializers*. I can't create an instance of the DrawingApp unless I have an object that conforms to the ShapeDrawer protocol to use as an initializer argument. Equally, I can't create a SketchComponent object unless I can pass its initializer an object that conforms to the AppSettings protocol. Listing 12-11 shows the adapter I created to solve the problem and integrate the classes with one another.

Listing 12-11. Creating an Adapter in the TwoWayAdapter.playground File

```
// application

protocol ShapeDrawer {
    func drawShape();
}

class DrawingApp {
    // ...statements omitted for brevity...
}
```

```
// component library

protocol AppSettings {
    var sketchRoundedShapes:Bool { get };
}

class SketchComponent {
    // ...statements omitted for brevity...
}

class TwoWayAdapter : ShapeDrawer, AppSettings {
    var app:DrawingApp?;
    var component:SketchComponent?

    func drawShape() {
        component?.sketchShape();
    }

    var sketchRoundedShapes: Bool {
        return app?.cornerRadius > 0;
    }
}
```

The adapter class—called TwoWayAdapter—conforms to the ShapeDrawer and AppSettings
protocols and implements the protocol methods using optional instances of the DrawingApp
and SketchComponent classes. This is the key to working around the competing demands of the
initializers, as Listing 12-12 shows.

Listing 12-12. Using the Adapter in the TwoWayAdapter.playground File

```
protocol ShapeDrawer {
    func drawShape();
}

class DrawingApp {
    // ...statements omitted for brevity...
}

// component library

protocol AppSettings {
    var sketchRoundedShapes:Bool { get };
}

class SketchComponent {
    // ...statements omitted for brevity...
}

class TwoWayAdapter : ShapeDrawer, AppSettings {
    // ...statements omitted for brevity...
}
```

```
let adapter = TwoWayAdapter();
let component = SketchComponent(settings: adapter);
let app = DrawingApp(drawer: adapter);

adapter.app = app;
adapter.component = component;

app.makePicture();
```

> **Note**   This is an adapter that cannot be created using Swift extensions because it needs to operate on two different classes.

I create an instance of the adapter, which conforms to the protocols that I need to create SketchComponent and DrawingApp objects. Then I set the adapter app and component properties so that the adapter has the objects it needs for its methods. The result is that both objects can call on the other through the adapter, and you can see the output in the playground debug console.

```
Sketch Square
```

Understanding the Pitfalls of the Adapter Pattern

The adapter pattern is useful only when integrating components that have similar functionality, meaning that the features provided by the classes are compatible even though the APIs are not.

In the example application, there is a component that consumes employee data (the SearchTool class) and a component that provides employee data (the NewCoDirectory class). The functionality of these classes is compatible, but I can't use the NewCoDirectory class as a source of data because it doesn't implement the protocol that the SearchTool class requires.

The adapter pattern is not helpful when the components provide different functionality. For example, the adapter pattern cannot be used to integrate a data source that provides details of employee parking spaces because there is no support for that data in the application, and no amount of adaptation of the API will change that. To use the adapter pattern effectively, focus purely on the API and keep the adaptations as simple as possible.

Examples of the Adapter Pattern in Cocoa

The adapter pattern is not exposed by Cocoa because its components set the standard for default behavior. If you want to integrate a component into Cocoa, then you implement a protocol. A good example is the NSCopying protocol that I used in Chapter 5 to implement the prototype pattern: if you want to integrate a class into Cocoa's support for object copying, then you make it conform to the NSCopying protocol even if it already has a custom approach to creating clones. Such is the position of the core API on any platform; if an adapter is needed, then it is your responsibility to define it in your code.

Applying the Pattern to the SportsStore Application

Not all adapters map a single type to integrate a component into an application, and to demonstrate this, I am going to create an adapter that implements the abstract factory pattern and that conforms to implementation protocols in order to do its job.

Preparing the Example Application

I added a file called `Euro.swift` to the example project and used it to define the class shown in Listing 12-13.

Listing 12-13. The Contents of the Euro.swift File

```swift
class EuroHandler {

    func getDisplayString(amount:Double) -> String {
        let formatted = Utils.currencyStringFromNumber(amount);
        return "€\(dropFirst(formatted))";
    }

    func getCurrencyAmount(amount:Double) -> Double {
        return 0.76164 * amount;
    }
}
```

The `EuroHandler` class converts dollar amounts to euros and creates formatted currency strings. This is the same type of functionality that I added to the SportsStore application to demonstrate the abstract factory pattern in Chapter 10, but the `EuroHandler` class does not fit directly into the model that the application expects and so requires an adapter.

Defining the Adapter Class

To adapt the `EuroHandler` class into the SportsStore application, I need to define a concrete factory class that produces `StockValueConverter` and `StockValueFormatter` objects. Listing 12-14 shows the changes I made to the `StockValueFactories.swift` file.

Listing 12-14. Defining the Adapter in the StockValueFactories.swift File

```swift
import Foundation

class StockTotalFactory {

    enum Currency {
        case USD
        case GBP
        case EUR
    }
```

```
    private(set) var formatter:StockValueFormatter?;
    private(set) var converter:StockValueConverter?;

    class func getFactory(curr:Currency) -> StockTotalFactory {
        if (curr == Currency.USD) {
            return DollarStockTotalFactory.sharedInstance;
        } else if (curr == Currency.GBP){
            return PoundStockTotalFactory.sharedInstance;
        } else {
            return EuroHandlerAdapter.sharedInstance;
        }
    }
}

// ...other factories omitted for brevity...

class EuroHandlerAdapter : StockTotalFactory,
        StockValueConverter, StockValueFormatter {

    private let handler:EuroHandler;

    override init() {
        self.handler = EuroHandler();
        super.init();
        super.formatter = self;
        super.converter = self;
    }

    func formatTotal(total:Double) -> String {
        return handler.getDisplayString(total);
    }

    func convertTotal(total:Double) -> Double {
        return handler.getCurrencyAmount(total);
    }

    class var sharedInstance:EuroHandlerAdapter {
        get {
            struct SingletonWrapper {
                static let singleton = EuroHandlerAdapter();
            }
            return SingletonWrapper.singleton;
        }
    }
}
```

> **Tip**   I have to define the factory class in the StockValueFactories.swift file because I need to set values for private properties in the StockTotalFactory class, and that means putting the adapter in the same file.

I have updated the StockTotalFactory class to add support for handling the euro and defined an adapter called EuroHandlerAdapter. The adapter is derived from the StockTotalFactory class and conforms to both the StockValueConverter and StockValueFormatter protocols. It adapts the EuroHandler class by creating an instance of it and mapping the functionality it provides to the methods specified by the protocols. I could have taken care of the protocols by defining an extension, but I prefer to keep adapters as a single type when possible.

Using the Adapted Functionality

In Listing 12-15, you can see how I have updated the displayStockTotal method of the ViewController class so that the euro is the chosen currency.

Listing 12-15. Using the Adapter in the ViewController.swift File

```
...
func displayStockTotal() {
    let finalTotals:(Int, Double) = productStore.products.reduce((0, 0.0),
        {(totals, product) -> (Int, Double) in
            return (
                totals.0 + product.stockLevel,
                totals.1 + product.stockValue
            );
        });

    var factory = StockTotalFactory.getFactory(StockTotalFactory.Currency.EUR);
    var totalAmount = factory.converter?.convertTotal(finalTotals.1);
    var formatted = factory.formatter?.formatTotal(totalAmount!);

    totalStockLabel.text = "\(finalTotals.0) Products in Stock. "
        + "Total Value: \(formatted!)";
}
...
```

The result is that the total value of the stock will be converted to euros and displayed at the bottom of the application layout, as shown in Figure 12-2.

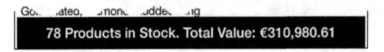

Go. .ateo, .non. .dde. .ig

78 Products in Stock. Total Value: €310,980.61

Figure 12-2. *The effect of the euro adapter*

Summary

In this chapter, I explained how the adapter pattern is used to make two classes with incompatible APIs work together. I demonstrated how to define an adapter by using an extension and creating a class that wraps around the object being adapted. In the next chapter, I describe the bridge pattern.

The Bridge Pattern

The bridge pattern can be confusing. It looks similar to the adapter pattern I described in Chapter 12, but its use can seem counterintuitive. In this chapter, I focus on the problem that the bridge pattern is most commonly used to resolve and explain why the biggest difference between the bridge and adapter patterns is intent rather than implementation. Table 13-1 puts the bridge pattern into context.

Table 13-1. *Putting the Bridge Pattern into Context*

Question	Answer
What is it?	The bridge pattern separates an abstraction from its implementation so that either can be changed without a corresponding change in the other. More commonly, the bridge pattern is used to resolve a problem known as an *exploding class hierarchy*, which usually arises through repeated but poorly thought-out refactoring and requires an ever-increasing number of classes to add new features to the application.
What are the benefits?	When the bridge pattern is applied to the exploding class hierarchy problem, the benefit is that adding a new feature to the application requires only a single class. More broadly, the pattern isolates the impact of a change when an abstraction or its implementation changes.
When should you use this pattern?	Use this pattern to resolve the exploding class hierarchy problem or to bridge between one API and another.
When should you avoid this pattern?	Do not use this pattern when attempting to integrate third-party components; use the adapter pattern I described in Chapter 12 instead.

(continued)

Table 13-1. (*continued*)

Question	Answer
How do you know when you have implemented the pattern correctly?	In the case of the exploding class hierarchy problem, the pattern is correctly implemented when adding a new feature or when support for a new platform can be done with a single class. More broadly, the pattern is implemented correctly when you can change an abstraction (such as a protocol or a closure signature) without having to make a corresponding change in its implementation.
Are there any common pitfalls?	The exploding class hierarchy will not be resolved if the common code is not separated from the platform-specific code.
Are there any related patterns?	Many of the structural patterns have similar implementations but different intents. Ensure that you select the correct pattern from the ones that I describe in this part of the book.

Preparing the Example Project

For this chapter I created a new OS X Command Line Tool project called Bridge. To prepare for this chapter, I added a file called **Comms.swift** and used it to define the types shown in Listing 13-1.

Listing 13-1. The Contents of the Comms.swift File

```swift
protocol ClearMessageChannel {
    func send(message:String);
}

protocol SecureMessageChannel {
    func sendEncryptedMessage(encryptedText:String);
}

class Communicator {
    private let clearChannel:ClearMessageChannel;
    private let secureChannel:SecureMessageChannel;

    init (clearChannel:ClearMessageChannel, secureChannel:SecureMessageChannel) {
        self.clearChannel = clearChannel;
        self.secureChannel = secureChannel;
    }

    func sendCleartextMessage(message:String) {
        self.clearChannel.send(message);
    }

    func sendSecureMessage(message:String) {
        self.secureChannel.sendEncryptedMessage(message);
    }
}
```

The **Communicator** class provides methods that allow standard and secure messages to be sent. The mechanisms by which these messages are processed are defined by the **ClearMessageChannel** and **SecureMessageChannel** protocols, each of which defines the methods required to handle one type of communication.

I am going to support two different networking mechanisms that can be used to transmit messages: landline and wireless. I created a file called **Channels.swift** and used it to create the classes shown in Listing 13-2.

Listing 13-2. The Contents of the Channels.swift File

```swift
class Landline : ClearMessageChannel {
    func send(message: String) {
        println("Landline: \(message)");
    }
}

class SecureLandLine : SecureMessageChannel {
    func sendEncryptedMessage(message: String) {
        println("Secure Landline: \(message)");
    }
}

class Wireless : ClearMessageChannel {
    func send(message: String) {
        println("Wireless: \(message)");
    }
}

class SecureWireless : SecureMessageChannel {
    func sendEncryptedMessage(message: String) {
        println("Secure Wireless: \(message)");
    }
}
```

To complete the preparations, I added code to the **main.swift** file that creates the channels it requires to send messages and uses them to create a **Communicator** object, as shown in Listing 13-3.

Listing 13-3. The Contents of the main.swift File

```swift
var clearChannel = Landline();
var secureChannel = SecureLandLine();

var comms = Communicator(clearChannel: clearChannel, secureChannel: secureChannel);

comms.sendCleartextMessage("Hello!");
comms.sendSecureMessage("This is a secret");
```

Running the project produces the following output in the Xcode debug console:

```
Landline: Hello!
Secure Landline: This is a secret
```

Understanding the Problem That the Pattern Solves

If the code I added to the example application seems poorly thought out, it is because I added all of the classes in one go. The problem that the bridge pattern solves is one that usually manifests itself gradually as features are added to an application and code is refactored.

What I have ended up with is two features (clear and secure messages) and two platforms on which those features are implemented (landlines and wireless networks). No one sets out to create this kind of hierarchy, and it usually gets created through the best of intentions. An application usually started with one feature and one platform, as shown in Figure 13-1.

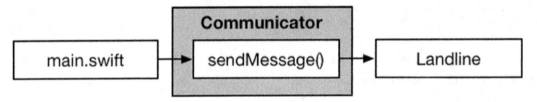

Figure 13-1. The simple starting point for an application

At some point, another platform is required, and the selection of that platform will need to change based on how the application is configured. Some judicious refactoring adds a protocol that identifies what the platform needs to do, and implementation classes that handle the details of the platform are created, as shown in Figure 13-2.

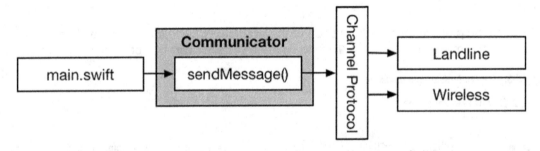

Figure 13-2. Dealing with multiple platforms

Later, there is a need to add a new feature—secure messaging—and so another protocol is added and implementation objects are created, as shown in Figure 13-3. This is the state of the application that I created in the previous section.

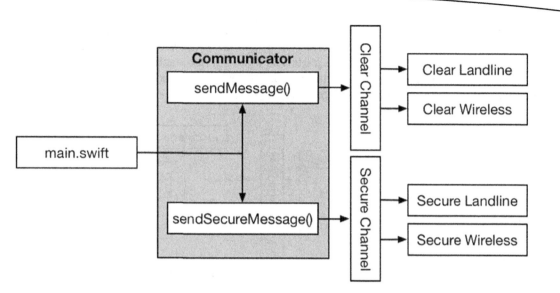

Figure 13-3. Dealing with multiple features

The problem is that the number of implementation classes increases sharply each time I add a new feature or a new platform. In fact, the total number of implementation classes is the product of the number and platforms, meaning that if I add a third feature to the application, the number of implementation classes will be six (the product of 3 and 2). Another platform will give require nine implementation classes (the product of 3 and 3).

This is known as the *exploding class hierarchy* problem, and it produces an unmanageable mess of protocols and implementation classes that are hard to keep track of and even harder to maintain. Exploding class hierarchies are usually not intentional, but they are easy to create when there is time pressure to add new features and keep the project moving along.

Understanding the Bridge Pattern

The bridge pattern separates an abstraction from its implementation so that the two can be changed independently from one another. It may sound counterintuitive, but the bridge pattern solves the exploding class hierarchy problem by creating two different hierarchies, separating the functionality that is specific to each platform from the functionality that is shared between them. A bridge class is created, which brings together both hierarchies.

Tip   Separating common and platform-specific functionality is the most frequent—and useful—way that the bridge pattern is applied, but it can be used to separate any abstraction from its implementation. See the "Applying the Pattern to the SportsStore Application" section for a more general example.

In the example application, the functionality that is specific to each platform is the transmission of a message over a particular type of network. The functionality that is common is the preparation of the message. The first step is to define protocols that describe each area—messaging and transmission—and then create implementation classes for them. Figure 13-4 shows the new hierarchies and the bridge class that brings them together.

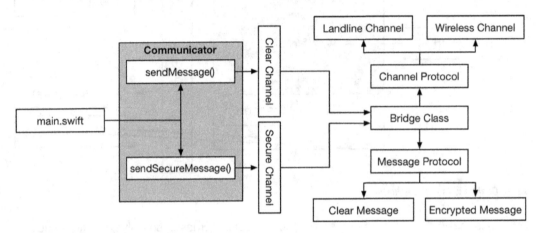

Figure 13-4. The bridge pattern

Tip   Don't worry if an abstract description doesn't make immediate sense. The bridge pattern can be hard to parse. If you are struggling to make sense of what's going on, then read the next sections to see how the pattern is implemented and then come back and read this description again.

The bridge class is responsible for combining the **Channel** and **Message** protocols to provide the functionality that the **Communicator** requires, using the protocols that the **Communicator** class relies on.

Note   Notice that I have not changed the **Communicator** class. The bridge class supports the API expected by the **Communicator** class and maps—or rather, *bridges*—to the new message and channel hierarchies. The **Communicator** class remains unmodified because the default assumption when implementing the bridge pattern is that there will be several other classes in the application that expect the same protocols. See the "Collapsing the Bridge" section for an alternative approach.

```
┌─────────────────────────────────────────────────────────────────────┐
│                    ISN'T THE BRIDGE JUST AN ADAPTER?                  │
└─────────────────────────────────────────────────────────────────────┘
```

The bridge pattern can look a lot like the adapter pattern I described in Chapter 12. After all, doesn't the bridge class adapt the **Channel** and **Message** protocols for the **Communicator** class, which relies on the **ClearChannel** and **SecureChannel** protocols?

The bridge and adapter patterns are similar, but they are used in different situations. The adapter pattern is used when you need to integrate a component whose code you cannot change, such as a third-party widget. You add the adapter to make the third-party component usable through an API that your application expects, but you can't change the way that the component works because you have only runtime components (or because your changes will be overwritten by the next release from the team that produces the component).

The bridge pattern is used when you *can* change the source code and *can* change the way that the components work and is applied when you have a class hierarchy that mixes common and platform-specific functionality. Applying the bridge pattern doesn't just involve creating the bridge class; it also requires refactoring the components to separate the common and platform-specific code.

Implementing the Bridge Pattern

Describing the bridge pattern can be useful, but a code example helps demonstrate how the pattern works. In the sections that follow, I'll refactor the example application to apply the bridge pattern and prevent the exploding class hierarchy.

Dealing with the Messages

The first step is to deal with the functionality that is common regardless of the network that is being used, which is the creation and preparation of a message. Listing 13-4 shows the contents of the **Messages.swift** file, which I added to the example project.

Listing 13-4. The Contents of the Messages.swift File

```
protocol Message {
    init (message:String);
    func prepareMessage();
    var contentToSend:String { get };
}

class ClearMessage : Message {
    private var message:String;

    required init(message:String) {
        self.message = message;
    }

    func prepareMessage() {
        // no action required
    }
```

```
    var contentToSend:String {
        return message;
    }
}

class EncryptedMessage : Message {
    private var clearText:String;
    private var cipherText:String?;

    required init(message:String) {
        self.clearText = message;
    }

    func prepareMessage() {
        cipherText = String(reverse(clearText));
    }

    var contentToSend:String {
        return cipherText!;
    }
}
```

I have defined a protocol called **Message**. The protocol defines a required initializer that accepts
the text of the message and defines a **prepareMessage** method that will be called so that classes
that conform to the protocol have an opportunity to process the message text. The get-only
contentToSend property will be used to get whatever text needs to be transmitted over a network.

I defined two classes that conform to the protocol. The first class is **ClearMessage**, which I will use to
represent messages that do not require encryption. I will use the **EncryptedMessage** class for those
messages for which encryption is needed. (Encryption, in this case, consists of simply reversing
the characters in the string—something that would not be adequate for a real project but will be
sufficient for an example application.)

Dealing with the Channels

The next step is to define the functionality that is unique to each network, which is the transmission
of messages. Listing 13-5 shows the changes I made to the **Channels.swift** file.

Listing 13-5. Revising the Contents of the Channels.swift File

```
protocol Channel {
    func sendMessage(msg:Message);
}

class LandlineChannel : Channel {

    func sendMessage(msg: Message) {
        println("Landline: \(msg.contentToSend)");
    }

}
```

```
class WirelessChannel : Channel {
    func sendMessage(msg: Message) {
        println("Wireless: \(msg.contentToSend)");
    }
}
```

I defined a protocol called **Channel** that has a method called **sendMessage**. Unlike the original version of the application, the channel is no longer responsible for dealing with different kinds of messages. Instead, the **sendMessage** method will be called with a **Message** object whose **contentToSend** property returns the content that should be transmitted. Channels are unaware of what type of message they are sending and can focus only on dealing with transmission.

I defined two classes that conform to the **Channel** protocol, reflecting landline and wireless networks. The implementation of the **sendMessage** method for both classes writes a message to the debug console indicating the channel and the content.

Creating the Bridge

Finally, I need to create a class that will act as a bridge between the **Communicator** class and the new **Message** and **Channel** protocols. Listing 13-6 shows the contents of the **Bridge.swift** file, which I added to the example project.

Listing 13-6. The Contents of the Bridge.swift File

```
class CommunicatorBridge : ClearMessageChannel, SecureMessageChannel {
    private var channel:Channel;

    init(channel:Channel) {
        self.channel = channel;
    }

    func send(message: String) {
        let msg = ClearMessage(message: message);
        sendMessage(msg);
    }

    func sendEncryptedMessage(encryptedText: String) {
        let msg = EncryptedMessage(message: encryptedText);
        sendMessage(msg);
    }

    private func sendMessage(msg:Message) {
        msg.prepareMessage();
        channel.sendMessage(msg);
    }
}
```

The **CommunicatorBridge** class implements the **ClearMessageChannel** and **SecureMessageChannel** protocols that the **Communicator** class relies on. It implements these protocols using the new **Message** and **Channel** protocols. The **CommunicatorBridge** class selects the appropriate **Message** implementation class based on which of its methods has been called and passes the **Message** object it creates to the **Channel** object given to its initializer.

Listing 13-7 shows how I have updated the **main.swift** file to use the **CommunicatorBridge** class to configure a **Communicator** object.

Listing 13-7. Using the CommunicatorBridge Class in the main.swift File

```
var bridge = CommunicatorBridge(channel: LandlineChannel());

var comms = Communicator(clearChannel: bridge, secureChannel: bridge);

comms.sendCleartextMessage("Hello!");
comms.sendSecureMessage("This is a secret");
```

Running the application results in the following output:

```
Landline: Hello!
Landline: terces a si sihT
```

Adding a New Message Type and Channel

To demonstrate the effect of the builder pattern, I am going to add a new type of message and a new channel to the application. The new messages will be for high-priority communications, and the new channel will be for satellite networks. To get started, I have added support for priority messages to the **Communicator** class, as shown in Listing 13-8. These are changes that would have to be applied regardless of whether the bridge pattern has been applied.

Listing 13-8. Adding Support for a New Message Type in the Comms.swift File

```
protocol ClearMessageChannel {
    func send(message:String);
}

protocol SecureMessageChannel {
    func sendEncryptedMessage(message:String);
}

protocol PriorityMessageChannel {
    func sendPriority(message:String);
}

class Communicator {
    private let clearChannel:ClearMessageChannel;
    private let secureChannel:SecureMessageChannel;
    private let priorityChannel:PriorityMessageChannel;
```

```
init (clearChannel:ClearMessageChannel, secureChannel:SecureMessageChannel,
    priorityChannel:PriorityMessageChannel) {
    self.clearChannel = clearChannel;
    self.secureChannel = secureChannel;
    self.priorityChannel = priorityChannel;
}

func sendCleartextMessage(message:String) {
    self.clearChannel.send(message);
}

func sendSecureMessage(message:String) {
    self.secureChannel.sendEncryptedMessage(message);
}

func sendPriorityMessage(message:String) {
    self.priorityChannel.sendPriority(message);
}
}
```

Under the original class hierarchy—without the bridge pattern—the addition of a new message and channel would have required five new classes, as shown in Figure 13-5.

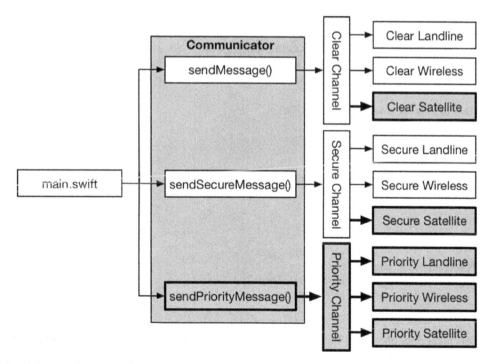

Figure 13-5. Adding new features to the application without the bridge pattern

This is the heart of the matter. Without the bridge pattern, I have to create even more classes when I add new features to the application. Adding the same message type and channel after the bridge pattern has been applied required only two new classes—one for the message type and one for the channel, as shown in Figure 13-6.

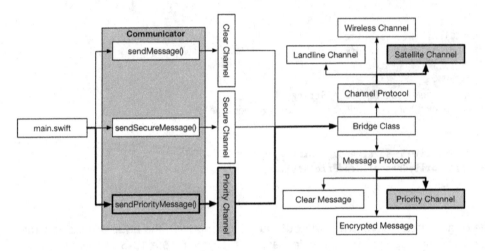

Figure 13-6. Adding new features to the application with the bridge pattern

The diagram looks more complicated, but that is because the bridge pattern puts more structure into the application (the bridge pattern is a structural pattern after all). In terms of the work required for the new features, much less effort is needed. Listing 13-9 shows the contents of the **NewFeatures.swift** file, which I added to the example project in order to implement the new message type and channel.

Listing 13-9. The Contents of the NewFeatures.swift File

```
class SatelliteChannel : Channel {

    func sendMessage(msg: Message) {
        println("Satellite: \(msg.contentToSend)");
    }
}

class PriorityMessage : ClearMessage {

    override var contentToSend:String {
        return "Important: \(super.contentToSend)";
    }
}
```

Having defined the new classes, I have to update the bridge so that it accepts the new message type from the **Communicator** class, as shown in Listing 13-10.

Listing 13-10. Adding Support for a New Message Type in the Bridge.swift File

```swift
class CommunicatorBridge : ClearMessageChannel,
        SecureMessageChannel, PriorityMessageChannel {

    private var channel:Channel;

    init(channel:Channel) {
        self.channel = channel;
    }

    func send(message: String) {
        let msg = ClearMessage(message: message);
        sendMessage(msg);
    }

    func sendEncryptedMessage(encryptedText: String) {
        let msg = EncryptedMessage(message: encryptedText);
        sendMessage(msg);
    }

    func sendPriority(message: String) {
        sendMessage(PriorityMessage(message: message));
    }

    private func sendMessage(msg:Message) {
        msg.prepareMessage();
        channel.sendMessage(msg);
    }
}
```

And now I can change the code in the **main.swift** file to test the new functionality, as shown in Listing 13-11.

Listing 13-11. Testing the New Message Type in the main.swift File

```swift
var bridge = CommunicatorBridge(channel: SatelliteChannel());
var comms = Communicator(clearChannel: bridge,secureChannel: bridge,
    priorityChannel: bridge);

comms.sendCleartextMessage("Hello!");
comms.sendSecureMessage("This is a secret");
comms.sendPriorityMessage("This is important");
```

Running the application produces the following output, which demonstrates the new message type and channel:

```
Satellite: Hello!
Satellite: terces a si sihT
Satellite: Important: This is important
```

Variations on the Bridge Pattern

The platform is selected at runtime and is usually set using a configuration file or some external setting. In the case of the example application, the platform is the channel over which messages are sent, and the choice of platform would be driven by the available networking hardware. In practice, I select the platform explicitly, like this:

```
...
var bridge = CommunicatorBridge(channel: SatelliteChannel());
...
```

This is unrealistic because the platform-specific implementation is selected at compile time, and I have to change the code and recompile to change the platform. I have done this because I don't want to create a configuration system or detect different kinds of networks to demonstrate the use of the pattern.

The simplest way to vary the pattern is to apply the factory method pattern so that the selection of the platform-specific implementation is hidden from the bridge class and from the rest of the application. Listing 13-12 shows how I have implemented the factory method—which I described in Chapter 9—in the example application.

Listing 13-12. Applying the Factory Method Pattern in the Channels.swift File

```swift
class Channel {

    enum Channels {
        case Landline;
        case Wireless;
        case Satellite;
    }

    class func getChannel(channelType:Channels) -> Channel {
        switch channelType {
            case .Landline:
                return LandlineChannel();
            case .Wireless:
                return WirelessChannel();
            case .Satellite:
                return SatelliteChannel();
        }
    }

    func sendMessage(msg:Message) {
        fatalError("Not implemented");
    }
}
```

```
class LandlineChannel : Channel {
    override func sendMessage(msg: Message) {
        println("Landline: \(msg.contentToSend)");
    }

}

class WirelessChannel : Channel {
    override func sendMessage(msg: Message) {
        println("Wireless: \(msg.contentToSend)");
    }
}
```

I have changed the definition of the **Channel** type so that it is a class rather than a protocol and have defined a nested **enum** called **Channels** that enumerates the set of platforms available: landline, wireless, and satellite. I have defined a class method called **getChannel** that accepts a **Channels** value and instantiates the class that represents the platform.

I had to apply the **override** keyword to the **sendMessage** method defined by the **LandlineChannel** and **WirelessChannel** classes because **Channel** has changed from a protocol to a class, and Listing 13-13 shows the corresponding change for the satellite implementation class.

Listing 13-13. Modifying a Method Declaration in the NewFeatures.swift File

```
class SatelliteChannel : Channel {
    override func sendMessage(msg: Message) {
        println("Satellite: \(msg.contentToSend)");
    }
}

class PriorityMessage : ClearMessage {
    override var contentToSend:String {
        return "Important: \(super.contentToSend)";
    }
}
```

Listing 13-14 shows the changes to the **CommunicatorBridge** class so that the initializer accepts a value from the enumeration rather than an *instance* of an implementation class.

Listing 13-14. Changing the Initializer in the Bridge.swift File

```
class CommunicatorBridge : ClearMessageChannel, SecureMessageChannel,
        PriorityMessageChannel {
    private var channel:Channel;

    init(channel:Channel.Channels) {
        self.channel = Channel.getChannel(channel);
    }

    func send(message: String) {
        let msg = ClearMessage(message: message);
        sendMessage(msg);
    }
```

```
    func sendEncryptedMessage(encryptedText: String) {
        let msg = EncryptedMessage(message: encryptedText);
        sendMessage(msg);
    }

    func sendPriority(message: String) {
        sendMessage(PriorityMessage(message: message));
    }

    private func sendMessage(msg:Message) {
        msg.prepareMessage();
        channel.sendMessage(msg);
    }
}
```

Finally, I need to update the code that selects the platform in the **main.swift** file, as shown in Listing 13-15.

Listing 13-15. Updating the main.swift File

```
var bridge = CommunicatorBridge(channel: Channel.Channels.Satellite);
var comms = Communicator(clearChannel: bridge,
    secureChannel: bridge, priorityChannel: bridge);

comms.sendCleartextMessage("Hello!");
comms.sendSecureMessage("This is a secret");
comms.sendPriorityMessage("This is important");
```

Collapsing the Bridge

When applying the bridge pattern, the standard assumption is that the protocols that are being bridged will be used elsewhere in the application. In the case of the example, this means there would be other classes similar to **Communicator** that will rely on the **ClearMessageChannel**, **SecureMessageChannel**, and **PriorityMessageChannel** protocols, which is why I left these—and the **Communicator** class—intact and applied the bridge to them.

In some applications, there will be only one class that relies on the protocols, and this allows it and the bridge to be merged and the redundant protocols removed.

The first step is to remove the **Bridge.swift** file from the project. The **CommunicatorBridge** class that it contains will not longer be required and will prevent Xcode from being able to build the project because it depends on protocols that I am going to remove. The next step is to add the bridge functionality to the **Communicator** class, as shown in Listing 13-16.

Listing 13-16. Adding the Bridge Functionality in the Comms.swift File

```
//protocol ClearMessageChannel {
//    func send(message:String);
//}
//
//protocol SecureMessageChannel {
//    func sendEncryptedMessage(message:String);
//}
//
//protocol PriorityMessageChannel {
//    func sendPriority(message:String);
//}

class Communicator {
    private let channnel:Channel;

    init (channel:Channel.Channels) {
        self.channnel = Channel.getChannel(channel);
    }

    private func sendMessage(msg:Message) {
        msg.prepareMessage();
        channnel.sendMessage(msg);
    }

    func sendCleartextMessage(message:String) {
        self.sendMessage(ClearMessage(message: message));
    }

    func sendSecureMessage(message:String) {
        self.sendMessage(EncryptedMessage(message: message));
    }

    func sendPriorityMessage(message:String) {
        self.sendMessage(PriorityMessage(message: message));
    }
}
```

I have commented out the old protocols and changed the **Communicator** class so that it operates directly on the **Message** and **Channel** protocols and no longer depends on a separate bridge class.

Caution   This variation is useful only when a single class uses the bridge. If you find that you have to make changes similar to the ones in Listing 13-16 to multiple classes, you have misapplied the pattern. The result may still be an improvement on the previous application structure, but you won't have applied the bridge pattern, and you won't benefit from isolating the implementation of the common and platform-specific functionality from the rest of the application.

I also have to update the code in the **main.swift** file that selects the platform and sends the messages, as shown in Listing 13-17.

Listing 13-17. Using the Collapsed Bridge in the main.swift File

```
var comms = Communicator(channel: Channel.Channels.Satellite);

comms.sendCleartextMessage("Hello!");
comms.sendSecureMessage("This is a secret");
comms.sendPriorityMessage("This is important");
```

> **Note** You won't be able to build the project if you have not removed the **Bridge.swift** file or at least commented out its contents.

Understanding the Pitfalls of the Bridge Pattern

The only pitfall is not recognizing which features are common across all platforms and which are platform-specific. A successful implementation of the bridge pattern separates common and specific functionality into different hierarchies, and it can be difficult to identify this split correctly.

As a rule of thumb, if you see groups of statements that are repeated in each platform class, they are candidates for being considered common functionality. Equally, control flow statements that deal with different platforms are platform-specific. That may seem like obvious advice, but it can be hard to figure out what is going on in a complex type hierarchy that has been poorly refactored several times and turned into a mess of cut-and-paste statements, hacks, and workarounds.

Examples of the Bridge Pattern in Cocoa

The bridge pattern hides the implementation details behind a public API, so it is not possible to know whether the pattern is used in the Cocoa frameworks.

Applying the Pattern to the SportsStore Application

Although the bridge pattern is generally applied to tidy up an exploding class hierarchy, it can be used to separate any abstraction from its implementation. In this section, I use this broader application of the pattern to create a bridge that makes the purpose of an API more obvious.

Preparing the Example Application

No preparation is required for this chapter, and I pick up the project from Chapter 12. Remember that you can download the SportsStore application and all of the other examples in this book from Apress.com.

Understanding the Problem

In Chapter 8, I added a feature that simulated getting the initial level of stock for a product from a remote server. The data that this process returns for each product becomes available after the product details have been displayed in the app layout, which led me to define a callback in the **ProductDataStore** class that is used to signal an update. Here is the signature of the callback:

```
...
var callback:((Product) -> Void)?;
...
```

The definition is simple: the **Product** object for which a stock level value is available is passed to the callback, which is not required to define a result.

This is a common way to define a notification callback, and it reflects the way that many developers focus their attention; at the time a new feature is being written, it is the most important feature in the application. Sadly, the style of callback doesn't consider that the recipient of the notification may have signed up with other event sources, each of which has also defined an egocentric callback. It becomes hard to figure out exactly what the change notification is for without having to define separate closures to deal with each one, which means that the source of the notification is implicit in directing the implementation of the recipient.

The bridge pattern can help address this problem by bridging the callback required by the event source and a more useful API that provides additional context to the recipient of the notification.

Defining the Bridge Class

The bridge class that I require is simple, and it has only to receive events using the callback whose signature I showed you in the previous section and map it to a more useful callback that provides more context information to the eventual recipient of the notification. Listing 13-18 shows the contents of the **EventBridge.swift** file that I added to the SportsStore project.

Listing 13-18. The Contents of the EventBridge.swift File

```
class EventBridge {
    private let outputCallback:(String, Int) -> Void;

    init(callback:(String,Int) -> Void) {
        self.outputCallback = callback;
    }

    var inputCallback:(Product) -> Void {
        return { p in self.outputCallback(p.name, p.stockLevel); }
    }
}
```

The **EventBridge** class is simple, but it separates the source of the events from the destination and provides the means by which either can be changed without needing to modify other. The key is that the **Product** object in the incoming notification isn't passed along as part of the outgoing notification—instead, just the name of the product and the new stock level are passed. This simpler notification suits the **ViewController** class, which doesn't really care about **Product** objects and is better focused on updating the value displayed to the client. Listing 13-19 shows how I have used the **EventBridge** class to simplify the **ViewController** code.

Listing 13-19. Applying the Bridge in the ViewController.swift File

```
import UIKit

// ...ProductTableCell class omitted for brevity...

class ViewController: UIViewController, UITableViewDataSource {

    @IBOutlet weak var totalStockLabel: UILabel!
    @IBOutlet weak var tableView: UITableView!

    var productStore = ProductDataStore();

    override func viewDidLoad() {
        super.viewDidLoad();
        displayStockTotal();
        let bridge = EventBridge(callback: updateStockLevel);
        productStore.callback = bridge.inputCallback;
    }

    func updateStockLevel(name:String, level:Int) {
        for cell in self.tableView.visibleCells() {
            if let pcell = cell as? ProductTableCell {
                if pcell.product?.name == name {
                    pcell.stockStepper.value = Double(level);
                    pcell.stockField.text = String(level);
                }
            }
        }
        self.displayStockTotal();
    }

    override func didReceiveMemoryWarning() {
        super.didReceiveMemoryWarning();
    }

    // ...other methods omitted for brevity...
}
```

This may not seem like a substantial change, but it means I am able to define a single method—**updateStockLevel**—to capture all stock level updates regardless of where in the application they originate. I may have to use a bridge in order to transform the original events so that the **updateStockLevel** can be called, but I no longer have to define closures for each individual event source that just sends me a **Product** object.

Summary

I described the bridge pattern in this chapter and explained how it can be used to deal with an exploding hierarchy of classes by separating common and platform-specific code. I also explained that the bridge pattern has a more general role of separating an abstraction from its implementation and demonstrated how this can be used to change the API used to receive events. In the next chapter, I describe the decorator pattern.

The Decorator Pattern

In this chapter, I describe the decorator pattern, which allows the behavior of an object to be selectively modified at runtime. This pattern has a number of uses but has the most impact when working with classes that cannot be modified. The idea of selective modification means that you can choose which objects are changed and which retain their original functionality. Table 14-1 puts the decorator pattern into context.

Table 14-1. Putting the Decorator Pattern into Context

Question	Answer
What is it?	The decorator pattern allows the behavior of individual objects to be changed without requiring changes to the classes that are used to create them or the components that consume them.
What are the benefits?	The changes in behavior defined with the decorator pattern can be combined to create complex effects without needing to create large numbers of subclasses.
When should you use this pattern?	Use this pattern when you need to change the behavior of objects without changing the class they are created from or the components that use them.
When should you avoid this pattern?	Do not use this pattern when you are able to change the class that creates the objects you want to modify. It is usually simpler and easier to modify the class directly.
How do you know when you have implemented the pattern correctly?	The pattern has been implemented correctly when you can select some of the objects created from a class to be modified without affecting all of them and without requiring changes to the class.
Are there any common pitfalls?	The main pitfall is implementing the pattern so that it affects all of the objects created from a given class rather than allowing changes to be applied selectively. A less common pitfall is implementing the pattern so that it has hidden side effects that are not related to the original purpose of the objects being modified.
Are there any related patterns?	Many of the structural patterns have similar implementations but different intents. Ensure that you select the correct pattern from the ones I describe in this part of the book.

Preparing the Example Project

Following the same approach I used in earlier chapters, I created a new OS X Command Line Tool project called Decorator. I added a file to the project called **Purchase.swift**, the contents of which are shown in Listing 14-1.

Listing 14-1. The Contents of the Purchase.swift File

```
class Purchase : Printable {
    private let product:String;
    private let price:Float;

    init(product:String, price:Float) {
        self.product = product;
        self.price = price;
    }

    var description:String {
        return product;
    }

    var totalPrice:Float {
        return price;
    }
}
```

The **Purchase** class represents a product selection made by a customer in a store. The class defines properties that store the name of the product and presents these publically through the calculated **description** and **totalPrice** properties. Next, I added a file called **CustomerAccount.swift** to the example project and used it to define the class shown in Listing 14-2.

Listing 14-2. The Contents of the CustomerAccount.swift File

```
import Foundation

class CustomerAccount {
    let customerName:String;
    var purchases = [Purchase]();

    init(name:String) {
        self.customerName = name;
    }

    func addPurchase(purchase:Purchase) {
        self.purchases.append(purchase);
    }
```

```
func printAccount() {
    var total:Float = 0;
    for p in purchases {
        total += p.totalPrice;
        println("Purchase \(p), Price \(formatCurrencyString(p.totalPrice))");
    }
    println("Total due: \(formatCurrencyString(total))");
}

func formatCurrencyString(number:Float) -> String {
    let formatter = NSNumberFormatter();
    formatter.numberStyle = NSNumberFormatterStyle.CurrencyStyle;
    return formatter.stringFromNumber(number) ?? "";
}
}
```

The **CustomerAccount** class maintains a collection of **Purchase** objects to represent the purchases made by a customer. New purchases are added to the account through the **addPurchase** method, and the **printAccount** method writes a summary of the account to the Xcode debug console. Listing 14-3 shows the statements that I added to the **main.swift** file to use the **Purchase** and **CustomerAccount** classes.

Listing 14-3. The Contents of the main.swift File

```
let account = CustomerAccount(name:"Joe");

account.addPurchase(Purchase(product: "Red Hat", price: 10));
account.addPurchase(Purchase(product: "Scarf", price: 20));

account.printAccount();
```

The **Purchase** class conforms to the **Printable** protocol, which means that the value of the **description** property is used when the object is passed to the **println** method. Running the example application produces the following output:

```
Purchase Red Hat, Price $10.00
Purchase Scarf, Price $20.00
Total due: $30.00
```

Understanding the Problem That the Pattern Solves

Imagine that I want to add some gift options to my customers, but I need to do so without modifying the **Purchase** or **CustomerAccount** class I defined in the previous section. There are lots of reasons why classes cannot be modified, but the most frequent is when they are part of a framework provided by a third party. In the case of my example application, the **Purchase** and **CustomerAccount** classes might be part of an off-the-shelf sales management system.

The customer can mix and match the gift options, each of which has a different price and can be applied independently. Table 14-2 shows the options and their costs.

Table 14-2. The Gift Options for Purchases

Gift Options	Cost
Gift wrap	$2
Ribbon	$1
Gift delivery	$5

The obvious way of adding support for the gift options is to create subclasses of the **Purchase** class, which will allow me to define new behaviors without needing to change the **Purchase** class or the **CustomerAccount** class, which expects to operate on **Purchase** objects.

Listing 14-4 shows the contents of the **Options.swift** file, which I added to the example project and used to define subclasses for the gift options.

Listing 14-4. The Contents of the Options.swift File

```
class PurchaseWithGiftWrap : Purchase {
    override var description:String { return "\(super.description) + giftwrap"; }
    override var totalPrice:Float { return super.totalPrice + 2;}
}

class PurchaseWithRibbon : Purchase {
    override var description:String { return "\(super.description) + ribbon"; }
    override var totalPrice:Float { return super.totalPrice + 1; }
}

class PurchaseWithDelivery : Purchase {
    override var description:String { return "\(super.description) + delivery"; }
    override var totalPrice:Float { return super.totalPrice + 5; }
}
```

Each of the three classes I have defined represents one of the options from Table 14-2 and overrides the **description** and **totalPrice** properties. Listing 14-5 shows how I can specify an option by using one of the subclasses rather than the **Purchase** base class.

Listing 14-5. Using a Purchase Subclass in the main.swift File

```
let account = CustomerAccount(name:"Joe");

account.addPurchase(Purchase(product: "Red Hat", price: 10));
account.addPurchase(Purchase(product: "Scarf", price: 20));
account.addPurchase(PurchaseWithGiftWrap(product: "Sunglasses", price: 25));

account.printAccount();
```

Running the application produces the following output in the debug console:

```
Purchase Red Hat, Price $10.00
Purchase Scarf, Price $20.00
Purchase Sunglasses + giftwrap, Price $27.00
Total due: $57.00
```

These subclasses work, but they don't meet my business requirements: customers cannot mix and match the options. Each subclass represents only a single option, and I have no way to represent a purchase that the customer wants gift wrapped and delivered. Clearly, I need another subclass to represent this combination, as shown in Listing 14-6.

Listing 14-6. Adding a Subclass for a Gift Option Combination in the Options.swift File

```
class PurchaseWithGiftWrap : Purchase {
    override var description:String { return "\(super.description) + giftwrap"; }
    override var totalPrice:Float { return super.totalPrice + 2;}
}

class PurchaseWithRibbon : Purchase {
    override var description:String { return "\(super.description) + ribbon"; }
    override var totalPrice:Float { return super.totalPrice + 1; }
}

class PurchaseWithDelivery : Purchase {
    override var description:String { return "\(super.description) + delivery"; }
    override var totalPrice:Float { return super.totalPrice + 5; }
}

class PurchaseWithGiftWrapAndDelivery : Purchase {
    override var description:String {
        return "\(super.description) + giftwrap + delivery"; }
    override var totalPrice:Float { return super.totalPrice + 5 + 2; }
}
```

This is only one of the possible combinations. To allow the customer a full range of choices, I need to create subclasses for all of the following combinations:

- Gift wrap
- Ribbon
- Delivery
- Gift wrap + Ribbon
- Gift wrap + Delivery
- Ribbon + Delivery
- Gift wrap + Ribbon + Delivery

The number of classes will keep increasing as I add options because I need to address all of the permutations that can exist. The volume of classes presents an error risk and makes maintenance difficult. As an example, changing the price of an option can require a massive number of changes, and it is easy to miss one or more classes that should be updated.

Understanding the Decorator Pattern

The decorator solves the permutation problem by creating decorator classes, which are wrappers around the original class that change its behavior. A decorator presents the same API as the wrapped class, and decorators can wrap other decorators in order to create permutations. Figure 14-1 illustrates the decorator pattern.

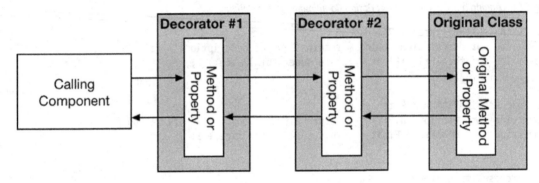

Figure 14-1. The decorator pattern

The decorators present the same methods and properties as the original class, which allows them to be used as substitutes without needing to modify the calling components. Decorators usually call the methods and properties of the objects they are wrapping, as shown in the figure. Since all of the objects involved present the same methods and properties, a decorator is unaware if the object it wraps is an instance of the original class or another decorator.

Implementing the Decorator Pattern

The decorator pattern is implemented by deriving from the class that cannot be changed in order to create a class that defines the same properties and methods and that can be used as a transparent substitute. The decorator class defines a `private` property that is the wrapped object and uses it to provide the base functionality that is decorated. Listing 14-7 shows how I replaced the individual classes from the previous section with decorators in the **Options.swift** file.

Listing 14-7. Defining Decorator Classes in the Options.swift File

```swift
class BasePurchaseDecorator : Purchase {
    private let wrappedPurchase:Purchase;

    init(purchase:Purchase) {
        wrappedPurchase = purchase;
        super.init(product: purchase.description, price: purchase.totalPrice);
    }
}

class PurchaseWithGiftWrap : BasePurchaseDecorator {
    override var description:String { return "\(super.description) + giftwrap"; }
    override var totalPrice:Float { return super.totalPrice + 2;}
}

class PurchaseWithRibbon : BasePurchaseDecorator {
    override var description:String { return "\(super.description) + ribbon"; }
    override var totalPrice:Float { return super.totalPrice + 1; }
}

class PurchaseWithDelivery : BasePurchaseDecorator {
    override var description:String { return "\(super.description) + delivery"; }
    override var totalPrice:Float { return super.totalPrice + 5; }
}
```

To reduce duplication, I have defined a **BasePurchaseDecorator** class that is derived from **Purchase** and defines an initializer that accepts a **Purchase** object and assigns it to a private stored variable.

The individual decorators inherit the **Purchase** variable and the initializer and override the **description** and **totalPrice** properties. Each decorator property calls the corresponding property of the wrapped **Purchase** object, manipulates the result, and then returns it to the caller. In the case of the **totalPrice** property, for example, each decorator gets the price from the wrapped object and adds the cost of the option it represents.

Tip   Some objects that require decoration will be defined by a protocol, and the implementation classes will not be exposed to you. This doesn't change the way that decorators are implemented. The decorator conforms to the protocol and wraps around an object that also conforms to the protocol.

The decorators are derived from the **Purchase** class and define an initializer that is wrapped that accepts a **Purchase** object, which means they can be combined to create permutations of objects, as shown in Listing 14-8.

Listing 14-8. Using the Decorator Classes in the main.swift File

```swift
let account = CustomerAccount(name:"Joe");

account.addPurchase(Purchase(product: "Red Hat", price: 10));
account.addPurchase(Purchase(product: "Scarf", price: 20));
account.addPurchase(PurchaseWithDelivery(purchase:
```

```
        PurchaseWithGiftWrap(purchase:
          Purchase(product: "Sunglasses", price:25))));
```

```
account.printAccount();
```

I create a **Purchase** object to represent the purchase of sunglasses and pass it to the initializer of the **PurchaseWithGiftWrap** decorator. I pass the decorator object to the initializer to the **PurchaseWithDelivery** to add a second decorator and add the twice-decorated purchase to the customer's account. I made no changes to the **Purchase** or **CustomerAccount** class, but the output produced by running the application shows that the decorator classes have allowed me to define the gift options:

```
Purchase Red Hat, Price $10.00
Purchase Scarf, Price $20.00
Purchase Sunglasses + giftwrap + delivery, Price $32.00
Total due: $62.00
```

The description of the purchase includes the options that have been selected, and the cost of those options is reflected in the price.

Variations on the Decorator Pattern

There are two variations on the decorator pattern, which I describe in the sections that follow.

Creating Decorators with New Functionality

The decorators that I defined in earlier sections presented the same API as the objects they decorated. This means decorators are essentially invisible to the classes that consume decorated objects, letting the application benefit from additional functionality—gift options in this case—without the need to make modifications.

The first pattern variation is to create decorators that define additional methods or properties beyond those defined by the original objects. This allows more flexibility in the kinds of enhancements that decorators can implement but does so by reducing the flexibility with which those enhancements can be applied. To demonstrate, I added a new file called **Discounts.swift** to the example project and used it to define the decorators shown in Listing 14-9.

Listing 14-9. The Contents of the Discounts.swift File

```swift
class DiscountDecorator: Purchase {
    private let wrappedPurchase:Purchase;

    init(purchase:Purchase) {
        self.wrappedPurchase = purchase;
        super.init(product: purchase.description, price: purchase.totalPrice);
    }

    override var description:String {
        return super.description;
    }
}
```

```
    var discountAmount:Float {
        return 0;
    }

    func countDiscounts() -> Int {
        var total = 1;
        if let discounter = wrappedPurchase as? DiscountDecorator {
            total += discounter.countDiscounts();
        }
        return total;
    }
}

class BlackFridayDecorator : DiscountDecorator {

    override var totalPrice:Float {
        return super.totalPrice - discountAmount;
    }

    override var discountAmount:Float {
        return super.totalPrice * 0.20;
    }
}

class EndOfLineDecorator : DiscountDecorator {

    override var totalPrice:Float {
        return super.totalPrice - discountAmount;
    }

    override var discountAmount:Float {
        return super.totalPrice * 0.70;
    }
}
```

I have defined the **DiscountDecorator** that wraps a **Purchase** object and exposes its **description** and **totalPrice** properties. The decorator also defines the **discountAmount** property, which returns the amount by which a price is discounted in a sale. The implementation of the **totalPrice** property uses the **discountAmount** value to reduce the price of a purchase. The **countDiscounts** method works out how many discounts have been applied to the purchase by looking to see whether the wrapped object is a discount decorator and working its way through the chain of wrapped objects to work out the total.

I have derived two decorator classes from **DiscountDecorator** that represent different sale conditions. Listing 14-10 shows how I applied the decorators to a purchase.

Listing 14-10. Applying the Discount Decorators in the swift.main File

```
let account = CustomerAccount(name:"Joe");

account.addPurchase(Purchase(product: "Red Hat", price: 10));
account.addPurchase(Purchase(product: "Scarf", price: 20));
account.addPurchase(EndOfLineDecorator(purchase:
    BlackFridayDecorator(purchase: PurchaseWithDelivery(purchase:
        PurchaseWithGiftWrap(purchase:Purchase(product: "Sunglasses", price:25))))));

account.printAccount();
```

I used both the **EndOfLineDecorator** and the **BlackFridayDecorator** to combine discounts on the sunglasses purchase. Running the application produces the following results:

```
Purchase Red Hat, Price $10.00
Purchase Scarf, Price $20.00
Purchase Sunglasses + giftwrap + delivery, Price $7.68
Total due: $37.68
```

The new decorators don't modify the description of the product, but they reduce the price from $32 to $25.60.

Using the New Functionality

The **countDiscounts** method that the new decorators present allows me to get information about the number of discounts that have been applied to a purchase, as shown in Listing 14-11.

Listing 14-11. Displaying the Number of Discounts in the main.swift File

```
let account = CustomerAccount(name:"Joe");

account.addPurchase(Purchase(product: "Red Hat", price: 10));
account.addPurchase(Purchase(product: "Scarf", price: 20));
account.addPurchase(EndOfLineDecorator(purchase:
    BlackFridayDecorator(purchase: PurchaseWithDelivery(purchase:
        PurchaseWithGiftWrap(purchase:Purchase(product: "Sunglasses", price:25))))));

account.printAccount();

for p in account.purchases {
    if let d = p as? DiscountDecorator {
        println("\(p) has \(d.countDiscounts()) discounts");
    } else {
        println("\(p) has no discounts");
    }
}
```

I check to see whether each of the **Purchase** objects stored by the **CustomerAccount** object is an instance of the **DiscountDecorator** class and call the **countDiscounts** method if it is. Running the application produces the following output:

```
Purchase Red Hat, Price $10.00
Purchase Scarf, Price $20.00
Purchase Sunglasses + giftwrap + delivery, Price $7.68
Total due: $37.68
Red Hat has no discounts
Scarf has no discounts
Sunglasses + giftwrap + delivery has 2 discounts
```

Understanding the Limitations of Decorators with New Functionality

Decorators that implement new functionality place limits on the way that decoration can be applied. To expose the new functionality, each instance of the decorator class requires at least one other component to be able to find it—either the calling component or the decorator that acts as a wrapper in the case of nested decorators.

The discount decorators I defined are sensitive to the order in which they are applied. In Listing 14-11, both discounts are applied to the total cost of the purchase, including the gift options that have been selected, like this:

```
...
account.addPurchase(EndOfLineDecorator(purchase:
    BlackFridayDecorator(purchase: PurchaseWithDelivery(purchase:
        PurchaseWithGiftWrap(purchase:Purchase(product: "Sunglasses", price:25))))));
...
```

Listing 14-12 shows how this statement changes if I want one of the discounts to apply only to the product price and exclude the options.

Listing 14-12. Changing the Application of a Discount in the main.swift File

```
let account = CustomerAccount(name:"Joe");

account.addPurchase(Purchase(product: "Red Hat", price: 10));
account.addPurchase(Purchase(product: "Scarf", price: 20));
account.addPurchase(EndOfLineDecorator(purchase:
        PurchaseWithDelivery(purchase:PurchaseWithGiftWrap(purchase:
            BlackFridayDecorator(purchase:
        Purchase(product: "Sunglasses", price:25))))));

account.printAccount();

for p in account.purchases {
    if let d = p as? DiscountDecorator {
        println("\(p) has \(d.countDiscounts()) discounts");
    } else {
        println("\(p) has no discounts");
    }
}
```

The **BlackFridayDecorator** reduces the price of the sunglasses only and does not affect the price of the gift options. Here is the output from running the application:

```
Purchase Scarf, Price $20.00
Purchase Sunglasses + giftwrap + delivery, Price $8.10
Total due: $38.10
Red Hat has no discounts
Scarf has no discounts
Sunglasses + giftwrap + delivery has 1 discounts
```

The price has been calculated correctly, but notice that only one discount is displayed by the summary. This happens because the gift option decorators have no knowledge of the discount decorators and the additional functionality they provide.

This kind of inflexibility doesn't mean you should avoid defining new features with decorators, but you should do so carefully and consider the impact it will have on the rest of the application, especially if there are other decorators already in use.

Creating Consolidated Decorators

So far, I have defined simple decorator classes because I wanted to emphasize how the pattern works and show how decorators can be selected and applied without modifying the classes they decorate or those that rely on them.

Decorators need not be so simple, and the pattern allows for any implementation of the methods and properties that the original class defines. A common variation is to create consolidated decorators that apply multiple changes to an object. Listing 14-13 shows how I have consolidated the gift option decorators into a single class.

> **Caution** Decorators are free to create their own implementations of methods and properties, but you should use them to perform only the same tasks as the original class's implementations. A good decorated implementation might apply sales tax to the **totalPrice** property in the example application, but a bad implementation would return the number of items in stock. Decorators should enhance or extend the functionality of the original class and not sneak new features into an existing API.

Listing 14-13. Creating a Single Decorator for Multiple Purchase Options in the Options.swift File

```swift
class GiftOptionDecorator : Purchase {
    private let wrappedPurchase:Purchase;
    private let options:[OPTION];

    enum OPTION {
        case GIFTWRAP;
        case RIBBON;
        case DELIVERY;
    }
```

```
init(purchase:Purchase, options:OPTION...) {
    self.wrappedPurchase = purchase;
    self.options = options;
    super.init(product: purchase.description, price: purchase.totalPrice);
}

override var description:String {
    var result = wrappedPurchase.description;
    for option in options {
        switch (option) {
            case .GIFTWRAP:
                result = "\(result) + giftwrap";
            case .RIBBON:
                result = "\(result) + ribbon";
            case .DELIVERY:
                result = "\(result) + delivery";
        }
    }
    return result;
}

override var totalPrice:Float {
    var result = wrappedPurchase.totalPrice;
    for option in options {
        switch (option) {
            case .GIFTWRAP:
                result += 2;
            case .RIBBON:
                result += 1;
            case .DELIVERY:
                result += 5;
        }
    }
    return result;
}
}
```

This is still a decorator; it allows me to selectively modify the behavior of **Purchase** objects, and it allows me to create combinations of gift options. The difference is that it consolidates the options so they can be applied in a single object. Listing 14-14 shows how I updated the code that creates the purchases to use the new decorator.

Tip   I prefer to use separate decorator classes for small projects. I find them more elegant and pleasant to work with. They are harder to maintain, however, and for more complex projects I switch to consolidated decorators that group related enhancements together. I find consolidated decorators less elegant but easier to manage.

Listing 14-14. Using the Consolidated Decorator in the main.swift File

```
let account = CustomerAccount(name:"Joe");

account.addPurchase(Purchase(product: "Red Hat", price: 10));
account.addPurchase(Purchase(product: "Scarf", price: 20));
account.addPurchase(EndOfLineDecorator(purchase: BlackFridayDecorator(purchase:
        GiftOptionDecorator(purchase: Purchase(product: "Sunglasses", price:25),
            options: GiftOptionDecorator.OPTION.GIFTWRAP,
                GiftOptionDecorator.OPTION.DELIVERY))));

account.printAccount();

for p in account.purchases {
    if let d = p as? DiscountDecorator {
        println("\(p) has \(d.countDiscounts()) discounts");
    } else {
        println("\(p) has no discounts");
    }
}
```

The code looks a little ugly because of the way that it has to be formatted to fit on the page, but the result is just the same as when I applied two of the individual decorator classes in the previous section.

Understanding the Pitfalls of the Decorator Pattern

There are two pitfalls to avoid when implementing the decorator pattern. The first is to try to decorate objects using Swift extensions. One of the main characteristics of the decorator pattern is that decoration is applied selectively to individual objects, but extensions change all objects of a specified type.

The Side-Effect Pitfall

The second pitfall arises when you are writing a decorator and you realize that you can use it to do more than just decorate the methods and properties of an object. It can be an appealing idea. For example, I could modify the decorator used to indicate the delivery option to automatically schedule the delivery.

This is a side effect because it isn't part of the original purpose of the object that was decorated. Side effects usually end up causing more problems than they solve and are the second pitfall associated with the decorator pattern.

Side effect decorators are hard to maintain, especially in a team development environment. Another programmer who sees the name of your **DeliveryDecorator** class is unlikely to realize it does anything more than to decorate an object. Problems with deliveries will start when the class is carelessly modified or reused elsewhere in the application.

Keep a narrow focus for your decorator classes and deal with related activities—such as deliveries—using separate classes.

Examples of the Decorator Pattern in Cocoa

The best-known use of the decorator pattern in Cocoa to handle scrolling windows. Rather than define scroll bars and the scrolling mechanism for every UI component that can be shown to the user, Cocoa decorates objects with **NSClipView**, which is in turn decorated by **NSScrollView.** **NSScrollView** displays the scroll bars and deals with user interaction and manages the **NSClipView** to determine which part of the UI component is visible to the user.

Applying the Pattern to the SportsStore Application

To put the decorator pattern into a broader context, I am going to apply it to the **Product** class in the SportsStore application to reduce the price of all products in the **Soccer** category and increase the price of any item for which there are four or fewer items in stock.

Preparing the Example Application

No preparation is required for this chapter, and I am going to pick up the SportsStore project as I left it in Chapter 13.

> **Tip**   Remember that all of the examples in this book are available as a free download from Apress.com.

Creating the Decorators

Once you know how the decorator pattern works, creating decorator classes is a simple process. Listing 14-15 shows the contents of the **ProductDecorators.swift** file, which I added to the SportsStore project.

Listing 14-15. The Contents of the ProductDecorators.swift File

```
class PriceDecorator : Product {
    private let wrappedProduct:Product;

    required init(name:String, description:String, category:String,
            price:Double, stockLevel:Int) {
        fatalError("Not supported");
    }

    init(product:Product) {
        self.wrappedProduct = product;
        super.init(name: product.name, description: product.productDescription,
            category: product.category, price: product.price,
                stockLevel: product.stockLevel);
    }
}
```

```
class LowStockIncreaseDecorator : PriceDecorator {

    override var price:Double {
        var price = wrappedProduct.price;
        if (stockLevel <= 4) {
            price = price * 1.5;
        }
        return price;
    }
}

class SoccerDecreaseDecorator : PriceDecorator {
    override var price:Double {
        return super.wrappedProduct.price * 0.5;
    }
}
```

The **PriceDecorator** class is the base for my decorators and is a subclass of the **Product** class. The **Product** class defines a **required** initializer that I have to add to **PriceDecorator** but don't want to use. I have used the **fatalError** function so that I don't have to implement the **required** initializer and defined a new initializer that accepts a **Product** object that will be decorated.

The **LowStockIncreaseDecorator** and **SoccerDecreaseDecorator** classes are the decorator classes, and they override the **price** property to change the prices of the products.

Applying the Decorators

I want to apply the decorators to **Product** objects as they are created. Listing 14-16 shows how I changed the **loadData** method in the **ProductDataStore** class.

Listing 14-16. Applying the Decorators in the ProductDataStore.swift File

```
...
private func loadData() -> [Product] {

    var products = [Product]();

    for product in productData {
        var p:Product = LowStockIncreaseDecorator(product: product);
        if (p.category == "Soccer") {
            p = SoccerDecreaseDecorator(product: p);
        }

        dispatch_async(self.networkQ, {() in
            let stockConn = NetworkPool.getConnection();
            let level = stockConn.getStockLevel(p.name);
            if (level != nil) {
                p.stockLevel = level!;
                dispatch_async(self.uiQ, {() in
```

```
                    if (self.callback != nil) {
                        self.callback!(p);
                    }
                })
            }
            NetworkPool.returnConnecton(stockConn);
        });
        products.append(p);
    }
    return products;
}
...
```

I decorate all **Product** objects with the **LowStockIncreaseDecorator** class but apply the **SoccerDecreaseDecorator** only to **Product** objects in the **Soccer** category. The effect is that the prices of all soccer products are permanently reduced, and those products whose stock level drops below five items will be increased.

Summary

In this chapter, I described the decorator pattern and explained how it can be used to change the behavior of objects at runtime. The decorator pattern is especially useful when dealing with classes that cannot be modified and makes it easy to enhance applications even when working with third-party or legacy frameworks. In the next chapter, I describe the composite pattern, which allows single instances and collections of objects to be treated consistently.

The Composite Pattern

The composite pattern is not as broadly applicable as some of the other design patterns I describe in this book, but it remains an important pattern because of the way it applies consistency to a data structure that contains different types of object. Table 15-1 puts the composite pattern in context.

Table 15-1. *Putting the Composite Pattern into Context*

Question	Answer
What is it?	The composite pattern allows a tree of individual objects and collections of objects to be treated consistently.
What are the benefits?	The consistency that the composite pattern brings means that components that operate on the tree structure are simpler and do not need to have knowledge of the different objects types that are in use.
When should you use this pattern?	Use this pattern when you have a tree structure that contains leaf nodes and collections of objects.
When should you avoid this pattern?	This pattern is applicable only to tree data structures.
How do you know when you have implemented the pattern correctly?	The pattern is implemented correctly when components that use the tree structure can treat all of the objects it contains using the same type or protocol.
Are there any common pitfalls?	This pattern is best suited to tree structures that are not modified once they have been created. Adding support for modifying the tree undermines the benefit of the pattern.
Are there any related patterns?	Many of the structural patterns have similar implementations but different intents. Ensure that you select the correct pattern from the ones I describe in this part of the book.

Preparing the Example Project

Following the same approach I used in earlier chapters, I created a new OS X Command Line Tool project called Composite. I added a file to the project called **CarParts.swift**, the contents of which are shown in Listing 15-1.

Listing 15-1. The Contents of the CarParts.swift File

```swift
class Part {
    let name:String;
    let price:Float;

    init(name:String, price:Float) {
        self.name = name; self.price = price;
    }
}

class CompositePart {
    let name:String;
    let parts:[Part];

    init(name:String, parts:Part...) {
        self.name = name; self.parts = parts;
    }
}
```

I have defined two classes to represent parts used to repair cars. The **Part** class represents a single self-contained part, such as a spark plug or a tire. The **CompositePart** class represents parts that are made up of other parts and that are typically purchased as a single unit, such as a wheel, which would comprise a tire, a wheel alloy, and some fixing nuts. The **CompositePart** class represents its constituent elements using a **Part** array. I also added a file called **Orders.swift**, the contents of which are shown in Listing 15-2.

Listing 15-2. The Contents of the Orders.swift File

```swift
import Foundation

class CustomerOrder {
    let customer:String;
    let parts:[Part];
    let compositeParts:[CompositePart];

    init(customer:String, parts:[Part], composites:[CompositePart]) {
        self.customer = customer;
        self.parts = parts;
        self.compositeParts = composites;
    }

    var totalPrice:Float {
        let partReducer = {(subtotal:Float, part:Part) -> Float in
            return subtotal + part.price};
```

```
        var total = reduce(parts, 0, partReducer);

        return reduce(compositeParts, total, {(subtotal, cpart) -> Float in
            return reduce(cpart.parts, subtotal, partReducer);
        });
    }

    func printDetails() {
        println("Order for \(customer): Cost: \(formatCurrencyString(totalPrice))");
    }

    func formatCurrencyString(number:Float) -> String {
        let formatter = NSNumberFormatter();
        formatter.numberStyle = NSNumberFormatterStyle.CurrencyStyle;
        return formatter.stringFromNumber(number) ?? "";
    }
}
```

The **CustomerOrder** class represents an order made up of **Part** and **CompositePart** objects. The **printDetails** method writes out the name of the customer and the total price of the order, which is obtained from the **totalPrice** property. Listing 15-3 shows the code I added to the **main.swift** file to create and populate a **CustomerOrder** object with **Part** and **CompositePart** objects.

Listing 15-3. The Contents of the main.swift File

```
let doorWindow = CompositePart(name: "DoorWindow", parts:
    Part(name: "Window", price: 100.50),
    Part(name: "Window Switch", price: 12));

let door = CompositePart(name: "Door", parts:
    Part(name: "Window", price: 100.50),
    Part(name: "Door Loom", price: 80),
    Part(name: "Window Switch", price: 12),
    Part(name: "Door Handles", price: 43.40));

let hood = Part(name: "Hood", price: 320);

let order = CustomerOrder(customer: "Bob", parts: [hood],
    composites: [door, doorWindow]);
order.printDetails();
```

The customer is **Bob**, and his order consists of a complete door, a door window, and a hood. Running the application produces the following output:

```
Order for Bob: Cost: $668.40
```

Understanding the Problem That the Pattern Solves

The classes in the example application exhibit two different problems, both of which stem from the fact that there are different types used to represent car parts in an order.

The first problem is that I am limited to simple hierarchies of parts. When I created the **CompositePart** object to represent a car door in Listing 15-3, I had to create a **Part** object for the **Window** and another for the **Window Switch**es. I had to create the same **Part** objects for the door window, even though the door contains a window. This limitation means that I need to keep two lists of parts up-to-date, even though one is a superset of the other.

The second problem is that classes that operate on parts need to know the details of the **CompositePart** and **Part** objects and how they relate to one another. You can see an example of this problem in the **CustomerAccount** class, in which a substantial portion of the code in the class deals with working out the total cost of all the **Part** objects that have been ordered.

```
...
var totalPrice:Float {
    let partReducer = {(subtotal:Float, part:Part) -> Float in
        return subtotal + part.price};

    var total = reduce(parts, 0, partReducer);

    return reduce(compositeParts, total, {(subtotal, cpart) -> Float in
        return reduce(cpart.parts, subtotal, partReducer);
    });
}
...
```

The need for the components that operate on parts to understand the relationship between the **Part** and **CompositePart** classes means that I have to duplicate this kind of code in each of those components.

Understanding the Composite Pattern

The composite pattern solves the problems I described by arranging objects into a tree hierarchy and defining a protocol that allows individual and composite objects to be treated consistently. The protocol is presented to the components that operate on the objects, which are unaware of which objects are single objects and which are collections.

The protocol is also used within the composite objects, which are then able to seamlessly collect together objects that represent individual objects and other collections. Figure 15-1 shows the way that the composite pattern is used to arrange objects, but this is a pattern that is most readily understood through a working implementation; see the next section for details.

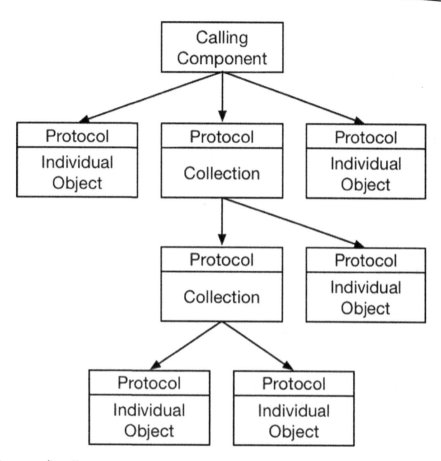

Figure 15-1. The composite pattern

Implementing the Composite Pattern

The objects used to represent individual objects are known as *leaf nodes* in the tree data structure. The objects used to represent a collection are known as *composites*. Both the leaf node and composite objects implement the same protocol, which hides the details of how collections are composed from the components that consume them.

The first step in implementation is to define the protocol, which is the heart of the pattern. Listing 15-4 shows the definition of the protocol for the example application, and the changes required make the **Part** and **CompositePart** classes conform to it.

Listing 15-4. Defining and Applying a Protocol in the CarParts.swift File

```swift
protocol CarPart {
    var name:String { get };
    var price:Float { get };
}

class Part : CarPart {
    let name:String;
    let price:Float;

    init(name:String, price:Float) {
        self.name = name; self.price = price;
    }
}

class CompositePart : CarPart {
    let name:String;
    let parts:[CarPart];

    init(name:String, parts:CarPart...) {
        self.name = name; self.parts = parts;
    }

    var price:Float {
        return reduce(parts, 0, {subtotal, part in
            return subtotal + part.price;
        });
    }
}
```

The **CarPart** protocol defines **name** and **price** properties, which correspond to the properties already defined by the **Part** class. This means that the only change for **Part** is to declare conformance to the protocol.

The changes for the **CompositePart** class are more profound. It is important that composite objects operate on the protocol and not the classes that conform to it, which means I have removed references to the **Part** class and replaced them with references to the **CarPart** protocol. In addition, I have defined the **price** property specified by the protocol, and its implementation uses the global **reduce** function to sum the value of the **price** properties of the **CarPart** objects it has been used to collect.

Applying the Pattern

The next step is to update the classes that operate on the left node and composite objects so that they rely on the protocol rather than its implementation classes. Listing 15-5 shows the changes that I made to the **CustomerOrder** class.

Listing 15-5. Applying the Protocol in the Orders.swift File

```
import Foundation

class CustomerOrder {
    let customer:String;
    let parts:[CarPart];

    init(customer:String, parts:[CarPart]) {
        self.customer = customer;
        self.parts = parts;
    }

    var totalPrice:Float {
        return reduce(parts, 0, {subtotal, part in
            return subtotal + part.price});
    }

    func printDetails() {
        println("Order for \(customer): Cost: \(formatCurrencyString(totalPrice))");
    }

    func formatCurrencyString(number:Float) -> String {
        let formatter = NSNumberFormatter();
        formatter.numberStyle = NSNumberFormatterStyle.CurrencyStyle;
        return formatter.stringFromNumber(number) ?? "";
    }
}
```

The **CustomerOrder** class no longer needs to have knowledge of the leaf node and composite classes and deals only with the **CartPart** protocol. The main impact is on the **totalPrice** property, which can simply sum the **price** property of the **CarPart** objects to get the total value of the order.

The final step is to change the code in the **main.swift** file so that I am able to create and reuse composite objects, as shown in Listing 15-6.

Listing 15-6. Reusing Composite Objects in the main.swift File

```
let doorWindow = CompositePart(name: "DoorWindow", parts:
    Part(name: "Window", price: 100.50),
    Part(name: "Window Switch", price: 12));

let door = CompositePart(name: "Door", parts:
    doorWindow,
    Part(name: "Door Loom", price: 80),
    Part(name: "Door Handles", price: 43.40));

let hood = Part(name: "Hood", price: 320);

let order = CustomerOrder(customer: "Bob", parts: [hood, door, doorWindow]);
order.printDetails();
```

> **Note**   The code that creates the data structure, which is in the **main.swift** file for the example, still needs to understand the differences between the leaf node and composite object in order to create the tree. The composite pattern affects the components that consume the tree structure, which no longer depend on being able to differentiate between the different types of object.

Rather than having to duplicate the parts required for a door window, I can simply create one composite object and pass it as an argument to the initializer of another. This means I can change the set of parts that define a door window in one place. Running the application produces the same output as before I implemented the composite pattern.

```
Order for Bob: Cost: $668.40
```

Understanding the Pitfalls of the Composite Pattern

The composite pattern works best when the tree structure that is created is fixed. The main pitfall for the composite pattern occurs when you need to be able to change the structure after it has been created. Listing 15-7 shows the changes I made to the **CompositePart** class to support changes.

Listing 15-7. Adding Support for Composite Collection Changes in the CarParts.swift File

```
...
class CompositePart : CarPart {
    let name:String;
    private var parts:[CarPart];

    init(name:String, parts:CarPart...) {
        self.name = name; self.parts = parts;
    }

    var price:Float {
        return reduce(parts, 0, {subtotal, part in
            return subtotal + part.price;
        });
    }

    func addPart(part:CarPart) {
        parts.append(part);
    }

    func removePart(part:CarPart) {
        for index in 0 ..< parts.count {
            if (parts[index].name  == part.name) {
                parts.removeAtIndex(index);
                break;
            }
```

```
        }
    }
}
...
```

The changes are simple enough. I redefined the constant **CarPart** array as a variable and added **addPart** and **removePart** methods. However, these changes mean that components that change the data structure need to know that the **CompositePart** class defines **addPart** and **removePart** methods and need to understand the difference between the **CompositePart** and **Part** classes in order to add and remove parts.

The changes in Listing 15-7 undermine the benefit of the composite pattern. A common attempt to address this problem is to include the methods in the protocol in order to harmonize the API implemented by the leaf node and composite objects, as shown in Listing 15-8.

Listing 15-8. Attempting to Harmonize the API in the CarParts.swift File

```
protocol CarPart {

    var name:String { get };
    var price:Float { get };

    func addPart(part:CarPart) -> Void;
    func removePart(part:CarPart) -> Void;
}

class Part : CarPart {
    let name:String;
    let price:Float;

    init(name:String, price:Float) {
        self.name = name; self.price = price;
    }

    func addPart(part: CarPart) {
        // do nothing
    }

    func removePart(part: CarPart) {
        // do nothing
    }
}

class CompositePart : CarPart {
    // ...statements omitted for brevity...
}
```

This is not a solution to the problem because the **Part** class has no way to implement the **addPart** and **removePart** methods. A component that calls these methods will expect the data structure to be modified, but, of course, nothing will happen, and the result is either data loss or an error.

Examples of the Composite Pattern in Cocoa

The most important use of the composite pattern in the Cocoa framework is the **UIView** class, which defines the common behavior for all the elements in an app layout. Individual view objects in the view hierarchy can be left nodes (like labels) or composites that contain collections of other views (like table view controllers).

Applying the Pattern to the SportsStore Application

To apply the composite pattern to the SportsStore application, I am going to create product sets that are comprised of individual products and that will be sold as a single unit.

Preparing the Example Application

To prepare for the composite pattern, I am going to simplify the **Product** class and remove some of the features that I added in earlier chapters. Listing 15-9 shows the changes I made.

Listing 15-9. Simplifying the Product Class in the Product.swift File

```
import Foundation

class Product : NSObject, NSCopying {
    private(set) var name:String;
    private(set) var productDescription:String;
    private(set) var category:String;
    private var stockLevelBackingValue:Int = 0;
    private var priceBackingValue:Double = 0;

    required init(name:String, description:String, category:String, price:Double,
        stockLevel:Int) {
            self.name = name;
            self.productDescription = description;
            self.category = category;
            super.init();
            self.price = price;
            self.stockLevel = stockLevel;
    }

    var stockLevel:Int {
        get { return stockLevelBackingValue;}
        set { stockLevelBackingValue = max(0, newValue);}
    }

    private(set) var price:Double {
        get { return priceBackingValue;}
        set { priceBackingValue = max(1, newValue);}
    }
```

```
    var stockValue:Double {
        get {
            return price * Double(stockLevel);
        }
    }

    func copyWithZone(zone: NSZone) -> AnyObject {
        return Product(name: self.name, description: self.description,
            category: self.category, price: self.price,
            stockLevel: self.stockLevel);
    }

    class func createProduct(name:String, description:String, category:String,
        price:Double, stockLevel:Int) -> Product {

        return Product(name:name, description: description, category: category,
            price: price, stockLevel: stockLevel);
    }
}
```

I have removed the category-specific subclasses from the **Product.swift** file and simplified the **Product** class itself so that it no longer deals with sales tax or upsell opportunities (which were the specializations provided by the subclasses).

Defining the Composite Class

When applying the composite pattern to an existing application, it isn't always possible to create a protocol to which both the leaf node and composite objects can conform. In these situations, I treat the existing class as both the definition of the common functionality and the template for the leaf nodes. This allows me to define the composite class as a subclass, as shown in Listing 15-10.

Listing 15-10. Defining the Composite Class in the Product.swift File

```
import Foundation

class Product : NSObject, NSCopying {
    // ...statements omitted for brevity...
}

class ProductComposite : Product {
    private let products:[Product];

    required init(name:String, description:String, category:String,
            price:Double, stockLevel:Int) {
        fatalError("Not implemented");
    }

    init(name:String, description:String, category:String, stockLevel:Int,
            products:Product...) {
        self.products = products;
        super.init(name: name, description: description, category: category,
            price: 0, stockLevel: stockLevel);
    }
```

```
      override var price:Double {
          get { return reduce(products, 0, {total, p in return total + p.price}); }
          set { /* do nothing */ }
      }
}
```

This approach is not as elegant as using a separate protocol, but it minimizes the number of changes that are required to implement the pattern. The **ProductComposite** class consists of subclasses from **Product** and maintains an immutable array of **Product** objects. The **price** property is overridden so that the value returned is calculated from the collected **Product** objects.

Applying the Pattern

The last step is to add a product set to the SportsStore catalog. Listing 15-11 shows the changes I made to the **ProductDataStore** class.

Listing 15-11. Defining Product Sets in the ProductDataStore.swift File

```
import Foundation

final class ProductDataStore {
    var callback:((Product) -> Void)?;
    private var networkQ:dispatch_queue_t
    private var uiQ:dispatch_queue_t;
    lazy var products:[Product] = self.loadData();

    init() {
        networkQ = dispatch_get_global_queue(DISPATCH_QUEUE_PRIORITY_BACKGROUND, 0);
        uiQ = dispatch_get_main_queue();
    }

    private func loadData() -> [Product] {
        // ...statements omitted for brevity...
    }

    private var productData:[Product] = [
        ProductComposite(name: "Running Pack",
            description: "Complete Running Outfit", category: "Running",
                stockLevel: 10, products:
            Product.createProduct("Shirt", description: "Running Shirt",
                category: "Running", price: 42, stockLevel: 10),
            Product.createProduct("Shorts", description: "Running Shorts",
                category: "Running", price: 30, stockLevel: 10),
            Product.createProduct("Shoes", description: "Running Shoes",
                category: "Running", price: 120, stockLevel: 10),
            ProductComposite(name: "Headgear", description: "Hat, etc",
                category: "Running", stockLevel: 10, products:
                Product.createProduct("Hat", description: "Running Hat",
                    category: "Running", price: 10, stockLevel: 10),
                Product.createProduct("Sunglasses", description: "Glasses",
                    category: "Running", price: 10, stockLevel: 10))
        ),
```

```
Product.createProduct("Kayak", description:"A boat for one person",
    category:"Watersports", price:275.0, stockLevel:0),
Product.createProduct("Lifejacket",
    description:"Protective and fashionable",
    category:"Watersports", price:48.95, stockLevel:0),

// ...statements omitted for brevity...
}
```

I have defined a new product called **Running Pack** that is made up of individual products. One of the products, **Headgear**, is itself a product set. Running the application shows the addition of the product to the catalog, as shown in Figure 15-2.

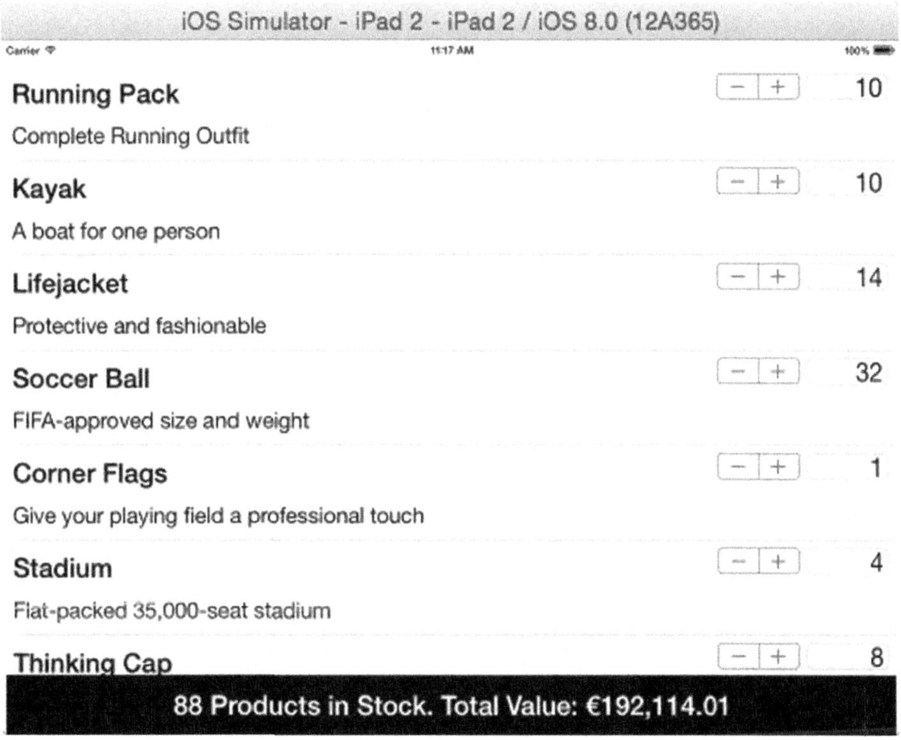

Figure 15-2. A product set in the SportsStore catalog

Summary

In this chapter I showed you how the composite pattern can be used so that different kinds of objects in a tree data structure can be treated consistently. In the next chapter, I describe the façade pattern, which allows complex APIs to be simplified for common tasks.

The Façade Pattern

The façade pattern is used to simplify the API presented by one or more classes so that common tasks can be performed more easily and the complexity required to use the API is consolidated in one part of the application. Table 16-1 puts the façade pattern into context.

Table 16-1. *Putting the Façade Pattern into Context*

Question	Answer
What is it?	The façade pattern simplifies the use of complex APIs to perform common tasks.
What are the benefits?	The complexity required to use an API is consolidated into a single class, which minimizes the impact of changes in the API and simplifies the components that consume the API functionality.
When should you use this pattern?	Use the façade pattern when you are working with classes that need to be used together but that don't have compatible APIs.
When should you avoid this pattern?	Do not use the façade pattern when integrating single components into the application; use the adapter pattern instead.
How do you know when you have implemented the pattern correctly?	The façade pattern is implemented when common tasks can be performed without calling components having any dependency on the underlying objects or their supporting data types.
Are there any common pitfalls?	The pitfall when implementing the façade pattern is to leak details of the underlying objects. This means that the calling components are still dependent on the underlying classes or supporting types and will require modification when they change.
Are there any related patterns?	Many of the structural patterns have similar implementations but different intents. Ensure that you select the correct pattern from the ones that I describe in this part of the book.

Preparing the Example Project

For this chapter, I created an Xcode OS X Command Line Tool project called Facade. I am going to create three classes on the theme of pirates. For the first, I created the **TreasureMap.swift** file, the contents of which are shown in Listing 16-1.

Listing 16-1. The Contents of the TreasureMap.swift File

```
class TreasureMap {

    enum Treasures {
        case GALLEON; case BURIED_GOLD; case SUNKEN_JEWELS;
    }

    struct MapLocation {
        let gridLetter: Character;
        let gridNumber: UInt;
    }

    func findTreasure(type:Treasures) -> MapLocation {
        switch type {
            case .GALLEON:
                return MapLocation(gridLetter: "D", gridNumber: 6);
            case .BURIED_GOLD:
                return MapLocation(gridLetter: "C", gridNumber: 2);
            case .SUNKEN_JEWELS:
                return MapLocation(gridLetter: "F", gridNumber: 12);
        }
    }
}
```

The **TreasureMap** class defines the **findTreasure** method, which accepts a value from the nested **Treasures** enumeration and returns a **MapLocation** that represents the location at which the specified type of treasure can be found. The second file I created is called **PirateShip.swift**, and its contents are shown in Listing 16-2.

Listing 16-2. The Contents of the PirateShip.swift File

```
import Foundation;

class PirateShip {

    struct ShipLocation {
        let NorthSouth:Int;
        let EastWest:Int;
    }

    var currentPosition:ShipLocation;
    var movementQueue = dispatch_queue_create("shipQ", DISPATCH_QUEUE_SERIAL);
```

```
init() {
    currentPosition = ShipLocation(NorthSouth: 5, EastWest: 5);
}

func moveToLocation(location:ShipLocation, callback:(ShipLocation) -> Void) {
    dispatch_async(movementQueue, {() in
        self.currentPosition = location;
        callback(self.currentPosition);
    });
}
}
```

As its name suggests, the **PirateShip** class represents a ship, which can be moved to new locations. Locations are specified using the nested **ShipLocation** struct and passed to the **moveToLocation** method. Ships take time to move to new locations, so the implementation of the **moveToLocation** method is asynchronous and uses a callback to send a notification when the ship is in the specified location. The asynchronous implementation is performed using a Grand Central Dispatch queue and block, which I described in Chapter 7. I have not added any delays to moving the ship, so the callback will be invoked immediately; that's enough for this chapter, where my emphasis is on dealing with complex APIs. The final file I added to the project is called **PirateCrew.swift**, and its contents are shown in Listing 16-3.

Listing 16-3. The Contents of the PirateCrew.swift File

```
import Foundation;

class PirateCrew {
    let workQueue = dispatch_queue_create("crewWorkQ", DISPATCH_QUEUE_SERIAL);

    enum Actions {
        case ATTACK_SHIP; case DIG_FOR_GOLD; case DIVE_FOR_JEWELS;
    }

    func performAction(action:Actions, callback:(Int) -> Void) {
        dispatch_async(workQueue, {() in
            var prizeValue = 0;
            switch (action) {
                case .ATTACK_SHIP:
                    prizeValue = 10000;
                case .DIG_FOR_GOLD:
                    prizeValue = 5000;
                case .DIVE_FOR_JEWELS:
                    prizeValue = 1000;
            }
            callback(prizeValue);
        });
    }
}
```

The **PirateCrew** class represents the crew of the ship, which can be assigned work through the **performAction** method. The work to be performed is expressed as a value from the **Actions** enumeration. The work itself is performed asynchronously, and a callback is used to signal when it has been completed. An **Int** value is passed to the callback that represents the worth of the treasure obtained as a result of the work.

Understanding the Problem That the Pattern Solves

The three classes in the example application have to be used together in order to generate any profit for the pirates. The **TreasureMap** class provides information on where there is treasure to be found, the **PirateShip** class provides the means for transporting the labor force required to retrieve the treasure, and the **PirateCrew** class provides the means to direct the labor force once it is in position.

These classes have to be used in a specific order. There is no point moving the ship until the location of treasure has been obtained from the map, and there is no point giving the crew work until the ship is in position.

To make the situation worse, the classes use different data types to represent their inputs and outputs. The **TreasureMap** class uses a different coordinate data type from the **PirateShip** class and a different enumeration from the **PirateCrew** class. And, finally, the methods defined by these classes have different characteristics; some produce results immediately, and others are asynchronous.

The problem this creates is that a degree of complexity is incurred to coordinate the use of these three classes in order to make any money. Listing 16-4 shows the code I defined in the **main.swift** file as a demonstration.

Listing 16-4. The Contents of the main.swift File

```
import Foundation;

let map = TreasureMap();
let ship = PirateShip();
let crew = PirateCrew();

let treasureLocation = map.findTreasure(TreasureMap.Treasures.GALLEON);

// convert from map to ship coordinates
let sequence:[Character] = ["A", "B", "C", "D", "E", "F", "G"];
let eastWestPos = find(sequence, treasureLocation.gridLetter);
let shipTarget = PirateShip.ShipLocation(NorthSouth:
    Int(treasureLocation.gridNumber), EastWest: eastWestPos!);

// relocate ship
ship.moveToLocation(shipTarget, callback: {location in
    // get the crew to work
    crew.performAction(PirateCrew.Actions.ATTACK_SHIP, {prize in
        println("Prize: \(prize) pieces of eight");
    });
});

NSFileHandle.fileHandleWithStandardInput().availableData;
```

The code in the **main.swift** file creates the **map**, **ship**, and **crew** objects and uses them in sequence to find and attack a treasure galleon. The code converts between the coordinates used by the map into the coordinates used by the ship and ensures that the instruction given to the crew (**ATTACK_SHIP**) corresponds with the map object at the ship's location (**GALLEON**). This code uses closures for the asynchronous callback methods to ensure that the crew is not given orders until the ship is in position and to get information about the prize money that is obtained.

> **Tip** I have used the NSFileHandle class in Listing 16-4 to stop the application from exiting before the asynchronous method calls made to the **PirateShip** and **PirateCrew** objects have completed. Applications don't wait for asynchronous GCD operations to complete, and **NSFileHandle** keeps the application alive by waiting to read data from the console.

This complexity will be duplicated throughout the application whenever the **TreasureMap**, **PirateShip**, and **PirateCrew** objects are used. The duplicated code will have to be carefully changed if any of the individual objects, the relationship between them, or the data types they use change. This kind of dependency leads to errors and produces code that is difficult to test effectively. Running the application produces the following output:

```
Prize: 10000 pieces of eight
```

Understanding the Façade Pattern

The façade pattern addresses the problem by creating a class that consolidates the complexity into a single location in the application and presents a simplified API to other components, as shown in Figure 16-1.

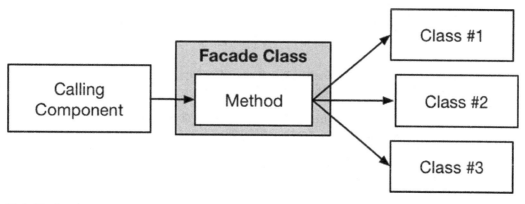

Figure 16-1. The façade pattern

The façade class takes care of the hard work and allows the calling component to take advantage of the functionality provided by the underlying classes without needing to know about them, the way they relate to one another, or the types they use to support their features. Changes in the underlying classes need be reflected only in the façade class, and the code in the calling classes is simpler and more focused on the task it needs to achieve.

Implementing the Façade Pattern

The façade pattern is simple to implement and requires the definition of a class that provides a simple API for using the complex classes. The façade class should not expose any of the details of the underlying classes or require the calling component to have any knowledge of them. Listing 16-5 shows the contents of the **Facade.swift** file, which I added to the example project in order to define a façade class.

Listing 16-5. The Contents of the Facade.swift File

```
import Foundation

enum TreasureTypes {
    case SHIP; case BURIED; case SUNKEN;
}

class PirateFacade {
    private let map = TreasureMap();
    private let ship = PirateShip();
    private let crew = PirateCrew();

    func getTreasure(type:TreasureTypes) -> Int? {

        var prizeAmount:Int?;

        // select the treasure type
        var treasureMapType:TreasureMap.Treasures;
        var crewWorkType:PirateCrew.Actions;

        switch (type) {
            case .SHIP:
                treasureMapType = TreasureMap.Treasures.GALLEON;
                crewWorkType = PirateCrew.Actions.ATTACK_SHIP;
            case .BURIED:
                treasureMapType = TreasureMap.Treasures.BURIED_GOLD;
                crewWorkType = PirateCrew.Actions.DIG_FOR_GOLD;
            case .SUNKEN:
                treasureMapType = TreasureMap.Treasures.SUNKEN_JEWELS;
                crewWorkType = PirateCrew.Actions.DIVE_FOR_JEWELS;
        }

        let treasureLocation = map.findTreasure(treasureMapType);
```

```
        // convert from map to ship coordinates
        let sequence:[Character] = ["A", "B", "C", "D", "E", "F", "G"];
        let eastWestPos = find(sequence, treasureLocation.gridLetter);
        let shipTarget = PirateShip.ShipLocation(NorthSouth:
            Int(treasureLocation.gridNumber), EastWest: eastWestPos!);

        let semaphore = dispatch_semaphore_create(0);

        // relocate ship
        ship.moveToLocation(shipTarget, callback: {location in
            self.crew.performAction(crewWorkType, {prize in
                prizeAmount = prize;
                dispatch_semaphore_signal(semaphore);
            });
        });

        dispatch_semaphore_wait(semaphore, DISPATCH_TIME_FOREVER);
        return prizeAmount;
    }
}
```

The **PirateFacade** class defines a method called **getTreasure** that is the façade for the **TreasureMap**, **PirateShip**, and **PirateCrew** classes. The implementation of the **getTreasure** method contains largely the same code but with two important differences.

The first difference is that the **PirateFacade** class relies on the **TreasureTypes** enumeration to work out what kind of treasure and what kind of crew work will be required. I could have relied on one of the enumerations defined by the classes behind the façade, but that would create a dependency on one of those classes, which is something that I want to avoid. Including an enumeration in the façade allows me to completely hide the implementation of the classes behind the façade.

The other difference is that the **getTreasure** method is synchronous and blocks while the calls to the asynchronous methods in the classes behind the façade are completed. This isn't required to implement the façade pattern, which can happily incorporate asynchronous methods, but I wanted to completely hide the underlying implementation details, which I have done using a Grand Central Dispatch semaphore. (I introduced the GCD semaphore in Chapter 7.)

Applying the Façade

All that remains is to revise the code in the **main.swift** file to take advantage of the façade class, as shown in Listing 16-6.

Listing 16-6. Using the Façade Class in the main.swift File

```
let facade = PirateFacade();
let prize = facade.getTreasure(TreasureTypes.SHIP);
if (prize != nil) {
    println("Prize: \(prize!) pieces of eight");
}
```

All of the complexity involved in using the **TreasureMap**, **PirateShip**, and **PirateCrew** classes is hidden away, and any component that needs to use these classes need deal only with the façade. Running the application produces the following output in the Xcode debug console:

```
Prize: 10000 pieces of eight
```

Variations on the Façade Pattern

The class I created in the previous section is an *opaque façade*, which means that no details of the underlying objects are exposed to the calling components. A variation on the pattern is to create a *transparent façade*, in which some or all of the underlying objects are exposed for calling components that require advanced features or finer-grained control over the work that is being done. In Swift, transparent façade classes simply provide access to the properties that store the underlying objects, as shown in Listing 16-7.

Listing 16-7. Creating a Transparent Façade in the Facade.swift File

```
import Foundation

enum TreasureTypes {
    case SHIP; case BURIED; case SUNKEN;
}

class PirateFacade {
    let map = TreasureMap();
    let ship = PirateShip();
    let crew = PirateCrew();

    func getTreasure(type:TreasureTypes) -> Int? {
        // ...statements omitted for brevity...
    }
}
```

I have removed the **private** keywords that were protecting the **map**, **ship**, and **crew** properties, and the effect is that calling components can choose to access those objects directly, rather than relying solely on the **getTreasure** method, as shown in Listing 16-8.

Listing 16-8. Using a Transparent Façade in the main.swift File

```
import Foundation;

let facade = PirateFacade();
let prize = facade.getTreasure(TreasureTypes.SHIP);
if (prize != nil) {
    facade.crew.performAction(PirateCrew.Actions.DIVE_FOR_JEWELS,
        callback: {secondPrize in
            println("Prize: \(prize! + secondPrize) pieces of eight");
        });
}

NSFileHandle.fileHandleWithStandardInput().availableData;
```

By accessing the **crew** property of the façade class, I am able to issue a second instruction without calling the **getTreasure** method, which would consult the map and move the ship. This is an advanced operation. Most of the time, the pirates attack a ship and move on, but in this instance, they also dive for sunken treasure at the same location. Creating a transparent façade allows me to deal with this advanced, and unusual, situation without adding additional complexity to the façade class.

The drawback of this approach is that it undermines the isolation offered by the façade class. The code in the **main.swift** file, which represents the calling component in this example, now needs to know about how the **PirateCrew** class is implemented, about its dependency on the **Actions** enumeration, and about the fact that the **performAction** method is implemented asynchronously. For this reason, the transparent variation on the façade pattern should be used sparingly and carefully. Running the application produces the following output:

```
Prize: 11000 pieces of eight
```

Understanding the Pitfalls of the Façade Pattern

There is only one pitfall when implementing the façade pattern: inadvertently exposing details of the underlying objects to the calling component. In an opaque façade class, exposing *any* detail is a problem. The façade should hide every detail, including associated data types, custom error messages, and anything else that would create a dependency between the component and the objects that the façade is hiding.

The situation is more complicated for transparent façades, which deliberately reveal at least some implementation details. Careful consideration should be given to which aspects of the underlying objects are exposed, and every effort should be taken to minimize the extent of the dependencies that will be created.

> **Caution**   I see the transparent variation of the pattern used most often as a retrospective reclassification of an opaque façade that has been hacked in order to implement last-minute changes. Façades should be classified as transparent during the design phase and not used as a label to mask problems in the application structure caused by time pressures. If you have to compromise a façade in order to get a product out the door, then do so, but don't pretend that it was supposed to be a transparent façade all along. You are only storing up trouble. Make the change, ship the product, and make sure you rework the code in a more considered manner when there is more time available.

Examples of the Façade Pattern in Cocoa

There are several examples of the façade pattern in the Cocoa frameworks, and the one that it used most commonly is the **UITextView** class, which provides a transparent façade for a set of complex classes used to manage the display of text. As a demonstration, I created a playground called **TextFacade.playground**, the contents of which are shown in Listing 16-9.

Listing 16-9. The Contents of the TextFacade.playground File

```
import UIKit

let textView = UITextView(frame: CGRectMake(0, 0, 200, 100));
textView.text = "The Quick Brown Fox";

textView;
```

The **UITextView** class provides a simplified API for displaying text. I have specified the frame associated with the view so that it will work in a playground, but otherwise, all I have to do is set the value of the **text** property to the text I want to display. Figure 16-2 shows how the text is displayed by default.

textView;

The Quick Brown Fox

Figure 16-2. The basic text view provided by the UITextView class

The UITextView class is a transparent façade, and I can take more control over how text is displayed by using the properties that provide access to the underlying objects that are doing the work behind the scenes. One of these objects is an instance of the NSLayoutManager class, which is accessed through the **layoutManager** property. The **NSLayoutManager** class provides different configuration options, including setting whether hidden characters are displayed. In Listing 16-10, you can see how I have used the façade transparency to change the visibility of hidden characters by directly accessing the **NSLayoutManager** object.

Listing 16-10. Accessing Advanced Features in the TextFacade.playground File

```
import UIKit

let textView = UITextView(frame: CGRectMake(0, 0, 200, 100));
textView.text = "The Quick Brown Fox";
textView.layoutManager.showsInvisibleCharacters = true;

textView;
```

I have changed the value of the **showInvisibleCharacters** property to **true**, and Figure 16-3 shows the effect on the way that the text is displayed.

×   textView;

The Quick Brown Fox

Figure 16-3. *The effect of setting an advanced configuration object*

Most of the time, applications won't need to display hidden characters, and the features provided by the **UITextView** façade class are sufficient. For those situations where hidden characters should be shown, calling components can use the transparency provided by **UITextView** to change the layout configuration, albeit at the cost of creating a dependency on the **NSLayoutManager** class.

Applying the Pattern to the SportsStore Application

I am going to apply the façade pattern to the SportsStore application to simplify the process of converting and formatting the total value of the stock. At the moment, several different steps are required. Here is the **displayStockTotal** method from the **ViewController** class:

```
...
func displayStockTotal() {
    let finalTotals:(Int, Double) = productStore.products.reduce((0, 0.0),
        {(totals, product) -> (Int, Double) in
            return (
                totals.0 + product.stockLevel,
                totals.1 + product.stockValue
            );
        });

    var factory = StockTotalFactory.getFactory(StockTotalFactory.Currency.EUR);
    var totalAmount = factory.converter?.convertTotal(finalTotals.1);
    var formatted = factory.formatter?.formatTotal(totalAmount!);

    totalStockLabel.text = "\(finalTotals.0) Products in Stock. "
        + "Total Value: \(formatted!)";
}
...
```

To display the total value, a component has to obtain a factory and then use a converter and a formatter to produce a string that can be shown to the user. I will create a simple façade that hides the details of the factory and the implementation object it provides.

Preparing the Example Application

No preparation is required for this chapter, and I pick up the SportsStore project just as I left it in Chapter 15.

> **Tip**   Remember that you don't have to build up the project step by step. The source code for every example is available as a free download from Apress.com.

Creating the Façade Class

I added a file called **StockTotalFacade.swift** to the SportsStore project and used it to define the class shown in Listing 16-11.

Listing 16-11. The Contents of the StockTotalFacade.swift File

```swift
class StockTotalFacade {

    enum Currency {
        case USD; case GBP; case EUR;
    }

    class func formatCurrencyAmount(amount:Double, currency: Currency) -> String? {
        var stfCurrency:StockTotalFactory.Currency;
        switch (currency) {
            case .EUR:
                stfCurrency = StockTotalFactory.Currency.EUR;
            case .GBP:
                stfCurrency = StockTotalFactory.Currency.GBP;
            case .USD:
                stfCurrency = StockTotalFactory.Currency.USD;
        }
        let factory = StockTotalFactory.getFactory(stfCurrency);
        let totalAmount = factory.converter?.convertTotal(amount);
        if (totalAmount != nil) {
            let formattedValue = factory.formatter?.formatTotal(totalAmount!);
            if (formattedValue != nil) {
                return formattedValue!;
            }
        }
        return nil;
    }
}
```

I have defined an opaque façade class called **StockTotalFacade** that provides a nested **Currency** enumeration so that currencies can be selected and a class method called **formatCurrencyAmount** that performs the conversion and formatting.

Applying the Façade Class

Applying the façade class is just a matter of revising the code in the **displayStockTotal** method defined by the **ViewController** class, as shown in Listing 16-12.

Listing 16-12. Applying the Façade Class in the ViewController.swift File

```
...
func displayStockTotal() {
    let finalTotals:(Int, Double) = productStore.products.reduce((0, 0.0),
        {(totals, product) -> (Int, Double) in
            return (
                totals.0 + product.stockLevel,
                totals.1 + product.stockValue
            );
        });

    let formatted = StockTotalFacade.formatCurrencyAmount(finalTotals.1,
        currency: StockTotalFacade.Currency.EUR);

    totalStockLabel.text = "\(finalTotals.0) Products in Stock. "
        + "Total Value: \(formatted!)";
}
...
```

I have removed the statements that deal with the factory, converter, and formatter classes and replaced them with a single call to the façade class. The application still converts and displays the total value of the products in stock, as shown in Figure 16-4, but the **ViewController** depends only on the façade class and not the underlying objects.

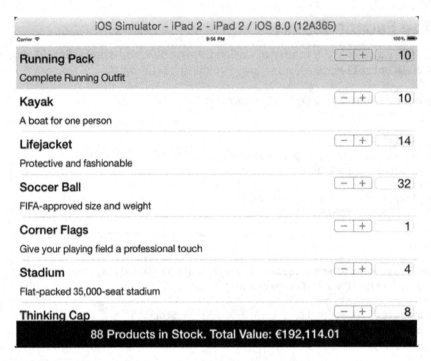

Figure 16-4. Using a façade class to calculate the total value of the stock

Summary

In this chapter I showed you how the façade pattern can be used to hide complex APIs and the coordination between objects required to perform a task. The façade presents a simplified API, which is consumed by calling components, and the effect is to consolidate the complexity into a single class. The façade pattern can be used to create opaque and transparent facades, which take different approaches to the way that the underlying complexity is made available. Opaque façades hide all of the complexity, while transparent façades allow calling components to access some or all of the underlying objects to perform advanced tasks. In the next chapter, I describe the flyweight pattern, which allows data to be shared between objects to reduce the memory footprint of an application.

The Flyweight Pattern

The flyweight pattern is applied when a number of similar objects all rely on the same set of data values. Rather than create a new set of data valued for each of the objects, the flyweight pattern shares one set between all of them, minimizing the amount of memory required to store the data and the amount of work required to create them. Table 17-1 puts the flyweight pattern into context.

Table 17-1. Putting the Flyweight Pattern into Context

Question	Answer
What is it?	The flyweight pattern shares common data objects between multiple calling components.
What are the benefits?	The flyweight pattern reduces the amount of memory needed to create the data objects required by the calling components and the amount of work required to create them. The impact of implementing the pattern increases with the number of calling components that share the data.
When should you use this pattern?	Use this pattern when you are able to identify and isolate sets of identical data objects that are used by calling components.
When should you avoid this pattern?	Do not use this pattern if there is no shared data or if the number of shared data objects is small and easy to create.
How do you know when you have implemented the pattern correctly?	The pattern has been implemented correctly when all of the calling components rely on the same set of immutable shared data objects (known as the *extrinsic* data) and have their own individual state data (known as the *intrinsic* data). The calling components should be able to concurrently modify the intrinsic data safely and not be able to modify the extrinsic data at all.
Are there any common pitfalls?	The common pitfalls include inadvertently creating more than one set of extrinsic data objects, not protecting against concurrent operations on the intrinsic data, allowing the extrinsic data to be modified, and over-optimizing the creation of extrinsic objects.
Are there any related patterns?	Many of the structural patterns have similar implementations but different intents. Ensure that you select the correct pattern from the ones I describe in this part of the book.

Preparing the Example Project

For this chapter, I created an Xcode OS X Command Line Tool project called Flyweight. I added a file called **Spreadsheet.swift**, the contents of which are shown in Listing 17-1.

Listing 17-1. The Contents of the Spreadsheet.swift File

```swift
func == (lhs: Coordinate, rhs: Coordinate) -> Bool {
    return lhs.col == rhs.col && lhs.row == rhs.row;
}

class Coordinate : Hashable, Printable {
    let col:Character;
    let row:Int;

    init(col:Character, row:Int) {
        self.col = col; self.row = row;
    }

    var hashValue: Int {
        return description.hashValue;
    }

    var description: String {
        return "\(col)(\row)";
    }
}

class Cell {
    var coordinate:Coordinate;
    var value:Int;

    init(col:Character, row:Int, val:Int) {
        self.coordinate = Coordinate(col: col, row: row);
        self.value = val;
    }
}

class Spreadsheet {
    var grid = Dictionary<Coordinate, Cell>();

    init() {

        let letters:String = "ABCDEFGHIJKLMNOPQRSTUVWXYZ";
        var stringIndex = letters.startIndex;
        let rows = 50;

        do {
            let colLetter = letters[stringIndex];
            stringIndex = stringIndex.successor();
            for rowIndex in 1 ... rows {
```

```
            let cell = Cell(col: colLetter, row: rowIndex, val: rowIndex);
            grid[cell.coordinate] = cell;
        }
    } while (stringIndex != letters.endIndex);
}

func setValue(coord: Coordinate, value:Int) {
    grid[coord]?.value = value;
}

var total:Int {
    return reduce(grid.values, 0,
        {total, cell in return total + cell.value});
}
}
```

The **Spreadsheet** class has a **Dictionary** property that stores a collection of **Cell** objects, each of which is indexed by a **Coordinate** object. The **Coordinate** stores a column and row value, such as A45, where A is the column and 45 is the row, in order to create a grid. The **Cell** object is used to store an **Int** value at a given position in the grid and also has details of the coordinate that its value relates to. The initializer for the **Spreadsheet** class creates a grid with 26 columns and 50 rows and sets the **value property** of each **Cell** to the row index. The **setValue** method changes the **value** property of a **Cell** at a specified **Coordinate**, and the **total** property computes the sum of the **value** properties of all the **Cell** objects in the grid.

Tip   The global function called **==** compares two **Coordinate** objects for equality, which allows them to be used as keys in a **Dictionary** collection.

Understanding the Problems That the Pattern Solves

The problem addressed by the flyweight pattern is the impact of creating large numbers of identical objects, both in terms of the memory that they consume and the amount of time taken to create them. The **Spreadsheet** class that I defined in the previous section creates **Cell** and **Coordinate** objects for every position in the grid it maintains, which means that each **Spreadsheet** object generates a relatively large number of objects. Listing 17-2 shows the code I added to the **main.swift** file to demonstrate the problem.

Listing 17-2. The Contents of the main.swift File

```
let ss1 = Spreadsheet();
ss1.setValue(Coordinate(col: "A", row: 1), value: 100);
ss1.setValue(Coordinate(col: "J", row: 20), value: 200);
println("SS1 Total: \(ss1.total)");
```

```
let ss2 = Spreadsheet();
ss2.setValue(Coordinate(col: "F", row: 10), value: 200);
ss2.setValue(Coordinate(col: "G", row: 23), value: 250);
println("SS2 Total: \(ss2.total)");

println("Cells created: \(ss1.grid.count + ss2.grid.count)");
```

I create two **Spreadsheet** objects, set values for different cells, and write out the totals. I then write out the total number of **Cell** objects that are in the **Dictionary** collections maintained by the **Spreadsheet** objects. Running the application produces the following output:

```
SS1 Total: 33429
SS2 Total: 33567
Cells created: 2600
```

I have ended up with a large number of **Cell** objects for such a simple operation, and most of them still have the default value that was assigned during instantiation.

Understanding the Flyweight Pattern

Each of the 2,600 **Cell** objects that I created in the previous section took time to create and memory to store. The flyweight pattern minimizes the CPU and memory impact by identifying and separating the data that is common across similar objects and sharing it, meaning that only one shared object has to be created. Figure 17-1 illustrates the flyweight pattern.

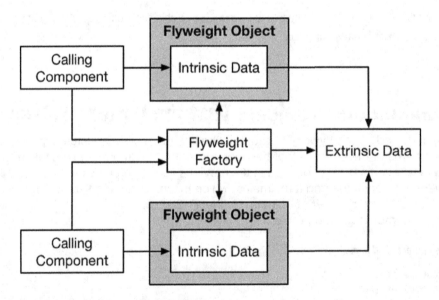

Figure 17-1. The flyweight pattern

In the flyweight pattern, the calling components are the objects that generate and rely on the large number of data objects. In the example project, the calling components are the **Spreadsheet** objects, and they rely on the **Cell** data objects.

The pattern uses a flyweight object to manage the data objects that the calling component needs. The flyweight object splits the data objects into *extrinsic* and *intrinsic* categories. The extrinsic data is common to all calling components; the intrinsic data is unique to each calling component.

The flyweight pattern minimizes the impact of creating objects by sharing the extrinsic state between flyweight objects, meaning that all of the calling components share the same set of data objects. Because it is shared, the extrinsic data is immutable and cannot be modified by the flyweights or the calling components.

The intrinsic data cannot be shared, so the amount of impact that the flyweight pattern has is driven by the ratio of extrinsic to intrinsic data objects.

The *flyweight factory* provides the calling components with a mechanism for obtaining flyweight objects and is responsible for providing the flyweights with access to the extrinsic data.

Implementing the Flyweight Pattern

I have chosen a spreadsheet as the example for this chapter because it provides some implementation challenges. When a new **Spreadsheet** object is created, every **Cell** object is identical and can easily be treated as extrinsic data. Each value that is set on a **Spreadsheet** is unique to that instance and becomes intrinsic data. My goal in implementing the pattern will be to make the transition from extrinsic to intrinsic data as seamless and simple as possible.

Creating the Flyweight Protocol

You don't have to define a protocol for your flyweights, but I like to do so because it makes it easier to introduce different implementations later in the application life cycle. I also find that using a protocol makes me pay more attention to the data I expose to the calling component because I have to explicitly define each method and property. Listing 17-3 shows the contents of the **Flyweight. swift** file that I added to the example project.

Listing 17-3. The Contents of the Flyweight.swift File

```
import Foundation;

protocol Flyweight {
    subscript(index:Coordinate) -> Int? { get set };
    var total:Int { get };
    var count:Int { get };
}
```

The data objects in the **Spreadsheet** class are stored in a **Dictionary** collection, and this is reflected in the **Flyweight** protocol. The subscript I have defined allows values to be gotten and set using **Coordinate** keys, and the **count** property will return the number of intrinsic data objects. (The number of objects is required to implement the pattern, but I will use it in the **main.swift** file to illustrate the impact of applying the pattern).

I don't want classes that consume the **Flyweight** protocol to have knowledge of the separation of intrinsic and extrinsic data, so I have added a **total** property, which will be used to compute the sum of the **value** property values of the intrinsic **Cell** objects.

Creating the Flyweight Implementation Class

The next step is to implement the flyweight implementation class that will conform to the **Flyweight** protocol. This is the class that will be responsible for managing the intrinsic data and that will be provided with access to the extrinsic data by the flyweight factory. Listing 17-4 shows the definition of the implementation class.

Listing 17-4. Defining the Flyweight Implementation Class in the Flyweight.swift File

```
import Foundation;

protocol Flyweight {
    subscript(index:Coordinate) -> Int? { get set };
    var total:Int { get };
    var count:Int { get };
}

class FlyweightImplementation : Flyweight  {
    private let extrinsicData:[Coordinate: Cell];
    private var intrinsicData:[Coordinate: Cell];

    private init(extrinsic:[Coordinate: Cell]) {
        self.extrinsicData = extrinsic;
        self.intrinsicData = Dictionary<Coordinate, Cell>();
    }

    subscript(key:Coordinate) -> Int? {
        get {
            if let cell = intrinsicData[key] {
                return cell.value;
            } else {
                return extrinsicData[key]?.value;
            }
        }
        set (value) {
            if (value != nil) {
                intrinsicData[key] = Cell(col: key.col,
                    row: key.row, val: value!);
            }
        }
    }
}
```

```
    var total:Int {
        return reduce(extrinsicData.values, 0, {total, cell in
            if let intrinsicCell = self.intrinsicData[cell.coordinate] {
                return total + intrinsicCell.value;
            } else {
                return total + cell.value
            }
        });
    }

    var count:Int {
        return intrinsicData.count;
    }
}
```

> **Tip**   Note that the flyweight does not modify the extrinsic data or allow the calling component to modify it. This is a critical characteristic of the flyweight pattern, and allowing the extrinsic data to be modified is a common pitfall.

The **FlyweightImplementation** class conforms to the **Flyweight** protocol and receives the extrinsic data as its initializer argument. The intrinsic data is used as an overlay on the extrinsic data, and requests for values fall through to the extrinsic data if there is no intrinsic **Cell** for the specified **Coordinate**. When a new value is set, a **Cell** object is created as part of the intrinsic data.

> **Note**   Not all intrinsic data has to correspond to an extrinsic equivalent. It is perfectly acceptable for a flyweight to manage intrinsic data that is not related to any extrinsic value. That said, I tend to define such data values in the calling component and leave the flyweight to focus on those intrinsic values that are related to the extrinsic data in some way.

Adding Concurrency Protections

The flyweight pattern doesn't put any limitations on how flyweight objects are used once they are obtained from the factory. This presents the kind of concurrency risk that I have described for other patterns; a flyweight can be shared between multiple threads, each of which tries to modify the intrinsic data at the same time. I need to modify the flyweight implementation class to protect against corrupting the intrinsic data or getting inconsistent results. Listing 17-5 shows how I have used Grand Central Dispatch (GCD) to protect the data.

Listing 17-5. Protecting Against Concurrency in the Flyweight.swift File

```swift
...
class FlyweightImplementation : Flyweight  {
    private let extrinsicData:[Coordinate: Cell];
    private var intrinsicData:[Coordinate: Cell];
    private let queue:dispatch_queue_t;

    private init(extrinsic:[Coordinate: Cell]) {
        self.extrinsicData = extrinsic;
        self.intrinsicData = Dictionary<Coordinate, Cell>();
        self.queue = dispatch_queue_create("dataQ", DISPATCH_QUEUE_CONCURRENT);
    }

    subscript(key:Coordinate) -> Int? {
        get {
            var result:Int?;
            dispatch_sync(self.queue, {() in
                if let cell = self.intrinsicData[key] {
                    result = cell.value;
                } else {
                    result = self.extrinsicData[key]?.value;
                }
            });
            return result;
        }
        set (value) {
            if (value != nil) {
                dispatch_barrier_sync(self.queue, {() in
                    self.intrinsicData[key] = Cell(col: key.col,
                        row: key.row, val: value!);
                });
            }
        }
    }

    var total:Int {
        var result = 0;
        dispatch_sync(self.queue, {() in
            result = reduce(self.extrinsicData.values, 0, {total, cell in
                if let intrinsicCell = self.intrinsicData[cell.coordinate] {
                    return total + intrinsicCell.value;
                } else {
                    return total + cell.value
                }
            });
        });
        return result;
    }
```

```
    var count:Int {
        var result = 0;
        dispatch_sync(self.queue, {() in
            result = self.intrinsicData.count;
        });
        return result;
    }
}
...
```

I want to allow multiple concurrent read operations but only one write operation at a time. I have defined a concurrent GCD queue, and I use the dispatch_sync function for the read operations, meaning those that don't modify the intrinsic data: getting a value with the **subscript** and getting the **total** and **count** values. When setting a value with the **subscript**, I use the dispatch_barrier_sync function, which ensures that no other request is processed while I am modifying the intrinsic data collection.

Creating the Flyweight Factory Class

The final class that I must define is the flyweight factory, which is used by calling components to obtain flyweights that have access to the extrinsic data. Listing 17-6 shows the definition of the class.

Listing 17-6. Creating the Flyweight Factory Class in the Flyweight.swift File

```
import Foundation;

protocol Flyweight {
    subscript(index:Coordinate) -> Int? { get set };
    var total:Int { get };
    var count:Int { get };
}

extension Dictionary {
    init(setupFunc:(() -> [(Key, Value)])) {
        self.init();
        for item in setupFunc() {
            self[item.0] = item.1;
        }
    }
}

class FlyweightFactory {

    class func createFlyweight() -> Flyweight {
        return FlyweightImplementation(extrinsic: extrinsicData);
    }
```

```
    private class var extrinsicData:[Coordinate: Cell] {
        get {
            struct singletonWrapper {
                static let singletonData = Dictionary<Coordinate, Cell> (
                    setupFunc: {() in
                        var results = [(Coordinate, Cell)]();
                        let letters:String = "ABCDEFGHIJKLMNOPQRSTUVWXYZ";
                        var stringIndex = letters.startIndex;
                        let rows = 50;
                        do {
                            let colLetter = letters[stringIndex];
                            stringIndex = stringIndex.successor();
                            for rowIndex in 1 ... rows {
                                let cell = Cell(col: colLetter, row: rowIndex,
                                    val: rowIndex);
                                results.append((cell.coordinate, cell));
                            }
                        } while (stringIndex != letters.endIndex);
                        return results;
                    }
                );
            }
            return singletonWrapper.singletonData;
        }
    }
}

class FlyweightImplementation : Flyweight  {
    // ...statements omitted for brevity...
}
```

The **FlyweightFactory** class defines a class method called **createFlyweight** that returns an object that conforms to the **Flyweight** protocol. The implementation of the **createFlyweight** creates a **FlyweightImplementation** object and passes the extrinsic data to it as an initializer argument. I create the extrinsic data using the singleton pattern that I described in Chapter 6. This ensures the extrinsic data is created in a lazy and thread-safe way.

To populate the dictionary collection, I have defined an extension that provides an initializer that accepts a function. The function is called to produce an array of key-value tuples that I add to the dictionary. This approach works around the limited support that Swift has for class variables and ensures that I can populate the dictionary with the extrinsic data as part of the singleton initialization.

Applying the Flyweight

The final step is to modify the **Spreadsheet** class so that it relies on a flyweight object to manage its data, as shown in Listing 17-7.

Listing 17-7. Using a Flyweight in the Spreadsheet.swift File

```
func == (lhs: Coordinate, rhs: Coordinate) -> Bool {
    return lhs.col == rhs.col && lhs.row == rhs.row;
}

class Coordinate : Hashable, Printable {
    // ...statements omitted for brevity...
}

class Cell {
    // ...statements omitted for brevity...
}

class Spreadsheet {
    var grid:Flyweight;

    init() {
        grid = FlyweightFactory.createFlyweight();
    }

    func setValue(coord: Coordinate, value:Int) {
        grid[coord] = value;
    }

    var total:Int {
        return grid.total;
    }
}
```

The **Spreadsheet** class obtains a flyweight from the factory and uses it to implement its API.
Listing 17-8 shows a minor change I made to the **main.swift** file to accurately report on the number
of **Cell** objects created by taking the extrinsic objects into account.

Listing 17-8. Counting the Extrinsic Cell Objects in the main.swift File

```
let ss1 = Spreadsheet();
ss1.setValue(Coordinate(col: "A", row: 1), value: 100);
ss1.setValue(Coordinate(col: "J", row: 20), value: 200);
println("SS1 Total: \(ss1.total)");

let ss2 = Spreadsheet();
ss2.setValue(Coordinate(col: "F", row: 10), value: 200);
ss2.setValue(Coordinate(col: "G", row: 23), value: 250);
println("SS2 Total: \(ss2.total)");

println("Cells created: \(1300 + ss1.grid.count + ss2.grid.count)");
```

Running the application produces the following output:

```
SS1 Total: 33429
SS2 Total: 33567
Cells created: 1304
```

Using the flyweight pattern leverages the same extrinsic data for each **Spreadsheet** object, and its impact increases as the number of **Spreadsheet** objects increases.

Variations on the Flyweight Pattern

The *copy-on-write* technique is a variation on the flyweight pattern that relies on an extrinsic object until the calling component wants to modify it. At this point, the extrinsic object is copied and then modified, and the flyweight no longer uses the extrinsic data. One part of the extrinsic data can be copied or the entire thing, as dictated by the needs of the application. The copy-on-write technique combines the flyweight pattern with the prototype pattern that I described in Chapter 5. Listing 17-9 shows the contents of the **CopyOnWrite.playground** file, which I created as a demonstration.

Listing 17-9. The Contents of the CopyOnWrite.playground File

```
import Foundation;

class Owner : NSObject, NSCopying {
    var name:String;
    var city:String;

    init(name:String, city:String) {
        self.name = name; self.city = city;
    }

    func copyWithZone(zone: NSZone) -> AnyObject {
        println("Copy");
        return Owner(name: self.name, city: self.city);
    }
}

class FlyweightFactory {

    class func createFlyweight() -> Flyweight {
        return Flyweight(owner: ownerSingleton);
    }

    private class var ownerSingleton:Owner {
        get {
            struct singletonWrapper {
                static let singleon = Owner(name: "Anonymous", city: "Anywhere");
            }
```

```
                return singletonWrapper.singleon;
            }
        }
    }
}

class Flyweight {
    private let extrinsicOwner:Owner;
    private var intrinsicOwner:Owner?;

    init(owner:Owner) {
        self.extrinsicOwner = owner;
    }

    var name:String {
        get {
            return intrinsicOwner?.name ?? extrinsicOwner.name;
        }
        set (value) {
            decoupleFromExtrinsic();
            intrinsicOwner?.name = value;
        }
    }

    var city:String {
        get {
            return intrinsicOwner?.city ?? extrinsicOwner.city;
        }
        set (value) {
            decoupleFromExtrinsic();
            intrinsicOwner?.city = value;
        }
    }

    private func decoupleFromExtrinsic() {
        if (intrinsicOwner == nil) {
            intrinsicOwner = extrinsicOwner.copyWithZone(nil) as? Owner;
        }
    }
}
```

The **FlyweightFactory** class uses the singleton pattern to define the extrinsic **Owner**, which is passed to new **Flyweight** objects. The **Flyweight** class uses the extrinsic **Owner** object to provide values for its **name** and **city** properties until either of the property setters is used. At this point, the prototype pattern is applied to copy the extrinsic object in order to create an intrinsic clone, to which the setter value is applied. Once a property setter has been used, the **Flyweight** object no longer uses the extrinsic object.

Understanding the Pitfalls of the Flyweight Pattern

There are several pitfalls to avoid when implementing the flyweight pattern. The flyweight pattern is not especially complex, especially compared to a pattern such as the object pool, which I described in Chapter 7, but it is easy to create an implementation that causes more problems than it solves.

Understanding the Extrinsic Duplication Pitfall

The easiest pitfall to fall victim to is creating more extrinsic data than you intended, undermining the efficacy of the flyweight pattern. In Swift, this will happen most often because of the difficulty in creating class variables and the limitations of doing so using a struct. You must ensure that the extrinsic data is created as part of the singleton initialization and that the data is created in a thread-safe way. It is for this reason that I defined an extension for the **Dictionary** class that allows me to specify a closure that will populate the extrinsic data collection in the example application.

Understanding the Mutable Extrinsic Data Pitfall

If you allow a calling component to modify the extrinsic data, you will create two different problems: the risk of concurrent accesses corrupting the data and flyweights getting inconsistent data. The extrinsic data used by a flyweight must be immutable, and letting it be modified is a common pitfall that causes odd behavior and runtime errors.

Understanding the Concurrent Access Pitfall

As I explained earlier in the chapter, the flyweight pattern doesn't apply any limits on how flyweight objects can be used, so it is important to protect the intrinsic data from concurrent access in the event that a calling component allows a flyweight to be used by multiple threads. You don't have to use the barrier-based approach I applied to the example flyweight class, and you don't even have to use GCD, but you must add some form of protection because many single-threaded applications are transformed into multithreaded applications at some point.

> **Tip**   You don't need to add protections for the extrinsic data, which should be immutable. Concurrency problems with the extrinsic data are an indication that your flyweight implementation is flawed.

Understanding the Over-optimization Pitfall

It is easy to get carried away with optimizing the creation of objects, to the extent that you end up with an implementation that makes it hard to modify the extrinsic data. The most common form of this pitfall arises when the values that the extrinsic objects represent are generated from a predictable algorithm. In the example application, I set the value of each **Cell** object to be the index of the row, which means that I could go further in my implementation of the flyweight factory class and create **Cell** objects only on request, using the row number to generate the object on the fly.

There are a couple of problems with this approach. The first is inflexibility. Algorithms used to generate values are rarely as simple as the one in my example, and the process for generating the values can be so complicated that the resulting code is hard to change when a different algorithm is implemented.

The second problem is that the flyweight class and the calling component must be able to carry out their business without knowing that objects are being created on demand. In the case of my example application, this would mean allowing flyweight classes to be able to get the total number of **Cell** objects and the sum of the **value** properties without needing to create all of the objects these tasks would usually require. The flyweight factory can provide this information only if it has deep insights into the extrinsic data, which further adds to the complexity and inflexibility of the code.

My advice is to accept that one set of shared extrinsic objects is a big enough optimization and that going any further yields little benefit but adds a lot of complexity and maintenance risk.

Understanding the Misapplication Pitfall

The final pitfall is to apply the flyweight pattern when it isn't required. To make the additional development time and testing worthwhile, the flyweight should be applied only in situations where a number of similar objects rely on a large common set of data values. If the extrinsic data isn't large or doesn't require substantial effort to create, then the work required to implement the flyweight pattern is unlikely to be justified.

Examples of the Flyweight Pattern in Cocoa

There are several flyweight implementations in the Cocoa frameworks. The one that I find most interesting is the NSNumber class, which is used to represent numeric values. Two **NSNumber** objects created with the same value will be managed so that the value is an extrinsic data item—something that can trip the unwary. Listing 17-10 shows the contents of the **Numbers.playground** file, which I created as a demonstration.

Listing 17-10. The Contents of the Numbers.playground File

```
import Foundation;

let num1 = NSNumber(int: 10);
let num2 = NSNumber(int: 10);

println("Comparison: \(num1 == num2)");
println("Identity:   \(num1 === num2)");
```

I create two **NSNumber** objects, both of which store the integer value **10**. I print out the results of using the comparison and identity operators. The debug console shows the following output:

```
Comparison: true
Identity: true
```

The result from the comparison operator makes sense, but the result from the identity operator may surprise you. Cocoa minimizes the amount of memory required for **NSNumber** objects by sharing them. This is a technique that many languages apply to string values, using a process known as *string interning* that reduces the amount of memory used to store strings and that speeds up string comparison. Cocoa does implement string interning for the **NSString** class, but it is difficult to use in Swift, and the **NSNumber** class provides simpler example.

Applying the Pattern to the SportsStore Application

The SportsStore application contains the **NetworkConnection** class, which I use to simulate network queries for stock level data. Each **NetworkConnection** instance contains a dictionary of stock values that it uses to satisfy the request for data. Here is the definition of the **NetworkConnection** class:

```
...
class NetworkConnection {

    private let stockData: [String: Int] = [
        "Kayak" : 10, "Lifejacket": 14, "Soccer Ball": 32,"Corner Flags": 1,
        "Stadium": 4, "Thinking Cap": 8, "Unsteady Chair": 3,
        "Human Chess Board": 2, "Bling-Bling King":4
    ];

    func getStockLevel(name:String) -> Int? {
        NSThread.sleepForTimeInterval(Double(rand() % 2));
        return stockData[name];
    }
}
...
```

In this section I am going to apply the flyweight pattern so that all of the **NetworkConnection** objects share the same dictionary object. The dictionary that I will be sharing isn't complicated to create and doesn't occupy much memory, but it still provides a foundation to which the flyweight pattern can be applied.

Preparing the Example Application

No preparation is required for this chapter, and I will pick up the SportsStore project as I left it at the end of Chapter 16.

Creating the Flyweight Protocol and Implementation Class

I always follow the same process when implementing the flyweight pattern: I define the protocol that will be used by the calling component, followed by the flyweight implementation class. This allows me to focus on the API that will be consumed publically in the protocol and separate the intrinsic and extrinsic data in the implementation class. Listing 17-11 shows the contents of the **NetworkConnectionFlyweight.swift** file that I added to the SportsStore project to implement the flyweight pattern.

Listing 17-11. The Contents of the NetworkConnectionFlyweight.swift File

```
protocol NetConnFlyweight {

    func getStockLevel(name:String) -> Int?;
}

class NetConnFlyweightImpl : NetConnFlyweight {
    private let extrinsicData:[String: Int];

    private init(data:[String: Int]) {
        self.extrinsicData = data;
    }

    func getStockLevel(name: String) -> Int? {
        return extrinsicData[name];
    }
}
```

This implementation of the pattern is simple, but I have chosen to expose the data values through a method rather than by providing a property that allows access to the dictionary. I have done this because it means I can change the way that the data is stored without having to update the protocol (and the components that consume it) and because it helps to ensure that I don't inadvertently allow the extrinsic data to be modified (which is easy to do when you allow direct access to the extrinsic data structures).

Creating the Flyweight Factory

One I have defined the protocol and implementation class, I complete the flyweight pattern by defining the factory and the extrinsic data that it manages. Listing 17-12 shows the definition of the factory class.

Listing 17-12. Defining the Flyweight Factory Class in the NetworkConnectionFlyweight.swift File

```
protocol NetConnFlyweight {

    func getStockLevel(name:String) -> Int?;
}

class NetConnFlyweightImpl : NetConnFlyweight {
    // ...statements omitted for brevity...
}

class NetConnFlyweightFactory {

    class func createFlyweight() -> NetConnFlyweight {
        return NetConnFlyweightImpl(data: stockData);
    }
```

```
    private class var stockData:[String: Int] {
        get {
            struct singletonWrapper {
                static let singleton = ["Kayak" : 10, "Lifejacket": 14,
                    "Soccer Ball": 32,"Corner Flags": 1, "Stadium": 4,
                    "Thinking Cap": 8, "Unsteady Chair": 3,
                    "Human Chess Board": 2, "Bling-Bling King":4
                ];
            }
            return singletonWrapper.singleton;
        }
    }
}
```

The **NetConnFlyweightFactory** class uses the singleton pattern to ensure that the extrinsic data is created once and defines a **createFlyweight** method that uses the extrinsic data to create instances of the implementation class.

Applying the Flyweight

The final step is to update the **NetworkConnection** class so that it uses the flyweight and shares a single immutable array of intrinsic stock data, as shown in Listing 17-13.

Listing 17-13. Using the Flyweight in the NetworkConnection.swift File

```
import Foundation

class NetworkConnection {
    private let flyweight:NetConnFlyweight;

    init() {
        self.flyweight = NetConnFlyweightFactory.createFlyweight();
    }

    func getStockLevel(name:String) -> Int? {
        NSThread.sleepForTimeInterval(Double(rand() % 2));
        return self.flyweight.getStockLevel(name);
    }
}
```

I have removed the local data array and changed the implementation of the **getStockLevel** method so that a flyweight is used to obtain the data value.

Summary

In this chapter, I explained how the flyweight pattern is used to share extrinsic data between objects in order to reduce the memory footprint of an application and the amount of work required to generate identical sets of data objects. In the next chapter, I describe the proxy pattern, which is used when an object is required to act as a representative of a resource or another object.

18

The Proxy Pattern

I describe the proxy pattern in this chapter, which is used when an object is required to act as an interface to another object or resource. There are three main ways in which the proxy pattern is applied, and I describe each of them and show you how to implement them. Table 18-1 puts the proxy pattern into context.

Table 18-1. *Putting the Proxy Pattern into Context*

Question	Answer
What is it?	The proxy pattern defines an object—the *proxy*—that represents some other resource, such as another object or a remote service. Calling components operate on the proxy, which in turn operates on the underlying resource.
What are the benefits?	Proxies allow close control over the way that the underlying resource is accessed, which is useful when you need to intercept and adapt operations.
When should you use this pattern?	Proxies are used in three main situations: to define an interface to a remote resource such as a web page or RESTful service, to manage the execution of expensive operations, and to restrict access to the methods and properties of other objects.
When should you avoid this pattern?	Do not use this pattern when the problem falls outside of the three situations that I describe in this chapter. Instead, use one of the other structural patterns.
How do you know when you have implemented the pattern correctly?	The pattern is implemented correctly when the proxy object can be used to perform operations on the resource it represents.
Are there any common pitfalls?	The only pitfall is allowing instances of the underlying class to be instantiated when a proxy is used to restrict access to an object.
Are there any related patterns?	Many of the structural patterns have similar implementations but different intents. Ensure that you select the correct pattern from the ones I describe in this part of the book.

Preparing the Example Project

For this chapter, I created an Xcode OS X Command Line Tool project called Proxy. Listing 18-1 shows the statements I added to the **main.swift** file to prepare for this chapter.

Listing 18-1. The Contents of the main.swift File

```
import Foundation;

func getHeader(header:String) {
    let url = NSURL(string: "http://www.apress.com");
    let request = NSURLRequest(URL: url!);
    NSURLSession.sharedSession().dataTaskWithRequest(request,
        completionHandler: {data, response, error in
        if let httpResponse = response as? NSHTTPURLResponse {
            if let headerValue
                    = httpResponse.allHeaderFields[header] as? NSString {
                println("\(header): \(headerValue)");
            }
        }
    }).resume();
}

let headers = ["Content-Length", "Content-Encoding"];
for header in headers {
    getHeader(header);
}

NSFileHandle.fileHandleWithStandardInput().availableData;
```

The code in the **main.swift** file makes HTTP requests to the Apress home page and prints the value of the **Content-Length** and **Content-Encoding** headers to the debug console. Running the application produces the following output:

```
Content-Encoding: gzip
Content-Length: 13960
```

You may see the **Content-Length** header displayed first. This is because the Foundation framework classes that perform the HTTP requests are asynchronous and the requests are performed concurrently, meaning that either request may complete first and write its result to the console. You will almost certainly see a different header values when you run the example application because Apress often changes the content on the home page of its website.

Understanding the Problems That the Pattern Solves

The proxy pattern is used to solve three different problems, each of which I explain in the sections that follow.

Understanding the Remote Object Problem

The remote object problem arises whenever you are dealing with resources that are accessed over a network, such as a web page or a RESTful web service. The code in the **main.swift** file accesses a web page, but it doesn't separate the feature it provides (getting an HTTP response header) from the mechanism used to make the request (the **NSURL**, **NSURLRequest**, and **NSURLSession** classes). There is no abstraction or encapsulation in this code, and changing the implementation will affect the way that the feature is consumed—something that is made worse if this kind of code is copied into any component that needs to read HTTP headers.

Understanding the Expensive Operation Problem

Tasks such as making HTTP requests are classified as *expensive operations*. The word *expensive* is used to refer to any aspect of an operation that should be minimized, such as the amount of computation required, the memory needed, the load on the device battery, the bandwidth consumed, and the elapsed time that the user has to wait.

For an HTTP request, the major expenses are elapsed time, bandwidth, and the work the server has to perform to generate the response. The code in the **main.swift** file doesn't attempt to optimize the way that the HTTP requests are performed to minimize the cost of the operation, and no thought has been given to the impact that this has on the user, the network, or the server that receives the requests.

Understanding the Restricted Access Problem

The need to restrict access to an object usually arises when a single-user framework is incorporated into a multiuser application. You can't change the definition of the objects that you need to protect because you don't have access to the source code or because there is already a dependency on the type elsewhere in the application, but equally, you cannot afford to let any user perform the operations that the object encapsulates.

Understanding the Proxy Pattern

The proxy pattern can be used whenever an object is required to represent some other resource. As you will see, the resource can be something abstract, such as a web page, or something local to the application, such as another object. Figure 18-1 shows the general form of the proxy pattern.

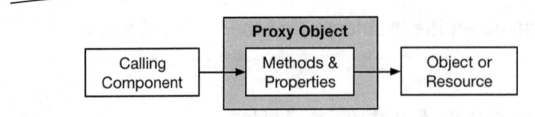

Figure 18-1. The proxy pattern

The general form of the proxy pattern lacks specificity, but that is because the pattern can be used in a wide range of situations. To put the pattern in context, in the following sections I explain how the pattern is used to solve the three common problems I described earlier in the chapter.

Solving the Remote Object Problem

The use of the proxy pattern to represent remote objects and resources has its roots in distributed systems such as CORBA, which provided a local object that exposes the same methods as a corresponding remote object on a server. The local object was the proxy, and calling one of its methods caused the corresponding method to be invoked on the remote object. CORBA took care of mapping the proxy object to the remote object and dealing with arguments and results.

CORBA isn't widely used anymore, but the proxy pattern has taken on a new importance as HTTP has become the transport of choice and RESTful services have become more popular. The proxy pattern can be applied to make it easy to work with remote resource and hide the implementation details from the functionality that the remote resource offers. This is the kind of thing that design patterns are especially good at solving: abstracting functionality so that the implementation mechanism can be altered without needing to change the way the feature is consumed and packaging up features so the implementation isn't repeated throughout an application. Figure 18-2 shows how a proxy can be used to represent a remote resource.

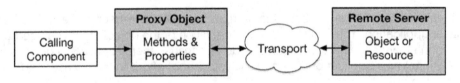

Figure 18-2. Using the proxy pattern to represent a remote resource

The proxy object hides the details of how the remote resource is accessed and just presents its data, which in the case of the example application is the value of HTTP headers. The use of the proxy consolidates the mechanism by which remote requests are made to a single class in the application and allows the implementation to be changed—to use alternative Cocoa classes, for example—without needing corresponding changes in the components that use the proxy.

Solving the Expensive Operation Problem

A proxy can be used to minimize the cost of expensive operations by decoupling the operation from its use. In the case of the example application, I can combine requests for multiple header values into a single request, as Figure 18-3 illustrates.

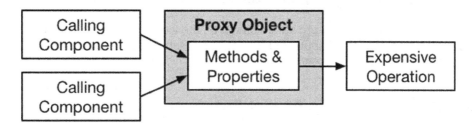

Figure 18-3. Using a proxy to combine operations

Obviously, I have the advantage of picking the example to suit the pattern, but expensive operations can often be combined or at least deferred until the cost of performing them is lower.

Solving the Restricted Access Problem

A proxy can be used as a wrapper around an object, adding additional logic to enforce some kind of restriction on its use, as shown in Figure 18-4.

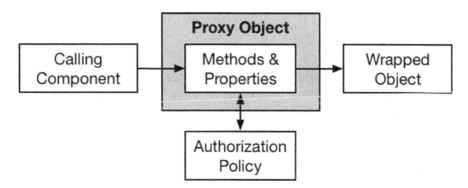

Figure 18-4. Restricting access with a proxy

The proxy usually conforms to a common protocol shared with the wrapped object, which means that proxy objects can be used as seamless replacements without having to modify the calling components. The proxy intercepts requests to access the properties and methods of the underlying object and will pass them on only if an access control policy has been satisfied.

Implementing the Proxy Pattern

The implementation of the proxy pattern varies based on the kind of problem that it is being used to solve. In the following sections, I show you how to implement the pattern for each of the three problems I described earlier in the chapter.

Implementing the Remote Object Proxy

The key to implementing the proxy pattern to access a remote object or pattern is to separate out the mechanism by which the remote operation is performed from the service or features that it provides to calling components.

For some applications, this will mean hiding the details of the network transport and protocol from the calling components. In the case of a proxy object that represents a RESTful service, the proxy object might hide details of the HTTP transport and the set of URLs that perform operations on the remote data objects.

I chose reading HTTP header values for the example in this chapter because doing so presents a different situation; the use of the HTTP transport can't be hidden since its use is a given. Instead, the proxy object hides away how the classes in the Foundation framework are used to perform HTTP requests and obtain header values.

Defining the Proxy Protocol

You don't have to define a protocol when implementing the proxy pattern for a remote object, but I find that it forces me to think more clearly about how I expose functionality to calling components (and, of course, it allows me to create alternative implementations should the need arise). Listing 18-2 shows the protocol that I defined to represent a web request, defined in a file called **Proxy.swift** that I added to the example project.

Listing 18-2. The Contents of the Proxy.swift File

```
protocol HttpHeaderRequest {

    func getHeader(url:String, header:String) -> String?;
}
```

The **HttpHeaderRequest** protocol defines a **getHeader** method that accepts the URL that will be targeted and the name of the header whose value is required. Notice that the **HttpHeaderRequest** method returns a synchronous result, rather than relying on a callback. Remote proxy objects have wide discretion in how they present their functionality, and I am going to define a proxy object that hides the fact that the Foundation framework classes I am using perform the request asynchronously.

Defining the Proxy Implementation Class

The next step is to define the class that conforms to the protocol and implements the mechanism by which the remote object is accessed. Listing 18-3 shows the proxy class I defined to make HTTP requests in order to get response header values.

Listing 18-3. Defining the Implementation Class in the Proxy.swift File

```
import Foundation;

protocol HttpHeaderRequest {

    func getHeader(url:String, header:String) -> String?;
}

class HttpHeaderRequestProxy : HttpHeaderRequest {
    private let semaphore = dispatch_semaphore_create(0);

    func getHeader(url: String, header: String) -> String? {

        var headerValue:String?;

        let nsUrl = NSURL(string: url);
        let request = NSURLRequest(URL: nsUrl!);
        NSURLSession.sharedSession().dataTaskWithRequest(request,
            completionHandler: {data, response, error in
                if let httpResponse = response as? NSHTTPURLResponse {
                    headerValue = httpResponse.allHeaderFields[header] as? NSString;
                }
                dispatch_semaphore_signal(self.semaphore);
        }).resume();
        dispatch_semaphore_wait(self.semaphore, DISPATCH_TIME_FOREVER);
        return headerValue;
    }
}
```

The **HttpHeaderRequestProxy** class conforms to the **HttpHeaderRequest** protocol and is the proxy for making requests. The implementation of the **getHeader** method uses the same **Foundation** classes I relied on at the start of this chapter, but with the addition of a (now familiar) GCD semaphore that allows me to hide the asynchronous nature of the Cocoa classes from calling components.

> **Tip**   I don't advocate hiding asynchronous operations in synchronous methods in real projects, not least because Swift closures make it easy to write code that handles asynchronous responses. The reason I have done so in this listing is to demonstrate that proxies can reveal as much or as little of their implementation detail as they choose.

Using the Remote Object Proxy

All that remains is to update the code in the **main.swift** file to use a proxy object rather than making HTTP requests directly, as shown in Listing 18-4.

Listing 18-4. Using a Proxy Object in the main.swift File

```
import Foundation;

let url = "http://www.apress.com";
let headers = ["Content-Length", "Content-Encoding"];

let proxy = HttpHeaderRequestProxy();

for header in headers {
    if let val = proxy.getHeader(url, header:header) {
        println("\(header): \(val)");
    }
}

NSFileHandle.fileHandleWithStandardInput().availableData;
```

The example application still makes the same number of HTTP requests, and it still uses the same Foundation classes to make those requests, but encapsulating the logic into a proxy means that I can make similar requests throughout the application without having to duplicate the implementation logic and—as you would expect by now—allows me to make changes to the manner in which HTTP requests are made without needing to make corresponding changes in the components that rely on the proxy.

Implementing the Expensive Operation Proxy

There are lots of strategies for optimizing the use of expensive resources and minimizing the number of expensive operations that are performed. Common examples include caching, lazy loading, and using other patterns such as the flyweight pattern I described in Chapter 17.

The expensive operation in the example application is the HTTP request. Reducing the number of HTTP requests that my application makes will have a substantial impact; the application will be more responsive to the user, consume less bandwidth (which can be important if the device is using a cell network), and reduce the request throughput at the server.

The obvious way to optimize the example application is to make a single request to service demand for multiple headers. This is a deliberately simple situation, but implementing it requires the same set of changes as any optimization. Listing 18-5 shows the changes I made to the proxy protocol and implementation class.

Listing 18-5. Optimizing HTTP Requests in the Proxy.swift File

```swift
import Foundation;

protocol HttpHeaderRequest {

    func getHeader(url:String, header:String) -> String?;
}

class HttpHeaderRequestProxy : HttpHeaderRequest {
    private let queue = dispatch_queue_create("httpQ", DISPATCH_QUEUE_SERIAL);
    private let semaphore = dispatch_semaphore_create(0);
    private var cachedHeaders = [String:String]();

    func getHeader(url: String, header: String) -> String? {

        var headerValue:String?;

        dispatch_sync(self.queue, {() in
            if let cachedValue = self.cachedHeaders[header] {
                headerValue = "\(cachedValue) (cached)";
            } else {
                let nsUrl = NSURL(string: url);
                let request = NSURLRequest(URL: nsUrl!);
                NSURLSession.sharedSession().dataTaskWithRequest(request,
                    completionHandler: {data, response, error in
                        if let httpResponse = response as? NSHTTPURLResponse {
                            let headers
                                = httpResponse.allHeaderFields as [String: String];
                            for (name, value) in headers {
                                self.cachedHeaders[name] = value;
                            }
                            headerValue
                                = httpResponse.allHeaderFields[header] as? NSString;
                        }
                        dispatch_semaphore_signal(self.semaphore);
                }).resume();
                dispatch_semaphore_wait(self.semaphore, DISPATCH_TIME_FOREVER);
            }
        });
        return headerValue;
    }
}
```

The **getHeader** method creates a cache of response header values that are used to satisfy subsequent requests, providing a mechanism by which the number of HTTP requests can be reduced. Running the application shows that one of the headers is obtained from the values obtained from the cache:

Content-Length: 13960
Content-Encoding: gzip (cached)

The changes to the **HttpHeaderRequestProxy** class rely on a GCD queue to ensure that one request callback is updating the dictionary of cached data when another callback is trying to read it.

Deferring the Operation

A common alternative implementation is to defer the execution of the expensive operation for as long as possible, often in the expectation that the user may cancel the task and the operation will not be required.

The benefit of this approach is that the expense of the operation may be avoided, but the drawback is that it requires an API change so that the calling component can signal that the operation should begin. Listing 18-6 shows the changes that I made to the proxy and its protocol to defer the HTTP request.

Listing 18-6. Deferring the HTTP Request in the Proxy.swift File

```
import Foundation;

protocol HttpHeaderRequest {
    init(url:String);
    func getHeader(header:String, callback:(String, String?) -> Void );
    func execute();
}

class HttpHeaderRequestProxy : HttpHeaderRequest {
    let url:String;
    var headersRequired:[String: (String, String?) -> Void];

    required init(url: String) {
        self.url = url;
        self.headersRequired = Dictionary<String, (String, String?) -> Void>();
    }

    func getHeader(header: String, callback: (String, String?) -> Void) {
        self.headersRequired[header] = callback;
    }
```

```
func execute() {
    let nsUrl = NSURL(string: url);
    let request = NSURLRequest(URL: nsUrl!);
    NSURLSession.sharedSession().dataTaskWithRequest(request,
        completionHandler: {data, response, error in
            if let httpResponse = response as? NSHTTPURLResponse {
                let headers = httpResponse.allHeaderFields as [String: String];
                for (header, callback) in self.headersRequired {
                    callback(header, headers[header]);
                }
            }
        }
    }).resume();
    }
}
```

I have changed the way that the proxy is used so that calling components call the **getHeader** method for each header that is required, supplying a callback for each of them. I have exposed the asynchronous nature of the underlying classes that make the HTTP requests because it is a nice fit with deferring the execution of the request itself.

When all of the headers and their callbacks have been registered, the **execute** method is called to perform the request and trigger the callbacks. If the user abandons the process before the **execute** method is called, then the HTTP request will not be performed, and the expense of the operation will not be incurred. The change in the **HttpHeaderRequest** protocol forces changes in the calling components, as shown in Listing 18-7.

Listing 18-7. Using the Revised Protocol in the main.swift File

```
import Foundation;

let url = "http://www.apress.com";
let headers = ["Content-Length", "Content-Encoding"];

let proxy = HttpHeaderRequestProxy(url: url);

for header in headers {
    proxy.getHeader(header, callback: {header, val in
        if (val != nil) {
            println("\(header): \(val!)");
        }
    });
}

proxy.execute();

NSFileHandle.fileHandleWithStandardInput().availableData;
```

Running the application produces the following output:

```
Content-Encoding: gzip
Content-Length: 13960
```

Implementing the Access Restriction Proxy

Proxies that restrict access to an object are defined as a wrapper around that object, which presents a different implementation path from the other proxy types.

Creating the Authorization Source

The first step is to define a source of authorization that will be used to check access. Separating the authorization check from the proxy allows the proxy to adopt the API of the object it is wrapping, which means that access can be restricted without having to propagate details of the authorization policy throughout the application. Listing 18-8 shows the contents of the **Auth.swift** file that I added to the example project.

Listing 18-8. The Contents of the Auth.swift File

```
class UserAuthentication {
    var user:String?;
    var authenticated:Bool = false;

    private init() {
        // do nothing - stops instances being created
    }

    func authenticate(user:String, pass:String) {
        if (pass == "secret") {
            self.user = user;
            self.authenticated = true;
        } else {
            self.user = nil;
            self.authenticated = false;
        }
    }

    class var sharedInstance:UserAuthentication {
        get {
            struct singletonWrapper {
                static let singleton = UserAuthentication();
            }
            return singletonWrapper.singleton;
        }
    }
}
```

The **UserAuthentication** class uses the singleton pattern to provide a simple mechanism for authenticating users—so simple, in fact, that any user who provides the password **simple** will be authenticated. In a real project, authentication is typically handled by a remote service, which may itself have its own proxy. For this example, any authenticated user is authorized to make HTTP requests.

Creating the Proxy Object

The next step is to define the proxy object so that it can be used as a seamless replacement for the object it wraps but with the enforcement of the authorization policy, as shown in Listing 18-9.

Listing 18-9. Defining the Access Restriction Proxy Class in the Proxy.swift File

```swift
import Foundation;

protocol HttpHeaderRequest {

    init(url:String);
    func getHeader(header:String, callback:(String, String?) -> Void );
    func execute();
}

class AccessControlProxy : HttpHeaderRequest {
    private let wrappedObject: HttpHeaderRequest;

    required init(url:String) {
        wrappedObject = HttpHeaderRequestProxy(url: url);
    }

    func getHeader(header: String, callback: (String, String?) -> Void) {
        wrappedObject.getHeader(header, callback: callback);
    }

    func execute() {
        if (UserAuthentication.sharedInstance.authenticated) {
            wrappedObject.execute();
        } else {
            fatalError("Unauthorized");
        }
    }
}

private class HttpHeaderRequestProxy : HttpHeaderRequest {
    let url:String;
    var headersRequired:[String: (String, String?) -> Void];

    // ...methods omitted for brevity...
}
```

The **AccessControlProxy** class conforms to the **HttpHeaderRequest** protocol and is a wrapper around an instance of the **HttpHeaderRequestProxy** class (there is no prohibition against proxies being used as stand-ins for objects that are themselves proxies). The **AccessControlProxy** implementation of the **execute** method calls the **UserAuthentication** class to determine whether value credentials have been provided. If the user has been authenticated, then the **execute** method of the wrapped object is called, and the **fatalException** method is called otherwise.

> **Tip**   Notice that I have applied the **private** keyword to the **HttpHeaderRequestProxy** class. There is
> no point implementing access restrictions if the proxy can be bypassed by creating an instance of the
> underlying class.

Applying the Proxy

The final step is to update the calling components so they use the new proxy class. In a real project,
I would typically provide a factory method to hide the details of the proxy class from the calling
components (as described in Chapter 9), but for this example I am going to instantiate the proxy
directly, as shown in Listing 18-10.

Listing 18-10. Using the Access Restriction Proxy in the main.swift File

```
import Foundation;

let url = "http://www.apress.com";
let headers = ["Content-Length", "Content-Encoding"];

let proxy = AccessControlProxy(url: url);

for header in headers {
    proxy.getHeader(header, callback: {header, val in
        if (val != nil) {
            println("\(header): \(val!)");
        }
    });
}

UserAuthentication.sharedInstance.authenticate("bob", pass: "secret");
proxy.execute();

NSFileHandle.fileHandleWithStandardInput().availableData;
```

Notice that I provide the user credentials before calling the **execute** method. In a real project,
the credentials are typically obtained from the user when the application first starts, and the
authentication/authorization status is unknown to the components that need to perform restricted
operations.

Variations on the Proxy Pattern

Proxy classes can be used to perform reference counting, which can be useful when resources
require active management and where you need to perform an action of some sort when a specific
number of references is reached, typically zero. To demonstrate this kind of proxy, I created another
Xcode OS X Command Line project called ReferenceCounting. I added a file called **NetworkRequest.**
swift to the project and used it to define the types shown in Listing 18-11.

Listing 18-11. The Contents of the NetworkRequest.swift File

```swift
import Foundation;

protocol NetworkConnection {
    func connect();
    func disconnect();
    func sendCommand(command:String);
}

class NetworkConnectionFactory {
    class func createNetworkConnection() -> NetworkConnection {
        return NetworkConnectionImplementation();
    }
}

private class NetworkConnectionImplementation : NetworkConnection {
    typealias me = NetworkConnectionImplementation;

    func connect() { me.writeMessage("Connect"); }
    func disconnect() { me.writeMessage("Disconnect"); }

    func sendCommand(command:String) {
        me.writeMessage("Command: \(command)");
        NSThread.sleepForTimeInterval(1);
        me.writeMessage("Command completed: \(command)");
    }

    private class func writeMessage(msg:String) {
        dispatch_async(self.queue, {() in
            println(msg);
        });
    }

    private class var queue:dispatch_queue_t {
        get {
            struct singletonWrapper {
                static let singleton = dispatch_queue_create("writeQ",
                    DISPATCH_QUEUE_SERIAL);
            }
            return singletonWrapper.singleton;
        }
    }
}
```

The **NetworkConnection** protocol defines the methods that are used to operate on a network connection to a hypothetical server. The **connect** method is called to establish a connection, the **sendCommand** connection is used to send work to the server, and the **disconnect** method is used to close the connection when the work is done.

The **NetworkConnectionImplementation** class conforms to the protocol and implements the methods by writing messages to the debug console. I have used the singleton pattern to define a GCD queue that is shared between all instances of the class so that messages written to the console are not corrupted when two objects write at the same time. The implementation of the **sendCommand** method incurs a one-second delay to simulate the server executing the command it has been sent.

I have used the factory method pattern to provide access to instances of the **NetworkConnectionImplementation** class, which is annotated with the **private** keyword and is inaccessible outside of the file in which it is defined. Listing 18-12 shows the statements I added to the **main.swift** file to create several simultaneous network requests.

Listing 18-12. The Contents of the main.swift File

```swift
import Foundation;

let queue = dispatch_queue_create("requestQ", DISPATCH_QUEUE_CONCURRENT);

for count in 0 ..< 3 {

    let connection = NetworkConnectionFactory.createNetworkConnection();

    dispatch_async(queue, {() in
        connection.connect();
        connection.sendCommand("Command: \(count)");
        connection.disconnect();
    });
}

NSFileHandle.fileHandleWithStandardInput().availableData;
```

I create three network requests, and on each of them I call the connect method to establish the connection, call the **sendCommand** method to send a job to the server, and then call the **disconnection** method. Running the application will produce results similar to the following:

```
Connect
Connect
Connect
Command: Command: 0
Command: Command: 1
Command: Command: 2
Command completed: Command: 0
Command completed: Command: 1
Command completed: Command: 2
Disconnect
Disconnect
Disconnect
```

You may see slightly different results because the connections may be processed in a different order. The important point to note from the output is that the network connections overlap and that a separate connection is used for each command that is sent to the server.

Implementing a Reference Counting Proxy

In this situation, a reference counting proxy can be used to manage the life cycle of a network connection so that it can be used to service multiple requests. Listing 18-13 shows the definition of the proxy class.

Listing 18-13. Defining a Reference Counting Proxy in the NetworkRequest.swift File

```swift
import Foundation;

protocol NetworkConnection {
    func connect();
    func disconnect();
    func sendCommand(command:String);
}

class NetworkConnectionFactory {
    class func createNetworkConnection() -> NetworkConnection {
        return connectionProxy;
    }

    private class var connectionProxy:NetworkConnection {
        get {
            struct singletonWrapper {
                static let singleton = NetworkRequestProxy();
            }
            return singletonWrapper.singleton;
        }
    }
}

private class NetworkConnectionImplementation : NetworkConnection {
    typealias me = NetworkConnectionImplementation;

    // ...methods omitted for brevity...
}

class NetworkRequestProxy : NetworkConnection {
    private let wrappedRequest:NetworkConnection;
    private let queue = dispatch_queue_create("commandQ", DISPATCH_QUEUE_SERIAL);
    private var referenceCount:Int = 0;
    private var connected = false;

    init() {
        wrappedRequest = NetworkConnectionImplementation();
    }

    func connect() { /* do nothing */ }
    func disconnect() { /* do nothing */ }
```

```
func sendCommand(command: String) {
    self.referenceCount++;
    dispatch_sync(self.queue, {() in
        if (!self.connected && self.referenceCount > 0) {
            self.wrappedRequest.connect();
            self.connected = true;
        }
        self.wrappedRequest.sendCommand(command);
        self.referenceCount--;
        if (self.connected && self.referenceCount == 0) {
            self.wrappedRequest.disconnect();
            self.connected = false;
        }
    });
}
}
```

I have revised the factory method class so that it uses the singleton pattern to return a shared instance of the **NetworkRequestProxy** class. The **NetworkRequestProxy** class conforms to the **NetworkRequest** protocol and is a wrapper around a **NetworkConnectionImplementation** object.

The goal with this kind of reference counting proxy is to take the control of the **connect** and **disconnect** methods away from the calling components and keep a connection open for as long as there are pending commands to be sent. I have used a serial GCD queue to ensure that only one command is processed at a time and to ensure that the reference counting is not affected by multiple concurrent accesses. Running the application will produce output similar to the following:

```
Connect
Command: Command: 0
Command completed: Command: 0
Command: Command: 1
Command completed: Command: 1
Command: Command: 2
Command completed: Command: 2
Disconnect
```

The commands are now processed serially over a single connection, reflected in the fact that there is one **Connect** and one **Disconnect** message. This kind of proxy trades one kind of expensive operation for another. Without the proxy, the expense is the number of concurrent requests and the demand this puts on the client, the network, and the server. The proxy reduces the request concurrency, but it serializes the commands sent to the server, which means that the combined workload takes longer to perform. The overall effect is to trade bandwidth and server capacity for the user's time.

Understanding the Pitfalls of the Proxy Pattern

The pitfalls associated with the proxy pattern depend on how it is being implemented, but the common theme is not to allow details of the implementation to leak out of the proxy class into the calling component. For remote object proxies, this means ensuring that no unnecessary details of the mechanism used to access the remote object are revealed. For proxies used to manage expensive operations, you should avoid exposing details of how the cost of the operation is being mitigated as far as it possible. For access restriction proxies, you should take care not to allow calling components to bypass the proxy and access the underlying object directly.

There are two specific pitfalls if you use the proxy pattern to implement the reference counting variation. First, do not use proxies to manage the life cycle of objects. Leave this to the built-in Swift support for automatic reference counting (ARC), which ensures that objects are destroyed when they are no longer required.

Second, do not use proxies to implement concurrency protections such as locks and semaphores. This is a reasonable thing to do if you are working with a language that doesn't have concurrency features, but Swift provides access to Grand Central Dispatch for high-level concurrency control, and if you don't like GCD, you can access a range of lower-level concurrency mechanisms. Writing your own concurrency code is stupid, dangerous, and almost impossible to get right. If you think you need to create your own concurrency protections, then you have either misunderstood the built-in features or misunderstood the problem you face in your project.

Examples of the Proxy Pattern in Cocoa

The framework provides excellent support for the proxy pattern through the **NSProxy** class, but it is available only to Objective-C programmers and cannot be used in Swift.

You don't call methods in Objective-C code. Instead, you send messages to objects. In most situations, this distinction doesn't have any real significance, and many Objective-C programmers are unaware of the difference. The **NSProxy** class is used to create classes that receive messages and forward them on to the resources or object for which they are proxies, which provides a nice mechanism by which messages can be changed or redirected on the fly.

None of this is available to Swift programmers, sadly, and attempting to derive a Swift class from **NSProxy** will generate a compiler error because it is impossible to call **super.init** from the derived class (because **NSProxy** doesn't define an initializer).

Applying the Pattern to the SportsStore Application

To demonstrate the use of the proxy pattern in the SportsStore application, I am going to create a proxy object that represents the product data on a remote server and then use the proxy to send stock level updates and to consolidate the code that gets the initial stock data when the application starts.

Preparing the Example Application

No preparation is required for this chapter, and I pick up the SportsStore application just as I left it in Chapter 17. Don't forget that you can download all of the code examples for this book, including projects for each chapter's version of the SportsStore application, from Apress.com.

Defining the Protocol, Factory Method, and Proxy Class

As I explained earlier, you don't need to define a protocol when creating a proxy, but I usually do. This is partly habit but mainly because it allows me to draw a clean line separating the functionality exposed to calling components from the implementation of the proxy class. Listing 18-14 shows the contents of the **Proxy.swift** file, which I added to the SportsStore project.

Listing 18-14. The Contents of the Proxy.swift File

```
protocol StockServer {

    func getStockLevel(product:String, callback: (String, Int) -> Void);
    func setStockLevel(product:String, stockLevel:Int);
}

class StockServerFactory {

    class func getStockServer() -> StockServer {
        return server;
    }

    private class var server:StockServer {
        struct singletonWrapper {
            static let singleton:StockServer = StockServerProxy();
        }
        return singletonWrapper.singleton;
    }
}

class StockServerProxy : StockServer {

    func getStockLevel(product: String, callback: (String, Int) -> Void) {
        // TODO - implement this method
    }

    func setStockLevel(product: String, stockLevel: Int) {
        // TODO - implement this method
    }
}
```

I have defined the **StockServer** protocol so that it contains **getStockLevel** and **setStockLevel** methods and created the **StockServerProxy** class, which acts as the proxy for the remote server. The glue between the protocol and the proxy class is the **StockServerFactory** class, which uses the singleton pattern to provide callers with a reference to a single proxy object. I have not yet implemented the proxy methods. I'll complete the proxy class once some of the other changes are in place.

Updating the Product Data Store

The **ProductDataStore** class supplies product data for the rest of the application and is the natural point at which to integrate the proxy, replacing the direct access to the **NetworkConnection** and **NetworkPool** classes that are currently in place. Listing 18-15 shows how I updated the **ProductDataStore** class to obtain its initial stock value data from the proxy.

Listing 18-15. Integrating the Proxy in the ProductDataStore.swift File

```
import Foundation

final class ProductDataStore {
    var callback:((Product) -> Void)?;
    private var networkQ:dispatch_queue_t
    private var uiQ:dispatch_queue_t;
    lazy var products:[Product] = self.loadData();

    init() {
        networkQ = dispatch_get_global_queue(DISPATCH_QUEUE_PRIORITY_BACKGROUND, 0);
        uiQ = dispatch_get_main_queue();
    }

    private func loadData() -> [Product] {

        var products = [Product]();

        for product in productData {
            var p:Product = LowStockIncreaseDecorator(product: product);
            if (p.category == "Soccer") {
                p = SoccerDecreaseDecorator(product: p);
            }

            dispatch_async(self.networkQ, {() in
                StockServerFactory.getStockServer().getStockLevel(p.name,
                    callback: { name, stockLevel in
                        p.stockLevel = stockLevel;
                        dispatch_async(self.uiQ, {() in
                            if (self.callback != nil) {
                                self.callback!(p);
                            }
                        })
                })
            });
        });
```

```
                products.append(p);
        }
        return products;
    }

    private var productData:[Product] = [
        ProductComposite(name: "Running Pack",
            description: "Complete Running Outfit", category: "Running",
                    stockLevel: 10, products:
    // ... statements omitted for brevity...
}
```

The change in the **loadData** method uses the proxy object to get its data value, and in Listing 18-16 you can see how I have updated the proxy **getStockLevel** method so that it obtains the stock data via the **NetworkPool** and **NetworkConnection** classes.

Listing 18-16. Implementing the getStockLevel Method in the Proxy.swift File

```
...
class StockServerProxy : StockServer {

    func getStockLevel(product: String, callback: (String, Int) -> Void) {
        let stockConn = NetworkPool.getConnection();
        let level = stockConn.getStockLevel(product);
        if (level != nil) {
            callback(product, level!);
        }
        NetworkPool.returnConnecton(stockConn);
    }

    func setStockLevel(product: String, stockLevel: Int) {
        // TODO - implement this method
    }
}
...
```

Sending Stock Level Updates

To use the proxy to send stock level changes, I need to update the **NetworkConnection** class, as shown in Listing 18-17.

Listing 18-17. Adding a New Command in the NetworkConnection.swift File

```
import Foundation

class NetworkConnection {
    private let flyweight:NetConnFlyweight;

    init() {
        self.flyweight = NetConnFlyweightFactory.createFlyweight();
    }
```

```
    func getStockLevel(name:String) -> Int? {
        NSThread.sleepForTimeInterval(Double(rand() % 2));
        return self.flyweight.getStockLevel(name);
    }

    func setStockLevel(name:String, level:Int) {
        println("Stock update: \(name) = \(level)");
    }
}
```

I don't have a real server to update, so the implementation of the **setStockLevel** method prints out a message to the debug console. With the update to the **NetworkConnection** class, I can complete the implementation of the proxy class, as shown in Listing 18-18.

Listing 18-18. Completing the Proxy Class in the Proxy.swift File

```
...
class StockServerProxy : StockServer {

    func getStockLevel(product: String, callback: (String, Int) -> Void) {
        let stockConn = NetworkPool.getConnection();
        let level = stockConn.getStockLevel(product);
        if (level != nil) {
            callback(product, level!);
        }
        NetworkPool.returnConnecton(stockConn);
    }

    func setStockLevel(product: String, stockLevel: Int) {
        let stockConn = NetworkPool.getConnection();
        stockConn.setStockLevel(product, level: stockLevel);
        NetworkPool.returnConnecton(stockConn);
    }
}
...
```

The final step is to call the proxy **setStockLevel** method from the **ViewController** class when the user makes a change, as shown in Listing 18-19.

Listing 18-19. Using the Proxy in the ViewController.swift File

```
...
@IBAction func stockLevelDidChange(sender: AnyObject) {
    if var currentCell = sender as? UIView {
        while (true) {
            currentCell = currentCell.superview!;
            if let cell = currentCell as? ProductTableCell {
                if let product = cell.product? {
                    if let stepper = sender as? UIStepper {
                        product.stockLevel = Int(stepper.value);
```

```
            } else if let textfield = sender as? UITextField {
                if let newValue = textfield.text.toInt()? {
                    product.stockLevel = newValue;
                }
            }
            cell.stockStepper.value = Double(product.stockLevel);
            cell.stockField.text = String(product.stockLevel);
            productLogger.logItem(product);

            StockServerFactory.getStockServer()
                .setStockLevel(product.name, stockLevel: product.stockLevel);
        }
        break;
    }
}
displayStockTotal();
    }
}
...
```

I have added a statement to the **stockLevelDidChange** method that uses the proxy to update the stock level. The effect of defining the proxy is that the implementation of the (simulated) network connection is known only to the proxy class and can be changed without needing to change the **ProductDataStore** or **ViewController** class. To test the changes, start the application and change one of the stock levels. You will see output similar to the following in the Xcode debug console:

```
Stock update: Thinking Cap = 9
```

Summary

In this chapter, I described how the proxy pattern is used to create stand-ins for objects and resources. I explained the three different ways in which proxies can be applied and showed you an example implementation of each of them. In the next part of the book, I show you the behavioral patterns, which increase the flexibility in the ways that objects work with one another.

Part IV

The Behavioral Patterns

The Chain of Responsibility Pattern

The chain of responsibility pattern is useful when there are multiple objects that could take responsibility for a request but you don't want to expose details of those objects to the calling component. Table 19-1 puts the chain of responsibility pattern into context.

Table 19-1. Putting the Chain of Responsibility Pattern into Context

Question	Answer
What is it?	The chain of responsibility pattern organizes sequentially a set of objects that may be able to take responsibility for a request from a calling component. The sequence of objects is referred to as a *chain*, and each object in the chain is asked to take responsibility for the request. The request moves along the chain until one of the objects takes responsibility or the end of the chain is reached.
What are the benefits?	The chain of responsibility allows objects that can process requests to be ordered into a preferential sequence that can be reordered, extended, or reduced without any impact on the calling component, which has no insight into the objects that comprise the chain.
When should you use this pattern?	Use this pattern when there are several objects that can handle a request, only one of which should be used.
When should you avoid this pattern?	Do not use this pattern when there is only one object that can handle a request or when the calling component needs to select the object.

(continued)

Table 19-1. (continued)

Question	Answer
How do you know when you have implemented the pattern correctly?	The pattern is implemented correctly when the set of objects that can take responsibility for a request are arranged sequentially and each is offered the chance to take responsibility in turn. The individual objects in the chain have no knowledge of one another (other than the next link in the chain).
Are there any common pitfalls?	The pitfall is leaking details of the objects in the chain, either to one another or to the calling component.
Are there any related patterns?	The chain of responsibility pattern shares some common concepts with the command pattern, described in Chapter 20.

Preparing the Example Project

For this chapter, I created an Xcode Command Line Tool project called ChainOfResp. I added a file called **Message.swift** to the project and used it to define the code shown in Listing 19-1.

Listing 19-1. The Contents of the Message.swift File

```
struct Message {
    let from:String;
    let to:String;
    let subject:String;
}
```

I defined a struct called **Message** that has constants representing different properties of a general message: the sender of the message, who the message is to, and the subject of the message. I have not defined a constant for the body of the message, which I don't need to demonstrate the chain of responsibility pattern. Listing 19-2 shows the contents of the **Transmitters.swift** file, in which I have defined a pair of classes that can process **Message** objects in order to transmit them elsewhere.

Listing 19-2. The Contents of the Transmitters.swift File

```
class LocalTransmitter {

    func sendMessage(message: Message) {
        println("Message to \(message.to) sent locally");
    }
}

class RemoteTransmitter {

    func sendMessage(message: Message) {
        println("Message to \(message.to) sent remotely");
    }
}
```

These classes represent the mechanisms by which messages are sent, either locally within a company or remotely to the wider world. Each transmitter class defines a **sendMessage** method that processes a **Message** object. I don't need to implement message routing to demonstrate the chain of responsibility pattern, and so the **sendMessage** methods write a message to the Xcode debug console. Listing 19-3 shows the code I added to the **main.swift** file to use the example classes.

Listing 19-3. The Contents of the main.swift File

```swift
let messages = [
    Message(from: "bob@example.com", to: "joe@example.com",
        subject: "Free for lunch?"),
    Message(from: "joe@example.com", to: "alice@acme.com",
        subject: "New Contracts"),
    Message(from: "pete@example.com", to: "all@example.com",
        subject: "Priority: All-Hands Meeting"),
];

let localT = LocalTransmitter();
let remoteT = RemoteTransmitter();

for msg in messages {
    if let index = find(msg.from, "@") {
        if (msg.to.hasSuffix(msg.from[Range<String.Index>(start:
                index, end: msg.from.endIndex)])) {
            localT.sendMessage(msg);
        } else {
            remoteT.sendMessage(msg);
        }
    } else {
        println("Error: cannot send message to \(msg.from)");
    }
}
```

I define an array of **Message** objects and use a **for** loop to examine each of them to choose between a **LocalTransmitter** object and a **RemoteTransmitter** object based on whether the **to** and **from** addresses share a common suffix. Running the example application produces the following results:

```
Message to joe@example.com sent locally
Message to alice@acme.com sent remotely
Message to all@example.com sent locally
```

Understanding the Problem That the Pattern Solves

The problem in the example application is that the components that use the transmitter classes to process **Message** objects have to know about those classes and understand when each should be used. This makes it hard to add new message handlers, to change the relationship between existing handlers, and to test and maintain the code overall. To demonstrate the problem, I have defined a new transmitter class, as shown in Listing 19-4.

Listing 19-4. Defining a New Transmitter Class in the Transmitters.swift File

```
class LocalTransmitter {

    func sendMessage(message: Message) {
        println("Message to \(message.to) sent locally");
    }
}

class RemoteTransmitter {

    func sendMessage(message: Message) {
        println("Message to \(message.to) sent remotely");
    }
}

class PriorityTransmitter {
    func sendMessage(message: Message) {
        println("Message to \(message.to) sent as priority");
    }
}
```

To properly handle **Message** objects, components need to be updated to reflect the new **PriorityTransmitter** class and know when it should be used. Listing 19-5 shows the changes required in the **main.swift** file, but in a real project these changes would be duplicated throughout the application.

Listing 19-5. Reflecting the Definition of a New Transmitter Class in the main.swift File

```
let messages = [
    Message(from: "bob@example.com", to: "joe@example.com",
        subject: "Free for lunch?"),
    Message(from: "joe@example.com", to: "alice@acme.com",
        subject: "New Contracts"),
    Message(from: "pete@example.com", to: "all@example.com",
        subject: "Priority: All-Hands Meeting"),
];

let localT = LocalTransmitter();
let remoteT = RemoteTransmitter();
let priorityT = PriorityTransmitter();
```

```
for msg in messages {
    if (msg.subject.hasPrefix("Priority")) {
        priorityT.sendMessage(msg);
    } else if let index = find(msg.from, "@") {
        if (msg.to.hasSuffix(msg.from[Range<String.Index>(start:
                index, end: msg.from.endIndex)])) {
            localT.sendMessage(msg);
        } else {
            remoteT.sendMessage(msg);
        }
    } else {
        println("Error: cannot send message to \(msg.from)");
    }
}
```

The changes themselves are simple, but the fact that calling components require so much insight into how the transmitter classes relate to one another and when to use them is a problem.

Understanding the Chain of Responsibility Pattern

The chain of responsibility pattern solves these problems by arranging the transmitters in a chain (which is where it gets the name). Each transmitter is a link in the chain and is able to inspect the **Message** object to determine whether it can take responsibility for the request. If a link in the chain is able to handle the **Message** request, then it does so. If not, then the request is passed to the next link in the chain, and the process is repeated until the request is handled or the last link in the chain is reached. Figure 19-1 illustrates the chain of responsibility pattern.

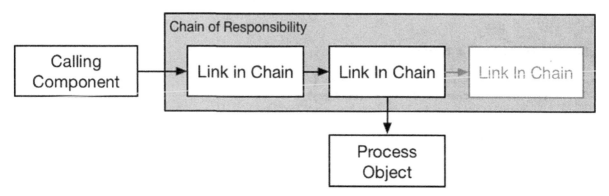

Figure 19-1. The chain of responsibility pattern

The calling component deals only with the first link in the chain and has no knowledge of subsequent links or the basis on which each link decides whether it can take responsibility for the request. In the figure, I have shown a chain with three links, where the second link takes responsibility for the request. In this situation, the third link in the chain doesn't participate in the process and is unaware of the request from the calling component.

Implementing the Chain of Responsibility Pattern

The implementation of the chain of responsibility pattern relies on hiding the details of the individual links that make up the chain from the calling components—something that is most readily achieved by defining a protocol or a base class. I usually rely on a base class because I like to deal with the next link in the chain using an optional property, which cannot be assigned new values when defined by a protocol. Listing 19-6 shows the base class I defined and applied to the transmitter classes.

Listing 19-6. Defining and Implementing a Base Class in the Transmitters.swift File

```
class Transmitter {
    var nextLink:Transmitter?;

    required init() {}

    func sendMessage(message:Message) {
        if (nextLink != nil) {
            nextLink!.sendMessage(message);
        } else {
            println("End of chain reached. Message not sent");
        }
    }

    private class func matchEmailSuffix(message:Message) -> Bool {
        if let index = find(message.from, "@") {
            return message.to.hasSuffix(message.from[Range<String.Index>(start:
                index, end: message.from.endIndex)]);
        }
        return false;
    }
}

class LocalTransmitter : Transmitter {

    override func sendMessage(message: Message) {
        if (Transmitter.matchEmailSuffix(message)) {
            println("Message to \(message.to) sent locally");
        } else {
            super.sendMessage(message);
        }
    }
}

class RemoteTransmitter : Transmitter {

    override func sendMessage(message: Message) {
        if (!Transmitter.matchEmailSuffix(message)) {
            println("Message to \(message.to) sent remotely");
        } else {
            super.sendMessage(message);
        }
    }
}
```

```
class PriorityTransmitter : Transmitter {

    override func sendMessage(message: Message) {
        if (message.subject.hasPrefix("Priority")) {
            println("Message to \(message.to) sent as priority");
        } else {
            super.sendMessage(message);
        }
    }
}
```

The **Transmitter** class defines the basic behavior of a transmitter, including referring a request to the next link in the chain. I have defined the code that checks e-mail suffixes in this class. (The **required** initializer is there so I can create instances of my transmitters from their types, which I do in the next section.)

Each of the individual transmitter classes is derived from **Transmitter** and overrides the **sendMessage** method. Each implementation checks to see whether the transmitter can take responsibility for the **Message** request. If the transmitter cannot take responsibility, it calls the base class implementation, which advances to the next link in the chain or reports an error if there are no further links.

Creating and Providing the Chain of Responsibility

The next step is to create the chain, instantiating the objects that I need and arranging them in the order in which they will be asked to take responsibility for a **Message**. You can use several of the design patterns that I described in Part 2 of this book to create the chain, but I am going to keep the example simple and implement a class method that creates a new chain each time it is called. Listing 19-7 shows the changes that I made to the **Transmitter** class to create the chain.

Listing 19-7. Creating the Chain in the Transmitters.swift File

```
...
class Transmitter {
    var nextLink:Transmitter?;

    required init() {}

    func sendMessage(message:Message) {
        if (nextLink != nil) {
            nextLink!.sendMessage(message);
        } else {
            println("End of chain reached. Message not sent");
        }
    }

    class func createChain() -> Transmitter? {

        let transmitterClasses:[Transmitter.Type] = [
            PriorityTransmitter.self,
            LocalTransmitter.self,
            RemoteTransmitter.self
        ];
```

```
        var link:Transmitter?;

        for tClass in transmitterClasses.reverse() {
            let existingLink = link;
            link = tClass();
            link?.nextLink = existingLink;
        }

        return link;
    }

    private class func matchEmailSuffix(message:Message) -> Bool {
        if let index = find(message.from, "@") {
            return message.to.hasSuffix(message.from[Range<String.Index>(start:
                index, end: message.from.endIndex)]);
        }
        return false;
    }
}
...
```

I have defined an array of **Transmitter** types to make it easy to add new transmitters or to change the order in which they appear in the chain. When I create the chain, I start with the last link and work my way back through the array of classes, creating each in turn and setting up the relationships between them.

> **Tip**   You don't need to use metatypes to create objects in a chain. I find this the clearest way to express the set of types in the chain, but I could have simply created the objects directly and explicitly set the **nextLink** property values.

Applying the Chain of Responsibility Pattern

The final step is to use the chain of responsibility to handle **Message** objects. Listing 19-8 shows the changes I made to the **main.swift** file.

Listing 19-8. Using the Chain of Responsibility in the main.swift File

```
let messages = [
    Message(from: "bob@example.com", to: "joe@example.com",
        subject: "Free for lunch?"),
    Message(from: "joe@example.com", to: "alice@acme.com",
        subject: "New Contracts"),
    Message(from: "pete@example.com", to: "all@example.com",
        subject: "Priority: All-Hands Meeting"),
];
```

```
if let chain = Transmitter.createChain() {
    for msg in messages {
        chain.sendMessage(msg);
    }
}
```

Applying the pattern simplifies the code in the calling components and hides the details of which objects will be asked to take responsibility for the **Message** object. When I need to add new transmitters to the application, I can do so by modifying just the **createChain** method of the **Transmitter** class; no changes are required in the calling components. Running the example application produces the following output:

```
Message to joe@example.com sent locally
Message to alice@acme.com sent remotely
Message to all@example.com sent as priority
```

Variations on the Chain of Responsibility Pattern

There are several common variations on the chain of responsibility pattern, each of which I describe in the following sections.

Applying the Factory Method Pattern

At the moment, all calls to the **Transmitters.createChain** method receive a chain of responsibility containing the same set of link objects. However, I can combine the chain of responsibility pattern with the factory method or abstract factory pattern (described in Chapters 9 and 10) to vary the links in the chains for different requests. Listing 19-9 shows the changes I made to the **Transmitter** class to support different configurations of chains.

Listing 19-9. Varying the Chain in the Transmitters.swift File

```
...
class func createChain(localOnly:Bool) -> Transmitter? {

    let transmitterClasses:[Transmitter.Type]
        = localOnly ? [PriorityTransmitter.self, LocalTransmitter.self]
        : [PriorityTransmitter.self, LocalTransmitter.self, RemoteTransmitter.self];

    var link:Transmitter?;

    for tClass in transmitterClasses.reverse() {
        let existingLink = link;
        link = tClass();
        link?.nextLink = existingLink;
    }

    return link;
}
...
```

There are lots of ways to approach varying the links in the chain, but I have settled on an argument to the **createChain** method that allows callers to specify whether the chain will be configured to handle local messages only. The effect of the argument is to include or exclude the **RemoteTransmitter** in the chain, although this difference is hidden from the calling component. Listing 19-10 shows how I use the **localOnly** argument in the **main.swift** file.

Listing 19-10. Specifying the Configuration of the Chain of Responsibility in the main.swift File

```
let messages = [
    Message(from: "bob@example.com", to: "joe@example.com",
        subject: "Free for lunch?"),
    Message(from: "joe@example.com", to: "alice@acme.com",
        subject: "New Contracts"),
    Message(from: "pete@example.com", to: "all@example.com",
        subject: "Priority: All-Hands Meeting"),
];

if let chain = Transmitter.createChain(true) {
    for msg in messages {
        chain.sendMessage(msg);
    }
}
```

I call the **createChain** method with a **localOnly** value of **true**, which means that one of the **Message** objects that I create will not be handled. You can see the effect by running the application, which produces the following output:

```
Message to joe@example.com sent locally
End of chain reached. Message not sent
Message to all@example.com sent as priority
```

Indicating Whether Responsibility Was Taken for the Request

At the moment, the calling component has no insight into whether the chain takes responsibility for a request. A common variation is to provide feedback to the calling component so that the chain of responsibility isn't a black hole. Listing 19-11 shows the changes I made to provide the calling component with the result.

Listing 19-11. Indicating Whether Responsibility Was Taken for a Request in the Transmitters.swift File

```
class Transmitter {
    var nextLink:Transmitter?;

    required init() {}

    func sendMessage(message:Message) -> Bool {
        if (nextLink != nil) {
            return nextLink!.sendMessage(message);
```

```
        } else {
            println("End of chain reached. Message not sent");
            return false;
        }
    }

    // ...methods omitted for brevity...
}

class LocalTransmitter : Transmitter {

    override func sendMessage(message: Message) -> Bool {
        if (Transmitter.matchEmailSuffix(message)) {
            println("Message to \(message.to) sent locally");
            return true;
        } else {
            return super.sendMessage(message);
        }
    }
}

class RemoteTransmitter : Transmitter {

    override func sendMessage(message: Message) -> Bool {
        if (!Transmitter.matchEmailSuffix(message)) {
            println("Message to \(message.to) sent remotely");
            return true;
        } else {
            return super.sendMessage(message);
        }
    }
}

class PriorityTransmitter : Transmitter {

    override func sendMessage(message: Message) -> Bool {
        if (message.subject.hasPrefix("Priority")) {
            println("Message to \(message.to) sent as priority");
            return true;
        } else {
            return super.sendMessage(message);
        }
    }
}
```

Each link in the chain knows only whether it can handle the message and has no insight into the capabilities of other links. The effect of this isolation is that a definitive **false** result, indicating that no link has taken responsibility for the request, requires all of the links in the chain to be consulted. A definitive **true** result is generated as soon as a link takes responsibility and handles the **Message** object. Listing 19-12 shows how I have used the result returned by the **sendMessage** methods in the **main.swift** file.

Listing 19-12. Receiving a Response from the Chain in the main.swift File

```
let messages = [
    Message(from: "bob@example.com", to: "joe@example.com",
        subject: "Free for lunch?"),
    Message(from: "joe@example.com", to: "alice@acme.com",
        subject: "New Contracts"),
    Message(from: "pete@example.com", to: "all@example.com",
        subject: "Priority: All-Hands Meeting"),
];

if let chain = Transmitter.createChain(true) {
    for msg in messages {
        let handled = chain.sendMessage(msg);
        println("Message sent: \(handled)");
    }
}
```

Running the application produces the following output, showing the effect of providing the calling component with a response:

```
Message to joe@example.com sent locally
Message sent: true
End of chain reached. Message not sent
Message sent: false
Message to all@example.com sent as priority
Message sent: true
```

Notifying All Links in the Chain

In the standard implementation of the chain of responsibility pattern, links in the chain are consulted only until one of them takes responsibility for the request. Links in the chain after the one that takes responsibility are unaware of the request.

A variation on the standard implementation is to notify all of the links in a chain about a request, even the ones that appear after the link that has accepted responsibility for the request. This is a variation that I rarely use but that can be helpful when links in the chain need to know when they have been preempted. Listing 19-13 shows the changes I made to implement the variation in **Transmitter** and its subclasses.

Listing 19-13. Notifying All Links in the Transmitters.swift File

```
class Transmitter {
    var nextLink:Transmitter?;

    required init() {}

    func sendMessage(message:Message, handled: Bool = false) -> Bool {
        if (nextLink != nil) {
            return nextLink!.sendMessage(message, handled: handled);
```

```
        } else if (!handled) {
            println("End of chain reached. Message not sent");
        }
        return handled;
    }

    // ...methods omitted for brevity...
}

class LocalTransmitter : Transmitter {

    override func sendMessage(message: Message, var handled:Bool) -> Bool {
        if (!handled && Transmitter.matchEmailSuffix(message)) {
            println("Message to \(message.to) sent locally");
            handled = true;
        }
        return super.sendMessage(message, handled: handled);
    }
}

class RemoteTransmitter : Transmitter {

    override func sendMessage(message: Message, var handled: Bool) -> Bool {
        if (!handled && !Transmitter.matchEmailSuffix(message)) {
            println("Message to \(message.to) sent remotely");
            handled = true;
        }
        return super.sendMessage(message, handled: handled);
    }
}

class PriorityTransmitter : Transmitter {
    var totalMessages = 0;
    var handledMessages = 0;

    override func sendMessage(message: Message, var handled:Bool) -> Bool {
        totalMessages++;
        if (!handled && message.subject.hasPrefix("Priority")) {
            handledMessages++;
            println("Message to \(message.to) sent as priority");
            println("Stats: Handled \(handledMessages) of \(totalMessages)");
            handled = true;
        }
        return super.sendMessage(message, handled: handled);
    }
}
```

I have changed the signature of the **sendMessage** method to define a **handled** parameter that I use to signal whether a link in the chain is being asked to take responsibility for a request or being notified about a request for which another link has already taken responsibility. I have also modified the **PriorityTransmitter** class so that it keeps track of the requests it handles and the total number of requests it processes. Running the application produces the following output:

```
Message to joe@example.com sent locally
Message sent: true
End of chain reached. Message not sent
Message sent: false
Message to all@example.com sent as priority
Stats: Handled 1 of 3
Message sent: true
```

Understanding the Pitfalls of the Pattern

The only pitfall when implementing the pattern is leaking details about the objects in the chain, either to the calling component or from one link in the chain to another. This pattern works by containing knowledge about the way that the chain has been created to a single method or class, and allowing the implementation detail to leak creates dependencies on a specific chain configuration that makes it difficult to change the chain later. Ensure that you present the calling components with a base class or protocol, and use the same base class or protocol when setting the **nextLink** properties of links in the chain.

If you are implementing the variation that returns a result to the calling component, then you must ensure that you do not inadvertently leak knowledge of the chain in the result. The chain of responsibility pattern works best with simple result types (like the **Bool** I used in the example), but if you use more complex types, then you must not include a reference to the link in the chain that has accepted responsibility for the request.

Examples of the Pattern in Cocoa

Cocoa relies on the chain of responsibility to handle user interface events. All UI components are derived from the **UIResponder** class (or the equivalent **NSResponder** for OS X apps). The links in the chain are individual UI components, arranged to reflect the hierarchy of interface components with the top-level view as the last link in the chain.

When the user interacts with a component—by clicking the mouse, for example—Cocoa sends the interaction event to the link in the chain that represents the component that has been clicked. The component is provided with the opportunity to take responsibility for handling the event, and the event moves along the chain until a component is found that will handle the event or the end of the chain is reached (which indicates that the application does not want or need to handle the event and it can be ignored).

Applying the Pattern to the SportsStore Application

To demonstrate the use of the chain of responsibility pattern, I will define a set of classes that format the background color of the table cells that display products in the SportsStore application.

Preparing the Example Application

I pick up the SportsStore project as I left it in Chapter 18, and no preparation for this chapter is required.

Defining the Chain and its Links

My chain is going to consist of a set of objects that will accept responsibility for formatting a table cell based on the category of the product that it displays. Listing 19-14 shows the contents of the **FormatterChain.swift** file that I added to the SportsStore project and used to implement the pattern.

Listing 19-14. The Contents of the FormatterChain.swift File

```
import UIKit;

class CellFormatter {
    var nextLink:CellFormatter?;

    func formatCell(cell: ProductTableCell) {
        nextLink?.formatCell(cell);
    }

    class func createChain() -> CellFormatter {
        let formatter = ChessFormatter();
        formatter.nextLink = WatersportsFormatter();
        formatter.nextLink?.nextLink = DefaultFormatter();
        return formatter;
    }
}

class ChessFormatter : CellFormatter {
    override func formatCell(cell: ProductTableCell) {
        if (cell.product?.category == "Chess") {
            cell.backgroundColor = UIColor.lightGrayColor();
        } else {
            super.formatCell(cell);
        }
    }
}
```

```
class WatersportsFormatter : CellFormatter {
    override func formatCell(cell: ProductTableCell) {
        if (cell.product?.category == "Watersports") {
            cell.backgroundColor = UIColor.greenColor();
        } else {
            super.formatCell(cell);
        }
    }
}

class DefaultFormatter : CellFormatter {
    override func formatCell(cell: ProductTableCell) {
        cell.backgroundColor = UIColor.yellowColor();
    }
}
```

All implementations of this pattern look alike, and the listing shows the common foundation that is shared with the earlier example. I have defined a base class (**CellFormatter**) that provides a class method for creating the chain and that provides the default behavior for navigating through the chain. The links in the chain are derived from the **CellFormatter** class, and they accept responsibility based on the product category. The formatting they perform is to change the background color of the cell. The **DefaultFormatter** class always sets the cell background to yellow and must be used to create the last link in the chain. Listing 19-15 shows how I use the chain of responsibility in the **ViewController** class.

Listing 19-15. Using the Chain of Responsibility in the ViewController.swift File

```
...
func tableView(tableView: UITableView,
    cellForRowAtIndexPath indexPath: NSIndexPath) -> UITableViewCell {
    let product = productStore.products[indexPath.row];
    let cell = tableView.dequeueReusableCellWithIdentifier("ProductCell")
        as ProductTableCell;

    cell.product = productStore.products[indexPath.row];
    cell.nameLabel.text = product.name;
    cell.descriptionLabel.text = product.productDescription;
    cell.stockStepper.value = Double(product.stockLevel);
    cell.stockField.text = String(product.stockLevel);

    CellFormatter.createChain().formatCell(cell);

    return cell;
}
...
```

You can see the effect of applying the formatting chain by running the application. The effect is garish but clearly indicates which link in the chain has accepted responsibility for each table cell, as shown in Figure 19-2.

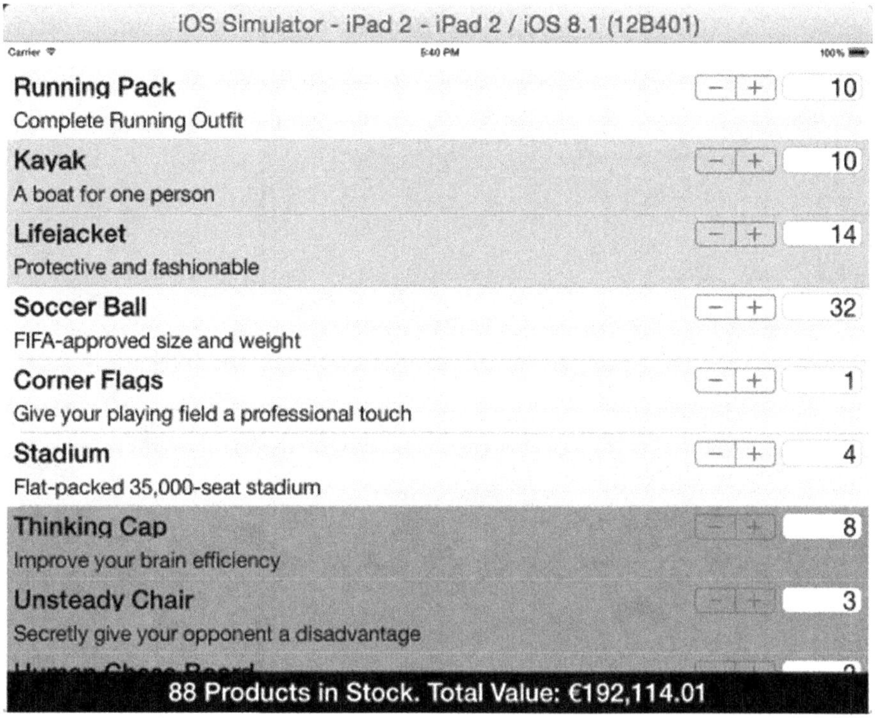

Figure 19-2. *Formatting table cells*

Summary

I described the chain of responsibility pattern in this chapter and explained how it can be used to find an object that will take responsibility for a request, while hiding details of which object is selected and the means by which the selection happens. In the next chapter, I describe the command pattern, which is used to encapsulate the details required to execute a method.

Chapter 20

The Command Pattern

The command pattern provides a mechanism by which details of how to invoke a method can be encapsulated so that the method can be invoked later or by a different component. Table 20-1 puts the command pattern into context.

Table 20-1. Putting the Command Pattern into Context

Question	Answer
What is it?	The command pattern is used to encapsulate details of how to invoke a method on an object in a way that allows the method to be invoked at a different time or by a different component.
What are the benefits?	There are lots of situations in which using a command is useful, but the most common ones are supporting undo operations and creating macros.
When should you use this pattern?	Use this pattern when you want to allow methods to be invoked by components that otherwise have no information about the object that will be used, the method that will be invoked, or the arguments that will be provided.
When should you avoid this pattern?	Do not use this pattern for regular method invocation.
How do you know when you have implemented the pattern correctly?	The pattern is implemented correctly when a component can use a command to invoke a method on an object without needing details of that object or the method itself.
Are there any common pitfalls?	The main pitfall is to require the component that executes the command to have knowledge of the method or object that will be used.
Are there any related patterns?	The memento pattern provides a model by which snapshots of an object's entire state can be used instead of individual operations.

Preparing the Example Project

To demonstrate the command pattern, I created an Xcode OS X Command Line Tool project called Command. I added a file called **Calculator.swift**, the contents of which are shown in Listing 20-1.

Listing 20-1. The Contents of the Calculator.swift File

```swift
class Calculator {
    private(set) var total = 0;

    func add(amount:Int) {
        total += amount;
    }

    func subtract(amount:Int) {
        total -= amount;
    }

    func multiply(amount:Int) {
        total = total * amount;
    }

    func divide(amount:Int) {
        total = total / amount;
    }
}
```

The **Calculator** class defines a stored **Int** property called **total**, whose value is changed by calling the **add**, **subtract**, **multiple**, and **divide** methods. Listing 20-2 shows the code I added to the **main.swift** file that uses the **Calculator** class to determine the value produced by several operations.

Listing 20-2. The Contents of the main.swift File

```swift
let calc = Calculator();
calc.add(10);
calc.multiply(4);
calc.subtract(2);

println("Total: \(calc.total)");
```

Running the application produces the following output:

```
Total: 38
```

Understanding the Problem That the Pattern Solves

The problem that the command pattern solves arises when you need to package a method invocation as an object so that it can be performed at a later date or be performed by another component without that component needing details of the method that will be invoked or the object that it will be invoked on.

Imagine that you are building an application where two components perform operations on the same object, such as an instance of the **Calculator** class I defined in the example application. Figure 20-1 shows the basic structure of the application, where each component invokes methods that update the **Calculator** total.

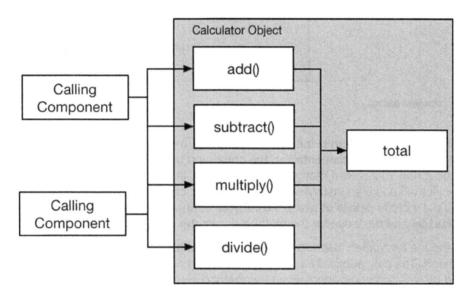

Figure 20-1. Two components performing operations on a common object

Now imagine that you need to implement support for undoing previous operations. One way to implement this is to have each component keep track of the operations it has performed so they can be undone in the future. The problem is that each component is unaware of the operations the other component has performed, and applying an undo operation without this information can corrupt the state of the shared object because the operations will be reversed in the wrong order.

I could get the components to coordinate with each other, but that just creates couplings between components and complicates the design of the application. What I require is a way to express undo operations independently of the components that performed them so that I can invoke them in a controlled way to gradually roll back the state of the shared object, and that, of course, is where the command pattern can help.

Understanding the Command Pattern

The command pattern represents a method invocation as an object so that it can be used to solve the undo problem and a range of related problems I describe in the "Variations on the Command Pattern" section. Figure 20-2 illustrates the command pattern.

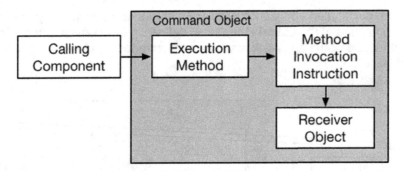

Figure 20-2. The command pattern

The heart of the command pattern is the *command object*, more often referred to simply as the *command*. Within its private implementation, the command has references to a *receiver object* and *instructions* about how to invoke a method on the receiver. In the context of the example application, the receiver object would be an instance of the **Calculator** class, and the method invocation instructions would include details of which **Calculator** method should be invoked (**add**, **subtract**, **multiply**, or **divide**) and the value for the method parameter.

The receiver and the invocation instructions are private and cannot be accessed by components that use the command. The only publically accessible facet of a command object is an *execution method* that is invoked by a calling component when the method invocation instructions should be executed on the receiver object (that is, call the specified method with the specified parameter values). In the language of the command pattern, the calling component is known as the *invoker* because it invokes the execution method.

Don't worry if this seems overly abstract. The command pattern is used in such a wide range of situations that it really begins to make sense only when you see it in context. The important point to note is that the method invocation instructions are not performed on the receiver object until the invoker calls the execution method. If you keep that in mind, everything else will fall into place when you see how the pattern is implemented.

Implementing the Command Pattern

For most people, the easiest way to understand the command pattern is to use it to solve a specific problem. In the sections that follow, I apply the pattern to create an undo facility for my example application. You may need to read through the implementation steps a couple of times to make sense of how the pattern fits together, but stick with it because the command pattern is worth taking the time to understand.

Defining the Command Protocol

The starting point for the command pattern is to define the protocol that provides invokers with an execution method. Listing 20-3 shows the contents of the **Commands.swift** file, which I added to the example project.

Listing 20-3. The Contents of the Commands.swift File

```
protocol Command {
    func execute();
}
```

A command allows the invoker to execute the command but not to see details of the receiver object or the instructions for invoking a method. To that end, the **Command** protocol I have defined in the listing defines an **execute** method but does not reveal any other details.

> **Tip**   The convention is to use the name **execute** for the execution method, but you can use any name that you prefer.

Defining the Command Implementation Class

The implementation class for the command pattern is simple to implement in Swift because the instructions for executing the receiver method can be expressed as a closure. Listing 20-4 shows the implementation class that I defined for the example project.

Listing 20-4. Defining the Command Implementation Class in the Commands.swift File

```
protocol Command {
    func execute();
}

class GenericCommand<T> : Command {
    private var receiver: T;
    private var instructions: T -> Void;

    init(receiver:T, instructions: T -> Void) {
        self.receiver = receiver; self.instructions = instructions;
    }
```

```
    func execute() {
        instructions(receiver);
    }

    class func createCommand(receiver:T, instuctions: T -> Void) -> Command {
        return GenericCommand(receiver: receiver, instructions: instuctions);
    }
}
```

I have defined a generic implementation class called **GenericCommand** that defines private properties that store the receiver object and the invocation instructions. The class conforms to the **Command** protocol, and the **execute** method invokes the execution instruction on the receiver object. I have also defined, simply as a convenience, a class method called **createCommand** that creates instances of **GenericCommand**.

Applying the Command Pattern

To apply the command pattern, I have extended the **Calculator** class so that it generates an array of **Command** objects that form the sequence of past undo operations. Listing 20-5 shows the changes I made.

Listing 20-5. Adding Undo Support in the Calculator.swift File

```
class Calculator {
    private(set) var total = 0;
    private var history = [Command]();

    func add(amount:Int) {
        addUndoCommand(Calculator.subtract, amount: amount);
        total += amount;
    }

    func subtract(amount:Int) {
        addUndoCommand(Calculator.add, amount: amount);
        total -= amount;
    }

    func multiply(amount:Int) {
        addUndoCommand(Calculator.divide, amount: amount);
        total = total * amount;
    }

    func divide(amount:Int) {
        addUndoCommand(Calculator.multiply, amount: amount);
        total = total / amount;
    }
```

```
    private func addUndoCommand(method:Calculator -> Int -> Void, amount:Int) {
        self.history.append(GenericCommand<Calculator>.createCommand(self,
            instuctions: {calc in
                method(calc)(amount);
            }));
    }

    func undo() {
        if self.history.count > 0 {
            self.history.removeLast().execute();
            // temporary measure - executing the command adds to the history
            self.history.removeLast();
        }
    }
}
}
```

> **Tip**   In this example, the receiver executes commands on itself. This is not a requirement of the command pattern, as I demonstrate in the "Variations on the Command Pattern" section.

Each of the four operation methods (**add**, **subtract**, and so on) calls the **addUndoCommand** method, passing in the method that will undo the operation and the amount that should be passed as the argument to that method. The **addUndoCommand** method creates the **Command** object and adds it to an array called **history**. I have also defined an **undo** method that removes the most recent **Command** from the **history** array and executes it, returning the **Calculator** object to an earlier state. Executing an undo **Command** causes a new **Command** to be added to the history, which is not the effect I want to create. For that reason, I remove and discard the last item in the **history** array after executing a **Command** in the **undo** method. This is a temporary measure that I remove in the next section.

WORKING WITH METHOD REFERENCES

In Listing 20-5, I pass references to methods as arguments to the **addUndoCommand** method, like this:

```
...
addUndoCommand(Calculator.add, amount: amount);
...
```

The first argument is a reference to the **add** method defined by the **Calculator** class. To receive this reference, I defined the **addUndoCommand** signature like this:

```
...
private func addUndoCommand(method:Calculator -> Int -> Void, amount:Int) {
...
```

The parameter called **method** is defined as a function that takes a **Calculator** object and that returns another function. The second function takes an **Int** and doesn't return a result. This can be confusing, but it relates to the way that Swift instance methods are implemented behind the scenes. Consider the following code:

```
class Printer {
    func printMessage(message:String) {
        println(message);
    }
}

let printerObject = Printer();
printerObject.printMessage("Hello");
```

I have defined a class called **Printer** that has a **printMessage** method. To use the **Printer** class, I create a new instance and then use that instance to call the method. The structure of the final statement is this:

```
<object reference>.<instance method name>(<argument value>)
```

This is the normal way of invoking a method, but there is an alternative:

```
...
Printer.printMessage(printerObject)("Hello");
...
```

This has the same effect as calling the method via the object reference. Here is the structure of this technique:

```
<class>.<instance method name>(<object reference>)(<argument value>)
```

Currying is the process of creating one function that fixes one or more arguments passed to another function. In this case, the first function returns a curried function that invokes the instance method on the specified object. The advantage of this approach is that the object reference is passed as an argument to the first function, which means that I can select the receiver for my commands dynamically and pass around references to methods as objects—something that becomes important when you want to change the receiver that a command targets (see the "Variations on the Command Pattern" section for an example).

Applying Concurrent Protections

The problem that I described at the start of this chapter included multiple components operating on a single **Calculator** object, and now that I have an array in the **Calculator** class, I need to add concurrency protection to avoid data protection. Listing 20-6 shows how I have used Grand Central Dispatch to serialize access to the **history** array.

Listing 20-6. Applying Concurrency Protections in the Calculator.swift File

```
import Foundation;

class Calculator {
    private(set) var total = 0;
    private var history = [Command]();
    private var queue = dispatch_queue_create("arrayQ", DISPATCH_QUEUE_SERIAL);
    private var performingUndo = false;

    func add(amount:Int) {
        addUndoCommand(Calculator.subtract, amount: amount);
        total += amount;
    }

    func subtract(amount:Int) {
        addUndoCommand(Calculator.add, amount: amount);
        total -= amount;
    }

    func multiply(amount:Int) {
        addUndoCommand(Calculator.divide, amount: amount);
        total = total * amount;
    }

    func divide(amount:Int) {
        addUndoCommand(Calculator.multiply, amount: amount);
        total = total / amount;
    }

    private func addUndoCommand(method:Calculator -> Int -> Void, amount:Int) {
        if (!performingUndo) {
            dispatch_sync(self.queue, {() in
                self.history.append(GenericCommand<Calculator>.createCommand(self,
                    instuctions: {calc in
                        method(calc)(amount);
                    }));
            });
        }
    }

    func undo() {
        dispatch_sync(self.queue, {() in
            if self.history.count > 0 {
                self.performingUndo = true;
                self.history.removeLast().execute();
                self.performingUndo = false;
            }
        });
    }
}
```

> **Note**   You don't have to add concurrency protection when implementing the command pattern, but I recommend that you at least consider it. As an application matures, the number of components that executes commands on a receiver may grow, increasing the chances of concurrent access and data corruption.

I have created a serial queue, and I use the **dispatch_**sync method in the **addUndoCommand** and **undo** methods to ensure that the **history** array is not modified concurrently. I have defined a variable called **performingUndo** that I set when executing an undo **Command** to prevent the **addUndoCommand** method from adding another command to the **history** array when called from one of the operation methods.

> **Tip**   Using a variable to signal whether I am executing an undo command prevents the application from locking up. Grand Central Dispatch doesn't support recursive locking, which means that the application freezes if I call a method that invokes the **dispatch_sync** function from inside a block that was also placed in the queue with the **dispatch_sync** function. The second call to **dispatch_async** blocks until the first call completes, which doesn't happen because the first call is waiting for the second one, a classic concurrency mistake.

Using the Undo Feature

The final step is to demonstrate the undo feature that I added to the **Calculator** class, as shown in Listing 20-7.

Listing 20-7. Using the Undo Feature in the main.swift File

```
let calc = Calculator();
calc.add(10);
calc.multiply(4);
calc.subtract(2);
println("Total: \(calc.total)");

for _ in 0 ..< 3 {
    calc.undo();
    println("Undo called. Total: \(calc.total)");
}
```

I use a **for** loop to call the **undo** method on the **Calculator** object three times, writing the new value of the **total** property to the debug console. Running the application produces the following output:

```
Total: 38
Undo called. Total: 40
Undo called. Total: 10
Undo called. Total: 0
```

Variations on the Command Pattern

The command pattern can be applied in a wide range of situations, but there are three main variations on the pattern that you will encounter, each of which I describe in the following sections.

Creating Composite Commands

The commands that I created in the **Calculator** object undo a single operation, but it is a simple matter to use the opacity of the **Command** protocol to create commands that perform multiple operations by acting as a wrapper around two or more other commands. Listing 20-8 shows how I defined a class that conforms to the **Command** protocol and that is a wrapper around other commands.

Listing 20-8. Defining a Command Wrapper in the Commands.swift File

```
protocol Command {
    func execute();
}

class CommandWrapper : Command {
    private let commands:[Command];

    init(commands:[Command]) {
        self.commands = commands;
    }

    func execute() {
        for command in commands {
            command.execute();
        }
    }
}

class GenericCommand<T> : Command {
    private var receiver: T;
    private var instructions: T -> Void;

    init(receiver:T, instructions: T -> Void) {
        self.receiver = receiver; self.instructions = instructions;
    }

    func execute() {
        instructions(receiver);
    }

    class func createCommand(receiver:T, instuctions: T -> Void) -> Command {
        return GenericCommand(receiver: receiver, instructions: instuctions);
    }
}
```

The **CommandWrapper** class defines a constant array of **Command** objects that are executed in sequence. Listing 20-9 shows how I have used **CommandWrapper** in the **Calculator** class to provide a snapshot of the undo commands.

Listing 20-9. Creating a Composite Command in the Calculator.swift File

```
import Foundation;

class Calculator {

    // ...properties and methods omitted for brevity...

    func getHistorySnaphot() -> Command? {
        var command:Command?;
        dispatch_sync(queue, {() in
            command = CommandWrapper(commands: self.history.reverse());
        });
        return command;
    }
}
```

The **getHistorySnapshot** method returns a **Command** that will undo all of the operations that have been performed by date. The implementation of the method creates an instance of the **CommandWrapper** class that copies the local array of undo commands. (See Chapter 5 for details of how Swift and Cocoa arrays are copied.)

> **Tip**   Notice that I reverse the array of commands that I pass to the **CommandWrapper** initializer. This is because the **Calculator** class processes its array in tail-first order, but the **CommandWrapper** class uses headfirst ordering. Reversing the order of the array means that the undo commands are applied in the same sequence as if they had been executed individually through the **undo** method.

Listing 20-10 shows the changes I made to the **main.swift** file to obtain and execute the composite command.

Listing 20-10. Using a Composite Command in the main.swift File

```
let calc = Calculator();
calc.add(10);
calc.multiply(4);
calc.subtract(2);

let snapshot = calc.getHistorySnaphot();
println("Pre-Snapshot Total: \(calc.total)");
snapshot?.execute();
println("Post-Snapshot Total: \(calc.total)");
```

Running the example application produces the following output, which demonstrates that each of the individual undo commands has been executed through the composite command:

```
Pre-Snapshot Total: 38
Post-Snapshot Total: 0
```

Using Commands as Macros

Commands are often used to create macros, which allows the same set of operations to be performed on different receive objects. To use commands as objects, the receiver must be passed to the **execute** method, rather than to the command object initializer. Listing 20-11 shows the changes I made to allow the receiver to be specified as an argument.

Listing 20-11. Modifying the Command Protocol and Implementation Classes in the Commands.swift File

```
protocol Command {
    func execute(receiver:Any);
}

class CommandWrapper : Command {
    private let commands:[Command];

    init(commands:[Command]) {
        self.commands = commands;
    }

    func execute(receiver:Any) {
        for command in commands {
            command.execute(receiver);
        }
    }
}

class GenericCommand<T> : Command {
    private var instructions: T -> Void;

    init(instructions: T -> Void) {
        self.instructions = instructions;
    }

    func execute(receiver:Any) {
        if let safeReceiver = receiver as? T {
            instructions(safeReceiver);
        } else {
            fatalError("Receiver is not expected type");
        }
    }

    class func createCommand(instuctions: T -> Void) -> Command {
        return GenericCommand(instructions: instuctions);
    }
}
```

I have added an **Any** parameter to the **execute** method defined by the **Command** protocol. I enforce type conformance in the execute method of the **GenericCommand** class by calling the global **fatalError** function if the object passed to the **execute** method doesn't match the generic type parameter. This isn't ideal because errors will be reported at runtime rather than by the compiler, but Swift makes it difficult to create and apply generic protocols.

In Listing 20-12, you can see how I have modified the **Calculator** class to remove the undo feature and replaced it with support for generating a macro command that will apply the operations that have been performed.

Listing 20-12. Adding Support for Macros in the Calculator.swift File

```swift
import Foundation;

class Calculator {
    private(set) var total = 0;
    private var history = [Command]();
    private var queue = dispatch_queue_create("arrayQ", DISPATCH_QUEUE_SERIAL);

    func add(amount:Int) {
        addMacro(Calculator.add, amount: amount);
        total += amount;
    }

    func subtract(amount:Int) {
        addMacro(Calculator.subtract, amount: amount);
        total -= amount;
    }

    func multiply(amount:Int) {
        addMacro(Calculator.multiply, amount: amount);
        total = total * amount;
    }

    func divide(amount:Int) {
        addMacro(Calculator.divide, amount: amount);
        total = total / amount;
    }

    private func addMacro(method:Calculator -> Int -> Void, amount:Int) {
        dispatch_sync(self.queue, {() in
            self.history.append(GenericCommand<Calculator>.createCommand(
                { calc in method(calc)(amount); }
            ));
        });
    }
}
```

```
    func getMacroCommand() -> Command? {
        var command:Command?;
        dispatch_sync(queue, {() in
            command = CommandWrapper(commands: self.history);
        });
        return command;
    }
}
```

Each operation method now calls the **addMacro** method, which builds up this history of the operations that have been performed on the **Calculator** instance (rather than the counter operations that were required for the undo feature). The important difference is that the **Calculator** object itself is not included in the **Command** objects that are created and subsequently packaged up by the **getMacroCommand** method. Instead, each command contains details of the operation method that will be invoked and the argument that will be passed to it, and it is the responsibility of the calling component to specify the **Calculator** object that will be the receiver for the commands. Listing 20-13 shows how I have used the macro feature in the **main.swift** file.

Listing 20-13. Creating and Applying a Macro in the main.swift File

```
let calc = Calculator();
calc.add(10);
calc.multiply(4);
calc.subtract(2);

println("Calc 1 Total: \(calc.total)");

let macro = calc.getMacroCommand();

let calc2 = Calculator();
macro?.execute(calc2);
println("Calc 2 Total: \(calc2.total)");
```

I apply a series of operations on one **Calculator** object and then use those commands as a macro to apply the same operations to a different **Calculator** object. Running the example application produces the following results:

```
Calc 1 Total: 38
Calc 2 Total: 38
```

Using Closures as Commands

The command pattern specifies the use of a command object, which is what I have used in all of the implementations so far in this chapter. However, a command is just a container for details of a method that should be invoked, the values for its argument, and—optionally—the receiver that will be targeted. All of these details can be encapsulated in Swift closures, without the need to define and use a **Command** protocol and its implementation.

I prefer to use **Command** objects. I find it makes the purpose of the pattern more obvious and produces code that it easier to read and maintain. You may feel differently, however, and in Listing 20-14, you can see how I have modified the **Calculator** class so that it uses closures to express commands and no longer relies on the **Command** protocol and the **GenericCommand** class.

Listing 20-14. Using Closures as Commands in the Calculator.swift File

```swift
import Foundation;

class Calculator {
    private(set) var total = 0;
    typealias CommandClosure = (Calculator -> Void);
    private var history = [CommandClosure]();
    private var queue = dispatch_queue_create("arrayQ", DISPATCH_QUEUE_SERIAL);

    func add(amount:Int) {
        addMacro(Calculator.add, amount: amount);
        total += amount;
    }

    func subtract(amount:Int) {
        addMacro(Calculator.subtract, amount: amount);
        total -= amount;
    }

    func multiply(amount:Int) {
        addMacro(Calculator.multiply, amount: amount);
        total = total * amount;
    }

    func divide(amount:Int) {
        addMacro(Calculator.divide, amount: amount);
        total = total / amount;
    }

    private func addMacro(method:Calculator -> Int -> Void, amount:Int) {
        dispatch_sync(self.queue, {() in
            self.history.append({ calc in  method(calc)(amount)});
        });
    }

    func getMacroCommand() -> (Calculator -> Void) {
        var commands = [CommandClosure]();
        dispatch_sync(queue, {() in
            commands = self.history
        });
```

```
        return { calc in
            if (commands.count > 0) {
                for index in 0 ..< commands.count {
                    commands[index](calc);
                }
            }
        };
    }
}
```

The changes in this listing may look minor, but writing this kind of code is mind-bending as you sort through the variables on which you want to close and those that you don't and figure out whether you need to curry from **Calculator -> Int -> Void** to **Calculator -> Void** or to **Int -> Void**.

If you are committed to this style of command, then notice that I used the **typealias** keyword to define an alias for use in arrays, like this:

```
...
typealias CommandClosure = (Calculator -> Void);
private var history = [CommandClosure]();
...
```

The Swift compiler doesn't like dealing with closure signatures as the data type for arrays but can be placated with an alias. Listing 20-15 shows the changes in the **main.swift** file to use the closure-based **Calculator** class.

Listing 20-15. Using the Closure-Based Calculator Class in the main.swift File

```
let calc = Calculator();
calc.add(10);
calc.multiply(4);
calc.subtract(2);
println("Calc 1 Total: \(calc.total)");

let macro = calc.getMacroCommand();

let calc2 = Calculator();
macro(calc2);
println("Calc 2 Total: \(calc2.total)");
```

The only change is to invoke the closure returned by the **getMacroCommand** method directly, rather than invoking an execute method defined by a **Command** object. Running the application produces the following output, showing that the closures work in just the same way as separate command objects:

```
Calc 1 Total: 38
Calc 2 Total: 38
```

Understanding the Pitfalls of the Command Pattern

The command pattern is relatively simple to implement as long as you don't expose details of the receiver object or the method invocation instructions to the calling component. When it comes to the implementation detail, ensure that you add concurrency protection if the commands may be used by multiple components and ensure that your closures operate on the object that you expect and are not closing on the wrong receiver objects.

Examples of the Command Pattern in Cocoa

The **Foundation** framework includes the **NSInvocation** class, which is used to implement the command pattern in Objective-C. However, because of the different ways that Swift and Objective-C invoke their methods, the **NSInvocation** class cannot be used in Swift code. A more specific implementation of the command pattern is available through the **NSUndoManager** class, which I use in the next section.

Applying the Pattern to the SportsStore Application

I am going to apply the command pattern to the SportsStore application to implement an undo feature for stock level changes. iOS includes a built-in undo management framework that is easy to use and that uses the command pattern.

Preparing the Example Application

The standard mechanism for triggering an iOS undo operation is to shake the device. To prepare for the command pattern, I am going to add support for receiving a notification when the shake motion is recognized. Listing 20-16 shows the change I made to the **ViewController** class.

Listing 20-16. Adding Shake Motion Support in the ViewController.swift File

```
class ViewController: UIViewController, UITableViewDataSource {

    @IBOutlet weak var totalStockLabel: UILabel!
    @IBOutlet weak var tableView: UITableView!

    let productStore = ProductDataStore();

    override func viewDidLoad() {
        super.viewDidLoad()
        displayStockTotal();
        let bridge = EventBridge(callback: updateStockLevel);
        productStore.callback = bridge.inputCallback;
    }

    override func motionEnded(motion: UIEventSubtype, withEvent event: UIEvent) {
        if (event.subtype == UIEventSubtype.MotionShake) {
            println("Shake motion detected");
        }
    }

    // ...methods omitted for brevity...
}
```

I have overridden the **motionEnded** method so that I check the type of the motion that has been detected and print out a message to the Xcode debug console if the motion is a shake. To test the change, start the SportsStore application and select Shake Gesture from the Hardware menu of the iOS simulator. You will see the following message displayed in the Xcode console:

```
Shake motion detected
```

Implementing the Undo Feature

The most direct way to implement the command pattern is to work with the **NSUndoManager** class. The NSUndoManager class is managed automatically through the **undoManager** property of the UI component classes' conformance to the **NSResponder** protocol, which means that creating an instance of the **NSUndoManager** is handled for you. There are two stages to working with the undo manager, and the first is to register the commands that will be invoked when the user requests an undo operation. Listing 20-17 shows the changes I made to the **ViewController** class.

Listing 20-17. Registering Undo Commands in the ViewController.swift File

```
...
@IBAction func stockLevelDidChange(sender: AnyObject) {
    if var currentCell = sender as? UIView {
        while (true) {
            currentCell = currentCell.superview!;
            if let cell = currentCell as? ProductTableCell {
                if let product = cell.product? {

                    let dict = NSDictionary(objects: [product.stockLevel],
                        forKeys: [product.name]);

                    undoManager?.registerUndoWithTarget(self,
                        selector: "undoStockLevel:",
                        object: dict);

                    if let stepper = sender as? UIStepper {
                        product.stockLevel = Int(stepper.value);
                    } else if let textfield = sender as? UITextField {
                        if let newValue = textfield.text.toInt()? {
                            product.stockLevel = newValue;
                        }
                    }
                    cell.stockStepper.value = Double(product.stockLevel);
                    cell.stockField.text = String(product.stockLevel);
                    productLogger.logItem(product);

                    StockServerFactory.getStockServer()
                        .setStockLevel(product.name,
                            stockLevel: product.stockLevel);
                }
```

```
                break;
            }
        }
        displayStockTotal();
    }
}

func undoStockLevel(data:[String:Int]) {
    let productName = data.keys.first;
    if (productName != nil) {
        let stockLevel = data[productName!];
        if (stockLevel != nil) {

            for nproduct in productStore.products {
                if nproduct.name == productName! {
                    nproduct.stockLevel = stockLevel!;
                }
            }

            updateStockLevel(productName!, level: stockLevel!);
        }
    }
}
...
```

The **undoManager** property is optional, and commands are registered with the **registerUndoWithTarget** method. The parameters for this method are the receiver of the command, the method that will be invoked, and an object that will be passed to that argument.

```
...
undoManager?.registerUndoWithTarget(self, selector: "undoStockLevel:", object: dict);
...
```

I have specified the view controller as the receiver, and I have specified a new method, called **undoStockLevel**. For the method argument, I have created an **NSDictionary** that contains the name of the product that has been modified and the old stock level.

NSUndoManager exposes some of its Objective-C roots. First, when I specify the name of the method to invoke, I follow the name with a colon, like this:

```
...
undoManager?.registerUndoWithTarget(self, selector: "undoStockLevel:", object: dict);
...
```

This relates to how methods are selected in Objective-C code, and omitting the colon will cause an exception when the command is executed. The other issue to be aware of is that I had to use an **NSDictionary** as the argument to be passed to the method because Swift built-in dictionaries are not supported. I had to define the **undoStockLevel** method because undo commands can provide only a single object. I unpack the data in the dictionary and use it to update the product object in the repository and to call the **updateStockLevel** method, which takes two arguments and therefore cannot be called directly by the undo manager.

Triggering an Undo Command

The result of calling the **registerUndoWithTarget** method is that a command is created behind the scenes, waiting to be executed when the user shakes the device. Listing 20-18 shows the change I made to the **motionEnded** method on the **ViewController** class.

Listing 20-18. Triggering Undo Commands in the ViewController.swift File

```
...
override func motionEnded(motion: UIEventSubtype, withEvent event: UIEvent) {
    if (event.subtype == UIEventSubtype.MotionShake) {
        println("Shake motion detected");
        undoManager?.undo();
    }
}
...
```

The **undo** method defined by the **NSUndoManager** class triggers the most recent undo command created by the **registerUndoWithTarget** method. To test the changes, start the application, change the value of one of the products, and then select Shake Gesture from the iOS simulator Hardware menu. The change that you made will be reversed, as illustrated by Figure 20-3.

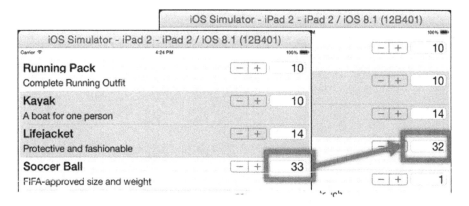

Figure 20-3. *Undoing a stock level change*

Summary

In this chapter I described the command pattern, which is used to encapsulate a method invocation so that it can be performed later or by another component. I demonstrated how the command pattern can be used to implement undo operations and to create sequences of invocations that act as macros. In the next chapter, I describe the mediator pattern, which is used to manage communication between groups of peer objects.

Chapter 21

The Mediator Pattern

The mediator pattern is used to simplify and rationalize the communication between groups of objects. This is one of the least well-known design patterns, but it solves a common problem and can simplify the design of an application significantly. Table 21-1 puts the mediator pattern into context.

Table 21-1. Putting the Mediator Pattern into Context

Question	Answer
What is it?	The mediator pattern simplifies peer-to-peer communication between objects by introducing a mediator object that acts as a communications broker between the objects.
What are the benefits?	Instead of having to keep track of and communicate with of all of its peers individually, an object just deals with the mediator.
When should you use this pattern?	Use this pattern when you are dealing with a group of objects that need to communicate freely between one another.
When should you avoid this pattern?	Don't use this pattern if you have one object that needs to send notifications to a range of disparate objects; use the observer pattern described in Chapter 22 instead.
How do you know when you have implemented the pattern correctly?	The mediator pattern is implemented correctly when each object deals only with the mediator and has no direct knowledge of its peers.
Are there any common pitfalls?	It is important that the mediator not provide peers with access to one another so that they might become interdependent.
Are there any related patterns?	This pattern is closely related to—and often combined with—the observer pattern that I describe in Chapter 22.

Preparing the Example Project

For this chapter I created an Xcode Command Line Tool project called Mediator and added to it a file called **Airplane.swift**, the contents of which are shown in Listing 21-1.

Listing 21-1. The Contents of the Airplane.swift File

```swift
struct Position {
    var distanceFromRunway:Int;
    var height:Int;
}

func == (lhs:Airplane, rhs:Airplane) -> Bool {
    return lhs.name == rhs.name;
}

class Airplane : Equatable {
    var name:String;
    var currentPosition:Position;
    private var otherPlanes:[Airplane];

    init(name:String, initialPos:Position) {
        self.name = name;
        self.currentPosition = initialPos;
        self.otherPlanes = [Airplane]();
    }

    func addPlanesInArea(planes:Airplane...) {
        for plane in planes {
            otherPlanes.append(plane);
        }
    }

    func otherPlaneDidLand(plane:Airplane) {
        if let index = find(otherPlanes, plane) {
            otherPlanes.removeAtIndex(index);
        }
    }

    func otherPlaneDidChangePosition(plane:Airplane) -> Bool {
        return plane.currentPosition.distanceFromRunway
                == self.currentPosition.distanceFromRunway
            && abs(plane.currentPosition.height
                - self.currentPosition.height) < 1000;
    }
```

```
func changePosition(newPosition:Position) {
    self.currentPosition = newPosition;
    for plane in otherPlanes {
        if (plane.otherPlaneDidChangePosition(self)) {
            println("\(name): Too close! Abort!");
            return;
        }
    }
    println("\(name): Position changed");
}

func land() {
    self.currentPosition = Position(distanceFromRunway: 0, height: 0);
    for plane in otherPlanes {
        plane.otherPlaneDidLand(self);
    }
    println("\(name): Landed");
}
}
```

The **Airplane** class represents the state of an aircraft as it approaches an airport and tracks its current position using the **Position** struct. There may be other planes approaching the airport, so each **Airplane** objects keeps track of those around it and ensures that its movements will not bring it too close to another plane. Listing 21-2 shows the statements that I added to the **main.swift** file to create and manipulate an instance of the **Airplane** class.

Listing 21-2. The Contents of the main.swift File

```
// initial setup
let british = Airplane(name: "BA706", initialPos: Position(distanceFromRunway: 11, height: 21000));

// plane approaches airport
british.changePosition(Position(distanceFromRunway: 8, height: 10000));
british.changePosition(Position(distanceFromRunway: 2, height: 5000));
british.changePosition(Position(distanceFromRunway: 1, height: 1000));
// plane lands
british.land();
```

I create an **Airplane** object to represent a British Airways flight and then call the **changePosition** method several times to reflect its progress toward the airport and then call the **land** method. Running the example application produces the following output:

```
BA706: Position changed
BA706: Position changed
BA706: Position changed
BA706: Landed
```

Understanding the Problem That the Pattern Solves

The problem with the example application becomes apparent when there are several **Airplane** objects used to represent approaches to the airport. Listing 21-3 shows the changes that I made to the **main.swift** file to add two additional **Airplane** objects.

Listing 21-3. Using Additional Airplane Objects in the main.swift File

```
// initial setup
let british = Airplane(name: "BA706", initialPos:
    Position(distanceFromRunway: 11, height: 21000));

// new plane arrives
let american = Airplane(name: "AA101", initialPos: Position(distanceFromRunway: 12, height: 22000));
british.addPlanesInArea(american);
american.addPlanesInArea(british);

// plane approaches airport
british.changePosition(Position(distanceFromRunway: 8, height: 10000));
british.changePosition(Position(distanceFromRunway: 2, height: 5000));
british.changePosition(Position(distanceFromRunway: 1, height: 1000));

// new plane arrives
let cathay = Airplane(name: "CX200", initialPos: Position(distanceFromRunway: 13, height: 22000));
british.addPlanesInArea(cathay);
american.addPlanesInArea(cathay);
cathay.addPlanesInArea(british, american);

// plane lands
british.land();

// plane moves too close
cathay.changePosition(Position(distanceFromRunway: 12, height: 22000));
```

Running the application produces the following output:

```
BA706: Position changed
BA706: Position changed
BA706: Position changed
BA706: Landed
CX200: Too close! Abort!
```

There are only three **Airplane** objects, but the complexity of the code in the **main.swift** file has increased sharply because each **Airplane** has to keep track of every other **Airplane**. Taking into account the amount of code required to keep track of the other aircraft inside the **Airplane** object, a substantial percentage of the application is given over just to managing the communication between **Airplane** objects. The result is a set of **Airplane** objects that know about each other and communicate by invoking methods directly on one another, as shown in Figure 21-1.

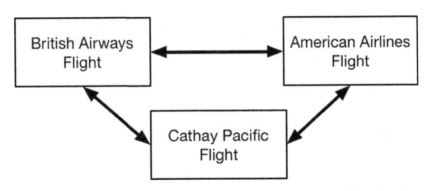

Figure 21-1. The peer communications problem

This is a problem that gets worse as the number of objects increases because every **Airplane** object has to be made aware of every other instance, creating an ever more complex set of dependencies in which it is easy to forget to establish a new connection, as shown in Figure 21-2.

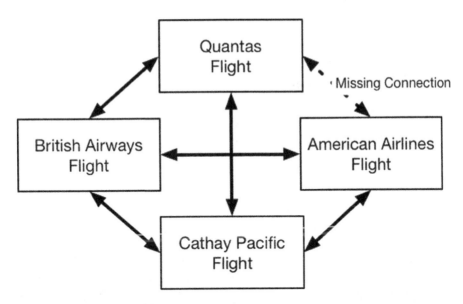

Figure 21-2. The effect of forgetting to establish a new connection

This kind of omission is nasty because it manifests itself as a problem when a feature relies on the missing connection. In this case, the collision-avoidance code in the **changePosition** method will always work unless the Qantas flight tries to move into the space occupied by the American Airlines flight. If this happens, the position of the American Airlines flight won't be checked, and collision-avoidance will have failed.

Understanding the Mediator Pattern

The mediator pattern solves the problem by introducing a *mediator* object that eases communication between two or more *peer objects*, often referred to as *colleagues*. The mediator keeps track of the peer objects and facilities the communication between them in order to break the dependencies between objects, avoid problems caused by omitted relationships, and simplify the overall application. Figure 21-3 illustrates the way that the mediator pattern transforms the **Airplane** problem.

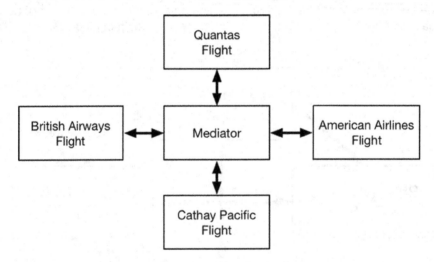

Figure 21-3. The mediator pattern

Each **Airplane** has a relationship with the mediator, rather than with its peers. It sends its messages to the mediator, and the mediator keeps track of the other **Airplane** objects and forwards the messages to them. The mediator reduces the number of dependencies in the application and ensures that all of the messages are dispatched to all of the peers, avoiding the missed connection problem.

Implementing the Mediator Pattern

The core of the mediator pattern is a pair of protocols: one that defines the functionality provided by the peers and one that defines the functionality for the mediator. You can see how I have defined the protocols in Listing 21-4, which shows the contents of the **Mediator.swift** file that I added to the example project.

Listing 21-4. The Contents of the Mediator.swift File

```
protocol Peer {
    var name:String {get};
    func otherPlaneDidChangePosition(position:Position) -> Bool;
}

protocol Mediator {
    func registerPeer(peer:Peer);
    func unregisterPeer(peer:Peer);
    func changePosition(peer:Peer, pos:Position) -> Bool;
}
```

The **Peer** protocol defines a **name** property for identification purposes and an otherPlaneDidChangePosition method that is called to check to see whether it is safe for another aircraft to move. The **Mediator** protocol defines **registerPeer** and **unregisterPeer** methods to add and remove objects from the set it mediates and defines a **changePosition** method that will call the **otherPlanChangePosition** method of the peers it mediates.

Defining the Meditator Class

The next step is to define a class that conforms to the **Mediator** protocol and that can be used to mediate the communication between a set of **Peer** objects. Listing 21-5 shows the class I defined.

Listing 21-5. Defining the Mediator Implementation in the Mediator.swift File

```
protocol Peer {
    var name:String {get};
    func otherPlaneDidChangePosition(position:Position) -> Bool;
}

protocol Mediator {
    func registerPeer(peer:Peer);
    func unregisterPeer(peer:Peer);
    func changePosition(peer:Peer, pos:Position) -> Bool;
}

class AirplaneMediator : Mediator {
    private var peers:[String:Peer];

    init() {
        peers = [String:Peer]();
    }
```

```
func registerPeer(peer: Peer) {
    self.peers[peer.name] = peer;
}

func unregisterPeer(peer: Peer) {
    self.peers.removeValueForKey(peer.name);
}

func changePosition(peer:Peer, pos:Position) -> Bool {
    for storedPeer in peers.values {
        if (peer.name != storedPeer.name
            && storedPeer.otherPlaneDidChangePosition(pos)) {
                return true;
        }
    }
    return false;
}
}
```

The implementation of the **AirplaneMediator** class is simple. I store the collection of **Peer** objects using a dictionary, which eases the implementation of the **changePosition** methods that must ensure that the caller of the method doesn't have its **otherPlaneDidchangePosition** method called for its own position change.

Conforming to the Peer Protocol

The next step is to update the **Airplane** class so that it conforms to the **Peer** protocol and no longer manages a list of its peers. Listing 21-6 shows the changes that I made.

Listing 21-6. Conforming to the Peer Protocol in the Airplane.swift File

```
struct Position {
    var distanceFromRunway:Int;
    var height:Int;
}

class Airplane : Peer {
    var name:String;
    var currentPosition:Position;
    var mediator:Mediator;

    init(name:String, initialPos:Position, mediator: Mediator) {
        self.name = name;
        self.currentPosition = initialPos;
        self.mediator = mediator;
        mediator.registerPeer(self);
    }
```

```swift
    func otherPlaneDidChangePosition(position:Position) -> Bool {
        return position.distanceFromRunway
                == self.currentPosition.distanceFromRunway
            && abs(position.height - self.currentPosition.height) < 1000;
    }

    func changePosition(newPosition:Position) {
        self.currentPosition = newPosition;
        if (mediator.changePosition(self, pos: self.currentPosition) == true) {
            println("\(name): Too close! Abort!");
            return;
        }
        println("\(name): Position changed");
    }

    func land() {
        self.currentPosition = Position(distanceFromRunway: 0, height: 0);
        mediator.unregisterPeer(self);
        println("\(name): Landed");
    }
}
```

The overall effect is to focus the class on its own state and rely on the meditator to manage the relationship with other peers on its behalf. Listing 21-7 shows how I updated the code in the **main.swift** file to use the mediator.

Listing 21-7. Using the Mediator in the main.swift File

```swift
let mediator:Mediator = AirplaneMediator();

// initial setup
let british = Airplane(name: "BA706", initialPos:
    Position(distanceFromRunway: 11, height: 21000), mediator:mediator);

// new plane arrives
let american = Airplane(name: "AA101", initialPos: Position(distanceFromRunway: 12, height: 22000),
mediator:mediator);

// plane approaches airport
british.changePosition(Position(distanceFromRunway: 8, height: 10000));
british.changePosition(Position(distanceFromRunway: 2, height: 5000));
british.changePosition(Position(distanceFromRunway: 1, height: 1000));

// new plane arrives
let cathay = Airplane(name: "CX200", initialPos: Position(distanceFromRunway: 13, height: 22000),
mediator:mediator);

// plane lands
british.land();

// plane moves too close
cathay.changePosition(Position(distanceFromRunway: 12, height: 22000));
```

I no longer need to notify each **Airplane** when I create another instance because the mediator will automatically keep track for me and ensure that I don't forget to create all of the connections required before the mediator was applied. Running the application produces the following output:

```
BA706: Position changed
BA706: Position changed
BA706: Position changed
BA706: Landed
CX200: Too close! Abort!
```

Implementing Concurrency Protections

Like with many of the patterns I describe in this book, implementing the mediator pattern means considering whether the peer objects will need to communicate with each other concurrently or whether peers will be registered or unregistered simultaneously. This won't be the case in all applications, but if there is likely to be concurrent use, then concurrency protections are required, as described in the following sections.

Implementing Concurrency Protections in the Mediator

Concurrency protection in the mediator ensures that the collection of peers isn't corrupted and that results returned by the mediator's methods are consistent. Listing 21-8 shows how I have used Grand Central Dispatch (GCD) to protect the mediator class.

Listing 21-8. Implementing Concurrency Protections in the Mediator.swift File

```
import Foundation;

protocol Peer {
    var name:String {get};
    func otherPlaneDidChangePosition(position:Position) -> Bool;
}

protocol Mediator {
    func registerPeer(peer:Peer);
    func unregisterPeer(peer:Peer);
    func changePosition(peer:Peer, pos:Position) -> Bool;
}

class AirplaneMediator : Mediator {
    private var peers:[String:Peer];
    private let queue = dispatch_queue_create("dictQ", DISPATCH_QUEUE_CONCURRENT);

    init() {
        peers = [String:Peer]();
    }
```

```
func registerPeer(peer: Peer) {
    dispatch_barrier_sync(self.queue, { () in
        self.peers[peer.name] = peer;
    });
}

func unregisterPeer(peer: Peer) {
    dispatch_barrier_sync(self.queue, { () in
        let removed = self.peers.removeValueForKey(peer.name);
    });
}

func changePosition(peer:Peer, pos:Position) -> Bool {
    var result = false;
    dispatch_sync(self.queue, { () in
        for storedPeer in self.peers.values {
            if (peer.name != storedPeer.name
                && storedPeer.otherPlaneDidChangePosition(pos)) {
                    result = true;
            }
        }
    });
    return result;
}
}
```

I want to allow multiple operations to read the data in the **peers** dictionary unless I am about to modify it. I have used a concurrent GCD queue with a call to the **dispatch**_sync function for read operations and with calls to the **dispatch_barrier**_sync function in the **registerPeer** and **unregisterPeer** method to gain exclusive access to the dictionary for making changes.

> **Tip** Notice that I have assigned the result of the call to the **removeValueForKey** method to a constant in the implementation of the **unregisterPeer** method. Swift tries to be helpful and takes the result returned from the call to the dictionary method as the result to return from the closure—which is a problem because closures used as GCD blocks may not return results. Assigning the result to a constant captures the value and prevents it from being treated as a result.

Implementing Concurrency Protections in the Peer

The concurrency protections I added to the mediator do not make any assumptions about the implementation of the peer objects and allow multiple simultaneous calls to the **otherPlanDidChangePosition** method. This means I need to modify the **Airplane** class so as to protect the integrity of its internal state data, as shown in Listing 21-9.

Listing 21-9. Adding Concurrency Protections in the Airplane.swift File

```swift
import Foundation

struct Position {
    var distanceFromRunway:Int;
    var height:Int;
}

class Airplane : Peer {
    var name:String;
    var currentPosition:Position;
    var mediator:Mediator;
    let queue = dispatch_queue_create("posQ", DISPATCH_QUEUE_CONCURRENT);

    init(name:String, initialPos:Position, mediator: Mediator) {
        self.name = name;
        self.currentPosition = initialPos;
        self.mediator = mediator;
        mediator.registerPeer(self);
    }

    func otherPlaneDidChangePosition(position:Position) -> Bool {
        var result = false;
        dispatch_sync(self.queue, {() in
            result = position.distanceFromRunway
                    == self.currentPosition.distanceFromRunway
                && abs(position.height - self.currentPosition.height) < 1000;
        });
        return result;
    }

    func changePosition(newPosition:Position) {
        dispatch_barrier_sync(self.queue, {() in
            self.currentPosition = newPosition;
            if (self.mediator.changePosition(self, pos:
                    self.currentPosition) == true) {
                println("\(self.name): Too close! Abort!");
                return;
            }
            println("\(self.name): Position changed");
        });
    }

    func land() {
        dispatch_barrier_sync(self.queue, { () in
            self.currentPosition = Position(distanceFromRunway: 0, height: 0);
            self.mediator.unregisterPeer(self);
            println("\(self.name): Landed");
        });
    }
}
```

The concurrency protection that I added to the class allows multiple concurrent calls to the **otherPlaneDidChangePosition** method, but calls to the **changePosition** and **land** methods use a barrier to ensure that they have exclusive access to make modifications.

Variations on the Mediator Pattern

The standard implementation of the mediator pattern is focused on managing the relationships with peers, but common variations extend the role of the mediator, as I describe in the following sections.

Putting More Logic Into the Mediator

The first variation is to add logic into the mediator implementation class to more actively manage the flow of messages between peers or to provide additional features. To demonstrate this variation, I am going to reduce the number of peer objects that are called by the mediator **changePosition** method by adding some basic logic to filter out those that are farther away from the airport than the airplane that wants to be (on the basis that all of the planes are trying to land and are moving in the same direction). The first step is to expand the information revealed by the **Peer** protocol so that the mediator can access its location data, as shown in Listing 21-10.

Listing 21-10. Revealing Additional Information in the Mediator.swift File

```
...
protocol Peer {
    var name:String {get};
    var currentPosition:Position {get};
    func otherPlaneDidChangePosition(position:Position) -> Bool;
}
...
```

Exposing the **currentPosition** property allows the mediator to be more selective about the peers whose methods it invokes, as shown in Listing 21-11.

Listing 21-11. Selectively Targeting Peers in the Mediator.swift File

```
...
func changePosition(peer:Peer, pos:Position) -> Bool {
    var result = false;
    dispatch_sync(self.queue, { () in

        let closerPeers = self.peers.values.filter({p in
            return p.currentPosition.distanceFromRunway
                <= pos.distanceFromRunway;
        });
```

```
    for storedPeer in closerPeers {
        if (peer.name != storedPeer.name
                && storedPeer.otherPlaneDidChangePosition(pos)) {
            result = true;
        }
    }
});
return result;
}
...
```

I use the **filter** method to eliminate those planes that are farther away and then invoke the **otherPlaneDidChangePosition** method on the remaining objects. Running the application produces the following output, which is the same as previous examples:

```
BA706: Position changed
BA706: Position changed
BA706: Position changed
BA706: Landed
CX200: Too close! Abort!
```

The benefit of this variation is that I make fewer calls to peer objects, and in doing so, I hope to speed up the process of changing the position of an airplane. The drawback of this approach is that I have now codified a behavior into the mediator that will need to be changed if the application is extended to include planes that are departing from the airport and not just those that are arriving.

Generalizing the Mediator-Peer Relationship

The standard implementation of the mediator pattern means that the mediator has some knowledge into the methods defined by the peers in order that it can call those methods as needed. This makes it difficult to reuse a mediator class for a different set of peers.

If you expect to need multiple mediators in an application, a common variation is to generalize the implementation of the pattern and create a mediator class that doesn't require any knowledge of the peers it is used with. There are two broad approaches to addressing this problem, although, as I explain in the following sections, both have their limitations.

Generalizing the Mediator with the Command Pattern

One approach is to combine the mediator pattern with the command pattern and have the mediator play the role of the invoker I described in Chapter 20. Listing 21-12 shows how I have defined a generalized command-based mediator class in a file called **CommandMediator.swift** that I added to the example project.

Listing 21-12. Defining a Generalized Mediator Class in the CommandMediator.swift File

```swift
protocol CommandPeer {
    var name:String { get };
}

class Command {
    let function:CommandPeer -> Any;

    init(function:CommandPeer -> Any) {
        self.function = function;
    }

    func execute(peer:CommandPeer) -> Any {
        return function(peer);
    }
}

class CommandMediator {
    private var peers = [String:CommandPeer]();

    func registerPeer(peer:CommandPeer) {
        peers[peer.name] = peer;
    }

    func unregisterPeer(peer:CommandPeer) {
        peers.removeValueForKey(peer.name);
    }

    func dispatchCommand(caller:CommandPeer, command:Command) -> [Any] {
        var results = [Any]();
        for peer in peers.values {
            if (peer.name != caller.name) {
                results.append(command.execute(peer));
            }
        }
        return results;
    }
}
```

Peers must conform to the **CommandPeer** protocol, in part to aid the implementation of the **Command** class and in part so that I can use the **name** property to prevent the mediator from executing a command on the object that created it.

> **Caution**   For simplicity I have implemented the **CommandMediator** class without concurrency protections. Using the command pattern doesn't protect the collection of peers, and you should apply protections to all mediators if concurrent use is possible. See the "Implementing Concurrency Protections" section for details.

The **Command** class represents the command that each peer will be asked to execute. As you saw in Chapter 20, there are different ways to arrange the definition and execution of a command, and the one that I have chosen to use means that the mediator will invoke the command, passing each peer into the **execute** method of the **Command** object. I have done this because I want to capture a result value from executing the command and present an array of those results to the calling peer.

The **CommandMediator** class is a variation of the mediator I used in the standard implementation of the pattern that presents a **dispatchCommand** method that accepts a **Command** object and passes each **CommandPeer** to its function. The results from executing the command on each peer are collected into an array and returned as the result to the calling peer.

Listing 21-13 shows how I updated the **Airplane** class to use the command-based mediator.

Listing 21-13. Using the CommandMediator in the Airplane.swift File

```
import Foundation

struct Position {
    var distanceFromRunway:Int;
    var height:Int;
}

class Airplane : CommandPeer {
    var name:String;
    var currentPosition:Position;
    var mediator:CommandMediator;
    let queue = dispatch_queue_create("posQ", DISPATCH_QUEUE_CONCURRENT);

    init(name:String, initialPos:Position, mediator: CommandMediator) {
        self.name = name;
        self.currentPosition = initialPos;
        self.mediator = mediator;
        mediator.registerPeer(self);
    }

    func otherPlaneDidChangePosition(position:Position) -> Bool {
        var result = false;
        dispatch_sync(self.queue, {() in
            result = position.distanceFromRunway
                    == self.currentPosition.distanceFromRunway
                && abs(position.height - self.currentPosition.height) < 1000;
        });
        return result;
    }

    func changePosition(newPosition:Position) {
        dispatch_barrier_sync(self.queue, {() in
            self.currentPosition = newPosition;
```

```
        let c = Command(function: {peer in
            if let plane = peer as? Airplane {
                return plane.otherPlaneDidChangePosition (self.currentPosition);
            } else {
                fatalError("Type mismatch");
            }
        });

        let allResults = self.mediator.dispatchCommand(self, command: c);
        for result in allResults {
            if result as? Bool == true {
                println("\(self.name): Too close! Abort!");
                return;
            }
        }
        println("\(self.name): Position changed");
    });
}

func land() {
    dispatch_barrier_sync(self.queue, { () in
        self.currentPosition = Position(distanceFromRunway: 0, height: 0);
        self.mediator.unregisterPeer(self);
        println("\(self.name): Landed");
    });
}
}
```

This approach creates a mediator that can handle any group of objects instantiated from a class that conforms to the **CommandPeer** protocol, but some caution is required because the **Command** objects that a peer creates have to make an assumption about the type of the peers against which the command will be executed. Since any peer can send a command, this means that all peers have to be derived from the same base class and that you cannot use the **CommandMediator** class to mediate between objects of differing types, even if they are all instantiated from classes that conform to the **CommandPeer** protocol.

The implementation of the **changePosition** method in the **Airplane** class creates a command that casts peer objects to the **Airplane** type and calls the **otherPlaneDidChangePosition** method. I call the global **fatalError** function if the peer cannot be cast as an **Airplane** because the behavior of a mediator in this situation is undefined.

The final change is to the **main.swift** file, in which I must create an instance of the **CommandMediator** class, as shown in Listing 21-14.

Listing 21-14. Using the CommandMediator Class in the main.swift File

```swift
let mediator = CommandMediator();

// initial setup
let british = Airplane(name: "BA706", initialPos:
    Position(distanceFromRunway: 11, height: 21000), mediator:mediator);

// new plane arrives
let american = Airplane(name: "AA101", initialPos:
    Position(distanceFromRunway: 12, height: 22000), mediator:mediator);

// plane approaches airport
british.changePosition(Position(distanceFromRunway: 8, height: 10000));
british.changePosition(Position(distanceFromRunway: 2, height: 5000));
british.changePosition(Position(distanceFromRunway: 1, height: 1000));

// new plane arrives
let cathay = Airplane(name: "CX200", initialPos:
    Position(distanceFromRunway: 13, height: 22000), mediator:mediator);

// plane lands
british.land();

// plane moves too close
cathay.changePosition(Position(distanceFromRunway: 12, height: 22000));
```

You can run the application to test that the changes don't affect the output, which is as follows:

```
BA706: Position changed
BA706: Position changed
BA706: Position changed
BA706: Landed
CX200: Too close! Abort!
```

Generalizing the Mediator with Messages

An alternative approach is to target a single method on peer objects and provide sufficient information to let the peer work out what response is needed. This avoids the assumptions about the type of the peer objects and allows peers of different types to be used with a single mediator, but it means that all peers need to have the same understanding about the range of messages that will be sent, which presents its own problems. Listing 21-15 shows how I have defined the protocol and implementation class required for the message-based mediator in a new file called **MessageMediator.swift** that I added to the example project.

Listing 21-15. The Contents of the MessageMediator.swift File

```
protocol MessagePeer {
    var name:String { get };
    func handleMessage(messageType:String, data:Any?) -> Any?;
}

class MessageMediator {
    private var peers = [String:MessagePeer]();

    func registerPeer(peer:MessagePeer) {
        peers[peer.name] = peer;
    }

    func unregisterPeer(peer:MessagePeer) {
        peers.removeValueForKey(peer.name);
    }

    func sendMessage(caller:MessagePeer, messageType:String, data:Any) -> [Any?] {
        var results = [Any?]();
        for peer in peers.values {
            if (peer.name != caller.name) {
                results.append(peer.handleMessage(messageType, data: data));
            }
        }
        return results;
    }
}
```

The **MessagePeer** protocol defines a **name** property so that the mediator can identify the sender of a message and defines a **handleMessage** method that is passed a string describing the message type and an optional **Any** data value, which will be used to provide data about the message to peers. The **MessageMediator** class keeps track of peers and also defines a **sendMessage** method that peers call to dispatch a message to their counterparts. The mediator gathers the set of results from the peers and returns them in an array to the caller. Listing 21-16 shows how I changed the implementation of the **Airplane** class to use the message-based mediator.

Listing 21-16. Using the Message-Based Mediator in the Airplane.swift File

```
import Foundation

struct Position {
    var distanceFromRunway:Int;
    var height:Int;
}

class Airplane : MessagePeer {
    var name:String;
    var currentPosition:Position;
    var mediator:MessageMediator;
    let queue = dispatch_queue_create("posQ", DISPATCH_QUEUE_CONCURRENT);
```

```
init(name:String, initialPos:Position, mediator: MessageMediator) {
    self.name = name;
    self.currentPosition = initialPos;
    self.mediator = mediator;
    mediator.registerPeer(self);
}

func handleMessage(messageType: String, data: Any?) -> Any? {
    var result:Any?;
    switch (messageType) {
        case "changePos":
            if let pos = data as? Position {
                result = otherPlaneDidChangePosition(pos);
            }
        default:
            fatalError("Unknown message type");

    }
    return result;

}

func otherPlaneDidChangePosition(position:Position) -> Bool {
    var result = false;
    dispatch_sync(self.queue, {() in
        result = position.distanceFromRunway
                == self.currentPosition.distanceFromRunway
            && abs(position.height - self.currentPosition.height) < 1000;
    });
    return result;
}

func changePosition(newPosition:Position) {
    dispatch_barrier_sync(self.queue, {() in
        self.currentPosition = newPosition;

        let allResults = self.mediator.sendMessage(self,
            messageType: "changePos", data: newPosition);
        for result in allResults {
            if result as? Bool == true {
                println("\(self.name): Too close! Abort!");
                return;
            }
        }
        println("\(self.name): Position changed");
    });
}
```

```
func land() {
    dispatch_barrier_sync(self.queue, { () in
        self.currentPosition = Position(distanceFromRunway: 0, height: 0);
        self.mediator.unregisterPeer(self);
        println("\(self.name): Landed");
    });
}
}
```

The advantage of this approach is that the **Airplane** class doesn't need to make any assumptions about the other peers—but this comes at the cost of needing to ensure that all peers know about the same set of message types and respond to them in a consistent and useful manner. This is harder than it sounds in a complex application, and it is easy to have multiple peer types whose message handling drifts apart as the application becomes more complex. To complete this implementation, I need to use the **MessageMediator** class in the **main.swift** file, as shown in Listing 21-17.

Listing 21-17. Using the MessageMediator Class in the main.swift File

```
let mediator = MessageMediator();

// initial setup
let british = Airplane(name: "BA706", initialPos:
    Position(distanceFromRunway: 11, height: 21000), mediator:mediator);

// new plane arrives
let american = Airplane(name: "AA101", initialPos:
    Position(distanceFromRunway: 12, height: 22000), mediator:mediator);

// plane approaches airport
british.changePosition(Position(distanceFromRunway: 8, height: 10000));
british.changePosition(Position(distanceFromRunway: 2, height: 5000));
british.changePosition(Position(distanceFromRunway: 1, height: 1000));

// new plane arrives
let cathay = Airplane(name: "CX200", initialPos:
    Position(distanceFromRunway: 13, height: 22000), mediator:mediator);

// plane lands
british.land();

// plane moves too close
cathay.changePosition(Position(distanceFromRunway: 12, height: 22000));
```

Understanding the Pitfalls of the Mediator Pattern

The most important pitfall to avoid is revealing details of one peer to another. The mediator should keep its peer collection private and not allow peers to locate or depend on one another, other than indirectly through the mediator. If you are implementing methods that return result, for example, then you must ensure that the peers do not return **self** as the result or, if they do, that the mediator doesn't pass the reference back to the calling peer. Programmers like shortcuts, and allowing direct peer-to-peer contact allows the lazy programmer to bypass the mediator and undermine the pattern implementation.

The Single Protocol Pitfall

A common pitfall is to make the peers and the mediator conform to a common protocol, such that the peers do not know that a mediator is being used, believing instead that they are dealing with a single peer object. This may seem like a clever idea, but it ends in messy and confusing code because there is rarely a one-to-one mapping of the methods that the mediator provides to the methods that must be exposed by the peers. My advice is to use separate protocols for the peers and the mediator, which ensures that implementation classes don't have to implement phantom methods or create tortured mappings between methods.

Examples of the Mediator Pattern in Cocoa

The **Foundation** framework includes a ready-made mediator called **NSNotificationCenter** that can be used to send notifications between objects. The NSNotificationCenter class is a message-based mediator; the class allows peers to specify the kinds of messages they want to receive and to restrict the peers from which messages can originate—but there is no support for receiving responses from peers. Messages flow in one direction only. I created an Xcode playground called **Notfications.playground** to demonstrate the use of the **NSNotificationCenter** class, as shown in Listing 21-18.

Listing 21-18. The Contents of the Notifications.playground File

```
import Foundation;

let notifier = NSNotificationCenter.defaultCenter();

@objc class NotificationPeer {
    let name:String;

    init(name:String) {
        self.name = name;
        NSNotificationCenter.defaultCenter().addObserver(self,
            selector: "receiveMessage:", name: "message", object: nil);
    }

    func sendMessage(message:String) {
        NSNotificationCenter.defaultCenter().postNotificationName("message",
            object: message);
    }

    func receiveMessage(notification:NSNotification) {
        println("Peer \(name) received message: \(notification.object)");
    }
}

let p1 = NotificationPeer(name: "peer1");
let p2 = NotificationPeer(name: "peer2");
let p3 = NotificationPeer(name: "peer3");
let p4 = NotificationPeer(name: "peer4");

p3.sendMessage("Hello!");
```

> **Note**   The **NSNotificationCenter** class also implements the observer pattern, which I describe in Chapter 22.

An instance of the **NSNotificationCenter** class is obtained through the class **defaultCenter** property and is used both to register peers to receive and send messages. Registration is performed using the **addObserver** method, like this:

```
...
NSNotificationCenter.defaultCenter().addObserver(self,
          selector: "receiveMessage:", name: "message", object: nil);
...
```

The first argument is the object that messages will be sent to, for which I have specified the current object. The **selector** argument specifies the method that the messages will be sent to, expressed as an Objective-C style selector, which means that the method name should be followed with a colon character. The **name** argument is used to select only messages that are sent using a specific label, and the **object** argument can be used to limit messages to those sent from a specific source. I have set the **name** to **message** and **object** arguments to **nil**, indicating that I want to receive all of the messages with the label **message**, regardless of the label and source.

> **Tip**   The method that is specified by the **selector** argument must be annotated with the @objc attribute or contained within a class that is annotated with **@objc**.

Messages are sent using the **postNotificationName** method, specifying a label and an object that will be sent to the peers, like this:

```
...
NSNotificationCenter.defaultCenter()
    .postNotificationName("message", object: message);
...
```

In the playground, I define a class called **NotificationPeer** that calls the **addObserver** method to register for messages to be sent to the **receiveMessage** method, and I use the **sendMessage** method to send messages via the **NSNotificationCenter**, using the label **message**.

When you register to receive messages, the method specified by the **selector** argument must take a single argument of the **NSNotification** type, which is used to represent messages and which defines the properties shown in Table 21-2.

Table 21-2. The Properties Defined by the NSNotification Class

Name	Description
name	The label used to send the message, set to `message` in the example
object	The optional data object associated with the message, set to the `message` parameter passed to the sendMessage method in the example
userInfo	An optional data value expressed as a dictionary that can be sent with an overloaded version of the postNotificationName method, not used in the example

I create four **NotificationPeer** objects in the playground and then call the **sendMessage** method on one of them, which produces the following output in the console:

```
Peer peer1 received message: Optional(Hello!)
Peer peer2 received message: Optional(Hello!)
Peer peer3 received message: Optional(Hello!)
Peer peer4 received message: Optional(Hello!)
```

The **NSNotificationCenter** can be a useful class, but I find not being able to obtain responses from peers to be a limitation in many projects, so I generally implement my own alternative, as described in the "Variations on the Mediator Pattern" section of this chapter.

Applying the Pattern to the SportsStore Application

There isn't a ready example for applying the mediator pattern on its own to the SportsStore for this chapter. Instead, in Chapter 22, I demonstrate how to use the mediator pattern and the command pattern together, which is a common combination.

Summary

In this chapter I described the mediator pattern and explained how it is used to handle communication between peer objects in order to reduce the complexity of an application and to ensure that no peer objects are left out. In the next chapter, I describe the observer pattern, which is used when an object needs to notify other objects when something interesting happens.

The Observer Pattern

The observer pattern is used to manage the process by which one object expresses interest in—and receives notification of—changes in another. The observer pattern allows large and complex groups of objects to cooperate with one another with few dependencies between them and is so widely used that you are likely to have come across it if you have developed an application using a modern UI component framework. Table 22-1 puts the observer pattern in context.

Table 22-1. Putting the Observer Pattern into Context

Question	Answer
What is it?	The observer pattern allows one object to register to receive notifications about changes in another object without needing to depend on the implementation of that object.
What are the benefits?	This pattern simplifies application design by allowing objects that provide notifications to do so in a uniform way without needing to know how those notifications are processed and acted on by the recipients.
When should you use this pattern?	Use this pattern whenever one object needs to receive notifications about changes in another object but where the sender of the notifications does not depend on the recipient to complete its work.
When should you avoid this pattern?	Do not use this pattern unless the sender of the notifications is functionally dependent from the recipients, such that the recipients could be removed from the application without preventing the sender from performing its work.
How do you know when you have implemented the pattern correctly?	The observer pattern is implemented correctly when an object can receive notifications without being tightly coupled to the object that sends them.
Are there any common pitfalls?	The biggest pitfall with this pattern is allowing the objects that send and receive notifications to become interdependent.
Are there any related patterns?	No.

Preparing the Example Project

For this chapter I created an Xcode OS X Command Line Tool project called Observer. I added a file to the project called **SystemComponents.swift** and used it to define the classes shown in Listing 22-1.

Listing 22-1. The Contents of the SystemComponents.swift File

```
class ActivityLog {
    func logActivity(activity:String) {
        println("Log: \(activity)");
    }
}

class FileCache {
    func loadFiles(user:String) {
        println("Load files for \(user)");
    }
}

class AttackMonitor {
    var monitorSuspiciousActivity: Bool = false {
        didSet {
            println("Monitoring for attack: \(monitorSuspiciousActivity)");
        }
    }
}
```

The three classes I have defined represent generic application components. I don't need to implement the components in any detail to demonstrate the pattern, and so they all write messages to the debug console to indicate they are being used. The **ActivityLog** represents a logging system that accepts details of system events, the **FileCache** class represents a cache that loads the files belonging to a given user, and the **AttackMonitor** class represents a security service that monitors system behavior when something suspicious has occurred. Listing 22-2 shows the contents of the **Authentication.swift** file, in which I defined a class that uses the system components.

Listing 22-2. The Contents of the Authentication.swift File

```
class AuthenticationManager {
    private let log = ActivityLog();
    private let cache = FileCache();
    private let monitor = AttackMonitor();

    func authenticate(user:String, pass:String) -> Bool {
        var result = false;
        if (user == "bob" && pass == "secret") {
            result = true;
            println("User \(user) is authenticated");
            // call system components
            log.logActivity("Authenticated \(user)");
            cache.loadFiles(user);
            monitor.monitorSuspiciousActivity = false;
        } else {
```

```
            println("Failed authentication attempt");
            // call system components
            log.logActivity("Failed authentication: \(user)");
            monitor.monitorSuspiciousActivity = true;
        }
        return result;
    }
}
```

The **AuthenticationManager** class represents a service that authenticates users with a password. The user's credentials are passed by a calling component to the **authenticate** method, which authenticates the user and writes a message to the debug console. To keep the example simple, the **AuthenticationManager** class allows a single username/password combination: the password **bob** with the password **secret**. Listing 22-3 shows the code I added to the **main.swift** file to use the **AuthenticationManager** class.

Listing 22-3. The Contents of the main.swift File

```
let authM = AuthenticationManager();

authM.authenticate("bob", pass: "secret");
println("-----");
authM.authenticate("joe", pass: "shhh");
```

The **authenticate** method of the **AuthenticationManager** class checks the credentials and authenticates the user. Once the authentication process has been completed, the component classes are called to set up the system for the user: logging a message, loading the user's file, and disabling the security monitor. The code in the **main.swift** file calls the **authenticate** method twice, once with credentials that will be authenticated and once with credentials that will fail. Running the application produces the following results:

```
User bob is authenticated
Log: Authenticated bob
Load files for bob
Monitoring for attack: false
-----
Failed authentication attempt
Log: Failed authentication: joe
Monitoring for attack: true
```

Understanding the Problem That the Pattern Solves

The structure of the code in the example application is commonly seen in real-world projects. Something happens that leads to a series of follow-on actions being performed. In the example, the starting event is a user authentication request, and the follow-on actions are logging, loading files, and configuring a monitoring service, as shown in Figure 22-1.

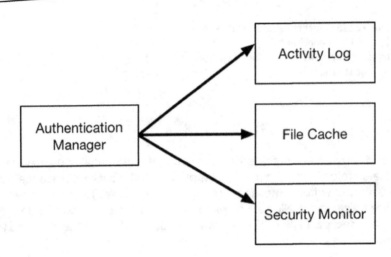

Figure 22-1. *An initial event and its follow-on action*

The problem is that the class that handles the initial activity—the **AuthenticationManager** class in the example—has to have detailed knowledge of the follow-on actions that are required, the classes responsible for those actions, and how those actions are performed. A change in one of the system components requires a change in the authentication manager class, and this presents the maintenance and testing problems that I have been referring to throughout this book. More broadly, the code in the authentication manager class spills over from the world of authentication and gets involved in completely different activities, something that makes the class more complex than it should be and more difficult to change.

Understanding the Observer Pattern

The observer pattern changes the relationship between objects by dividing them into *subjects* and *observers*. The subject objects maintain collections of dependent objects, the observers, and notify them about important changes or actions. In the example application, the subject would be the authentication manager class, and the observers would be the system component classes.

Without the observer pattern, a class like **AuthenticationManager** has to know which system components need to be called when an authentication request succeeds or fails, what changes should be applied to each of them, and how those changes should be performed.

The observer pattern reshapes this model so that the subject notifies its observers that the initial event has occurred—a authentication request was made—and leaves it to the observers to respond in whatever way is required. The subject doesn't need to know what the observer objects do or how they do it—just that they want to be told about important events.

The observer pattern standardizes the way that the observers receive notifications so that no knowledge of individual observers is required. Each subject knows only that there are observers that want to receive notifications and is responsible only for sending them to a well-defined method that all of the observers implement (conventionally named **notify**). Figure 22-2 illustrates the observer pattern, although the impact of this pattern is best seen through an implementation.

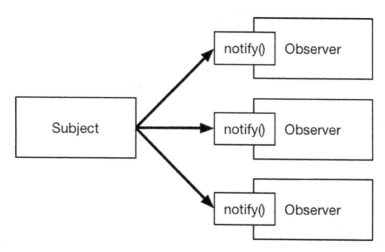

Figure 22-2. The observer pattern

Implementing the Observer Pattern

To key to implementing the observer pattern is to define the interactions between the subjects and observers using protocols. Listing 22-4 shows the protocols I defined in a new file called **Observer.swift**.

Listing 22-4. The Contents of the Observer.swift File

```
protocol Observer : class {
    func notify(user:String, success:Bool);
}

protocol Subject {
    func addObservers(observers:Observer...);
    func removeObserver(observer:Observer);
}
```

The names of the protocols reflect the roles that classes that conform to them play in the observer pattern. Classes that conform to the **Observer** protocol implement the **notify** method to receive notifications from classes that conform to the **Subject** protocol. In the observer pattern, subjects are responsible for keeping track of their observers, so I have defined the **addObservers** and **removeObserver** methods to allow observers to register and unregister their interest in receiving notifications from the subject. Notice that the **addObservers** method can accept multiple **Observer** objects. This makes it easier to set up the **Subject** object, as you will see in the "Consuming the Pattern" section.

> **Tip**   Notice that I have used the class keyword when defining the **Observer** protocol. This will make it possible for me to compare objects that implement the protocol when managing the observers in a class that conforms to the **Subject** protocol, as shown in Listing 22-5.

Creating the Base Subject Class

In the observer pattern, the subject is responsible for keeping track of its observers. To avoid duplicating the code that creates and manages the collection of observers, I create a base class that manages the observers and provides a method that subject implementation classes can use to send a notification. Since Swift collections are not thread-safe and there is the potential for the collection of observers to be accessed concurrently, I use Grand Central Dispatch (GCD) to protect the observer collection, as shown in Listing 22-5.

Listing 22-5. Defining a Base Subject Class in the Observer.swift File

```
import Foundation;

protocol Observer : class {
    func notify(user:String, success:Bool);
}

protocol Subject {
    func addObservers(observers:Observer...);
    func removeObserver(observer:Observer);
}

class SubjectBase : Subject {
    private var observers = [Observer]();
    private var collectionQueue = dispatch_queue_create("colQ",
        DISPATCH_QUEUE_CONCURRENT);

    func addObservers(observers: Observer...) {
        dispatch_barrier_sync(self.collectionQueue, { () in
            for newOb in observers {
                self.observers.append(newOb);
            }
        });
    }
```

```
    func removeObserver(observer: Observer) {
        dispatch_barrier_sync(self.collectionQueue, { () in
            self.observers = filter(self.observers, {$0 !== observer});
        });
    }

    func sendNotification(user:String, success:Bool) {
        dispatch_sync(self.collectionQueue, { () in
            for ob in self.observers {
                ob.notify(user, success: success);
            }
        });
    }
}
```

Conforming to the Subject Protocol

The next step is to update the **AuthenticationManager** class so that it conforms to the **Subject** protocol and to remove direct references to the system component classes that perform the follow-on actions. Listing 22-6 shows the changes that I made, relying on the **SubjectBase** class that I defined in the previous section.

Listing 22-6. Applying the Pattern in the Authentication.swift File

```
class AuthenticationManager : SubjectBase {

    func authenticate(user:String, pass:String) -> Bool {
        var result = false;
        if (user == "bob" && pass == "secret") {
            result = true;
            println("User \(user) is authenticated");
        } else {
            println("Failed authentication attempt");
        }
        sendNotification(user, success: result);
        return result;
    }
}
```

The effect is to simplify the class and return its focus to authenticating users. The references to individual component classes have been replaced with a single call to the **sendNotification** method, which in turn calls the **notify** method defined by each of the **Observer** objects that have been registered through the **addObservers** method provided by the **SubjectBase** class.

Conforming to the Observer Protocol

The next step is to update the component classes so they conform to the **Observer** protocol and can receive notifications from a **Subject**. Listing 22-7 shows the changes I made.

Listing 22-7. Conforming to the Observer Protocol in the SystemComponents.swift File

```
class ActivityLog : Observer {

    func notify(user: String, success: Bool) {
        println("Auth request for \(user). Success: \(success)");
    }

    func logActivity(activity:String) {
        println("Log: \(activity)");
    }
}

class FileCache : Observer {

    func notify(user: String, success: Bool) {
        if (success) {
            loadFiles(user);
        }
    }

    func loadFiles(user:String) {
        println("Load files for \(user)");
    }
}

class AttackMonitor : Observer {

    func notify(user: String, success: Bool) {
        monitorSuspiciousActivity = !success;
    }

    var monitorSuspiciousActivity: Bool = false {
        didSet {
            println("Monitoring for attack: \(monitorSuspiciousActivity)");
        }
    }
}
```

The additions make each class responsible for its own response to successful and failed authentication requests, which breaks the tight coupling with the authentication manager class.

Consuming the Pattern

All that remains is to update the code in the **main.swift** file to create the observers and register them with the subject, as shown in Listing 22-8.

Listing 22-8. Consuming the Observer Pattern in the main.swift File

```
let log = ActivityLog();
let cache = FileCache();
let monitor = AttackMonitor();

let authM = AuthenticationManager();
authM.addObservers(log, cache, monitor);

authM.authenticate("bob", pass: "secret");
println("-----");
authM.authenticate("joe", pass: "shhh");
```

I create instances of the individual observers and pass them to the **addObservers** method of the **AuthenticationManager** class. The **AuthenticationManager** class deals only with the observers through the **Observer** protocol and the **notify** method it defines and has no knowledge of the individual classes and what they do when the **notify** method is called. Running the application produces the following results:

```
User bob is authenticated
Auth request for bob. Success: true
Load files for bob
Monitoring for attack: false
-----
Failed authentication attempt
Auth request for joe. Success: false
Monitoring for attack: true
```

Using the **Observer** protocols makes it easy to extend the application without having to modify the subject; new **Observer** objects are simply passed to the subject's **addObservers** method.

Variations on the Observer Pattern

The observer pattern has a number of useful variations, each of which I describe in the following sections.

Generalizing Notifications

The standard pattern implementation I created in the previous section is dedicated to dealing with authentication requests. You can see this in the signature of the **notify** method defined by the **Observer** protocol.

```
...
func notify(user:String, success:Bool);
...
```

The **notify** method can be used only to process authentication request notifications, and this can be a problem when there are multiple subjects in the same application, each of which ends up defining its own version of the **Observer** protocol and the **notify** method.

A common variation is to generalize the **Observer** protocol so that it can be used to receive a wider range of notifications, each of which may originate from a different subject. The most robust approach is to define a class that represents a notification and encapsulates details of the notification type and any associated data, as shown in Figure 22-3.

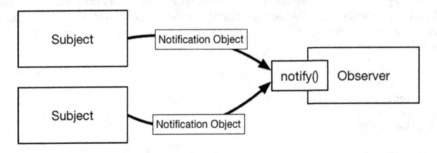

Figure 22-3. An observer receiving notification objects from multiple subjects

Listing 22-9 shows how I have added support for a notification object to the example application.

Listing 22-9. Adding a Notification Object in the Observer.swift File

```swift
import Foundation;

enum NotificationTypes : String {
    case AUTH_SUCCESS = "AUTH_SUCCESS";
    case AUTH_FAIL = "AUTH_FAIL";
}

struct Notification {
    let type:NotificationTypes;
    let data:Any?;
}
```

```
protocol Observer : class {
    func notify(notification:Notification);
}

protocol Subject {
    func addObservers(observers:Observer...);
    func removeObserver(observer:Observer);
}

class SubjectBase : Subject {
    private var observers = [Observer]();
    private var collectionQueue = dispatch_queue_create("colQ",
        DISPATCH_QUEUE_CONCURRENT);

    func addObservers(observers: Observer...) {
        dispatch_barrier_sync(self.collectionQueue, { () in
            for newOb in observers {
                self.observers.append(newOb);
            }
        });
    }

    func removeObserver(observer: Observer) {
        dispatch_barrier_sync(self.collectionQueue, { () in
            self.observers = filter(self.observers, {$0 !== observer});
        });
    }

    func sendNotification(notification:Notification) {
        dispatch_sync(self.collectionQueue, { () in
            for ob in self.observers {
                ob.notify(notification);
            }
        });
    }
}
```

I have defined a struct called **Notification** that indicates its type through a value from the **NotificationTypes** enumeration and that provides the data observers will need to process the notification as an optional constant called **data**. I have updated the **Observer** protocol so that the **notify** method receives a **Notification** object and updated the **sendNotification** method in the **SubjectBase** class to receive a **Notification** object. Listing 22-10 shows how I updated the observer classes so they conform to the modified protocol.

> **Tip**   You don't have to use an enumeration to detail the notification types in an application. The alternative is to use a **String** to provide the name of the notification. I generally start with an enumeration because it reduces the chance of mistyping a notification name in an observer, causing it to respond unexpectedly. For larger projects, I usually switch to using string values because having a single enumeration to define all of the notifications can become unwieldy, especially when multiple developers are defining different notifications on the same project.

Listing 22-10. Conforming to the Revised Observer Protocol in the SystemComponents.swift File

```swift
class ActivityLog : Observer {

    func notify(notification:Notification) {
        println("Auth request for \(notification.type.rawValue) "
            + "Success: \(notification.data!)");
    }

    func logActivity(activity:String) {
        println("Log: \(activity)");
    }
}

class FileCache : Observer {

    func notify(notification:Notification) {
        if (notification.type == NotificationTypes.AUTH_SUCCESS) {
            loadFiles(notification.data! as String);
        }
    }

    func loadFiles(user:String) {
        println("Load files for \(user)");
    }
}

class AttackMonitor : Observer {

    func notify(notification: Notification) {
        monitorSuspiciousActivity
        = (notification.type == NotificationTypes.AUTH_FAIL);
    }

    var monitorSuspiciousActivity: Bool = false {
        didSet {
            println("Monitoring for attack: \(monitorSuspiciousActivity)");
        }
    }
}
```

Finally, I revised the subject class so that it uses the **Notification** struct, as shown in Listing 22-11.

Listing 22-11. Using Notification Objects in the AuthenticationManager.swift File

```
class AuthenticationManager : SubjectBase {

    func authenticate(user:String, pass:String) -> Bool {
        var nType = NotificationTypes.AUTH_FAIL;
        if (user == "bob" && pass == "secret") {
            nType = NotificationTypes.AUTH_SUCCESS;
            println("User \(user) is authenticated");
        } else {
            println("Failed authentication attempt");
        }
        sendNotification(Notification(type: nType, data: user));
        return nType == NotificationTypes.AUTH_SUCCESS;
    }
}
```

Running the example application produces the following output:

```
User bob is authenticated
Auth request for AUTH_SUCCESS Success: bob
Load files for bob
Monitoring for attack: false
-----
Failed authentication attempt
Auth request for AUTH_FAIL Success: joe
Monitoring for attack: true
```

Understanding the Notification Object Pitfall

The changes seem modest, but there is a potential pitfall when applying this variation. The observers have to know what data type to expect to be associated with a notification, and the subjects have to honor that expectation.

In the case of the example application, the subject—the **AuthenticationManager** class—sends the name of the user who has requested authentication expressed as a **String** value, and the observers have to know what type the subject uses and, as importantly, what that value means. The pitfall arises when two subjects use the same notification types with different data types or—more dangerously—use the same data type but intend the value to express different meanings.

The surest way of avoiding this problem is to define subclasses for each notification that refine the meaning of the associated data value. This is not a guarantee against deliberate misuse, but it does guard against accidental problems. Listing 22-12 shows how I have defined a notification subclass in the example application.

Listing 22-12. Defining a Notification Subclass in the Observers.swift File

```swift
import Foundation;

enum NotificationTypes : String {
    case AUTH_SUCCESS = "AUTH_SUCCESS";
    case AUTH_FAIL = "AUTH_FAIL";
    case SUBJECT_CREATED = "SUBJECT_CREATE";
    case SUBJECT_DESTROYED = "SUBJECT_DESTROYED";
}

class Notification {
    let type:NotificationTypes;
    let data:Any?;

    init(type:NotificationTypes, data:Any?) {
        self.type = type; self.data = data;
    }
}

class AuthenticationNotification: Notification {

    init(user:String, success:Bool) {
        super.init(type: success ? NotificationTypes.AUTH_SUCCESS
            : NotificationTypes.AUTH_FAIL, data: user);
    }

    var userName : String? {
        return self.data? as String?;
    }

    var requestSuccessed : Bool {
        return self.type == NotificationTypes.AUTH_SUCCESS;
    }
}

protocol Observer : class {
    func notify(notification:Notification);
}

protocol Subject {
    func addObservers(observers:Observer...);
    func removeObserver(observer:Observer);
}

class SubjectBase : Subject {
    // ...statements omitted for brevity...
}
```

I have changed **Notification** from a **struct** to a class so that I can derive the
AuthenticationNotification class from it and define computed properties that present the
property values in a more useful manner.

You can create more specialized versions of the **Observer** protocol that deliver only notification-specific objects, but I find that implementation classes that receive multiple notification types from multiple subjects quickly become complex to implement and test. Instead, I prefer to use a general-purpose **Observer** protocol and have the implementation classes test to see which types they receive, as shown in Listing 22-13.

Listing 22-13. Receiving a Notification-Specific Object in the SystemComponents.swift File

```
...
class FileCache : Observer {
    func notify(notification:Notification) {
        if let authNotification = notification as? AuthenticationNotification {
            if (authNotification.requestSuccessed              && authNotification.userName != nil) {
                loadFiles(authNotification.userName!);
            }
        }
    }

    func loadFiles(user:String) {
        println("Load files for \(user)");
    }
}
...
```

This approach means that any observer can still receive any notification through a single method but can opt to check for more specialized types and take advantage of them as required. The other two classes in the **SystemComponents.swift** file do not check for the **AuthenticationNotification** type, but they are still perfectly able to receive and process the notifications sent by the authentication manager class.

Using Weak References

Swift uses strong references for objects by default, which can lead to an odd situation where a reference from a subject is the only one keeping an observer from being destroyed. This is a dangerous situation to be in because the observer may still be responding to notifications long after it should have been released, creating unexpected behavior and potentially keeping other objects alive longer than intended.

Swift provides support for weak references that are not used in the automatic reference counting process and that can be used in applications that have short-lived observers that may not have the chance to deregister from their subjects. Swift arrays don't work with weakly referenced objects directly, so a wrapper is required, as shown in Listing 22-14.

Listing 22-14. Using Weak References to Observers in the Observer.swift File

```swift
import Foundation;

// ...statements omitted for brevity...

private class WeakObserverReference {
    weak var observer:Observer?;

    init(observer:Observer) {
        self.observer = observer;
    }
}

class SubjectBase : Subject {
    private var observers = [WeakObserverReference]();
    private var collectionQueue = dispatch_queue_create("colQ",
        DISPATCH_QUEUE_CONCURRENT);

    func addObservers(observers: Observer...) {
        dispatch_barrier_sync(self.collectionQueue, { () in
            for newOb in observers {
                self.observers.append(WeakObserverReference(observer: newOb));
            }
        });
    }

    func removeObserver(observer: Observer) {
        dispatch_barrier_sync(self.collectionQueue, { () in
            self.observers = filter(self.observers, { weakref in
                return weakref.observer != nil && weakref.observer !== observer;
            });
        });
    }

    func sendNotification(notification:Notification) {
        dispatch_sync(self.collectionQueue, { () in
            for ob in self.observers {
                ob.observer?.notify(notification);
            }
        });
    }
}
```

I have defined a class called **WeakObserverReference** that acts as a wrapper around a weakly referenced **Observer** object through the use of the **weak** keyword. The **WeakObserverRerence** objects are strongly referenced by the collection maintained by the **SubjectBase** class and won't be destroyed, even when the observer they weakly refer to has been.

Dealing with Short-Lived Subjects

The standard implementation of the observer pattern assumes that an application reaches a sort of steady state, in which the observer and subject objects have been created and associated with one another, allowing a steady of flow of notifications for the life of the application.

This isn't always the case, of course, and a common variation is to adapt the pattern so that observers automatically receive notifications from subjects that have a relatively short life. In this situation, it is helpful to arrange for observers to be notified when a new subject has been created. The way I manage this situation is to combine the observer pattern with the mediator pattern I described in Chapter 21. The mediator provides a handy mechanism through which subjects can notify observers that they have been created—a kind of meta-observer pattern. The first step is to define two new types of notification, which I will use to indicate when a subject is created and destroyed, as shown in Listing 22-15.

Listing 22-15. Defining New Notification Types in the Observer.swift File

```
...
enum NotificationTypes : String {
    case AUTH_SUCCESS = "AUTH_SUCCESS";
    case AUTH_FAIL = "AUTH_FAIL";
    case SUBJECT_CREATED = "SUBJECT_CREATE";
    case SUBJECT_DESTROYED = "SUBJECT_DESTROYED";
}
...
```

Listing 22-16 shows the contents of the **MetaObserver.swift** file that I added to the example project and that I used to define the protocol and classes required to handle short-lived subjects automatically.

Listing 22-16. The Contents of the MetaObserver.swift File

```
protocol MetaObserver : Observer {
    func notifySubjectCreated(subject:Subject);
    func notifySubjectDestroyed(subject:Subject);
}

class MetaSubject : SubjectBase, MetaObserver {

    func notifySubjectCreated(subject: Subject) {
        sendNotification(Notification(type: NotificationTypes.SUBJECT_CREATED,
            data: subject));
    }

    func notifySubjectDestroyed(subject: Subject) {
        sendNotification(Notification(type: NotificationTypes.SUBJECT_DESTROYED,
            data: subject));
    }
```

```
    class var sharedInstance:MetaSubject {
        struct singletonWrapper {
            static let singleton = MetaSubject();
        }
        return singletonWrapper.singleton;
    }

    func notify(notification:Notification) {
        // do nothing - required for Observer conformance
    }
}

class ShortLivedSubject : SubjectBase {

    override init() {
        super.init();
        MetaSubject.sharedInstance.notifySubjectCreated(self);
    }

    deinit {
        MetaSubject.sharedInstance.notifySubjectDestroyed(self);
    }
}
```

At the heart of this variation is the **MetaObserver** protocol, which extends **Observer** and adds method that will be called when new short-lived subjects are created and destroyed. I need a mechanism to track meta-observers and dispatch notifications to them, so I created the mediator in the form of the **MetaSubject** class, which is derived from **SubjectBase** (so I inherit thread-safe observer tracking) and conforms to the **MetaObserver** protocol (so that individual subjects can announce their creation and destruction). The final addition is the **ShortLivedSubject** class, which is derived from **SubjectBase** and implements an initializer and de-initializer that calls the methods of the **MetaSubject** class. Listing 22-17 shows how I have updated the **AuthenticationManager** class so that it participates in the new functionality.

Listing 22-17. Creating a Short-Lived Subject in the Authentication.swift File

```
class AuthenticationManager : ShortLivedSubject {

    func authenticate(user:String, pass:String) -> Bool {
        var nType = NotificationTypes.AUTH_FAIL;
        if (user == "bob" && pass == "secret") {
            nType = NotificationTypes.AUTH_SUCCESS;
            println("User \(user) is authenticated");
        } else {
            println("Failed authentication attempt");
        }
        sendNotification(Notification(type: nType, data: user));
        return nType == NotificationTypes.AUTH_SUCCESS;
    }
}
```

I only need to change the base class because all of the behavior I require is inherited. Listing 22-18 shows the changes I made to transform one of the observer classes into a meta-observer.

Listing 22-18. Creating a Meta-observer in the SystemComponents.swift File

```
...
class AttackMonitor : MetaObserver {

    func notifySubjectCreated(subject: Subject) {
        if (subject is AuthenticationManager) {
            subject.addObservers(self);
        }
    }

    func notifySubjectDestroyed(subject: Subject) {
        subject.removeObserver(self);
    }

    func notify(notification: Notification) {
        monitorSuspiciousActivity
            = (notification.type == NotificationTypes.AUTH_FAIL);
    }

    var monitorSuspiciousActivity: Bool = false {
        didSet {
            println("Monitoring for attack: \(monitorSuspiciousActivity)");
        }
    }
}
...
```

The implementation of the **notifySubjectCreated** method checks the type of the newly created subject and registers for notifications only for instances of the **AuthenticationManager** class. The final step is to change the way that the observer is created and applied in the **main.swift** file, as shown in Listing 22-19.

Listing 22-19. Using a Meta-observer in the main.swift File

```
// create meta observer
let monitor = AttackMonitor();
MetaSubject.sharedInstance.addObservers(monitor);

// create regular observers
let log = ActivityLog();
let cache = FileCache();

let authM = AuthenticationManager();
// register only the regular observers
authM.addObservers(cache, monitor);

authM.authenticate("bob", pass: "secret");
println("-----");
authM.authenticate("joe", pass: "shhh");
```

The **AttackMonitor** object is registered as a meta-observer with the **MetaSubject** class. This ensures that the **AttackMonitor** object is notified when the subject object is created and has the option of registering for notifications. Running the application produces the following output, which demonstrates that the meta-observer receives notifications from the subject:

```
Monitoring for attack: false
User bob is authenticated
Monitoring for attack: false
-----
Failed authentication attempt
Monitoring for attack: true
```

Understanding the Pitfalls of the Observer Pattern

There are no serious pitfalls for the standard implementation of the observer pattern as long as you ensure that your observers receive notifications only through the **notify** method and that the subject doesn't try to cast the observers to their implementation types.

When creating variations on the observer pattern, you should make sure you don't lose sight of the division of responsibilities between the subject and the observer; it is easy to create an implementation that blurs the lines between subject and observer and that undermines the simplicity and directness of the pattern.

Examples of the Observer Pattern in Cocoa

There are several examples of the observer pattern in the Cocoa frameworks. In Chapter 21, I described the **NSNotificationCenter** class as an example of the mediator protocol, but this class also implements the observer pattern. This is the same combination that I used to handle short-lived subjects earlier in the chapter, and, in fact, you can use the **NSNotificationCenter** as a way to notify meta-observers that subjects have been created or destroyed. I use the **NSNotificationCenter** to apply the mediator and command patterns to the SportsStore application later in this chapter.

User Interface Events

The Cocoa implementation of the observer pattern that most programmers encounter is in the UI frameworks, where user interactions and changes in UI component state are expressed using *events*, which are notifications by another name. Within the Cocoa frameworks, there are protocols for different categories of event, each of which has its equivalent of the **notify** method that I defined in the **Observer** protocol in the "Implementing the Observer Pattern" section of this chapter. As an example, here is the method I added to the SportsStore application to respond when the user shakes the iOS device to perform an undo operation:

```
...
override func motionEnded(motion: UIEventSubtype, withEvent event: UIEvent) {
    if (event.subtype == UIEventSubtype.MotionShake) {
        println("Shake motion detected");
        undoManager?.undo();
    }
}
...
```

The **motionEnded** method is defined by the **UIResponder** protocol, to which the **ViewController** class conforms through its base class. Rather than signal all UI notifications through a single **notify** method, the **UIResponder** protocol defines methods for each major type of user interaction, and the **UIEventSubtype** enumeration is used to indicate the specific motion has been performed. You will encounter events in all applications that use UI components, but you will typically implement only the observer and rely on the components as subjects.

Observing Property Changes

Objective-C has a feature called *key-value observing* (KVO) that allows one object to receive notifications when the value of another object's property changes. You can use KVO to communicate between Swift objects as long as both of them are derived from **NSObject**, and you use the **dynamic** keyword when defining the property that will be observed.

To demonstrate how to use KVO in Swift, I created a new Xcode Command Line Tool project called KVO and used the **main.swift** file to define the code shown in Listing 22-20.

Listing 22-20. Using KVO in the main.swift File

```
import Foundation;

class Subject : NSObject {
    dynamic var counter = 0;
}

class Observer : NSObject {

    init(subject:Subject) {
        super.init();
        subject.addObserver(self, forKeyPath: "counter",
            options: NSKeyValueObservingOptions.New, context: nil);
    }

    override func observeValueForKeyPath(keyPath: String, ofObject object: AnyObject,
        change: [NSObject : AnyObject], context: UnsafeMutablePointer<Void>) {

        println("Notification: \(keyPath) = \(change[NSKeyValueChangeNewKey]!)");
    }
}
```

```
let subject = Subject();
let observer = Observer(subject: subject);
subject.counter++;
subject.counter = 22;
```

> **Tip**   I had to use an Xcode project for this simple example because the limitations of playgrounds prevent KVO from working properly.

The **Subject** class uses the **dynamic** keyword to define a variable called **counter**. This is the property that I will observe using KVO, and the **dynamic** keyword prevents the implementation of the property from being optimized by the compiler, allowing the KVO feature to replace it at runtime with the equivalent of a computed property that notifies its observers of changes.

The **Observer** class registers its interest in the property using the **addObserver** method, like this:

```
...
subject.addObserver(self, forKeyPath: "counter",
    options: NSKeyValueObservingOptions.New, context: nil);
...
```

The arguments to the **addObserver** method specify the observer, the property to be observed, and a value from the **NSKeyValueObservingOptions** enumeration that specifies which value should be included in the notification when there is a change. I specified the **New** value, indicating that the value assigned to the subject property should be used.

Notifications are sent to the observer's **observeValueForKeyPath** method, containing details of the subject, the property that changed, and the new value. In this example, I write out the name of the property and its value. Running the example produces the following output in the Xcode console:

```
Notification: counter = 1
Notification: counter = 22
```

Applying the Pattern to the SportsStore Application

In this chapter, I am going to use the **NSNotificationCenter** class to apply both the mediator and command patterns to the SportsStore application.

Preparing the Example Application

No preparation to the SportsStore application is required, and I pick up the project as I left it in Chapter 20. Don't forget that you can get the SportsStore project from Apress.com as part of the free source code download that accompanies this book if you don't want to type the changes yourself.

Applying the Pattern

I am going to apply the observer pattern to the product class so that it acts as a subject that sends out notifications when the stock level changes. Rather than define custom protocols and classes, I am going to use the **NSNotificationCenter** class to handle the notifications and to act as a mediator so that the subjects and observers can find one another. Listing 22-21 shows the change I made to the **Product** class so that it sends notifications.

Listing 22-21. Sending Notifications in the Product.swift File

```
...
var stockLevel:Int {
    get { return stockLevelBackingValue;}
    set {
        stockLevelBackingValue = max(0, newValue);
        NSNotificationCenter.defaultCenter().postNotificationName("stockUpdate",
            object: self);
    }
}
...
```

The advantage of using the **NSNotificationCenter** class is that notifications can be added to an application with the minimum of effort, although care is still required to make sure that notifications sent by different parts of the application don't clash with one another. Now that the **Product** class is sending out notifications, I can observe them anywhere the stock level information is of interest. Listing 22-22 shows how I have changed the **ProductTableCell** class so that it updates its UI components in response to a stock level notification.

Listing 22-22. Responding to Notifications in the ViewController.swift File

```
...
class ProductTableCell : UITableViewCell {

    @IBOutlet weak var nameLabel: UILabel!
    @IBOutlet weak var descriptionLabel: UILabel!
    @IBOutlet weak var stockStepper: UIStepper!
    @IBOutlet weak var stockField: UITextField!

    var product:Product?;

    required init(coder aDecoder: NSCoder) {
        super.init(coder: aDecoder);
        NSNotificationCenter.defaultCenter().addObserver(self,
            selector: "handleStockLevelUpdate:", name: "stockUpdate", object: nil);
    }
```

```
        func handleStockLevelUpdate(notification:NSNotification) {
            if let updatedProduct = notification.object as? Product {
                if updatedProduct.name == self.product?.name {
                    stockStepper.value = Double(updatedProduct.stockLevel);
                    stockField.text = String(updatedProduct.stockLevel);
                }
            }
        }
    }
}
...
```

The **ProductTableCell** class sets the values of the **UIStepper** and **UITextField** components when a notification for the **Product** that is being displayed changes. This means I can remove the statements that explicitly altered the UI components from the **stockLevelDidChange** method in the **ViewController** class, as shown in Listing 22-23.

Listing 22-23. Removing Statements from the ViewController.swift File

```
...
@IBAction func stockLevelDidChange(sender: AnyObject) {
    if var currentCell = sender as? UIView {
        while (true) {
            currentCell = currentCell.superview!;
            if let cell = currentCell as? ProductTableCell {
                if let product = cell.product? {

                    let dict = NSDictionary(objects: [product.stockLevel],
                        forKeys: [product.name]);

                    undoManager?.registerUndoWithTarget(self,
                        selector: "undoStockLevel:", object: dict);

                    if let stepper = sender as? UIStepper {
                        product.stockLevel = Int(stepper.value);
                    } else if let textfield = sender as? UITextField {
                        if let newValue = textfield.text.toInt()? {
                            product.stockLevel = newValue;
                        }
                    }

//                  cell.stockStepper.value = Double(product.stockLevel);
//                  cell.stockField.text = String(product.stockLevel);
                    productLogger.logItem(product);
```

```
            StockServerFactory.getStockServer()
                .setStockLevel(product.name,
                    stockLevel: product.stockLevel);
        }
        break;
    }
}
displayStockTotal();
    }
}
...
```

Summary

In this chapter I described the observer pattern, which is used to standardize the process by which objects express interest in and receive notifications of changes in other objects. The observer pattern is a powerful tool because it allows components to cooperate with one another while remaining loosely coupled, which in turn makes it easier to test and make changes to those components. In the next chapter, I describe the memento pattern, which is used to manage the state of an object.

The Memento Pattern

The memento pattern is a close relative of the command pattern I described in Chapter 20, with the important difference that it is used to capture the complete state of an object so that it can be subsequently reset. Table 23-1 puts the memento pattern in context.

Table 23-1. *Putting the Memento Pattern into Context*

Question	Answer
What is it?	The memento pattern captures the complete state of an object into a memento that can be used to reset the object at a later date.
What are the benefits?	The memento pattern allows a complete reset of an object without the need to track and apply individual undo commands.
When should you use this pattern?	Use this pattern when there is a "known-good" point in an object's life that you may want to return to at some point in the future.
When should you avoid this pattern?	This pattern should be used only when you need to return an object to an earlier state. Use the command pattern, as described in Chapter 20, if you need to add support for undoing the effect of only the most recent operation.
How do you know when you have implemented the pattern correctly?	The pattern is implemented correctly if the object can be returned to an earlier state from any starting position.
Are there any common pitfalls?	The most common pitfall is to not completely capture or set the state.
Are there any related patterns?	The memento and command patterns share a common philosophy.

Preparing the Example Project

I created an Xcode Command Line Tool project called Memento for this chapter and added to it a file called **Ledger.swift**, the contents of which are shown in Listing 23-1.

Listing 23-1. The Contents of the Ledger.swift File

```swift
class LedgerEntry {
    let id:Int;
    let counterParty:String;
    let amount:Float;

    init(id:Int, counterParty:String, amount:Float) {
        self.id = id; self.counterParty = counterParty; self.amount = amount;
    }
}

class LedgerCommand {
    private let instructions:Ledger -> Void;
    private let receiver:Ledger;

    init(instructions:Ledger -> Void, receiver:Ledger) {
        self.instructions = instructions; self.receiver = receiver;
    }

    func execute() {
        self.instructions(self.receiver);
    }
}

class Ledger {
    private var entries = [Int:LedgerEntry]();
    private var nextId = 1;
    var total:Float = 0;

    func addEntry(counterParty:String, amount:Float) -> LedgerCommand {
        let entry = LedgerEntry(id: nextId++, counterParty: counterParty, amount: amount);
        entries[entry.id] = entry;
        total += amount;
        return createUndoCommand(entry);
    }

    private func createUndoCommand(entry:LedgerEntry) -> LedgerCommand {
        return LedgerCommand(instructions: {target in
            let removed = target.entries.removeValueForKey(entry.id);
            if (removed != nil) {
                target.total -= removed!.amount;
            }
        }, receiver: self);
    }
}
```

```
    func printEntries() {
        for id in entries.keys.array.sorted(<) {
            if let entry = entries[id] {
                println("#\(id): \(entry.counterParty) $\(entry.amount)");
            }
        }
        println("Total: $\(total)");
        println("----");
    }
}
```

The **Ledger** class represents an account record of the kind of ledger that banks use to record transactions, albeit massively simplified. The **Ledger** class defines an **addEntry** method that accepts details of the counterparty and an amount and uses them to create a **LedgerEntry** object. With each call to the **addEntry** method, a dictionary of **LedgerEntry** objects is built up, indexed by a unique ID.

The **Ledger** class provides support for undoing operations using the command pattern that I described in Chapter 20. A call to the **addEntry** method returns a **LedgerCommand** object, whose **execute** method will locate and remove a **LedgerEntry** object. Finally, the **Ledger** class defines a **total** property that is updated when entries are added or undone. Listing 23-2 shows the code I added to the **main.swift** file to use the **Ledger** class.

Listing 23-2. The Contents of the main.swift File

```
let ledger = Ledger();

ledger.addEntry("Bob", amount: 100.43);
ledger.addEntry("Joe", amount: 200.20);
let undoCommand = ledger.addEntry("Alice", amount: 500);
ledger.addEntry("Tony", amount: 20);

ledger.printEntries();
undoCommand.execute();
ledger.printEntries();
```

The statements in the **main.swift** file create a **Ledger** object and call the **addEntry** method to create four entries. I then print out the contents of the ledger, execute an undo command for one of the four entries, and print out the contents again to see the effect. Running the application produces the following output:

```
#1: Bob $100.43
#2: Joe $200.2
#3: Alice $500.0
#4: Tony $20.0
Total: $820.63
----
#1: Bob $100.43
#2: Joe $200.2
#4: Tony $20.0
Total: $320.63
```

Understanding the Problem That the Pattern Solves

I used the command pattern to implement the undo feature for the **Ledger** class in the example application, using the same techniques I described in Chapter 20. I like the command pattern because it is endlessly powerful and flexible, but the way that I have applied the pattern to create the undo feature has a potential flaw that limits its applicability in some applications.

As things stand, I can undo individual operations. When I execute the undo command for the **LedgerEntry** whose counterparty is **Alice**, the effect is to reverse the effect of a single call to the **addEntry** method. What I can't easily do, however, is return the **Ledger** to an earlier state so that the entry that I have undone and all subsequent entries are removed. I have removed the **Alice** entry, but doing so didn't remove the **Tony** entry.

In some applications, undoing a single operation isn't enough; you need to be able to return the state of an object to a specific point, a process referred to as *unwinding* or *rewinding* the object's state. This is often the case with transactional data, such as ledgers, where returning to a checkpoint or snapshot is needed in order to be sure of the integrity of an application and its data.

One approach is for the calling component to keep track of all the undo commands it receives and execute them in reverse order to undo the effects of each operation, as shown in Listing 23-3.

Listing 23-3. Manually Unwinding the State of a Ledger in the main.swift File

```
let ledger = Ledger();

ledger.addEntry("Bob", amount: 100.43);
ledger.addEntry("Joe", amount: 200.20);
let aliceUndoCommand = ledger.addEntry("Alice", amount: 500);
let tonyUndoCommand = ledger.addEntry("Tony", amount: 20);

ledger.printEntries();
tonyUndoCommand.execute();
aliceUndoCommand.execute();
ledger.printEntries();
```

This is a messy approach because it relies on one component having access to all of the undo commands and knowing the order in which they should be applied, which is hard to arrange if there are multiple components operating on a single **Ledger** object. Each component will have only some of the undo commands, and the order in which they should be applied is unknown.

In short, trying to unwind or reset the state of an object using individual undo commands is a problem; what I need is a more flexible approach that doesn't place the burden of responsibility on the calling component to keep track of the changes that need to be applied to return to a trusted snapshot or checkpoint.

Understanding the Memento Pattern

There are two participants in the memento patterns: the *originator* and the *caretaker*. The originator is the object whose state may be unwound, such as the **Ledger** in the example application. The caretaker is the calling component that will tell the originator when its state should be unwound, which is the code in the **main.swift** file in the example.

The originator provides the caretaker with a *memento*, which is an object that contains instructions or data required to return the originator to an earlier state. The details of the memento are hidden from the caretaker, which cannot modify or manipulate the state it contains. At some point in the future, the caretaker returns the memento to the originator, which uses the instructions or data to unwind its state. Figure 23-1 illustrates the memento pattern.

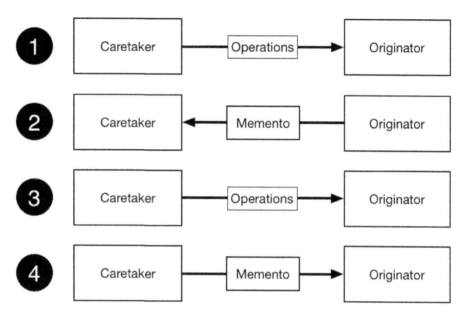

Figure 23-1. The memento pattern

The easiest way to understand the memento pattern is to focus on the four phases that underpin it, as numbered in the figure.

In the first phase, the caretaker performs normal operations on the originator, each of which modifies its state. In the second phase, the caretaker requests a memento from the originator. The creation of the memento object doesn't change the state of the originator; it just captures the present state so that the originator can return to it later.

In the third phase, the caretaker performs further operations on the originator, which further modify its state. In the fourth and final phase, the caretaker returns the memento object to the originator, which uses it to restore its state to the point at which the memento was created.

By encapsulating a snapshot of the originator's state into an object, the memento pattern avoids the problems I encountered when using undo commands to unwind state. The caretaker doesn't need to keep track of the operations that have been performed or worry about operations performed by other components; it simply returns the memento to the originator when it wants the state to be unwound.

Using a memento allows for a lot of flexibility. The memento object can be used by a different component than the original caretaker, it can be used to repeatedly unwind the state to the same point, and it can be used to transfer the state of one object to another.

Implementing the Memento Pattern

The implementation of the memento pattern is based on two protocols: one for the originator and one for the memento. The caretaker doesn't require its own protocol since it is just a calling component that takes advantage of the functionality provided by the originator. Listing 23-4 shows the contents of the **Memento.swift** file, which I added to the example project.

Listing 23-4. The Contents of the Memento.swift File

```
import Foundation

protocol Memento {
    // no methods or properties defined
}

protocol Originator {
    func createMemento() -> Memento;
    func applyMemento(memento:Memento);
}
```

The **Memento** protocol doesn't define any methods or properties, and that's because all of its implementation details are private, meaning that the only purpose of the protocol is to denote that an object is a memento.

The **Originator** protocol defines a **createMemento** that will produce a memento of the current state and an **applyMemento** method that accepts a memento and uses it to restore the originator to the state it defines.

Implementing the Memento Class

The implementation detail of a memento is entirely at the discretion of the originator as long as two basic conditions are met. The first condition is that the caretaker should not be able to modify the state that the memento contains in any way. The second condition is that the memento should always work, regardless of the current state of the originator.

In practice, this means an originator either contains a static snapshot of the state data or consists of a set of operations that reset the state and are then applied in sequence, rather like the command macros I described in Chapter 20. Listing 23-5 shows how I have the pattern in the example project. (I have also removed the undo commands to keep the example simple, but there is no reason why the command and memento patterns cannot coexist in an application).

Listing 23-5. Creating the Memento and Originator in the Ledger.swift File

```swift
import Foundation

class LedgerEntry {
    let id:Int;
    let counterParty:String;
    let amount:Float;

    init(id:Int, counterParty:String, amount:Float) {
        self.id = id; self.counterParty = counterParty; self.amount = amount;
    }
}

class LedgerMemento : Memento {
    private let entries = [LedgerEntry]();
    private let total:Float;
    private let nextId:Int;

    init(ledger:Ledger) {
        self.entries = ledger.entries.values.array;
        self.total = ledger.total;
        self.nextId = ledger.nextId;
    }

    func apply(ledger:Ledger) {
        ledger.total = self.total;
        ledger.nextId = self.nextId;
        ledger.entries.removeAll(keepCapacity: true);
        for entry in self.entries {
            ledger.entries[entry.id] = entry;
        }
    }
}

class Ledger : Originator {
    private var entries = [Int:LedgerEntry]();
    private var nextId = 1;
    var total:Float = 0;

    func addEntry(counterParty:String, amount:Float) {
        let entry = LedgerEntry(id: nextId++, counterParty: counterParty, amount: amount);
        entries[entry.id] = entry;
        total += amount;
    }

    func createMemento() -> Memento {
        return LedgerMemento(ledger: self);
    }
}
```

```
func applyMemento(memento: Memento) {
    if let m = memento as? LedgerMemento {
        m.apply(self);
    }
}

    func printEntries() {
        for id in entries.keys.array.sorted(<) {
            if let entry = entries[id] {
                println("#\(id): \(entry.counterParty) $\(entry.amount)");
            }
        }
        println("Total: $\(total)");
        println("----");
    }
}
```

It is important that the memento sets or re-creates every aspect of the state of the originator. In the case of the example application, this means I need to set the **nextId** and **total** properties directly and populate the dictionary of ledger entries.

Using the Memento

The final step is to obtain and use a memento in the **main.swift** file, which plays the role of the caretaker in the example. Listing 23-6 shows the changes I made.

Listing 23-6. Using a Memento in the main.swift File

```
let ledger = Ledger();

ledger.addEntry("Bob", amount: 100.43);
ledger.addEntry("Joe", amount: 200.20);

let memento = ledger.createMemento();

ledger.addEntry("Alice", amount: 500);
ledger.addEntry("Tony", amount: 20);

ledger.printEntries();

ledger.applyMemento(memento);

ledger.printEntries();
```

The memento restores the ledger to its earlier state. Running the application produces the following output:

```
#1: Bob $100.43
#2: Joe $200.2
#3: Alice $500.0
#4: Tony $20.0
Total: $820.63
----
#1: Bob $100.43
#2: Joe $200.2
Total: $300.63
```

The effect is the same as when I used the command pattern to create individual undo commands, but the implementation is more robust and flexible.

Variations on the Memento Pattern

The only common variation on the memento pattern is to represent the state of the originator so that it can be stored persistently. This allows the memento data to be sent to a remote server or stored in a database until it is required again.

You can use any data format that suits your project, but I tend to use JSON because it has become the de facto standard for representing objects, especially in web services. Apple provides JSON support through the **NSJSONSerialization** class, but the process of converting a Swift object to and from JSON is awkward. Listing 23-7 shows the changes I made to the **LedgerMemento** class so that it expresses the state data as JSON.

Listing 23-7. Expressing State as JSON in the Ledger.swift File

```
...
class LedgerMemento : Memento {
    let jsonData:String?;

    init(ledger:Ledger) {
        self.jsonData = stringify(ledger);
    }

    init(json:String?) {
        self.jsonData = json;
    }

private func stringify(ledger:Ledger) -> String? {

        var dict = NSMutableDictionary();
        dict["total"] = ledger.total;
        dict["nextId"] = ledger.nextId;
        dict["entries"] = ledger.entries.values.array;
        var entryArray = [NSDictionary]();
```

```
        for entry in ledger.entries.values {
        var entryDict = NSMutableDictionary();
            entryArray.append(entryDict);
            entryDict["id"] = entry.id;
            entryDict["counterParty"] = entry.counterParty;
            entryDict["amount"] = entry.amount;
        }
        dict["entries"] = entryArray;

        if let jsonData = NSJSONSerialization.dataWithJSONObject(dict,
                options: nil, error: nil) {
            return NSString(data: jsonData, encoding: NSUTF8StringEncoding);
        }
        return nil;
    }

    func apply (ledger:Ledger) {

        if let data = jsonData?.dataUsingEncoding(NSUTF8StringEncoding,
                    allowLossyConversion: false) {
            if let dict = NSJSONSerialization.JSONObjectWithData(data, options: nil,
                    error: nil) as? NSDictionary {
                ledger.total = dict["total"] as Float;
                ledger.nextId = dict["nextId"] as Int;
                ledger.entries.removeAll(keepCapacity: true);
                if let entryDicts = dict["entries"] as? [NSDictionary] {
                    for dict in entryDicts {
                        let id = dict["id"] as Int;
                        let counterParty = dict["counterParty"] as String;
                        let amount = dict["amount"] as Float;
                        ledger.entries[id] = LedgerEntry(id: id,
                            counterParty: counterParty, amount: amount);
                    }
                }
            }
        }
    }
}
...
```

Unfortunately, the **NSJSONSerialization** class operates only on foundation types, which means that I have to convert the state of a **Ledger** object into an **NSMutableDictionary** containing key-value pairs for each data item. I define keys for **total** and **nextId** and assign their values directly. To represent the ledger entries, I create an array of **NSMutableDictionary** objects, each of which contains key-value pairs for the **id**, **counterParty**, and **amount** properties. The result is a JSON string like this, which I have formatted to make it easier to read:

```
{ "total": 300.63,
  "nextId": 3,
  "entries": [
    { "id": 2, "counterParty": "Joe", "amount": 200.2 },
    { "id": 1,"counterParty": "Bob", "amount": 100.43}]
}
```

The process of parsing a JSON string to re-create the state of a **Ledger** object is equally awkward. The string is converted into a dictionary that is then processed to extract the data values. Overall, the process is difficult and error-prone, but I expect the JSON support for Swift to improve in future versions of Swift because it has become so prevalent as a data format. Listing 23-8 shows the changes that I made to the **main.swift** file to get hold of the JSON data and use it to set the state of an originator object.

Listing 23-8. Using a Persistent Memento in the main.swift File

```
let ledger = Ledger();

ledger.addEntry("Bob", amount: 100.43);
ledger.addEntry("Joe", amount: 200.20);

let memento = ledger.createMemento() as LedgerMemento;

let newMemento = LedgerMemento(json: memento.jsonData);
ledger.applyMemento(newMemento);

ledger.printEntries();
```

I have used two **LedgerMemento** objects to demonstrate how the JSON string can be used as a persistent representation of an object's state. Running the example application produces the following output:

```
#1: Bob $100.43
#2: Joe $200.2
Total: $300.63
```

Understanding the Pitfalls of the Memento Pattern

Most problems with the memento pattern arise when the implementation doesn't conform to the two rules I listed earlier in the chapter, such that the caretaker is able to change the state stored by the memento or the memento doesn't correctly set every aspect of the originator's state. As long as you bear these two rules in mind, you should not encounter any problems implementing the memento pattern.

Test carefully if you are using a data format such as JSON to persistently store mementos. As Listing 23-7 showed, generating and parsing the persistent representation for even a simple object can be complex and can produce hard-to-read code.

Examples of the Memento Pattern in Cocoa

Cocoa provides an implementation of the memento pattern through the **NSCoding** protocol. An originator object conforms to the protocol and works with an **NSCoder** object to produce a snapshot of its state. **NSCoder** can be subclassed to support different data formats, or the built-in implementations can be used. Listing 23-9 shows how I have changed the **Ledger** class so that it conforms to the protocol.

Listing 23-9. Conforming to the NSCoding Protocol in the Ledger.swift File

```
import Foundation;

class LedgerEntry {
    let id:Int;
    let counterParty:String;
    let amount:Float;

    init(id:Int, counterParty:String, amount:Float) {
        self.id = id; self.counterParty = counterParty; self.amount = amount;
    }
}

class LedgerMemento : Memento {

    let data:NSData;

    init(data:NSData) { self.data = data;}
}

class Ledger : NSObject, Originator, NSCoding {
    private var entries = [Int:LedgerEntry]();
    private var nextId = 1;
    var total:Float = 0;

    override init() {
        // do nothing - required to allow instances
        // to be created without a coder
    }

    required init(coder aDecoder: NSCoder) {
        self.total = aDecoder.decodeFloatForKey("total");
        self.nextId = aDecoder.decodeIntegerForKey("nextId");
        self.entries.removeAll(keepCapacity: true);
        if let entryArray = aDecoder.decodeDataObject()
                as AnyObject? as? [NSDictionary] {
```

```
        for entryDict in entryArray {
            let id = entryDict["id"] as Int;
            let counterParty = entryDict["counterParty"] as String;
            let amount = entryDict["amount"] as Float;
            self.entries[id] = LedgerEntry(id: id, counterParty: counterParty,
                amount: amount);
        }
    }
}

func encodeWithCoder(aCoder: NSCoder) {
    aCoder.encodeFloat(total, forKey: "total");
    aCoder.encodeInteger(nextId, forKey: "nextId");
    var entriesArray = [NSMutableDictionary]();
    for entry in self.entries.values {
        var dict = NSMutableDictionary();
        dict["id"] = entry.id;
        dict["counterParty"] = entry.counterParty;
        dict["amount"] = entry.amount;
        entriesArray.append(dict);
    }
    aCoder.encodeObject(entriesArray);
}

func createMemento() -> Memento {
    return LedgerMemento(data:
        NSKeyedArchiver.archivedDataWithRootObject(self));
}

func applyMemento(memento: Memento) {
    if let lmemento = memento as? LedgerMemento {
        if let obj = NSKeyedUnarchiver.unarchiveObjectWithData(lmemento.data)
                as? Ledger {
            self.total = obj.total;
            self.nextId = obj.nextId;
            self.entries = obj.entries;
        }
    }
}

func addEntry(counterParty:String, amount:Float) {
    let entry = LedgerEntry(id: nextId++, counterParty: counterParty,
        amount: amount);
    entries[entry.id] = entry;
    total += amount;
}
```

```
func printEntries() {
    for id in entries.keys.array.sorted(<) {
        if let entry = entries[id] {
            println("#\(id): \(entry.counterParty) $\(entry.amount)");
        }
    }
    println("Total: $\(total)");
    println("----");
}
}
```

> **Note**   The NSCoding protocol isn't the only way that Apple supports object persistence. You can also use the Core Data framework, which is a framework that allows objects to be stored persistently and manipulated. Wikipedia provides a nice overview of Core Data at http://en.wikipedia.org/wiki/Core_Data.

Using the **NSCoding** protocol means encoding the originator's state as an **NSData** object, so the first change is to make the **LedgerMemento** class a wrapper around an **NSData** object. I don't want to expose the technique the originator uses to represent its state to the caretaker, and the easiest way to do this is to keep using the **Memento** protocol.

A class that conforms to the NSCoding protocol must be derived from **NSObject**, which provides some of the features that are required to create mementos. The protocol defines the **encodeWithEncoder** method, which is used to create mementos. Rather like the JSON serialization I used earlier in the chapter, I have to represent the internal state of the originator as a set of key-value pairs, and you can see the obvious similarities in the method implementation, although individual objects are added to the memento through the methods of the encoder.

In the **createMemento** method specified by my **Originator** protocol, I select the coder that will be used to represent the data, like this:

```
...
func createMemento() -> Memento {
    return LedgerMemento(data: NSKeyedArchiver.archivedDataWithRootObject(self));
}
...
```

The NSKeyedArchiver is one of the built-in coder implementations provided by Apple, and calling its **archivedDataWithRootObject** method encodes the state of the originator within an NSData object that I wrap in a **LedgerMemento** and return as the method result.

The NSCoding protocol specifies a required initializer for decoding a memento. The initializer creates a new instance of the originator class from the memento rather than setting the state of an existing object, so I have to explicitly copy the data values in the **applyMemento** method, like this:

```
...
```

```
func applyMemento(memento: Memento) {
    if let lmemento = memento as? LedgerMemento {
        if let obj = NSKeyedUnarchiver.unarchiveObjectWithData(lmemento.data)
                as? Ledger {
            self.total = obj.total;
            self.nextId = obj.nextId;
            self.entries = obj.entries;
        }
    }
}
...
```

The required initializer is invoked by my call to the **unarchiveObjectWithData** method of the NSKeyedUnarchiver class, which accepts the **NSData** memento and decodes it so that I can read the key-value pairs and extract the state data it contains. Listing 23-10 shows the changes I made to the **main.swift** file to use the modified memento.

Listing 23-10. Using Coding in the main.swift File

```
let ledger = Ledger();

ledger.addEntry("Bob", amount: 100.43);
ledger.addEntry("Joe", amount: 200.20);

let memento = ledger.createMemento();

ledger.applyMemento(memento);

ledger.printEntries();
```

Running the example application produces the following results:

```
#1: Bob $100.43
#2: Joe $200.2
Total: $300.63
```

Applying the Pattern to the SportsStore Application

In this section, I am going to combine the command and memento patterns to replace the undo feature I added in Chapter 20 with the ability to reset the application entirely.

Most implementations of the memento pattern are based on taking and returning to multiple snapshots, but that is only one interpretation of how a memento should work. As I explained, the way that a memento works is entirely down to the implementation, and it need not contain the data values that an object contained. It can also be a trigger for some other kind of action, including discarding any changes made by the user and reloading the original data. In this case, the memento will be a command that calls a method that resets the data in the application.

Preparing the Example Application

In preparation for the pattern, I need to add a method to the **ProductDataStore** class that will reset the data and discard any changes made by the user. Listing 23-11 shows the addition I made.

Listing 23-11. Adding a Reset Method in the ProductDataStore.swift File

```
import Foundation

final class ProductDataStore {
    var callback:((Product) -> Void)?;
    private var networkQ:dispatch_queue_t
    private var uiQ:dispatch_queue_t;
    lazy var products:[Product] = self.loadData();

    init() {
        networkQ = dispatch_get_global_queue(DISPATCH_QUEUE_PRIORITY_BACKGROUND, 0);
        uiQ = dispatch_get_main_queue();
    }

    func resetState() {

        self.products = loadData();
    }

    // ...method and statements omitted for brevity...
}
```

Implementing the Pattern

To add support for resetting the application, all I need to do is define a method that the **NSUndoManager** will invoke when the device is shaken and that will, in turn, call the **resetState** method that I defined in Listing 23-11. Listing 23-12 shows the change that I made to the **ViewController** class.

Listing 23-12. Adding Support for Resetting the Application in the ViewController.swift File

```
...
class ViewController: UIViewController, UITableViewDataSource {

    @IBOutlet weak var totalStockLabel: UILabel!
    @IBOutlet weak var tableView: UITableView!

    let productStore = ProductDataStore();

    // ...methods omitted for brevity...

    @IBAction func stockLevelDidChange(sender: AnyObject) {
        if var currentCell = sender as? UIView {
            while (true) {
                currentCell = currentCell.superview!;
```

```
                    if let cell = currentCell as? ProductTableCell {
                        if let product = cell.product? {

//                          let dict = NSDictionary(objects: [product.stockLevel],
//                              forKeys: [product.name]);

                            undoManager?.registerUndoWithTarget(self,
                                selector: "resetState",
                                object: nil);

                            if let stepper = sender as? UIStepper {
                                product.stockLevel = Int(stepper.value);
                            } else if let textfield = sender as? UITextField {
                                if let newValue = textfield.text.toInt()? {
                                    product.stockLevel = newValue;
                                }
                            }
//                              cell.stockStepper.value = Double(product.stockLevel);
//                              cell.stockField.text = String(product.stockLevel);
                            productLogger.logItem(product);

                            StockServerFactory.getStockServer()
                                .setStockLevel(product.name,
                                    stockLevel: product.stockLevel);
                        }
                        break;
                    }
                }
            displayStockTotal();
        }
    }

func resetState() {

self.productStore.resetState();

    }

//    func undoStockLevel(data:[String:Int]) {
//        let productName = data.keys.first;
//        if (productName != nil) {

//            let stockLevel = data[productName!];
//            if (stockLevel != nil) {
//
//                for nproduct in productStore.products {
//                    if nproduct.name == productName! {
//                        nproduct.stockLevel = stockLevel!;
//                    }
//                }
//
```

```
//                updateStockLevel(productName!, level: stockLevel!);
//            }
//        }
//    }

    func displayStockTotal() {
        let finalTotals:(Int, Double) = productStore.products.reduce((0, 0.0),
            {(totals, product) -> (Int, Double) in
                return (
                    totals.0 + product.stockLevel,
                    totals.1 + product.stockValue
                );
            });

        let formatted = StockTotalFacade.formatCurrencyAmount(finalTotals.1,
            currency: StockTotalFacade.Currency.EUR);

        totalStockLabel.text = "\(finalTotals.0) Products in Stock. "
            + "Total Value: \(formatted!)";
    }
}
...
```

I changed the selector for the undo manager callback so that it calls the **resetState** method and so that shaking the device triggers a reload of the product data, which has the effect of discarding any changes made by the user. To test the changes, start the application and make some changes to the stock levels. Select Shake Gesture from the iOS Simulator Hardware menu, and the values will be reset.

Summary

In this chapter I showed you how to describe and apply the state of an object using the memento pattern. This is one of the least used patterns and tends to be overshadowed by the more general command pattern, but the idea of describing the entire state of an object can be a powerful one. In the next chapter, I describe the strategy pattern, which defines classes that can be extended without being modified or subclassed.

Chapter 24

The Strategy Pattern

The strategy pattern is used to create classes whose functionality can be extended without being modified or subclassed, which can be useful when you are delivering frameworks to third-party developers or when any changes, however small, to key classes will trigger extensive and expensive testing and validation procedures. Table 24-1 puts the strategy pattern into context.

Table 24-1. Putting the Strategy Pattern into Context

Question	Answer
What is it?	The strategy pattern is used to create classes that can be extended without modification, through the application of algorithm objects that conform to a well-defined protocol.
What are the benefits?	The strategy pattern allows third-party developers to change the behavior of classes without modifying them and can allow low-cost changes to be made in projects that have expensive and lengthy validation procedures for specific classes.
When should you use this pattern?	Use this pattern when you need classes that can be extended without being modified.
When should you avoid this pattern?	There is no reason to avoid this pattern.
How do you know when you have implemented the pattern correctly?	The strategy pattern is implemented correctly when you can extend the behavior of a class by defining and applying a new strategy without needing to make any changes to the class itself.
Are there any common pitfalls?	No. The strategy pattern is simple to implement.
Are there any related patterns?	The strategy and visitor patterns are often used together.

Preparing the Example Project

For this chapter, I created an Xcode OS X Command Line Tool project called Strategy. I added a file called **Sequence.swift** and used it to define the class shown in Listing 24-1.

Listing 24-1. The Contents of the Sequence.swift File

```swift
class Sequence {
    private var numbers:[Int];

    init(_ numbers:Int...) {
        self.numbers = numbers;
    }

    func addNumber(value:Int) {
        self.numbers.append(value);
    }

    func compute() -> Int {
        return numbers.reduce(0, combine: {$0 + $1});
    }
}
```

The **Sequence** class maintains an array of **Int** values that are defined through the initializer and added to through the **addNumber** method. The **compute** method uses the **reduce** function to sum the values and return a result. Listing 24-2 shows the code I added to the **main.swift** file to consume the **Sequence** class.

Listing 24-2. The Contents of the main.swift File

```swift
let sequence = Sequence(1, 2, 3, 4);
sequence.addNumber(10);
sequence.addNumber(20);

let sum = sequence.compute();
println("Sum: \(sum)");
```

I create a **Sequence** object, call the **addNumber** method twice, and then call the **compute** method to produce the total, which I write to the Xcode console. Running the application produces the following output:

```
Sum: 40
```

Understanding the Problem That the Pattern Solves

The **Sequence** class that I defined in the example application contains a simple algorithm. When the **compute** method is called, the **reduce** method is used to add together all of the **Int** values in the collection.

If I want to add another algorithm, then I have a choice. I can modify the code of the **Sequence** class to add the new algorithm alongside the existing one, or I can create a new subclass that overrides the existing algorithm and effectively replaces it.

Modifying or subclassing to add features runs counter to the open/closed design principle, which states that classes should be open to being extended and should be closed to being modified, or, put another way, that is preferable to be able to add to the functionality provided by a class without needing to modify it or to create a new subclass.

There is nothing intrinsically wrong with modifying source code or creating new subclasses, but for some projects, doing so can trigger requirements for extensive unit, system, and integration testing before a change can be deployed into a production system. This process is often driven by regulatory requirements or sometimes by a corporate policy that places the emphasis on quality rather than time to market. To set the scene for the chapter, Listing 24-3 shows a simple change applied to the **Sequence** class to define a second algorithm.

Listing 24-3. Defining a New Algorithm in the Sequence.swift File

```swift
enum ALGORITHM {
    case ADD; case MULTIPLY;
}

class Sequence {
    private var numbers:[Int];

    init(_ numbers:Int...) {
        self.numbers = numbers;
    }

    func addNumber(value:Int) {
        self.numbers.append(value);
    }

    func compute(algorithm:ALGORITHM) -> Int {
        switch (algorithm) {
            case .ADD:
                return numbers.reduce(0, combine: {$0 + $1});
            case .MULTIPLY:
                return numbers.reduce(1, combine: {$0 * $1});
        }
    }
}
```

There are lots of ways I could have added the new algorithm, but I have chosen to define a enumeration that specifies the algorithm, which I then use in a **switch** statement in the **compute** method. In projects that have a heavy-weight testing and validation process, the simple addition of a multiplication algorithm would trigger weeks of expensive testing. For completeness, Listing 24-4 shows the corresponding changes to the **main.swift** file to use the new **Sequence** feature.

Listing 24-4. Using the New Sequence Algorithm in the main.swift File

```swift
let sequence = Sequence(1, 2, 3, 4);
sequence.addNumber(10);
sequence.addNumber(20);

let sum = sequence.compute(ALGORITHM.ADD);
println("Sum: \(sum)");

let multiply = sequence.compute(ALGORITHM.MULTIPLY);
println("Multiply: \(multiply)");
```

Running the example application produces the following results:

```
Sum: 40
Multiply: 4800
```

Understanding the Strategy Pattern

The strategy pattern supports the open/closed principle by defining a protocol to which different algorithm classes can conform. This allows for the algorithm to be selected and changed at runtime and for new algorithms to be added to the application without needing to change the class that uses them. Figure 24-1 illustrates the strategy pattern.

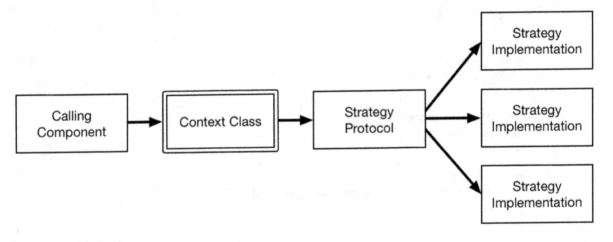

Figure 24-1. The strategy pattern

In the strategy pattern, the class that is being extended is known as the *context class*. Rather than implementing a feature directly, the context class delegates its implementation to a class that conforms to the strategy protocol. The strategy pattern doesn't specify how a specific strategy implementation class is selected, but the most common approach is to let the calling component make the choice.

Implementing the Strategy Pattern

The heart of the strategy pattern is the protocol that is used to specify an algorithm. Listing 24-5 shows the contents of the **Strategies.swift** file, which I added to the example project.

Listing 24-5. The Contents of the Strategies.swift File

```
protocol Strategy {
    func execute(values:[Int]) -> Int;
}
```

The strategy protocol doesn't specify any aspect of an algorithm other than the inputs and outputs. In this case, the strategy operates on an **Int** array and produces a single **Int** value.

Defining the Strategies and the Context Class

The next step is to define strategy classes for each of the algorithms required by the application. Listing 24-6 shows the classes I defined for the example applications.

Listing 24-6. Defining the Strategy Classes in the Strategies.swift File

```
protocol Strategy {
    func execute(values:[Int]) -> Int;
}

class SumStrategy: Strategy {

    func execute(values: [Int]) -> Int {
        return values.reduce(0, combine: {$0 + $1});
    }
}

class MultiplyStrategy: Strategy {

    func execute(values: [Int]) -> Int {
        return values.reduce(1, combine: {$0 * $1});
    }
}
```

I have defined strategies that sum and multiply the **Int** values, each of which conforms to the **Strategy** protocol. You can see how the strategy protocol is used in the context class in Listing 24-7, which shows how I replaced the directly implementing algorithms with delegation to a strategy that is specified as an argument to the **compute** method.

Listing 24-7. Delegating to a Strategy in the Sequence.swift File

```
final class Sequence {
    private var numbers:[Int];

    init(_ numbers:Int...) {
        self.numbers = numbers;
    }

    func addNumber(value:Int) {
        self.numbers.append(value);
    }

    func compute(strategy:Strategy) -> Int {
        return strategy.execute(self.numbers);
    }
}
```

The objective when implementing the strategy pattern is to define a context class that doesn't need to be modified or subclassed. In addition to revising the **compute** method, I have marked the class as **final**.

Consuming the Pattern

The final step is to revise the calling component so that it selects strategies. I have followed the most common approach in my implementation, which is to have the calling component create instances of the strategy implementation objects and pass them to the context class, as shown in Listing 24-8.

Listing 24-8. Selecting and Using Strategies in the main.swift File

```
let sequence = Sequence(1, 2, 3, 4);
sequence.addNumber(10);
sequence.addNumber(20);

let sumStrategy = SumStrategy();
let multiplyStrategy = MultiplyStrategy();

let sum = sequence.compute(sumStrategy);
println("Sum: \(sum)");

let multiply = sequence.compute(multiplyStrategy);
println("Multiply: \(multiply)");
```

Running the example application produces the following output:

```
Sum: 40
Multiply: 4800
```

Variations on the Strategy Pattern

Swift makes it easy to define strategies as closures rather than as objects that conform to a protocol. The advantage of using closures is that a calling component can close on its own methods and properties to define more complex strategies. The drawback of closures is that they can be harder to read, and passing them around as objects requires close attention to detail.

A compromise approach is to create a class that conforms to a strategy protocol but that relies on a closure as its implementation. Listing 24-9 shows the addition I made to the **Strategies.swift** file to define such a class.

Listing 24-9. Defining a Closure Strategy Class in the Strategies.swift File

```
protocol Strategy {

    func execute(values:[Int]) -> Int;
}

class ClosureStrategy : Strategy {
    private let closure:[Int] -> Int;

    init(_ closure:[Int] -> Int) {
        self.closure = closure;
    }

    func execute(values: [Int]) -> Int {
        return self.closure(values);
    }
}

class SumStrategy: Strategy {

    func execute(values: [Int]) -> Int {
        return values.reduce(0, combine: {$0 + $1});
    }
}

class MultiplyStrategy: Strategy {

    func execute(values: [Int]) -> Int {
        return values.reduce(1, combine: {$0 * $1});
    }
}
```

The **ClosureStrategy** class conforms to the **Strategy** protocol and accepts a closure as its initializer argument, which is then used in the implementation of the **execute** method. Listing 24-10 shows how I can use the **ClosureStrategy** class to close on a property in the **main.swift** file.

Listing 24-10. Using a Closure in the main.swift File

```
let sequence = Sequence(1, 2, 3, 4);
sequence.addNumber(10);
sequence.addNumber(20);

let sumStrategy = SumStrategy();
let multiplyStrategy = MultiplyStrategy();

let sum = sequence.compute(sumStrategy);
println("Sum: \(sum)");

let multiply = sequence.compute(multiplyStrategy);
println("Multiply: \(multiply)");

let filterThreshold = 10;
let cstrategy = ClosureStrategy({values in
    return values.filter({ $0 < filterThreshold }).reduce(0, {$0 + $1});
});
let filteredSum = sequence.compute(cstrategy);
println("Filtered Sum: \(filteredSum)");
```

I use the **ClosureStrategy** class to close on the **filterThreshold** constant and use it to select a subset of values to sum. Running the application produces the following results:

```
Sum: 40
Multiply: 4800
Filtered Sum: 10
```

Understanding the Pitfalls of the Strategy Pattern

There are no pitfalls associated with the strategy pattern, which is simple to implement and use.

Examples of the Strategy Pattern in Cocoa

The strategy pattern is used extensively in Cocoa to allow the behavior of framework classes to be changed without modification or subclassing. The Cocoa implementations of strategies tend to fall into two categories: those defined by protocols and those defined by selectors. I give an example of each in the sections that follow.

Cocoa Protocol-Based Strategies

Cocoa uses protocols to define strategies for its UI components, and one of the classic examples is using a protocol to define the strategy for generating rows in a table view. The class that implements the table view is called **UITableView**, and it relies on a class that conforms to the **UITableViewDataSource** protocol to implement the strategy for providing data, allowing third-party developers to extend the behavior of the **UITableView** class without needing to modify it or to create a subclass. As a simple demonstration, I created an Xcode iOS playground called **ProtocolStrategy.playground** and used it to define the code shown in Listing 24-11.

Listing 24-11. The Contents of the ProtocolStrategy.playground File

```
import UIKit

class DataSourceStrategy : NSObject, UITableViewDataSource {
    let data:[Printable];

    init(_ data:Printable...) {
        self.data = data;
    }

    func tableView(tableView: UITableView,
            numberOfRowsInSection section: Int) -> Int {
        return data.count;
    }

    func tableView(tableView: UITableView,
            cellForRowAtIndexPath indexPath: NSIndexPath) -> UITableViewCell {

        let cell = UITableViewCell();
        cell.textLabel.text = data[indexPath.row].description;
        return cell;

    }
}

let dataSource = DataSourceStrategy("London", "New York", "Paris", "Rome");
let table = UITableView(frame: CGRectMake(0, 0, 400, 200));
table.dataSource = dataSource;
table.reloadData();

// required for display in assistant editor
table;
```

I have defined a class called **DataSourceStrategy** that conforms to the **UITableViewDataSource** protocol and implements the two methods required to provide data values from an array of **Printable** objects. I create an instance of the strategy class and use it as the data source for a **UITableView** object, producing the result shown in Figure 24-2.

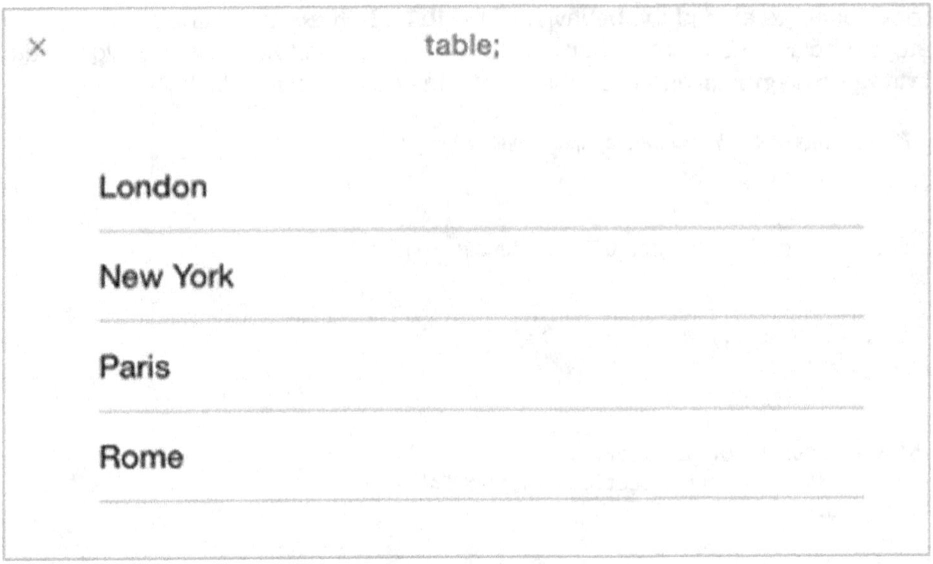

Figure 24-2. Using a protocol-based UIKit strategy

Cocoa Selector-Based Strategies

Not all Cocoa classes rely on protocols to define strategies. Some use selectors to specify methods that are called on to extend the functionality of a class. As a demonstration, I created an Xcode OS X playground called **SelectorStrategy.playground**, which is shown in Listing 24-12.

Listing 24-12. The Contents of the SelectorStrategy.playground File

```
import Foundation;

@objc class City {
    let name:String;

    init(_ name:String) {
        self.name = name;
    }

    func compareTo(other:City) -> NSComparisonResult {
        if (self.name == other.name) {
            return NSComparisonResult.OrderedSame;
        } else if (self.name < other.name) {
            return NSComparisonResult.OrderedDescending;
        } else {
            return NSComparisonResult.OrderedAscending;
        }
    }
}
```

```
let nsArray = NSArray(array: [City("London"), City("New York"), City("Paris"), City("Rome")]);
let sorted = nsArray.sortedArrayUsingSelector("compareTo:");

for city in sorted {
    println(city.name);
}
```

The **NSArray** class can be used to sort its contents using a selector to refer to the method that defines the strategy for comparing two objects. In the example, I define an object called **City** that has a method called **compareTo**. The **compareTo** method accepts another **City** object and compares it to the current instance, returning a value from the **NSComparisonResult** enumeration.

I define an **NSArray** of **City** objects and sort the array by calling the **sortedArrayUsingSelector** method, specifying that the **compareTo** method contains the strategy for comparing **City** objects. The result is a sorted array of objects written to the console, as follows:

```
Rome
Paris
New York
London
```

Applying the Pattern to the SportsStore Application

The SportsStore application already relies on the strategy pattern because the **ViewController** class implements the **UITableViewDataSource** protocol in order to provide data items to a **UITableView** component.

```
...
class ViewController: UIViewController, UITableViewDataSource {
...
```

Summary

I described the strategy design pattern in this chapter, which is used to extend the functionality of a class without modifying it or creating a new subclass. In the next chapter, I describe the visitor pattern, which allows the behavior of collection classes to be extended without modification or subclassing.

Chapter 25

The Visitor Pattern

The visitor pattern is similar to the strategy pattern in that it allows the behavior of a class to be extended without modifying its source code or creating a new subclass, except that the visitor pattern is applied to collections of heterogeneous objects. Table 25-1 puts the visitor pattern into context.

Table 25-1. *Putting the Visitor Pattern into Context*

Question	Answer
What is it?	The visitor pattern allows new algorithms to operate on collections of heterogeneous objects without needing to modify or subclass the collection class.
What are the benefits?	The visitor pattern is useful when you want to provide collection classes as part of frameworks without requiring third-party developers to modify the source code. This pattern is also useful in projects where modifying core classes triggers expensive testing procedures.
When should you use this pattern?	Use this pattern when you have classes that manage collections of mismatched objects and you want to perform operations on them.
When should you avoid this pattern?	There is no need to use this pattern when all of the objects are of the same type or when the collection class can be readily modified.
How do you know when you have implemented the pattern correctly?	The pattern is implemented correctly when a visitor class can extend the behavior of the collection class by defining methods that handle each type of object in the collection.
Are there any common pitfalls?	The only pitfall is trying to avoid using the double dispatch technique, which I describe in the "Understanding Double Dispatch" sidebar.
Are there any related patterns?	The visitor pattern is another way to conform to the open/closed principle supported by the strategy pattern I described in Chapter 24.

Preparing the Example Project

For this chapter I created an OS X Command Line Tool project called Visitor. I added a file called **Shapes.swift** and used it to define the classes shown in Listing 25-1.

Listing 25-1. The Contents of the Shapes.swift File

```
import Foundation;

class Circle {
    let radius:Float;

    init(radius:Float) {
        self.radius = radius;
    }
}

class Square {
    let length:Float;

    init(length:Float) {
        self.length = length;
    }
}

class Rectangle {
    let xLen:Float;
    let yLen:Float;

    init(x:Float, y:Float) {
        self.xLen = x;
        self.yLen = y;
    }
}

class ShapeCollection {
    let shapes:[Any];

    init() {
        shapes = [
            Circle(radius: 2.5), Square(length: 4), Rectangle(x: 10, y: 2)
        ];
    }

    func calculateAreas() -> Float {
        return shapes.reduce(0, combine: {total, shape in
            if let circle = shape as? Circle {
                println("Found Circle");
                return total + (3.14 * powf(circle.radius, 2));
            } else if let square = shape as? Square {
                println("Found Square");
                return total + powf(square.length, 2);
```

```
            } else if let rect = shape as? Rectangle {
                println("Found Rectangle");
                return total + (rect.xLen * rect.yLen);
            } else {
                // unknown type - do nothing
                return total;
            }
        });
    }
}
```

I have defined three classes that represent shapes—**Circle**, **Square**, and **Rectangle**—and a class called **ShapeCollection** that manages a collection of shape objects. The **ShapeCollection** class contains a method called **calculateAreas** that enumerates the collection and calculates the total area of the shapes it contains. Listing 25-2 shows the code I defined in the **main.swift** file to demonstrate the example classes.

Listing 25-2. The Contents of the main.swift File

```
let shapes = ShapeCollection();
let area = shapes.calculateAreas();
println("Area: \(area)");
```

Running the application produces the following results:

```
Found Circle
Found Square
Found Rectangle
Area: 55.625
```

Understanding the Problem That the Pattern Solves

In the example application, the **ShapeCollection** class manages a heterogeneous collection of objects that do not share a common base class or conform to a common protocol. To perform operations on the objects in the collection, I have to try to cast each object to different types, which leads to a set of conditional statements like the one in the **calculateAreas** method.

```
...
func calculateAreas() -> Float {
    return shapes.reduce(0, combine: {total, shape in
        if let circle = shape as? Circle {
            println("Found Circle");
            return total + (3.14 * powf(circle.radius, 2));
        } else if let square = shape as? Square {
            println("Found Square");
            return total + powf(square.length, 2);
```

```
        } else if let rect = shape as? Rectangle {
            println("Found Rectangle");
            return total + (rect.xLen * rect.yLen);
        } else {
            // unknown type - do nothing
            return total;
        }
    });
}
...
```

Each time I add a new feature, I have to modify or subclass the **ShapeCollection** class and create another set of conditional statements that cast each object in the collection. Not only will this trigger comprehensive and expensive testing in some projects, but it will also produce code that is duplicative, inflexible, and error-prone. Listing 25-3 shows how I added another method to the **ShapeCollection** class.

Listing 25-3. Adding a New Method to the ShapeCollection Class in the Shapes.swift File

```
...
class ShapeCollection {
    let shapes:[Any];

    init() {
        shapes = [
            Circle(radius: 2.5), Square(length: 4), Rectangle(x: 10, y: 2)
        ];
    }

    func calculateAreas() -> Float {
        return shapes.reduce(0, combine: {total, shape in
            if let circle = shape as? Circle {
                println("Found Circle");
                return total + (3.14 * powf(circle.radius, 2));
            } else if let square = shape as? Square {
                println("Found Square");
                return total + powf(square.length, 2);
            } else if let rect = shape as? Rectangle {
                println("Found Rectangle");
                return total + (rect.xLen * rect.yLen);
            } else {
                // unknown type - do nothing
                return total;
            }
        });
    }

    func countEdges() -> Int {
        return shapes.reduce(0, combine: {total, shape in
            if let circle = shape as? Circle {
                println("Found Circle");
                return total + 1;
```

```
            } else if let square = shape as? Square {
                println("Found Square");
                return total + 4;
            } else if let rect = shape as? Rectangle {
                println("Found Rectangle");
                return total + 4;
            } else {
                // unknown type - do nothing
                return total;
            }
        });
    }
}
...
```

The new method is called **countEdges**, and it totals the number of shape edges in the collection. Listing 25-4 shows the statements I added to the **main.swift** file to test the new method.

Listing 25-4. Using the New Method in the main.swift File

```
let shapes = ShapeCollection();
let area = shapes.calculateAreas();
println("Area: \(area)");
println("---");
let edges = shapes.countEdges();
println("Edges: \(edges)");
```

Running the application produces the following results:

```
Found Circle
Found Square
Found Rectangle
Area: 55.625
---
Found Circle
Found Square
Found Rectangle
Edges: 9
```

Each new feature faces the same problem when enumerating the objects in the collection, producing similarly ugly code.

Understanding the Visitor Pattern

The visitor pattern solves the problem by separating the algorithm that operates on the collection into a separate object and ensures that it defines methods that can handle each collected type. This allows the algorithm to be selected at runtime, which means that new behavior can be defined without having to modify or subclass the type that maintains the collection, conforming to the open/closed principle I described in Chapter 23.

Ensuring that the algorithm object has a method to handle each collected type avoids the conditional casting code and relies on the built-in type management features of Swift to select the right method to process a collection object. Figure 25-1 illustrates the visitor pattern.

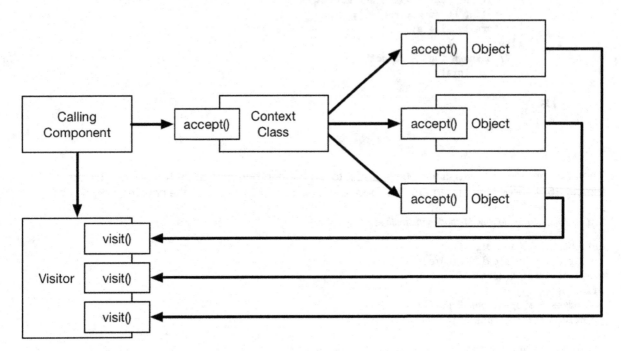

Figure 25-1. The visitor pattern

The *visitor* is a class that defines methods called **visit** that receive each of the types in the collection managed by the context class. The calling component provides the visitor to the context class, which in turn passes it on to the **accept** method defined by each object in the collection. Upon receipt of the visitor, each object calls the **visit** method, relying on Swift to select the right version of the method; this is a technique known as *double dispatch*. Don't worry if this double method invocation doesn't make sense; it will become more obvious when you see the implementation code in the next section, and I explain the reason that double dispatch works in the "Understanding Double Dispatch" sidebar.

Implementing the Visitor Pattern

The starting point to implementing the visitor pattern is to create protocols that define the visitor and ensure that the objects in the collection implement an **accept** method. Listing 25-5 shows the contents of the **Visitor.swift** file, which I added to the example project.

Listing 25-5. The Contents of the Visitor.swift File

```
import Foundation;

protocol Shape {
    func accept(visitor:Visitor);
}

protocol Visitor {
    func visit(shape:Circle);
    func visit(shape:Square);
    func visit(shape:Rectangle);
}
```

The **Shape** protocol defines the **accept** method, and the **Visitor** protocol defines **visit** methods that accept each of the shape types in the application, which is essential for double dispatch to work.

UNDERSTANDING DOUBLE DISPATCH

Double dispatch underpins the visitor pattern, and it relies on Swift to select a method based on the parameter type. Consider the following protocol and classes:

```
...
protocol MyProtocol {
    func dispatch(handler:Handler);
}

class FirstClass : MyProtocol {
    func dispatch(handler: Handler) {
        handler.handle(self);
    }
}

class SecondClass : MyProtocol {
    func dispatch(handler: Handler) {
        handler.handle(self)
    }
}
...
```

The **FirstClass** and **SecondClass** both conform to **MyProtocol**. The **dispatch** method defined by the protocol and implemented by the classes is the key to the double dispatch technique, although the best way to understand double dispatch is to see what happens without it. Here is the definition of the **Handler** class that is accepted by the **dispatch** method:

```
...
class Handler {
    func handle(arg:MyProtocol) {
        println("Protocol");
    }

    func handle(arg:FirstClass) {
        println("First Class");
    }

    func handle(arg:SecondClass) {
        println("Second Class");
    }
}
...
```

Consider what happens when I create an array of **FirstClass** and **SecondClass** objects and pass them to a **Handler** object, like this:

```
...
let objects:[MyProtocol] = [FirstClass(), SecondClass()];
let handler = Handler();

for object in objects {
    handler.handle(object);
}
...
```

This is regular single dispatch, in which I simply call the method of the **Handler** object for each of the objects in the array. To be able to store a **FirstClass** object and a **SecondClass** object in the same array, I have to specify its type as **MyProtocol**, and this affects the version of the **handle** method selected by Swift in the **for** loop, producing the following results:

```
Protocol
Protocol
```

Both objects are dealt with using the type of the array. To enable double dispatch, I have to change the method call in the **for** loop, like this:

```
...
for object in objects {
    object.dispatch(handler);
}
...
```

The **dispatch** method implementations result in the **Handler.handle** method being called from within the classes, but with the **self** argument. The effect is to call the version of the **handle** method with the most specific type, producing the following results:

```
First Class
Second Class
```

Calling the **handle** method from within an objects method has the effect of calling the method version with the most specific argument type without needing to perform any casts, which is the central technique in the visitor pattern.

Conforming to the Shape Protocol

The next step is to update the shape classes so they confirm to the **Shape** pattern. As Listing 25-6 shows, each shape class has the same implementation of the **accept** method.

Listing 25-6. Conforming to the Shape Protocol in the Shapes.swift File

```
import Foundation;

class Circle : Shape {
    let radius:Float;

    init(radius:Float) {
        self.radius = radius;
    }

    func accept(visitor: Visitor) {
        visitor.visit(self);
    }
}

class Square : Shape {
    let length:Float;

    init(length:Float) {
        self.length = length;
    }
```

```
        func accept(visitor: Visitor) {
            visitor.visit(self);
        }
}

class Rectangle : Shape {
    let xLen:Float;
    let yLen:Float;

    init(x:Float, y:Float) {
        self.xLen = x;
        self.yLen = y;
    }

    func accept(visitor: Visitor) {
visitor.visit(self);

    }
}

class ShapeCollection {
let shapes:[Shape];

    init() {
        shapes = [
            Circle(radius: 2.5), Square(length: 4), Rectangle(x: 10, y: 2)
        ];
    }

    func accept(visitor: Visitor) {
        for shape in shapes {
            shape.accept(visitor);
        }
    }
}
```

> **Tip** I have modified the collection classes directly to conform to the protocol, but don't forget you can use Swift extensions to add protocol conformance to classes without modifying them.

I have also added an **accept** method to the **ShapeCollection** class, which receives a **Visitor** object and calls the **accept** method of each object in the collection, which I have changed to a **Shape** array.

Creating the Visitors

With the basic infrastructure in place, I can create the visitor classes that operate on the collection of shape objects, as shown in Listing 25-7.

Listing 25-7. Defining the Visitors in the Visitor.swift File

```swift
import Foundation;

protocol Shape {
    func accept(visitor:Visitor);
}

protocol Visitor {
    func visit(shape:Circle);
    func visit(shape:Square);
    func visit(shape:Rectangle);
}

class AreaVisitor : Visitor {
    var totalArea:Float = 0;

    func visit(shape: Circle) {
        totalArea += (3.14 * powf(shape.radius, 2));
    }

    func visit(shape: Square) {
        totalArea += powf(shape.length, 2);
    }

    func visit(shape: Rectangle) {
        totalArea += (shape.xLen * shape.yLen);
    }
}

class EdgesVisitor : Visitor {
    var totalEdges = 0;

    func visit(shape: Circle) {
        totalEdges += 1;
    }

    func visit(shape: Square) {
        totalEdges += 4;
    }

    func visit(shape: Rectangle) {
        totalEdges += 4;
    }
}
```

The use of double dispatch means that the appropriate version of the **visit** method will be called for each object in the collection. This means I can access the type-specific properties defined by the shape classes, without having to cast from one type to another.

Applying the Visitors

The final step is to update the calling component to create and use **Visitor** objects to operate on the collection. Listing 25-8 shows the changes I made to the **main.swift** file.

Listing 25-8. Using the Visitors in the main.swift File

```
let shapes = ShapeCollection();
let areaVisitor = AreaVisitor();
shapes.accept(areaVisitor);
println("Area: \(areaVisitor.totalArea)");
println("---");
let edgeVisitor = EdgesVisitor();
shapes.accept(edgeVisitor);
println("Edges: \(edgeVisitor.totalEdges)");
```

Running the application produces the following results:

```
Area: 55.625
---
Edges: 9
```

New algorithms can be defined by creating new visitors and passing them to the **accept** method. In this way, new behaviors and features can be created without needing to modify or subclass the collection class.

Variations on the Visitor Pattern

There are no common variations on the visitor pattern.

Understanding the Pitfalls of the Visitor Pattern

The only pitfall when implementing the visitor pattern is to try to sidestep the use of double dispatch. Although this technique looks awkward, it is not possible to implement the visitor pattern without it.

Examples of the Visitor Pattern in Cocoa

The Cocoa frameworks do not contain examples of the visitor pattern.

Applying the Pattern to the SportsStore Application

There is no suitable heterogeneous collection in the SportsStore application to which the visitor pattern can be applied.

Summary

I described the visitor pattern in this chapter and explained how it can be used to extend the behavior of heterogeneous collections without having to modify or subclass the collection class. In Chapter 26, I describe the template method pattern, which allows steps in an algorithm to be selectively replaced.

The Template Method Pattern

The template method pattern allows for individual steps in an algorithm to be changed, which is useful when you are writing classes with default behavior that you want to allow to be changed by other developers. This is a simple pattern to understand and to implement, but it is widely used and can be found throughout most public frameworks, including those provided by Apple. Table 26-1 puts the template method pattern into context.

Table 26-1. *Putting the Template Method Pattern into Context*

Question	Answer
What is it?	The template method pattern allows specific steps in an algorithm to be replaced by implementations provided by a third-party, either by specifying functions as closures or by creating a subclass.
What are the benefits?	This pattern is useful when you are writing frameworks that you want to allow other developers to extend and customize.
When should you use this pattern?	Use this pattern to selectively permit steps in any algorithm to be changed without modifying the original class.
When should you avoid this pattern?	Do not use this pattern if the entire algorithm can be changed. See the other patterns in this part of the book for alternatives.
How do you know when you have implemented the pattern correctly?	This pattern is implemented correctly when selected steps in an algorithm can be changed without modifying the class that defines the algorithm.
Are there any common pitfalls?	No.
Are there any related patterns?	This pattern has similar goals to the strategy and visitor patterns I described in Chapters 24 and 25.

Preparing the Example Project

For this chapter I created an Xcode OS X Command Line Tool project called TemplateMethod. I created a file called **Donors.swift**, the contents of which are shown in Listing 26-1.

Listing 26-1. The Contents of the Donors.swift File

```swift
struct Donor {
    let title:String;
    let firstName:String;
    let familyName:String;
    let lastDonation:Float;

    init (_ title:String, _ first:String, _ family:String, _ last:Float) {
        self.title = title;
        self.firstName = first;
        self.familyName = family;
        self.lastDonation = last;
    }
}

class DonorDatabase {
    private var donors:[Donor];

    init() {
        donors = [
            Donor("Ms", "Anne", "Jones", 0),
            Donor("Mr", "Bob", "Smith", 100),
            Donor("Dr", "Alice", "Doe", 200),
            Donor("Prof", "Joe", "Davis", 320)];
    }

    func generateGalaInvitations(maxNumber:Int) -> [String] {

        // step 1 - filter out non-donors
        var targetDonors:[Donor] = donors.filter({$0.lastDonation > 0});

        // step 2 - order donors by last donation
        targetDonors.sort({ $0.lastDonation > $1.lastDonation});

        // step 3 - limit the number of invitees
        if (targetDonors.count > maxNumber) {
            targetDonors = Array(targetDonors[0..<maxNumber]);
        }

        // step 4 - generate the invitations
        return targetDonors.map({ donor in
            return "Dear \(donor.title). \(donor.familyName)";
        })
    }
}
```

The example for this chapter is based on an imaginary charity that solicits contributions from donors. Each donor is represented by a **Donor** object, and the set of objects is collected by the **DonorDatabase** class.

The **DonorDatabase** class defines a **generateGalaInvitations** method that processes the **Donor** objects to generate salutations for invitations to a gala concert. Listing 26-2 shows the code I added to the **main.swift** file to generate the set of salutations.

Listing 26-2. The Contents of the main.swift File

```
let donorDb = DonorDatabase();

let galaInvitations = donorDb.generateGalaInvitations(2);
for invite in galaInvitations {
    println(invite);
}
```

Running the example produces the following output in the Xcode console:

```
Dear Prof. Davis
Dear Dr. Doe
```

Understanding the Problem That the Pattern Solves

The algorithm for generating greetings for the gala has four distinct stages.

1. Filtering out those donors who have not made a donation

2. Sorting the donors by their recent donations

3. Selecting the number of donors for which there are invitations

4. Generating the salutations for the invitations

These are the same four basic steps that the charity will need to perform in order to generate greetings for any communication with the donors: *filter*, *sort*, *select*, and *generate*. The problem addressed by the template method pattern is a variation of the problem addressed by the strategy and visitor patterns I described in Chapters 24 and 25: how to extend the behavior of a class without modifying it.

In this case, the problem is applied to algorithms that have well-defined steps that can be varied to create different results, such as the algorithm used to generate salutations in the **DonorDatabase** class. Unlike the other patterns, however, the template method pattern is useful when you need to ensure that some parts of an algorithm can be varied while other parts remain fixed, ensuring that, say, sorting and selecting are always handled in the same way but that the filtering and generating steps can be changed to create new results for different kinds of donor communication.

Understanding the Template Method Pattern

The template method relies on an implementation of an algorithm that defines only the parts that are to remain fixed. The remaining parts of the algorithm are provided by the calling component to complete the algorithm and generate the required results, as illustrated by Figure 26-1.

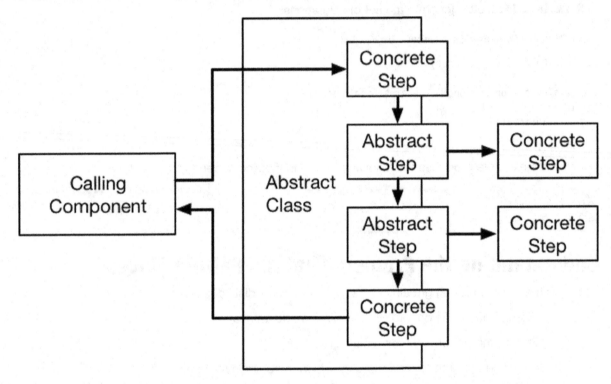

Figure 26-1. The template method pattern

Implementing the Template Method Pattern

In other languages, the template pattern is implemented by defining a class that requires subclasses to complete the algorithm and provide the missing steps. Swift doesn't support abstract classes, but it does allow functions to be treated as objects, which allows an implementation of the pattern to be created anyway.

The first step is to generalize the class that contains the algorithm so that only the fixed parts of the algorithm are defined and the parts that can be changed are specified as functions that can be set using properties. Listing 26-3 shows the changes I made to the **Donors.swift** file.

Listing 26-3. Redefining the Algorithm in the Donors.swift File

```swift
struct Donor {
    let title:String;
    let firstName:String;
    let familyName:String;
    let lastDonation:Float;

    init (_ title:String, _ first:String, _ family:String, _ last:Float) {
        self.title = title;
        self.firstName = first;
        self.familyName = family;
        self.lastDonation = last;
    }
}

class DonorDatabase {
    private var donors:[Donor];
    var filter: ([Donor] -> [Donor])?;
    var generate: ([Donor] -> [String])?;

    init() {
        donors = [
            Donor("Ms", "Anne", "Jones", 0),
            Donor("Mr", "Bob", "Smith", 100),
            Donor("Dr", "Alice", "Doe", 200),
            Donor("Prof", "Joe", "Davis", 320)];
    }

    func generate(maxNumber:Int) -> [String] {

        // step 1 - filter out non-donors
        var targetDonors:[Donor] = filter?(donors)
            ?? donors.filter({$0.lastDonation > 0});

        // step 2 - order donors by last donation
        targetDonors.sort({ $0.lastDonation > $1.lastDonation});

        // step 3 - limit the number of invitees
        if (targetDonors.count > maxNumber) {
            targetDonors = Array(targetDonors[0..<maxNumber]);
        }

        // step 4 - generate the invitations
        return generate?(targetDonors) ?? targetDonors.map({ donor in
            return "Dear \(donor.title). \(donor.familyName)";
        })
    }
}
```

I have defined **filter** and **generate** properties that can be used to override the default steps for the filter and generate steps in the algorithm. I have changed the name of the algorithm method to **generate**, and I fall back to the default steps if the new properties are not set.

Listing 26-4 shows the changes I made to the **main.swift** file to use the modified **DonorDatabase** class and to define a new algorithm.

Listing 26-4. Consuming the Template Method Pattern in the main.swift File

```
let donorDb = DonorDatabase();

let galaInvitations = donorDb.generate(2);
for invite in galaInvitations {
    println(invite);
}

donorDb.filter = { $0.filter({$0.lastDonation == 0})};
donorDb.generate = { $0.map({ "Hi \($0.firstName)"})};

let newDonors = donorDb.generate(Int.max);
for invite in newDonors {
    println(invite);
}
```

I run the standard version of the algorithm and then define new functions for the **filter** and **generate** properties using closures, selecting those donors who have yet to make a contribution and generating a more causal greeting. Running the application produces the following output:

```
Dear Prof. Davis
Dear Dr. Doe
Hi Anne
```

Variations on the Template Method Pattern

You can create a more traditional implementation of the template method pattern by implementing each step of the algorithm as a method and allowing subclasses to override them, as shown in Listing 26-5.

Listing 26-5. Using Methods to Define Algorithm Steps in the Donors.swift File

```
...
class DonorDatabase {
    private var donors:[Donor];

    init() {
        donors = [
            Donor("Ms", "Anne", "Jones", 0),
            Donor("Mr", "Bob", "Smith", 100),
            Donor("Dr", "Alice", "Doe", 200),
            Donor("Prof", "Joe", "Davis", 320)];
    }
```

```swift
func filter(donors:[Donor]) -> [Donor] {
    return donors.filter({$0.lastDonation > 0});
}

func generate(donors:[Donor]) -> [String] {
    return donors.map({ donor in
        return "Dear \(donor.title). \(donor.familyName)";
    })
}

func generate(maxNumber:Int) -> [String] {

    // step 1 - filter out non-donors
    var targetDonors = filter(self.donors);

    // step 2 - order donors by last donation
    targetDonors.sort({ $0.lastDonation > $1.lastDonation});

    // step 3 - limit the number of invitees
    if (targetDonors.count > maxNumber) {
        targetDonors = Array(targetDonors[0..<maxNumber]);
    }

    // step 4 - generate the invitations
    return generate(targetDonors);
    }
}
...
```

I have defined the **filter** and **generate** steps as separate methods that can be overridden by subclasses, as shown in Listing 26-6.

Listing 26-6. Creating a Subclass in the main.swift File

```swift
let donorDb = DonorDatabase();

let galaInvitations = donorDb.generate(2);
for invite in galaInvitations {
    println(invite);
}

class NewDonors : DonorDatabase {

    override func filter(donors: [Donor]) -> [Donor] {
        return donors.filter({ $0.lastDonation == 0});
    }

    override func generate(donors: [Donor]) -> [String] {
        return donors.map({ "Hi \($0.firstName)"});
    }
}
```

```
let newDonor = NewDonors();
for invite in newDonor.generate(Int.max) {
    println(invite);
}
```

I prefer the closure-based technique, but it is a matter of personal preference, and you should choose whichever approach suits your coding style better.

Understanding the Pitfalls of the Pattern

There are no pitfalls associated with the template method pattern, which is simple to implement and test. If you choose to implement the variation I showed in the previous section, take care to define as methods only the steps that you want to permit to be changed.

Examples of the Template Method Pattern in Cocoa

The template method pattern is used throughout Cocoa and is particularly visible in the UI components. You can see an example in the SportsStore application where the **ViewController** class is derived from the **UIViewController** class and overrides the **viewDidLoad** method, which is called when the user interface is created, as follows:

```
...
override func viewDidLoad() {
    super.viewDidLoad();
    displayStockTotal();
    let bridge = EventBridge(callback: updateStockLevel);
    productStore.callback = bridge.inputCallback;
}
...
```

You may not think of user interface initialization as an algorithm, but it is one that you will have used in all iOS projects in some form, and it allows Apple to define a set of fixed classes with default behaviors that can be overridden by third-party developers.

Applying the Pattern to the SportsStore Application

As noted in the previous section, the SportsStore application already relies on the template method pattern.

Summary

I described the template method pattern in this chapter and explained how it can be used to allow some steps in an algorithm to be modified, either by defining new functions using closures or by creating a subclass. I turn my attention to the one of the most important and misunderstood patterns in the next part of this book: the Model/View/Controller (MVC) pattern.

Part V

The MVC Pattern

Chapter 27

The Model/View/Controller Pattern

The Model/View/Controller (MVC) pattern has become increasingly prevalent in recent years and underpins a lot of modern software development, including iOS app projects. In this chapter, I put the MVC pattern into context, explain why it is important, and describe how it relates to the other design patterns I have described in this book. Table 27-1 puts the MVC pattern into context.

Table 27-1. *Putting the MVC Pattern into Context*

Question	Answer
What is it?	The MVC pattern adds structure to an entire application rather than to an individual component.
What are the benefits?	The sections of an application can be developed, tested, and maintained more easily.
When should you use this pattern?	Use this pattern for any complex project.
When should you avoid this pattern?	The amount of planning and infrastructure required to implement this pattern isn't justified for short-lived or simple projects.

(continued)

Table 27-1. (*continued*)

Question	Answer
How do you know when you have implemented the pattern correctly?	Implementing the MVC pattern involves a lot of judgment and the expression of personal preferences, which means that it is hard to give a definitive explanation of when the pattern is implemented correctly. In general terms, the individual sections of the application—the model, the views, and the controllers—should be loosely coupled to the extent that they can be readily isolated for testing, and changes can be made to the implementation of one section without requiring corresponding changes in the other sections.
Are there any common pitfalls?	The only pitfall is to create a suboptimal implementation by putting functionality into the wrong section. Identifying the correct section is a matter of experience and preference, and there are few absolute right and wrong decisions.
Are there any related patterns?	The implementation of the MVC pattern often relies on the patterns described elsewhere in this book.

Preparing the Example Project

For this chapter I created an Xcode OS X Command Line Tool project called MVC. No other preparation is required other than to create the project.

Understanding the Problem That the Pattern Solves

The MVC pattern adds structure to a project in order to simplify development, testing, and maintenance. However, rather than focusing on the relationship or interaction between specific objects and types, the MVC pattern is applied to the entire application.

Understanding the MVC Pattern

If you have some spare time and find yourself in the mood to experiment, find two or three developers and ask them to describe the MVC pattern. Push for details and you will realize two important facts about the MVC pattern. The first fact is that every developer has a different understanding of the MVC pattern. The second fact is that most developers' understanding of MVC comprises of a vague collection of ideas, usually built around the phrase "separation of concerns."

The MVC pattern is expressed with incredible variety in different platforms and frameworks. A developer who has built a web application using Microsoft's MVC framework will have a different understanding from a developer who has used Apple's **UIKit** framework to build an iOS app. Both frameworks follow the MVC pattern but have different perspectives on how components are arranged to make a well-designed application. And the components needed to build a web application are different from the components required for an iOS app, which leads to further differences. There are so many different expressions of the MVC pattern and so many different variations that it can hardly be surprising that a dozen developers will produce (at least) a dozen different interpretations.

Caution   Arguing about the application of the MVC pattern is the go-to activity of any developer who isn't in the mood to write code. This can, if left unchecked, lead to a job as a software architect and, in extreme cases, an enterprise architect. As one who has led enterprise architecture in some of the world's largest companies, let me just say that writing code is a lot more interesting than spending all day talking about it.

At the heart of the MVC pattern is the idea of *separation of concerns*, which is why this phrase often comes up. Separation of concerns just means keeping the different sections of an application apart from one another and is done to make those parts easier to develop, maintain, and test.

Separation of concerns will seem like a familiar idea by this point because it is a theme that emerges from many of the design patterns that I have described in this book. The MVC pattern follows a convention of using four different sections in an application:

- The *model*, which is the *M* in MVC. The model contains the application's data.

- The *view*, which is the *V* in MVC. The view generates the output from the model that is shown to the user.

- The *controller*, which is the *C* in MVC. The controller responds to user interaction and is responsible for updating the model and the view to reflect change in the application state.

- The *cross-cutting concerns*. As you will learn, not everything can fit neatly into the model, view, and controller sections of the application, and the cross-cutting concerns are sections of the application that span two or more other sections.

As you will learn, the crisp definitions I have given for each section of the MVC pattern become a lot more blurred when it comes to applying the pattern to a real project, but keeping these simple definitions in mind can be helpful, as is understanding the interactions between each section, which I have shown in Figure 27-1.

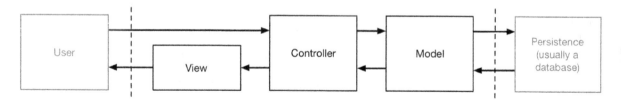

Figure 27-1. The Model/View/Controller pattern

User interaction is received by the controller, which contains the logic required to update the data in the model to reflect the interaction. The updated application state is passed by the controller to the view, which generates the representation shown to the user, reflecting the effect of the original interaction.

As a simple example, imagine an application that displays a list of names. There has to be a beginning, so the first instruction from the user is to list all of the names. This produces the following sequence:

1. The controller receives the instruction from the user.

2. The controller asks the model for all of the names.

3. The model obtains the requested data from its storage mechanism and returns it to the controller.

4. The controller gives the list of names to the view and asks it to present them to the user.

5. The view generates a representation of the list along with details of the commands that can be performed on it.

The same basic sequence of actions is played out for every interaction. Imagine that the user performs the action to delete a name from the list. Here is the sequence of actions that plays out:

1. The controller receives the instruction from the user, which includes details of the name to be deleted.

2. The controller asks the model to delete the specified name.

3. The model deletes the name from its storage mechanism and returns the modified list to the controller.

4. The controller gives the revised list of names to the view and asks it to present them to the user.

5. The view generates a representation of the list along with details of the commands that can be performed on it.

The separation of concerns means that each section of the application has a particular role and well-defined relationship with the other sections. Each section relies on the others to perform its role but doesn't have any knowledge or dependency on how it is implemented, which means that the implementation of one section can be changed without requiring corresponding changes in the other sections. The best example of this is the mechanism that the model uses to persistently store the application's data. This is typically a relational database, but details of which one and how the data is represented are part of the model's implementation and are entirely unknown to the controller and view sections. The relational database could be replaced with a completely different type of storage without requiring any changes to the controller, which just deals with data objects and doesn't care how they are stored, or to the view, which doesn't directly interact with the model at all.

Understanding the MVC Application Sections

Applying the MVC pattern can be an intimidating process at first, but it need not be if you keep focused on what the MVC pattern tries to achieve. The goal of the MVC pattern—like all of the design patterns I have described in this book—is to create code that is simpler to write, modify, and maintain, and achieving this goal is your only objective when implementing the MVC pattern.

It is not to conform to someone else's rigid definition of what MVC means. There are no fixed rules about how to decide which bits of an application belong in the model, view, and controller sections—just guidelines that you have to interpret to make the best judgments you can.

Like all of the patterns I have described in this book, applying MVC effectively requires flexibility and adaptations to the current project. Some pieces of an application will be easier to deal with than others, but every project has some features or functions that could reasonably be placed in at least two sections.

> **Tip**   Don't worry if these following sections don't make immediate sense. It can take a while to process the structure of the MVC pattern. You may find the simple example application that I create in the "Implementing the MVC Pattern" section helpful for putting some of the ideas into context.

Understanding the Model

Models contain the data that users work with. There are two broad types of model. The first model type is the *domain model*, which contains the application data along with the operations, transformations, and rules for creating, storing, and manipulating that data, collectively referred to as the *model logic*. This is the kind of model shown in Figure 27-1 and is what usually is being referred to when the word *model* is used.

Many developers new to the MVC pattern get confused with the idea of including logic in the data model, believing that the goal of the MVC pattern is to separate data from logic. This is a misapprehension; the goal of the MVC framework is to divide an application into three functional areas, each of which may contain both logic *and* data. The goal isn't to eliminate logic from the model. Rather, it is to ensure that the model contains only the logic for creating and managing the model data. The domain model in an application built using the MVC pattern *should* do the following:

- Contain the domain data
- Contain the logic for creating, managing, and modifying the domain data (even if that means executing remote logic via web services)
- Provide a clean API that exposes the model data and operations on it

The domain model *should not* do the following:

- Expose details of how the model data is obtained or managed (that is, details of the data storage mechanism or the remote web service should not be exposed to controllers and views)
- Contain logic that transforms the model based on user interaction (this is the controller's job)
- Contain logic for displaying data to the user (this is the view's job)

The benefit of ensuring that the domain model is isolated from the controller and views is that you can test your logic more easily and that enhancing and maintaining the overall application is simpler and easier.

```
GETTING IT WRONG
```

Many developers are hesitant to apply the MVC pattern because they worry about "getting it wrong," which generally means putting features into the wrong section. In other words, code that belongs in a controller ends up in a view.

My advice is not to worry. Dive right in and start making mistakes as quickly as you can. The only way you can develop a solid understanding of the MVC pattern is to weigh the decisions about the structure of specific applications, and you learn just as much when you make decisions that you later come to realize you would make differently.

Code is fluid and malleable, and in most projects you will have the opportunity to refactor the application. This can be a tedious process, but it isn't the end of the world and can give you useful insights as well. Don't worry even if you don't have time to refactor because the impact of a decision you would like to revise is minimal, and most "wrong" decisions are really decisions that run counter to your evolving preferences and experiences.

The second kind of model is the *view model*, which represents data passed from the controller to the view in order that it can be represented to the user. Usually, view models are just a subset of the data in the domain model, such as the results of a query, but a view model can also contain extra information that the view needs that is not part of the domain model, such as hints about the state of the current user session.

Understanding Controllers

Controllers are the connective tissue in an MVC application, responding to user interaction and acting as a conduit between the model and views. A controller built using the MVC *should* do the following:

- Contain the logic required to initialize the model
- Contain the logic/behaviors required by the view to present data from the model
- Contain the logic/behaviors required to update the model based on user interaction

The controller *should not* do the following:

- Contain logic that displays data to the user (that is the job of the view)
- Contain logic that manages the persistence of data (that is the job of the model)
- Manipulate data outside of the scope

Controllers implement the logic of the application, often referred to as the domain logic or the business logic. This logic is broken up into *actions* or *commands* that the user can invoke, which perform operations on the model and then use a view to represent the effect of the action to the user.

Understanding Views

Views are responsible for displaying a view model to the user. The means by which this is done varies, and it can be anything from generating an HTML page to creating or updating a set of **UIKit** components, depending on the application.

Views are usually created using a framework, such as **UIKit**, because creating the infrastructure required to display data is a complex process and does not need to re-created from scratch for every application. Views *should* do the following:

- Contain the logic and markup required to present data to the user

Views *should not* do the following:

- Contain complex logic (this is better placed in a controller)
- Contain logic that creates, stores, or manipulates the model

Views *can* contain logic, but it should be simple and used sparingly. Putting anything but the most simple method calls or expressions in a view makes the overall application harder to test and maintain.

Understanding Cross-Cutting Concerns

Cross-cutting concerns are those parts of the application that do not fit into the other sections. The classic examples are logging and authorization, which are generally required throughout an application. It doesn't make sense to create duplicate logging or security features for different sections, and so a single implementation is used by multiple sections so that, for example, once a user has been authenticated, the user's identity is propagated through the different sections without the need to further verification.

The danger with cross-cutting concerns is that features and functions that more properly belong in the model, view, or controller end up being defined as cross-cutting concerns, distorting the shape of the application and undermining the clean separation between the sections of the application.

There are few genuine cross-cutting concerns in any application, which means that once you have implemented logging and security, you should treat any other features implemented as cross-cutting concerns with suspicion and consider whether the feature may actually belong in the model, view, or controller.

Implementing the MVC Pattern

The best way to learn about the MVC pattern is to implement it. The more experience you have in separating the concerns in an application into models, views, and controllers, the more natural the process will become. In the sections that follow, I am going to use the MVC pattern to create a simple command-line application. I walk through the process and explain the decisions I made along the way. As I explained earlier, the MVC pattern leaves a lot of room for personal style and interpretation, and inevitably the implementation will reflect the way that I think about software and development and be shaped by the kinds of projects I usually work on. This doesn't mean you should slavishly follow my techniques. Instead, you should feel free to follow your own path and make the decisions that have the most beneficial impact in your development environment and on the kinds of projects you develop.

The example application will manage a list of people and the cities they live in. This isn't especially useful as an application in its own right, but there is just enough complexity to allow me to implement the MVC pattern without the application features getting in the way.

Defining the Common Code

In any project, there are functions that you need to use throughout an application. Common code isn't the same thing as a cross-cutting concern. As a rule of thumb, functions and static methods that you define to avoid duplication are common code; features that have common state across sections are cross-cutting concerns.

I started defining the application by defining extensions that I will rely on to manipulate strings into arrays, to remove duplicate objects in arrays, and to find the first object in an array that matches a specified test. I added a file called **Extensions.swift** to the example project, the contents of which are shown in Listing 27-1.

Listing 27-1. The Contents of the Extensions.swift File

```
import Foundation

extension String {

    func split() -> [String] {
        return self.componentsSeparatedByCharactersInSet(
            NSCharacterSet.whitespaceAndNewlineCharacterSet())
            .filter({$0 != ""});
    }
}

extension Array {

    func unique<T: Equatable>() -> [T] {
        var uniqueValues = [T]();

        for value in self {
            if !contains(uniqueValues, value as T) {
                uniqueValues.append(value as T);
            }
        }
        return uniqueValues;
    }

    func first<T>(test:T -> Bool) -> T? {
        for value in self {
            if test(value as T) {
                return value as? T;
            }
        }
        return nil;
    }
}
```

These extensions are not related to the structure of the MVC pattern, and I have defined them to avoid code duplication in the project.

Defining the Framework

The model, views, and controllers do not exist in isolation. They need a framework of some sort to connect the sections to one another, to receive and process interactions from the user, and to display content on the screen. Without an underlying framework, every application would have to re-create the same set of low-level functions, which would be extremely tedious. As a Swift developer, the frameworks that you are likely to use most often are **UIKit** and **AppKit**, which include all of the low-level features, such as translating mouse clicks into events and drawing complex UI components on the screen.

There is no handy MVC framework for Command Line Tool projects, so I am going to have to create one. This would be a serious (and unwise) undertaking in a real project, but one of the advantages of book examples is simplicity, and creating a basic framework is a useful means of demonstrating how the sections of the MVC pattern fit together.

The example application will read commands from the Xcode console, which will also be used to display data to the user. Listing 27-2 shows the contents of the **Commands.swift** file, which I have used to define the commands that the application will support.

Listing 27-2. The Contents of the Commands.swift File

```
import Foundation

enum Command : String {
    case LIST_PEOPLE = "L: List People";
    case ADD_PERSON = "A: Add Person";
    case DELETE_PERSON = "D: Delete Person";
    case UPDATE_PERSON = "U: Update Person";
    case SEARCH = "S: Search";

    static let ALL = [Command.LIST_PEOPLE, Command.ADD_PERSON,
        Command.DELETE_PERSON, Command.UPDATE_PERSON, Command.SEARCH];

    static func getFromInput(input:String) -> Command? {
        switch (input.lowercaseString) {
        case "l":
            return Command.LIST_PEOPLE;
        case "a":
            return Command.ADD_PERSON;
        case "d":
            return Command.DELETE_PERSON;
        case "u":
            return Command.UPDATE_PERSON;
        case "s":
            return Command.SEARCH;
        default:
            return nil;
        }
    }
}
```

The **Command** enumeration defines values for each of the commands that the application will support, allowing the user to list all of the people in the application, add or delete people, modify a person's detail, and perform a simple search.

Swift enumerations don't make it easy to get a list of all defined values, so I have defined a static constant called **ALL**, which is set to an array of the enumeration values. I have also defined a static method called **getFromInput**, which maps a **String** to an enumeration value. I'll use the **getFromInput** method to select a command based on values read from the command line.

Creating the Model

I have put enough of the infrastructure in place to allow me to start implementing the MVC sections. The model is the best place to start when implementing MVC because the model types are used throughout the application. Listing 27-3 shows the contents of the **Model.swift** file, which I added to the example project.

Listing 27-3. The Contents of the Model.swift File

```
import Foundation

func == (lhs:Person, rhs:Person) -> Bool {
    return lhs.name == rhs.name && lhs.city == rhs.city;
}

class Person : Equatable, Printable {
    var name:String;
    var city:String;

    init(_ name:String, _ city:String) {
        self.name = name;
        self.city = city;
    }

    var description: String {
        return "Name: \(self.name), City: \(self.city)";
    }
}
```

In a real project, there can be a wide range of model types to represent the different data objects that an application handles, but the **Person** class is the only model type in the example application. The **Person** class defines two stored properties, which I will use for the name of a person and the city in which they live.

Implementing the Repository Pattern

I like to implement the repository pattern when writing MVC applications, in which the data types are defined separately from the mechanism that is used to store and retrieve them, which is known as the *model repository*. This is why the **Person** class is so simple; it only needs to store its data values and doesn't need to pay attention about how those values are obtained or persisted.

The advantage of the repository pattern is that it allows the storage mechanism to be changed without needing to make corresponding changes in the application's model types. This can be helpful for testing the application because you can replace the real repository with one that uses predefined test values that are stored in memory. When starting a new MVC application, I usually create an in-memory repository and only replace it with an implementation that persists data to a database when the core functionality of the application is in place.

The key to a good repository is to start with a protocol through which the other components in the application will perform data operations, and Listing 27-4 shows the repository protocol I defined in the example application.

Listing 27-4. Defining the Repository Protocol in the Model.swift File

```swift
import Foundation

func == (lhs:Person, rhs:Person) -> Bool {
    return lhs.name == rhs.name && lhs.city == rhs.city;
}

class Person : Equatable, Printable {
    var name:String;
    var city:String;

    init(_ name:String, _ city:String) {
        self.name = name;
        self.city = city;
    }

    var description: String {
        return "Name: \(self.name), City: \(self.city)";
    }
}

protocol Repository {

    var People:[Person] { get };

    func addPerson(person:Person);
    func removePerson(name:String);
    func updatePerson(name:String, newCity:String);
}
```

Tip   The **Person** class that I define in Listing 27-4 implements the **Equatable** and **Printable** protocols. The **Equatable** protocol works with the **==** function I create in the listing to allow **Person** objects to be compared to one another. The **Printable** protocol is used when an object is passed to the **println** function, which writes out the value of the **description** property.

I have defined a read-only property called **People** that will return all of the **Person** objects stored in the repository, as well as methods that add, remote, and modify objects.

> **Tip**   Exposing all of the model objects as a collection such as an array makes it easy to consume the data in other sections of the application, but doing so assumes that the data can be retrieved efficiently. This should be done only if there are small amounts of data in the application or if the storage mechanism is capable of delivering content only when the elements in the collection are accessed.

In this chapter, I am only going to implement a nonpersistent in-memory repository, which has the benefit of being simple and being reset to a known state each time the application is restarted. Listing 27-5 shows how I defined the repository implementation class.

Listing 27-5. Defining the Repository Implementation in the Model.swift File

```
...
protocol Repository {

    var People:[Person] { get };

    func addPerson(person:Person);
    func removePerson(name:String);
    func updatePerson(name:String, newCity:String);
}

class MemoryRepository : Repository {
    private var peopleArray:[Person];

    init() {
        peopleArray = [
            Person("Bob", "New York"),
            Person("Alice", "London"),
            Person("Joe", "Paris")];
    }

    var People:[Person] {
        return self.peopleArray;
    }

    func addPerson(person: Person) {
        self.peopleArray.append(person);
    }

    func removePerson(name: String) {
        let nameLower = name.lowercaseString;
        self.peopleArray = peopleArray .filter({$0.name.lowercaseString != nameLower});
    }
```

```
    func updatePerson(name: String, newCity: String) {
        let nameLower = name.lowercaseString;
        let test:Person -> Bool = {p in return p.name.lowercaseString == nameLower};
        if let person = peopleArray.first(test) {
            person.city = newCity;
        }
    }
}
...
```

The repository uses a standard Swift array to store its model objects, and the array is populated with some sample objects in the class initializer. As I explained in Chapter 5, Swift arrays are value types, which means that a copy of the array is created when a calling component assigns the array returned by the **People** property to a local variable or constant. It is for this reason that I have implemented separate methods for adding, removing, or modifying data objects because the array that a calling component operates on will be different.

> **Note**   I have explained the importance of concurrency protections in many of the chapters in this book. This project is a rare example of an application that doesn't need them. It will be accessed by only one thread at a time because I will be reading instructions from the command line and then executing them. In a real project, however, you must ensure that your repository is thread-safe, either because you use a mechanism like Grand Central Dispatch in your implementation class or because the storage mechanism you are relying on is inherently thread-safe.

Defining the View

Views are used to display data to the user and, typically, provide the user with the controls or commands used for interaction, such as buttons and text fields. It usually makes sense for the view to display the controls because the set of interactions that are allowed depends on the data that is being displayed. A view that gathers the values required to create a new model object may display Create and Cancel buttons, whereas a view that displays a list of model objects may just have a Reload button.

I have taken a different approach for the example application because the user will be able to use the same set of interactions throughout the life of the application, something that is possible only because the project is so simple. This means that the views in the application are responsible only for displaying data to the user. I started by defining a protocol that all views in the application will conform to. Listing 27-6 shows the protocol, which I defined in a new file called **Views.swift**.

Listing 27-6. The Contents of the Views.swift File

```
protocol View {

    func execute();
}
```

The **View** protocol defines a single method called **execute** that will be invoked to display content to the user. A project usually contains views that display the application data in different ways, and views are selected by a controller in response to user interaction, a process that will make sense once I define a controller in the "Defining the Controller" section.

I need only one view to get started, which I will use to display a list of **Person** objects. Listing 27-7 shows the view class I created.

Listing 27-7. Defining a View Class in the Views.swift File

```
protocol View {

    func execute();
}

class PersonListView : View {
    private let people:[Person];

    init(data:[Person]) {
        self.people = data;
    }

    func execute() {
        for person in people {
            println(person);
        }
    }
}
```

The **PersonListView** class is simple; it accepts an array of **Person** objects as its initializer argument, and the **execute** method prints out each of them in turn using the global **println** function. (The **Person** class conforms to the **Printable** protocol, which means that the String returned by the **description** property is written to the console by the **println** function.)

Notice that the view doesn't deal directly with the repository; its only knowledge of the **Person** objects it operates on comes from the initializer argument. This reflects the separation of concerns principle and means that the same class can be used to display different data sets, which you will see when I implement the controller in the next section.

Defining the Controller

The final MVC section to implement is the controller, but the reality is that I tend to develop the initial views and controllers in an application in parallel, moving between them to get the basic behavior I am looking for. A book chapter doesn't lend itself to describing this kind of development process and makes example projects look linear, but I find that implementing the MVC pattern is easiest when I implement the model and then work on the other sections simultaneously. But, in linear book chapter style, I have defined a controller that acts as the connective tissue between the model and the view. Listing 27-8 shows the contents of the **Controllers.swift** file, in which I have defined a common base class for controllers in the example application.

Listing 27-8. The Contents of the Controllers.swift File

```
class ControllerBase {
    private let repository:Repository;
    private let nextController:ControllerBase?;

    init(repo:Repository, nextController:ControllerBase?) {
        self.repository = repo;
        self.nextController = nextController;
    }

    func handleCommand(command:Command, data:[String]) -> View? {
        return nextController?.handleCommand(command, data:data);
    }
}
```

I have used a base class rather than a protocol because I am going to use the chain of responsibility pattern (as described in Chapter 19) to find a controller that can handle a command selected by the user. The initializer accepts a **Repository** object so that the controller has access to the model data and the next controller in the chain.

The **handleCommand** method will be called when the user selects a command. Controllers can elect to handle the command or pass it on to the next controller in the chain. If none of the controllers in the chain handles the command, then **nil** will be returned by the base class implementation of the **handleCommand** method. The **handleCommand** returns a **View**, which is how controllers act as the link between the model (via the repository initializer argument) and the views. The **View** object selected by the controller will be executed by the framework, which I'll set up in the "Completing the Framework" section.

> **Tip**   The mechanism that the application framework uses to find a controller to respond to a command varies based on the type of application that is being built. There is usually a predefined map of URLs to controllers in web applications, and native GUI applications usually send commands to the controller most closely associated with the currently displayed view.

Having defined the base functionality for a controller, I can now create a concrete implementation that will respond to the commands I defined in the **Command** enumeration. I am going to start with a single controller that will handle all of the commands defined in the **Command** enumeration, but I'll lay the foundation for additional controllers in the "Completing the Framework" section and add a second controller that follows the same pattern in the "Extending the Application" section. Listing 27-9 shows the controller I created.

Listing 27-9. Defining a Concrete Controller in the Controllers.swift File

```swift
class ControllerBase {
    private let repository:Repository;
    private let nextController:ControllerBase?;

    init(repo:Repository, nextController:ControllerBase?) {
        self.repository = repo;
        self.nextController = nextController;
    }

    func handleCommand(command:Command, data:[String]) -> View? {
        return nextController?.handleCommand(command, data:data);
    }
}

class PersonController : ControllerBase {

    override func handleCommand(command: Command, data:[String]) -> View? {
        switch command {
            case .LIST_PEOPLE:
                return listAll();
            case .ADD_PERSON:
                return addPerson(data[0], city: data[1]);
            case .DELETE_PERSON:
                return deletePerson(data[0]);
            case .UPDATE_PERSON:
                return updatePerson(data[0], newCity:data[1]);
            case .SEARCH:
                return search(data[0]);
            default:
                return super.handleCommand(command, data: data);
        }
    }

    private func listAll() -> View {
        return PersonListView(data:repository.People);
    }

    private func addPerson(name:String, city:String) -> View {
        repository.addPerson(Person(name, city));
        return listAll();
    }

    private func deletePerson(name:String) -> View {
        repository.removePerson(name);
        return listAll();
    }

    private func updatePerson(name:String, newCity:String) -> View {
        repository.updatePerson(name, newCity: newCity);
        return listAll();
    }
```

```
    private func search(term:String) -> View {
        let termLower = term.lowercaseString;
        let matches = repository.People.filter({ person in
            return person.name.lowercaseString.rangeOfString(termLower) != nil
                || person.city.lowercaseString.rangeOfString(termLower) != nil});
        return PersonListView(data: matches);
    }
}
```

The **PersonController** class is derived from **ControllerBase**, and the implementation of the **handleCommand** method contains a **switch** statement that routes requests for all of the commands defined in the **Command** enumeration to one of the **private** methods it defines.

The basic pattern for the **private** methods is the same. Perform an operation on the model and then select the data that will be displayed by the **PersonListView** view. The **addPerson**, **deletePerson**, and **updatePerson** methods display all of the model data, so I return the result of calling the **listAll** method, which uses the repository **People** property to initialize a **PersonListView** object. The **search** method is a little more complex and filters the objects in the repository to locate those **Person** objects whose **name** or **city** property contains a specified term.

Completing the Framework

I have implemented the model, a controller, and a view, and it is now time to complete the framework in order to gather commands from the user, select controllers to handle those commands, and execute the views that the controllers select. Listing 27-10 shows the additions I made to the **main.swift** file to complete the application.

Listing 27-10. Completing the Framework in the main.swift File

```
import Foundation

let repository = MemoryRepository();
let controllerChain = PersonController(repo: repository, nextController: nil);

var stdIn = NSFileHandle.fileHandleWithStandardInput();
var command = Command.LIST_PEOPLE;
var data = [String]();

while (true) {

    if let view = controllerChain.handleCommand(command, data:data) {
        view.execute();
        println("--Commands--");
        for command in Command.ALL {
            println(command.rawValue);
        }
    } else {
        fatalError("No view");
    }
```

```
    let input:String = NSString(data: stdIn.availableData,
        encoding: NSUTF8StringEncoding) ?? "";

    let inputArray:[String] = input.split();

    if (inputArray.count > 0) {
        command = Command.getFromInput(inputArray.first!) ?? Command.LIST_PEOPLE;
        if (inputArray.count > 1) {
            data = Array(inputArray[1...inputArray.count - 1]);
        } else {
            data = [];
        }
    }
    println("Command \(command.rawValue) Data \(data)");
}
```

The code that I added read a string from the standard input and breaks it into a command (which is translated into a value from the **Command** enumeration) and data values. Both the command and the data values are passed to the first controller in the chain of responsibility, although there is only one controller at the moment.

This cycle of interaction, controller selection, and view selection is at the heart of the MVC model although it is rarely seen because few projects require the creation of a framework in which to host the MVC sections.

Running the Application

Run the project to test the application. The framework will display the initial set of data objects in the model in the Xcode console, along with the set of commands that can be selected, like this:

```
Name: Bob, City: New York
Name: Alice, City: London
Name: Joe, City: Paris
--Commands--
L: List People
A: Add Person
D: Delete Person
U: Update Person
S: Search
```

You can enter commands by clicking in the Xcode console and typing one of the command letters shown in the previous output, followed by the data used by the command. Table 27-2 shows examples of how to use each command that the application supports.

Table 27-2. Using the Commands Supported by the Example Application

Command	Example	Description
L	L	Prints all of the Person objects in the model
A <name> <city>	A Anne Berlin	Adds a new Person to the model using the specified values for the name and city properties
D <name>	D Joe	Deletes the Person whose name property matches the specified value
U <name> <city>	U Joe Paris	Changes the city property of the Person object whose name property has the specified value
S <term>	S ari	Searches for Person objects whose name or city property contains the specified term

There is no way to clear the text shown in the Xcode console, so each command adds to the output shown by the application. Here is the output shown when using the search command:

```
s n
Command S: Search Data [n]
Name: Bob, City: New York
Name: Alice, City: London
--Commands--
L: List People
A: Add Person
D: Delete Person
U: Update Person
S: Search
```

I entered **s n** and hit Enter, which specifies a search for the letter *N*. The search matches the **Bob** and **Alice** model objects, both of which have **city** properties that contain the search term.

Extending the Application

The entire point of the MVC pattern is to create applications that are each to test and maintain. I am not going to get into the details of effective testing in this book, but I am going to demonstrate how to extend the example application so that it contains multiple controllers and views. The new features that I will add to the project will focus on the **city** property defined by the **Person** class.

Defining the New Commands

The first step is to extend the set of commands that the application supports, as shown in Listing 27-11.

Listing 27-11. Defining New Commands in the Commands.swift File

```swift
import Foundation

enum Command : String {
    case LIST_PEOPLE = "L: List People";
    case ADD_PERSON = "A: Add Person";
    case DELETE_PERSON = "D: Delete Person";
    case UPDATE_PERSON = "U: Update Person";
    case SEARCH = "S: Search";
    case LIST_CITIES = "LC: List Cities";
    case SEARCH_CITIES = "SC: Search Cities";
    case DELETE_CITY = "DC: Delete City";

    static let ALL = [Command.LIST_PEOPLE, Command.ADD_PERSON,
        Command.DELETE_PERSON, Command.UPDATE_PERSON, Command.SEARCH,
        Command.LIST_CITIES, Command.SEARCH_CITIES, Command.DELETE_CITY];

    static func getFromInput(input:String) -> Command? {
        switch (input.lowercaseString) {
        case "l":
            return Command.LIST_PEOPLE;
        case "a":
            return Command.ADD_PERSON;
        case "d":
            return Command.DELETE_PERSON;
        case "u":
            return Command.UPDATE_PERSON;
        case "s":
            return Command.SEARCH;
        case "lc":
            return Command.LIST_CITIES;
        case "sc":
            return Command.SEARCH_CITIES;
        case "dc":
            return Command.DELETE_CITY;
        default:
            return nil;
        }
    }
}
```

I have added new commands to search for a city, to delete all of the **Person** objects with a specific **city** value, and to list all of the unique city values in the model.

Defining the New View

The new view will accept a collection of **Person** objects and write out a list of the **city** property values when executed, as shown in Listing 27-12.

Listing 27-12. Adding a View in the Views.swift File

```
protocol View {

    func execute();
}

class PersonListView : View {
    private let people:[Person];

    init(data:[Person]) {
        self.people = data;
    }

    func execute() {
        for person in people {
            println(person);
        }
    }
}

class CityListView : View {
    private let cities:[String];

    init(data:[String]) {
        self.cities = data;
    }

    func execute() {
        for city in self.cities {
            println("City: \(city)");
        }
    }
}
```

Defining the New Controller

The view I created in the previous section displays the city information, but I need a controller to handle the new commands I defined, as shown in Listing 27-13.

Listing 27-13. Defining a New Controller in the Controllers.swift File

```swift
class ControllerBase {
    private let repository:Repository;
    private let nextController:ControllerBase?;

    init(repo:Repository, nextController:ControllerBase?) {
        self.repository = repo;
        self.nextController = nextController;
    }

    func handleCommand(command:Command, data:[String]) -> View? {
        return nextController?.handleCommand(command, data:data);
    }
}

class PersonController : ControllerBase {

    // ...statements omitted for brevity...
}

class CityController : ControllerBase {

    override func handleCommand(command: Command, data: [String]) -> View? {
        switch command {
            case .LIST_CITIES:
                return listAll();
            case .SEARCH_CITIES:
                return search(data[0]);
            case .DELETE_CITY:
                return delete(data[0]);
            default:
                return super.handleCommand(command, data: data);
        }
    }

    private func listAll() -> View {
        return CityListView(data: repository.People.map({$0.city}).unique());
    }
```

```
    private func search(city:String) -> View {
        let cityLower = city.lowercaseString;
        let matches:[Person] = repository.People
            .filter({ $0.city.lowercaseString == cityLower });
        return PersonListView(data: matches);
    }

    private func delete(city:String) -> View {
        let cityLower = city.lowercaseString;
        let toDelete = repository.People .filter({ $0.city.lowercaseString == cityLower });
        for person in toDelete {
            repository.removePerson(person.name);
        }
        return PersonListView(data: repository.People);
    }
}
```

The **CityController** class follows the same pattern as the existing controller and uses the **handleCommand** method to select one of the **private** command-specific methods, which operate on the model through the repository and select a view.

Notice that only the **listAll** method uses the newly defined view, while the **search** and **delete** methods rely on the original **PersonListView** class. There is no tie between views and controllers, and in most MVC applications controllers can select any view that can display the data generated by the command being processed.

Updating the Framework

The final step is to add the new controller to the chain of responsibility maintained by the framework in the **main.swift** file so that a **CityController** object is offered the chance to handle commands, as shown in Listing 27-14.

Listing 27-14. Extending the Chain of Responsibility in the main.swift File

```
...
let repository = MemoryRepository();

let controllerChain = PersonController(repo: repository, nextController:
    CityController(repo: repository, nextController: nil));

var stdIn = NSFileHandle.fileHandleWithStandardInput();
var command = Command.LIST_PEOPLE;
var data = [String]();
...
```

Testing the Changes

You can test the changes by running the application and entering commands into the Xcode debug console. As an example, here is the output shown when I search for a **city** value:

```
sc london
Command SC: Search Cities Data [london]
Name: Alice, City: London
--Commands--
L: List People
A: Add Person
D: Delete Person
U: Update Person
S: Search
LC: List Cities
SC: Search Cities
DC: Delete City
```

Notice how I have been able to extend the functionality of the example application without needing to change any of the existing model, view, or controller code. I defined a new set of commands and then added new code to respond to them and display the data that was generated. Each of the components in the application is focused on a narrow range of tasks and is loosely coupled to the other components, making it easy to isolate a component for testing or to add or change features.

Variations on the MVC Pattern

There are many variations in the way that the MVC pattern is implemented and variations on the pattern itself. The only variation that matters to Swift developers is using a predefined MVC framework. The most commonly used frameworks are **UIKit** and **AppKit**. Creating your own MVC framework is an interesting experiment, and it reveals a lot about how the different sections of the pattern fit together, but for real applications, stick to the MVC frameworks provided by Apple, which provide a lot of ready-made functionality and which have been thoroughly tested.

Understanding the Pitfalls of the MVC Pattern

The most common pitfall is to define code in one section that belongs in another. As I explained at the start of the chapter, this isn't always a clear-cut decision, and the best way to avoid this pitfall is through experience. Implementing the MVC pattern successfully depends on understanding the way that your development processes work, and the more often you apply the MVC pattern, the better your understanding of what works for your projects and what doesn't. Take your time to think through what you are doing, be prepared to refactor when you change your mind about a feature, and leave yourself opportunities to experiment.

Examples of the MVC Pattern in Cocoa

The most obvious examples of the MVC pattern are the **AppKit** and **UIKit** frameworks, which use MVC to enforce structure in UI applications.

Summary

In this chapter I described the MVC pattern and explained how it is used to add structure to a complete application. I explained the different sections that make up the MVC pattern and created an example application and framework as an example implementation.

And that is all I have to teach you about design patterns. I have described each of the most important design patterns that you can apply to a Swift project and explained that you should use the implementations I provided as a starting point for your own applications, adapting the patterns as needed to suit your needs, preferences, and coding style. I wish you every success in your Swift project, and I can only hope you have enjoyed reading this book as much as I have enjoyed writing it.

Index

Get the eBook for only $10!

> Now you can take the weightless companion with you anywhere, anytime. Your purchase of this book entitles you to 3 electronic versions for only $10.

This Apress title will prove so indispensible that you'll want to carry it with you everywhere, which is why we are offering the eBook in 3 formats for only $10 if you have already purchased the print book.

Convenient and fully searchable, the PDF version enables you to easily find and copy code—or perform examples by quickly toggling between instructions and applications. The MOBI format is ideal for your Kindle, while the ePUB can be utilized on a variety of mobile devices.

Go to www.apress.com/promo/tendollars to purchase your companion eBook.

Apress®
THE EXPERT'S VOICE™